AF412829

SYSTEMS
CONTROL

SYSTEMS CONTROL

The Serious Pilot's Guide
to Aircraft Components and Their Operation

by DAN MANNINGHAM

and the Editors of *Business and Commercial Aviation*

Ziff-Davis Publishing Company/New York

Contents

Preface

In the beginning, airplanes were conceived, designed, built and flown by rugged individuals. Those early pilots understood the aircraft very well because it was all their creation.

In time, there devolved a rather natural separation of the basic machine into two basic parts, airframe and motor. Pilots reviewed the basic structure of fuselage and airfoils and memorized the elementary operational procedures for the engine. The word "systems" was not even part of an aviation vocabulary.

Gradually, but inevitably, the airplane has become more intricate. Modern aircraft are immensely complex machines. So much so, in fact, that they are best understood as a group of interrelated units working together for the common purpose of flight. Those units have come to be known as systems.

Even the most basic new airplane available is made up of several systems: airframe, engine, fuel, electrical, avionics. Many new airplanes are additionally complicated with pneumatics and pressurization, propellers, hydraulics, oxygen, anti-ice and even flush toilets. Each one of those marvelous conveniences contributes to the efficiency and comfort of flight. And each one creates an added burden for the pilot who must cope with their operation and potential failure. Systems are a blessing and a curse at the same time.

As a pilot or operator, you are caught in the middle. Either you will master those complex, and often devious, systems or they will master you. This volume is designed to give you the knowledge to keep the upper hand.

Business and Commercial Aviation magazine is the world's largest publication solely dedicated to the serious pilot. Over the years, hundreds of comprehensive and award-winning articles of permanent value have appeared in this most excellent periodical. This volume, *Systems Control,* is an anthology of the best of those articles from previous issues of *B/CA.* You will not learn how to build an airplane in these pages but you will learn how to maintain and operate your airplane's systems more safely and efficiently.

Dan Manningham

Mansfield, Ohio
March 1980

RECORD KEEPING I

I

Aircraft systems have become extraordinarily complex. Reliability improves with each new generation, but sooner or later all components require some expensive and time-consuming attention. Careful record keeping is absolutely essential for documenting individual aircraft or systems performance and for monitoring entire fleets of aircraft by type. As a pilot or operator you should be keeping records of your own airplane's performance. You can also benefit from the careful records kept by the FAA on fleet experience. Record keeping and systems information can be as vital to flight safety as proper engine care.

Carefully kept records help the airlines to save millions in operational dollars. Business and commercial operators can save money, too, by carefully noting aircraft performance. The chapter titled "Aircraft Performance Log" explains the benefits and presents a comprehensive system for recording your airplane's performance. When it is time for maintenance, that basic health record will be invaluable in making some difficult decisions.

Airworthiness Directives are government edicts which mandate specific maintenance action for all aircraft or accessories of a given type. They are often resented because of the expense and downtime involved. Serious aviation professionals should understand the process by which ADs are issued in order to gain a healthy respect for them. In the chapter called "Airworthiness Directives" the whole scheme from defect detection to government edict is detailed.

In a secluded office at the Aeronautical Center in Oklahoma City, the FAA maintains a computerized library of

Aircraft Performance Log 1

Aircraft and engines are becoming increasingly reliable and efficient, but there is no escape from wear and performance degradation even if misuse and mishaps are avoided. Sooner or later all aircraft components must be repaired, overhauled or replaced.

Since that can be expensive and time-consuming, it is important that a maintenance program and operational procedures be utilized that will encourage the longest possible service life from each component. The pilot can participate by using his equipment in accordance with authorized or recommended guidelines.

Equally as important, he can also monitor the performance of his aircraft and its equipment in order to detect discrepancies as soon as they become apparent and arrange for corrective action. In many cases the latter practice will help prevent a failure that could lead to needless expense and downtime—or an accident.

The trouble is, discrepancies often do not become apparent until the failure has already occurred. Even if a pilot flies the same airplane all the time, deterioration in performance of some component can be so gradual and subtle it may not be noticed until it's too late.

The best way to maximize early detection of an impending failure is to maintain a performance log designed to reveal trends. The log does not have to indicate *why* a change is taking place—that is the responsibility of the maintenance shop—only that a change has in fact taken place or is still in progress.

Keeping track of performance trends is not a new idea; the airlines have followed the practice for years to reduce maintenance costs and improve safety and they now employ highly computerized systems for the purpose. Most corporate flight operations that use large aircraft also have some form of performance trend monitoring program.

For those operators of sophisticated and large equipment the performance log, be it manual or computerized, pays off handsomely. The airlines, for instance, save millions of dollars just by paying attention to airspeed and fuel flow. A downward trend in airspeed at a given power setting alerts them to poorly fitting gear doors, worn or misadjusted gap seals at the control surfaces, misrigged flaps or leading edge devices and pressurization leaks. They have reduced this computerized trend watching to such a science that it tells them when the paint job has become so scuffed it makes economic sense to repaint the aircraft.

Fuel flows tell the airlines when it's economically advantageous to pull an engine down for a thorough inspection and repair.

A manually kept flight log for your single or twin can do almost as much for you. Kept over a long period, you will see the effect of a gear door out of rig almost instantly. In time, you'll also see the effect of worn door seals, power loss due to ring and valve wear, drag rise due to deteriorating paint and the performance loss in various systems and components.

This will assist you in determining when certain repairs are economically feasible. It will also—and this is very important—give you a talking point with your mechanic. Every aircraft operator has had the experience of being told he's a dummy by his mechanic. You try to explain to the A&P that your oil temperature is running higher than normal and he looks at you as though he thinks you belong in a padded cell and says curtly, "Yeah, it's summertime."

If you can get him to run the engine up, he'll just remark, "It's in the green," and no amount of arguing that it's lower than it was *last* summer will impress him.

A log of last summer's temperatures, however, should cause him to take a closer look at your oil cooler, the oil temperature bypass valve and whatnot. The same will be true for vacuum pressure, flap and gear motors, gyros and manifold pressure gauges. A record leaves no doubt that a change has occurred and something more than a superficial look is warranted.

One final thought before moving on to the log itself: a record must not be allowed to turn you into an aeronautical hypochondriac. Changes in performance are normal and to be expected. Having a long record of them will simply give you and your mechanic a better handle on the magnitude and rate of degradation.

It is impossible to standardize a performance trend log because different aircraft have different components and specifications. Even individual airplanes in the same model line can be equipped so independently that a trend log suitable for one might be inappropriate for another. Thus, you will have to construct a log tailored to the particular plane you fly.

What parameters should a performance trend log include? That too is an individual decision, but since the idea is to detect changes, the log should provide for the monitoring of anything that is critical to flight, can change in degrees and is subject to monitoring.

It should not be overdone, however. If the log calls for too many data inputs, the tendency will be to skip it on too many flights.

In that regard, the log does not have to be filled out *every* flight. But on most flights you have a half hour or so with nothing better to do, so you can occupy yourself with filling in the blanks for five minutes of it.

We prepared a sample log after consulting maintenance people and taking notes from the cockpit of the several aircraft we operate. Some of the parameters on it may not be pertinent to your aircraft, or your own log may need additions. In the case of a twin, two columns will be needed for engine and systems data.

Notice that the log format allows the recording of performance-related data for a number of flights or flight legs on the same sheet. This is very important. By keeping as many items on one sheet as possible, one can detect a trend simply by scanning a line. If you use separate sheets for each flight or leg, you will have to thumb through a stack to detect trends and that will defeat the purpose.

In fact, we recommend that the list of parameters down the left side be on one piece of paper and that the columns for data entry be on another. With that arrangement, as each sheet of data entries is filled, it can be taped to the previous one to create a running scroll of data lasting years if you like. Then you can run horizontally along a line—oil pressure, for instance—and instantly spot both seasonal and permanent trends.

Now let's go through the parameters one by one and examine the how and why. Note that we've broken our log into two sections: things to be entered in flight and things to be entered on the ground.

Date—This one is self-explanatory. For space reasons, we've elected to not show the year for each entry; we just jot it into the upper margin, as illustrated.

Trip Time—Trip Time might more logically belong down in the ground section, but we prefer it here next to the date so we can go back at the end of several days flying and use this log to bring our pilot log up to date at one setting. Use tachometer time for this entry if possible because it's more closely tied to how the engine was run (rpm) as in Hobbs time.

Altitude—This is the altitude of the point the following data was recorded. If you have two altimeters (and you should), record the deviation in the number two altimeter for a cross accuracy check at altitude.

Weight—Use an estimated weight at the time of recording the data.

OAT—Self-explanatory.

Climb—Record the climb rate at the same altitude each time—say, passing through 6000—at the same power and same indicated airspeed. A downward trend would most likely indicate deteriorating power output

5

	Date							
FLIGHT	Trip Time							
	Altitude							
	Weight							
	OAT							
	Climb							
	MP							
	RPM							
	Fuel Flow							
	EGT 1							
	2							
	3							
	4							
	5							
	6							
	CHT							
	Oil Temp.							
	Oil Pressure							
	Vacuum							
	IAS							
	TAS							
	DG Precession							
	Flap Speed							
	Gear Speed							
GROUND	Mags							
	Carb. Heat							
	Gen./Alt.							
	Vacuum							
	Oil Pressure							
	Altimeters							
	MP							
	Gyro Rundown							
	Fuel Added							
	Oil Added							

This is an example of what your own performance log might look like. We recommend that you attach the information on the left permanently to a clipboard. The vertical rules should be on a separate sheet of paper so a continuous log can be created.

from the engine(s), but it might also indicate a drag rise in the airframe.

MP—Manifold pressure is recorded to set the conditions for the following data, of course, but in nonturbocharged aircraft it should also be watched for trends. A down trend might indicate air leaks in the intake box or a deteriorating air filter. A trend might also indicate a degradation in gauge accuracy, but a cross-check on that is provided in the ground portion of the log.

RPM—Again, the primary purpose for recording RPM is to establish a standard for the following data.

Fuel Flow—This will vary depending on altitude, power setting and how the engine has been leaned, but trends will show up. Those trends could indicate a number of things ranging from an actual increase or decrease in fuel flow at a given power setting to a degradation in the accuracy of associated instrumentation, such as the tachometer or manifold pressure. An actual change in fuel flow would most likely be due to some change in the flow to an individual cylinder in an injected engine. In that case, it should show up in the EGT recordings. Gauge accuracy can be cross-checked against the specific consumption calculated later.

EGT—These should be recorded with the engine leaned in the usual way. Alternately, as we've done here, one cylinder can be leaned up to an index and the others measured relative to that index. Trends might indicate a bad spark plug, dirt in an injector, a leaking valve, a leaking induction system or a host of other things. You'll want to watch this one closely.

CHT—Since most cylinder head temperature gauges in small aircraft aren't marked off properly, we suggest a dab of white paint on the glass over the point where the needle normally sets. Then record excursions in needle widths above or below the white dot. Also, since the CHT thermocouple is usually on the hottest cylinder in a full throttle climb, it's best to make a mental note of the reading during climb for entry later. If you're leaning in the climb, the EGT should be about the same for each recording. If the trend is to a higher CHT, have your mechanic inspect your engine baffling, the baffle seals and the cowl flap rigging.

Oil Temp.—Again, you'll probably have to use a white dot and needle-width technique for recordings. Make certain the oil temperature has stabilized before taking the reading. If you spot a trend, check to see if it's following the trend of the OAT. If not, make sure you're running the same weight and quantity of oil in the engine before talking with your mechanic.

Oil Pressure—Record relative to a white dot at a stabilized oil temperature. In cruise, this is a check against the oil pressure relief valve; however, in very cold weather—at $-10°C$ or colder—you may see a dramatic increase or decrease in oil pressure during cruise. That's normal for many engines.

Vacuum—This too may be a check against the vacuum relief setting. At higher altitudes, however, it will indicate a deterioration in vacuum pump capacity.

IAS—As discussed above, a downward trend in indicated airspeed will most likely be due to increased drag. Have your mechanic check gear and cabin door rigging and seals, flap rigging and all fairings. A decreasing IAS might also be due to inaccuracies in various gauges.

TAS—Compared to IAS, true airspeed doesn't tell you much except what altitude you're trending to fly. But you'll be curious.

DG Precession—Record both the precession and the heading. Often a DG will precess more on one heading than another and that's good to know. The use of the eight cardinal points—N, SE, NW—is close enough.

Flap Speed—We recommend timing the full extension at a given speed and don't expect to record a dramatic trend. Flap motors tend to work forever or not at all. But occasionally a gross difference will pop up and that should receive the attention of a mechanic.

Gear Speed—It's best to record the retraction time and here you may spot a trend due to binding, poor hydraulic seals or a weakening motor. Have it checked out.

After you've landed and cleared the runway, you can get down to the serious checking.

Mags—We recommend that you stop briefly out on the ramp for a quick mag check. If you've got a problem, better to find it upon arrival rather than when you're in a hurry to crank up and fly home that night. Record the drop on each side.

Carb. Heat—Check the carburetor heat drop or alternate air system at this time.

Gen./Alt.—Next turn on all the electrical appliances you can and check to see what rpm is required to zero the amp meter. (Obviously, this check is feasible in some aircraft and not in others.) An upward trend in the rpm required will reveal a weakness in the generator or alternator. This check should be conducted at the end of a day flight, of course, when the battery is presumably fully charged.

Vacuum—Now check the rpm required to bring the vacuum pressure (or instrument *pressure*) to a given value.

Oil Pressure—Using rpm as the gauge, bring the oil pressure up to a given value. In some airplanes this check cannot be done on a cool day because of a high pressure value even at dead idle. On others you'll have to use different summer and winter index values. Experimentation is required. This check will tell you quite a lot about engine bearing wear, but it cannot tell you when an overhaul is a must. If the rpm required begins to concern you, perform the same check on other like aircraft to establish a norm.

Now you can taxi in and shut down for the rest of the checks.

Altimeters—Set the current altimeter as given by the tower and record the deviation from field elevation. In the case of an unlevel airport, you may have to defer this check until you taxi out to the touchdown zone and compare readings against the altitude shown on the approach plate.

MP—With the engine off, record the manifold pressure deviation from the aircraft altimeter setting. This is a check on the gauge accuracy. Few will be right, but the deviation should be consistent.

Gyro Rundown—The length of time it takes a gyro to run down indicates the condition of its bearings. Therefore, it's a good idea to time the rundown occasionally. If you have exceptionally quiet instruments, a screwdriver held against the cases will help you hear them. No time has been established as a norm, but if you discover any trend, consult an instrument repairman.

Fuel Added—We record this as specific consumption by dividing the pounds consumed by the trip time. To make it a more meaningful number that can be compared for both long and short trips, subtract taxi and takeoff fuel from the total added. For a 200-hp engine that's about nine pounds, ranging up to 15 pounds for a 300-hp model.

Oil Added—Each quart of oil added should be recorded, but periodically —perhaps once each 10 trips—the sum should be divided into the hours flown to establish a specific consumption figure.

At first all this may seem a lot of work for a small return, but it'll do several things for you, all of them good.

For one thing, it'll keep you aware of what's going on with your aircraft. You'll begin to have a feel for it you never possessed before and that will cause you to notice things not even covered by the log.

Also, keeping a log will increase your confidence in your aircraft. It's surprising, but just *knowing* that your airplane is performing properly, and *knowing* that you'll spot it quickly if something does begin to degrade, actually adds to both the utility and utilization.

Airworthiness Directives

2

by Gerard M. Bruder, Jr

On the night of June 30, 1977, the cabin door of a Learjet 23 suddenly opened and separated from the airframe as the aircraft was rotated for takeoff from Wichita's Mid-Continent Airport. Although the door struck the tail, damage was minor and the pilot completed the takeoff, declared an emergency and successfully returned to the field.

There was nothing sensational about the incident, and it attracted little attention—even in the Wichita press. Yet, the incident ultimately affected every operator of the Learjet 23, 24 and 25 series in the world; it prompted the issuance of an airworthiness directive that required replacement of the upper door-handle bolt on such aircraft.

That AD was one of 310 the FAA issued in 1977. Like taxes and occasional mechanical problems, ADs are inevitable for just about all aircraft and thus contribute to operating costs. Many ADs actually involve relatively minor expenses and downtime (a few require only a one-time inspection with no teardown), but some are significant enough to threaten the economic viability of certain operations—and destroy the future marketability of the affected aircraft model.

Because both operating costs and the number of ADs have increased in recent years, you, as an operator or maintenance chief, should understand the AD-formulation process and the considerations it includes. You should also realize that you can play a role in that process in a variety of ways.

The first "ADs" were issued in the 1920s by the Bureau of Air Commerce of the Department of Commerce, but then they were called "maintenance notes"; federal inspectors performing annual relicensing inspections of aircraft would describe serious deficiencies in the "notes" section of their relicensing forms, and if a particular deficiency were later discovered on one or more aircraft of the same model, a mandatory, fleetwide correction would be prescribed.

Air safety was of deep concern to the government even in those early days of aviation, and it became more so as manufacturers produced higher performance aircraft, public acceptance of air travel increased and the full potential of aviation became evident. Thanks both to technology and federal regulations, flight safety gradually increased—a trend that continues today and that, because of its positive nature, constantly inspires ever more stringent regulations and standards. (Paradoxically, air disasters are now so infrequent that when one does occur, it receives publicity that gives the uninformed public the delusion that flying actually is *unsafe.*)

Several years after the Civil Aeronautics Authority was formed in 1940 to regulate the growing aviation industry, maintenance notes were renamed ADs, and the system of formulating them continued to evolve into the structure which is in effect today.

The present AD-formulation process involves four main steps: discovery of the deficiency, fact-gathering, evaluation/decision and implementation.

Discovery can occur from accident investigation; maintenance Malfunction or Defect Reports (repair stations are required to submit them, and company maintenance personnel are encouraged to do so); manufacturers' service bulletins; reports from pilots and operators of unusual or abnormal mechanical developments; and patterns or profiles that become evident from a series of incidents.

Accident investigation plays a major role in the creation of an AD, especially if the circumstances of a particular crash are "suspicious," as was the case in the inflight breakup of a Cessna 441 Conquest November 15, 1977; the 441 was a new aircraft and the pilot reported severe vibration. The FAA required the installation of a dual trim-tab elevator system on all 441s, and while the NTSB has not concluded its investigation of the accident, it recommended that similar trim-tab systems be installed on all Cessna 400-series aircraft—a recommendation subsequently rejected by the FAA.

However, the April 25 crash of another new airplane—the Beech 76 Duchess—was not suspicious (it apparently was weather-related) and has thus far resulted in no ADs or recommendations.

The FAA and the NTSB work closely together on accident investigations, even though the former has no legal accident investigative authority. The FAA usually is delegated the responsibility to analyze nonfatal accidents and is invited to participate in all fatals, but only the Safety Board may determine probable cause.

Thus, the FAA is in a position to discover flagrant design problems as promptly as the NTSB is. But not all flaws are obvious, and the FAA relies heavily on the Safety Board's studied analyses and subsequent recommendations in areas where accident causes are not easily determined.

The relationship between the FAA and the NTSB was not always one of complete confidence, however, and even now the two agencies occasionally have differences of opinion.

For several years after the NTSB was formed in 1967, the FAA reportedly ignored many NTSB recommendations on the assumption that the Board was not really qualified to issue them. The Board did, in fact, make some recommendations that were highly controversial. For instance, just three days after its offices opened, the NTSB asked the FAA to ground all Beech 18s until a final fix was found to a wing-spar problem that had already caused six fatal accidents and been the subject of 12 ADs. Because there were several thousand Beech 18s in the field at the time, some of which constituted entire fleets, the FAA regarded such a recommendation as economically unfeasible—and unnecessary from a safety standpoint.

But the agency did issue an AD that required visual, magnetic-particle and X-ray inspections of thin-wall Beech 18 wing spars prior to subsequent flight. One operator in Texas who used 20 Beech 18s for mail and cargo flights was irate over that AD and charged that it would ruin his business. Then he discovered a crack in one of his aircraft's wing spars and "became a staunch supporter," an FAA official said. (But some operators ignored the AD or performed cursory inspections, and the Beech 18 wing-spar problem caused another three fatal accidents and prompted seven more ADs, some of which were intended to clarify or expand previous ADs.)

Eventually, the NTSB established its credibility, and now the FAA complies with 75 to 85 percent of NTSB recommendations for ADs, according to Safety Board figures. The Board made 113 AD recommendations from 1967 to 1977.

Several times Congress has asked the Safety Board if it wishes authority to issue decrees instead of recommendations, but the Board maintains that it could not remain impartial and politically "removed" with such authority. For example, an NTSB spokesman says, if the Board ordered a certain structural change to correct a deficiency in a business jet and a year later several accidents in that model occurred because the change actually had been unrelated to the problem, the Board would be under pressure to defend its action.

One NTSB recommendation the FAA wishes it had complied with immediately concerned the rear cargo door on the DC-10. One such door suddenly blew off of an American Airlines DC-10 en route to New York City from Los Angeles June 12, 1972, causing decompression, extensive damage and critical flight control problems. Although there were no fatalities or serious injuries, the captain had to make an emergency landing and was unable to keep the aircraft on the runway.

The NTSB recommended that the FAA require two changes: (1) modifications to the DC-10 rear cargo door to preclude future inflight separations, and (2) the installation of relief vents between the cabin and aft cargo compartment to minimize the pressure loading on the cabin floor should a recurrence take place.

1. REGISTRATION NO. N-34DC	DEPARTMENT OF TRANSPORTATION FEDERAL AVIATION ADMINISTRATION **MALFUNCTION OR DEFECT REPORT**			Form Approved Budget Bureau No. 04-R0003	8. DATE SUB. 7/26/78	**FOR FAA USE ONLY** CONTROL NO.					
	A. MAKE	B. MODEL	C. SERIAL NO.	7A. COMMENTS (Describe the malfunction or defect and the circumstances under which it occurred. State probable cause and recommendations to prevent recurrence.)							
2. AIRCRAFT	Adanac	Pegasus (385 shp)	10-503	Experienced unusual vibration of airframe on three occasions when airspeed was above 200 knots. Unable to determine cause.							
3. POWERPLANT	TurbPowerCo.	RME-385	2984								
4. PROPELLER	BladeCorp.	4-bladed full feather	CS-1067								
5. APPLIANCE/COMPONENT (assy. that includes part)											
A. NAME	B. MAKE	C. MODEL	D. SERIAL NO.								
	N/A										Continue on reverse
6. SPECIFIC PART (of component) CAUSING TROUBLE				SUBMITTED BY							
A. NAME	B. NUMBER	C. PART/DEFECT LOCATION									
	N/A										
FAA USE	E. PART TT	F. PART TSO	G. PART CONDITION	B.	C.	D.	E.	F.	G.	H.	I.
D. ATA CODE	N/A			REP. STA.	OPER.	MECH.	AIR TAXI	MFG.	FAA	OTHER	

FAA FORM 8330-2 (9-70) SUPERSEDES PREVIOUS EDITIONS

The FAA's Malfunction or Defect Reports are an important source of information on potential fleetwide design problems. The report is fictitious but represents a typical report.

But those fixes represented investments of millions of dollars for McDonnell Douglas, manufacturer of the DC-10, and then-FAA Administrator John H. Shaffer decided against an AD in favor of a "gentleman's agreement" between the agency and the manufacturer that the latter would resolve the problem—presumably in a manner and a time frame more economically attractive than the provisions of an AD would have been. The gentleman's agreement approach was, in fact, an accepted FAA policy in certain situations—particularly those in which the affected fleet was relatively small. The official FAA *AD Handbook* at the time even sanctioned that approach.

Almost two years later, on March 3, 1974, a Turkish Airlines DC-10 crashed near Paris, killing all 346 persons aboard in what was until recently the worst aviation accident in history.

An investigation revealed that the aircraft's rear cargo door had blown off—and that modifications to the door had not been completed. The official French report contained this comment (translated):

"The Commission recommends that the mandatory procedure of 'airworthiness directives,' whatever the financial repercussions, should be selected whenever safety could be at serious risk."

Such sentiment was echoed in the United States, where public and Congressional criticism of the FAA was scathing. The result was a significant AD policy change, one that is largely responsible for the increased number of ADs you've noticed in the past several years: The agency held NTSB recommendations in higher regard, abandoned its gentleman's agreement approach, began reviewing each and every manufacturer service bulletin and, through ADs, converted into law those bulletins that were safety-related.

It should be noted that in many cases ADs that follow service bulletins are superfluous because the necessary fixes have already been accomplished by the time the AD is issued.

"Often, the manufacturer can move faster than we can," an FAA engineer at the agency's Washington, D.C., headquarters says. "This is especially true when the AD is preceded by a proposal."

Nonetheless, the AD is still issued so that the agency will be protected from lawsuits and criticism in case subsequent accidents occur to aircraft whose owners failed to comply with the fix.

The NTSB was not entirely blameless in the DC-10 cargo door scandal because it neglected to check to see if corrective action had been taken. After the Paris disaster, the Safety Board instituted an automatic follow-up program on its recommendation (in *all* areas of transportation) and now sends a formal and public letter of inquiry to the appropriate regulatory agency whenever a recommendation has not brought at least an acknowledgment within 90 days.

Accident investigation and service bulletins do not account for all discoveries of design deficiencies, of course; Malfunction or Defect Reports (the FAA says it gets such reports on about 25 percent of all significant repairs) and letters or phone calls from operators contribute their share.

But the discovery of a serious problem in an aircraft airframe, engine or system does not automatically produce an AD because in many instances the problem is a result of abuse, faulty installation or simple wear and tear. The purpose of the second step in the AD-formulation process—fact-gathering—is to obtain sufficient information about a deficiency to determine if the problem is fleetwide or unique. To accomplish that the FAA contacts the manufacturer (who in turn contacts customers) and conducts tests.

One day the leading edge of a Cessna 401 wing literally exploded when the pilot turned off the landing lights while taxiing at Silver City, New Mexico. None of the occupants were injured, but the wing was destroyed, and had the incident occurred in flight it undoubtedly would have been fatal. An investigation determined that fumes from a fuel leak in the leading edge area had been ignited when the landing lights were deactivated. However, the FAA found that the leak and explosion in the 401 had resulted from a combination of faulty maintenance and improper fuel management and that the series' fuel system design was sound; no AD was issued, although 401 fuel system inspection advice was later included in a maintenance advisory circular.

On another occasion, a Beech King Air 90 operator discovered that the autopilot elevator servo had pulled the elevator control cable off its track, resulting in so much friction that only one cable strand was still intact. Beech sent a service bulletin to its King Air owners urging them to inspect the elevator control cables in their aircraft and immediately report any wear. One operator found wear, and four days later the FAA issued an emergency AD requiring modification of the H-14 autopilot elevator servo on models A90, B90, C90 and E90.

When the FAA is unable to obtain enough information through informal channels, it often issues a "fact-finding" AD instructing owners to inspect a suspect part or system and report the results to the FAA. Later, if the comments warrant, another AD is issued to prescribe corrective action and/or periodic inspections.

The FAA says it now enjoys excellent cooperation with manufacturers in isolating and correcting design deficiencies, but this was not always the case. "Ten years ago," says a project engineer from the FAA's Central Region, "manufacturers pretty much considered ADs to be stigmas on their products and even went to Washington in an attempt to have them revoked. Now, companies *ask* for ADs on things we often consider to be too minor; the number of [product-liability] lawsuits has increased, and they realize they're in a better position legally if they've asked us for an AD—whether or not we actually issue an AD."

But such requests are often valid and thus do justify ADs. Manufacturers' product-liability concerns and the other factors we've mentioned were responsible for the issuance by the Central Region of 45 ADs in 1975 and the same number in 1976 for Cessna, Beech and Gates Learjet products compared to just six in 1966 and seven in 1967. (The Central Region issues more ADs because more airframe models are within its area of jurisdiction.)

Once the FAA has gathered sufficient data on an incident or suspected deficiency, the agency moves into the evaluation/decision phase of the AD-formulation process. This is perhaps the most critical stage, for an error in judgment here can result in fatal crashes later on or unnecessary expenses for both operators and the manufacturer, either of which weakens the FAA's credibility and thus the weight of future ADs. In fact, the FAA is required by law to justify formally each AD. The justification is published in the *Federal Register*, where all ADs are officially recorded. Consequently, the evaluation process is painstakingly thorough and involves a continual exchange of information and ideas among FAA personnel and the manufacturer.

For example, in the Central Region, the project engineer assigned to a case studies the facts, consults with other engineers and the manufacturer and makes a recommendation. The office chief then reviews the recommen-

15

dation and either concurs or remands it for additional study and justification.

If there is concurrence, the recommendation is sent to the Engineering and Manufacturing Branch of the region, where it is reviewed for concurrence and conformance with FAA standards and policy. Next, the recommendation goes to the region's divisional level for more review. Now the recommendation moves on to the legal division for proper preparation and format.

A copy is sent to Washington headquarters for approval, and finally the regional director signs the recommendation; it is then law. In rare cases in which an AD would have a major economic or political impact—as in the DC-10 rear cargo door problem—it is reviewed by the FAA Administrator.

Four times a year a review board—composed of 10 to 20 persons, including the Central Regional director—meets in an all-day session to discuss recent action, review the status of current AD proposals and resolve any difficulties that may have arisen.

These basic steps are followed in the formulation of each AD, regardless of its source or urgency. Procedures vary somewhat in other regions, but the format in them is similar.

Safety is always the primary consideration in evaluation of an AD proposal, but close behind that is the potential economic impact on owners, operators and the manufacturer. Some FAA officials unofficially concede that the 16 ADs issued on the Beech 99 between 1969 and 1977 probably crippled the marketability of that commuter aircraft. (Beech officials say

---

AD Information, Please

Thinking about buying an aircraft and want to know which ADs are outstanding on that particular model? You have several sources of information.

If an FAA General Aviation District Office is nearby, you can stop by and review a listing of all current ADs. Some FAA district engineering and manufacturing branches also maintain such lists.

You can obtain your own copy of all current ADs (on airframes, engines, avionics and other equipment) by subscribing to the FAA's "Summary of Airworthiness Directives." The summary is published in two versions; Volume I is for aircraft under 12,500 pounds, while Volume II covers aircraft over 12,500 pounds. Each volume is updated in even-numbered years.

Make checks or money orders payable to the FAA and write to the FAA, Aeronautical Center, Attention: ACC-23, P.O. Box 25461, Oklahoma City, Ok. 73125.

If you are interested in AD information on one model or series of aircraft (except pure jets), AeroTech Publications, Old Bridge, New Jersey, offers several excellent services that provide, at a glance, current, comprehensive maintenance data on the aircraft and all applicable equipment. Information is available from the company at P.O. Box 528, Old Bridge, New Jersey 08857.

production of the 99 was suspended due to decreasing market demand but that there is now renewed interest in acquisition of the aircraft.) The FAA realizes that public outcries over excessive ADs could have major repercussions in the agency's structure and among its top personnel.

"We try to find a balance between safety and economics whenever possible," one FAA regional director says. "If there are two ways of complying with an AD, we'll choose the less expensive one even if it is slightly less desirable."

In fact, the government was sensitive to public reaction to mandatory fixes way back in the budding days of aviation. A 1930 Department of Commerce memo to inspectors describing modifications to the tail of Travel Air aircraft (produced by the Travel Air Manufacturing Company) contained the following admonition:

"Not a little diplomacy will be needed in handling some of these owners, no doubt, and as we have no wish to broadcast any details that would be damaging to Travel Air, it is particularly requested that nothing that could be construed as an arbitrary attitude be adopted by our inspectors in handling such of these cases as come under their jurisdiction."

When an AD is likely to generate considerable controversy, the FAA often issues a press release to amplify the need for the measure. The recent Beech Queen Air/Twin Bonanza AD is an example. Four Queen Airs and one Twin Bonanza crashed between 1972 and 1978—four in 1977—after engine fires started forward of the firewall (on the outboard side of the engine, out of the crew's line of sight), spread and weakened the wing spar before they were detected. The AD called for installation of a closed-loop fire-detection system, new fire-resistant hoses and preflight inspections of the engine compartments while the fuel boost pumps are on. One FAA source estimated the individual cost of compliance at $3,000 to $5,000, and many operators of the 839 affected aircraft claimed that AD would ruin the resale value of the aircraft.

"We recognize the economic impact on owners and operators of the aircraft, and every effort—consistent with safety—has been made toward minimizing the potential cost of modifying these airplanes," said Central Region Director C. R. Melugin, Jr., in a press release on the AD. "However, the overriding safety considerations and our responsibilities to the flying public demand that this action be taken."

In an attempt to ease the AD economic burden on owners and operators, the FAA often grants compliance deadline extensions and makes provisions for temporary inspections for ferrying affected aircraft to repair stations. The agency recently extended the deadline for complying with an AD issued on the Cessna 210 landing gear because Cessna was suffering a strike and a backlog had developed on necessary parts. Without the extension, a large number of 210s would have been grounded.

ADs may be challenged in court, but the FAA says that they rarely are.

The urgency of an AD governs how quickly implementation—the last step in the AD-formulation process—takes place. The FAA is not required to solicit comments on proposed measures, although if the time factor is not critical it usually does in the form of a notice of proposed rulemaking (NPRM). Sometimes the agency even issues an advance NPRM, followed later by an NPRM.

One FAA official admits that the *Federal Register* is not a good medium for solicitation of comments because few owners and operators read it. Thus, many NPRMs receive little response (creating a delusion of public apathy) until the NPRM becomes an AD; "then people scream." *B/CA* and other aviation publications serve as a more effective forum, he says.

Occasionally, when an NPRM does generate comments that bring additional facts to light, the FAA withdraws the proposal. For example, the agency rescinded an NPRM to require adjustments to the elevator trim tab system of Beech Barons and Travel Airs to correct excessive play after many operators argued that this was a maintenance problem rather than a design deficiency.

However, most NPRMs eventually become ADs. "We give them very careful thought," according to an FAA project engineer, who adds that when an NPRM is withdrawn, the agency reserves the right to reissue it at a later time.

If immediate corrective action is imperative in the interest of safety, the FAA issues an emergency AD (the same formulation steps are followed, but efforts are concentrated and a number of personnel work full-time on the AD). Most emergency ADs require a fix or inspection before the next flight, which in effect grounds the entire fleet until compliance takes place (in the case of the Conquest, the agency withdrew the aircraft's airworthiness certificate, an extremely rare action).

The implementation process can take as long as six months or as little as three days, depending on the safety factor. In all cases, however, copies of the AD are sent to all registered owners of the affected airplane, engine or avionics from the FAA's computerized registration list in Oklahoma City.

ADs involving U.S. registered foreign-manufactured aircraft are handled through Washington headquarters and are sent to an appropriate embassy or agency in the country of manufacture.

Similarly, when another country becomes aware of a design flaw in an American-made airplane based there, it forwards its version of an AD to Washington. Cooperation between government and industry is practically universal, according to the FAA.

When action prescribed in an AD is especially critical—as in the case of the Beech 18 wing—the agency often requires written reports of compliance. Usually, however, the FAA assumes that the owner or operator will have enough common and self-preservation sense to comply with the AD. Since discovery of noncompliance is automatic grounds for issuance of a "violation"—usually a fine—and since such violations are "very rare," in the words of an FAA inspector, that assumption apparently is correct (although a case may be made that many instances of noncompliance go undetected).

Tougher certification standards have undoubtedly precluded a great number of design problems and subsequent ADs. For instance, the FAA says it would not certify the Beech 18 with its original wing-spar design today. Given composite materials, continued technological advances, increased use of computerization in the aviation field and retirement of older aircraft, it may be possible to reach the day when the FAA will have to find something else for its AD people to do.

The FAA's Service Difficulty Program 3

by Dan Manningham

The FAA's Aeronautical Center is strategically located at Will Rogers World Airport in Oklahoma City. This bustling, campus-like complex houses the activities of several dozen individual departments and divisions from air traffic controller training to development of new flight standards. On the second floor of the Aircraft Records Building, in Room 217, is the Safety Data Branch, a little-known service arm of the FAA. The Safety Data Branch has several specific functions, but its most interesting and valuable contribution to general aviation is the Service Difficulty Program.

The Service Difficulty Program deals with broken parts. In operation it is designed to promote flight safety by providing an open exchange of mechanical and maintenance irregularity information. Mechanics, inspectors, pilots and operators contribute their individual aircraft malfunction or defect experiences, which are incorporated into a bank of useful data available to anyone with an interest. If you would like to know the service history of any given aircraft or system, this is the place to start. Globe Swift landing gear difficulties, JetRanger engine malfunctions and King Air pressurization problems, for example, are all catalogued in the data bank.

The basic authority for this sort of service is FAR 145.63:

"(a) Each certificated domestic repair station shall report to the Administrator within 72 hours after it discovers any serious defect in, or other recurring unairworthy condition of, an aircraft, powerplant or propeller, or any component of any of them."

Despite this and other FARs that mandate reports from certain segments, such as certificated repair stations and air taxi operators, the vast majority of reports are submitted voluntarily by mechanics, inspectors, pilots and operators. In reality, information flows in and out of the Service Difficulty Program on a grass-roots, free-wheeling basis that belies the precise processing, control and storage that is this program's forte. Individual reports, often received in scrawled handwriting on grease-stained postcards, are collected, edited and electronically processed. All information is available to the general public without restraint and at only token cost. The concept of liberal data interchange is essential to the program's purpose of enhanced safety without unnecessary regulation.

The Service Difficulty Program is the combined effort of the Safety Data Branch's three individual sections—Data Review, Maintenance Analysis, and Aircraft and Agency, each with clearly delineated responsibilities. The Maintenance Analysis Center (MAC) has received some attention recently although that section is merely the most visible element of the total Service Difficulty Program. The process begins at the Data Review Section.

The Data Review Section processes all input to the Service Difficulty Program. Information comes into this office on postcards and neatly typed air carrier forms and by telephone. Basically, there are three types of reports that convey service difficulty information from the field to the office:

• The Malfunction or Defect Report (FAA Form 8330-2) is an oversized, postpaid postcard available to repair facilities from the local general aviation district office. When a mechanic, or any other qualified individual, finds a problem related to design, materials or workmanship, he fills out the card and drops it in the mail. The GADO reviews the cards to detect problems in products or maintenance systems within the district and forwards them to the Data Review Section.

From every M or D Report, specialists at Data Review carefully process the information into a form acceptable to the computer. Some editing of the comments section may be done here to accommodate the computer's limited word storage capacity of 115 characters per report, but all M or D Reports are microfilmed and readily retrievable. Actually, M or D Reports are simply transposed into the same format used routinely by air carriers and air taxi operators. That format, known as the Service Difficulty Report, is another form of input to the Data Review Section.

• The Service Difficulty Report (FAA Form 8070-1) is the final document for all computer inputs and is used by air carriers and air taxi operators to report the same sort of discrepancies general aviation mechanics would report on the M or D Report. The Service Difficulty Report is more formal than the M or D Report and is used by those operators accustomed to the idiosyncrasies of Air Transport Association coding systems. The purpose and content are identical to those of M or D Reports, which are transposed to this format at Data Review anyway.

• Maintenance Difficulty Records are simply telephoned reports, usually of an alert or hazardous nature, such as structural failures, control-system failures or fires. Maintenance Difficulty Reports are also processed into the standardized Service Difficulty Report format at the Data Review Section. Most Maintenance Difficulty Reports come from within the FAA, but anyone may call the Safety Data Branch at (405) 686–4171/4173 to report a hazardous situation.

In all cases these input reports should be as complete and accurate as possible. Pictures, sketches and/or defective parts are extremely helpful in the process and should be included whenever possible.

The U.S. civil aircraft fleet numbers about 190,000 units. There are approximately 3,600 certificated repair stations. In 1977 the Safety Data Branch received just over 16,000 reports of service difficulty, a paltry sum estimated to be 10 percent or less of actual service difficulties. Even if each repair station submitted just one M or D Report per month the totals would nearly triple. One major engine overhauler, an FAA certificated repair station, reports it just isn't organized to submit M or Ds and seldom uses them. This is unfortunate because everyone benefits from accurate, timely reporting to the central data bank.

A serious potential deterrent to participation in the program is that submitters of M or D Reports or Service Difficulty Reports are not granted immunity from legal or administrative action. The Safety Data Branch is not given to issuing violations, but many potential contributors may be intimidated by even the suggestion of liability. The fact is that the Service Difficulty Program probably would receive far more support if the FAA would specifically declare immunity for submitters, as the agency has done with the Aviation Safety Reporting Program. In the meantime, if you are concerned about incriminating yourself, your company or your aircraft, just submit the report without names or identifiable numbers. It is less useful than a complete report but far better than no report at all.

The Maintenance Analysis Center is the section of the Safety Data Branch that is responsible for statistical output. Information that has been edited and processed into the computer data bank by the Data Review Section is retrieved and disseminated by the Maintenance Analysis Center. Several statistical outputs are routinely generated here for internal FAA and NTSB use, but business and commercial operators will find the MAC's tailored outputs to be most useful.

When requested, the Maintenance Analysis Center will extract specific data concerning service difficulties with any single aircraft, model fleet or system/subsystem. Computer printouts are available for any U.S.-certificated aircraft, engine, propeller, component or appliance. Data are retained for the past five-year period and printouts are available for any portion thereof. These computer-printed Service Difficulty Reports do not include the cause of a failure or problem, but they do describe the circumstances.

If, for instance, you were interested in the service history of the Piper Aztec, the Maintenance Analysis Center could supply service difficulty information for all aircraft of that model for up to the past five years. Really complete coverage requires separate reports for that aircraft model,

22

the appropriate engine and the applicable propeller. Separate engine and propeller reports provide all available service difficulty information for those components regardless of aircraft model. In this case the Lycoming 540 engine and the Hartzell propeller are widely used on other aircraft so that separate engine and propeller Service Difficulty Reports would include all information from those installations.

The Maintenance Analysis Center can generate these reports in 21 formats and 26 sorts tailored to your individual needs. (Format is the horizontal arrangement of data across the report, such as part number, manufacturer's name, etc. Sort is the vertical sequence of data arranged according to system, N-number, make and model, etc.) Formats and sorts are best selected by discussing your requirements with Maintenance Analysis Center personnel on the phone. If they understand your needs, they can readily prescribe the best format and sort.

Regardless of the specific format or sort, Service Difficulty Reports from the Maintenance Analysis Center contain a wealth of information. Each incident is detailed in a three-line printout that summarizes the original Malfunction or Defect Report or Service Difficulty Report. Arrangement of the data varies with the selected format, but one typical report, which was extracted from a service difficulty program that included over 600 individual three-line reports for a certain model of turboshaft engine, included the following information:

- Component make—N.A.
- Component model—N.A.
- Component serial number—N.A.
- Part name—"coupling nut"
- Part number—6871338
- Condition—"failed"
- Location—"outer position"
- Aircraft model—N.A.
- Aircraft serial number—N.A.
- Engine model—N.A.
- Engine serial-number—N.A.
- Text—"Power turbine outer coupling nut failed at liftoff causing three and four turbine wheels to disintegrate."

At the far right-hand corner of each report is a code group of condensed information that can easily be deciphered with a reader template supplied by the Maintenance Analysis Center. In this case the code group revealed that:

- This incident was reported by an FAA inspector via telephone from the Pacific region.
- The incident involved engine stoppage, inflight separation and multiple failures during the takeoff.

• The original report contains a lengthy verbal description that may be reviewed by requesting a copy of microfilm frame number DZ 0331.

• The subject engine had accumulated 1,375 hours total time.

The Service Difficulty Program is a virtual library of service problems assembled in a highly condensed form. A complete reading of every individual item could take hours or days, but few operators would benefit from such minute scrutiny.

In most cases requesters will find more useful information by scanning the Service Difficulty Reports for specific items and patterns. In the case of our turboshaft-engine report, for instance, it is immediately obvious that fuel control problems have dominated (485 out of 660 incidents) and that each of the two fuel controllers for that engine has been responsible for a surprisingly similar number of problems (215 versus 240).

The Service Difficulty Program can be tailored to include only information recorded for a specific aircraft by its N-number or information on any single system for a fleet, such as Learjet pressurization, Hughes 500 tail rotors or Cessna Citation windows. Service Difficulty Reports are normally mailed within 24 hours after the Maintenance Analysis Center receives the request, although in a few instances it may take up to 48 hours. At B/CA we have received Service Difficulty Reports in the mail within two days of a telephone request. In all cases we have found Maintenance Analysis Center personnel to be courteous and very helpful.

At present most interrogations to the Maintenance Analysis Center are from lawyers involved in aviation cases, so that the primary purpose of the Service Difficulty Program has, unfortunately, been prostituted. Certainly, it's appropriate for lawyers to make use of this information, but it is somewhat ironic that service difficulty information is used more for product liability litigation than for safety.

The third section of the Safety Data Branch and the last element in the Service Difficulty Program is the Aircraft and Agency Section.

Aircraft and Agency uses service difficulty information from the data bank to create analytical outputs. Its most familiar product was the *General Aviation Inspection Aids*, AC 20-7, which was recently replaced by new Advisory Circular 43-16, General Aviation Airworthiness Alerts.

AW Alerts is a monthly publication consisting of a selection of the most pertinent information of assistance to maintenance and inspection people.

Individual items can be thought of as voluntary AD notes, ranging from the correct routing of a fuel line to avoid chafing to the proper tensioning of control cables. *AW Alerts* is a vital output from the Service Difficulty Program. All material in the issues is advisory, but it is unthinkable that a professional mechanic or operator would ignore this excellent compilation of potential service problems.

Unfortunately, unlike the old *Inspection Aids, AW Alerts* are not being offered on a subscription basis. Instead, they are being distributed, free of charge, only to the following: GADOs, state aeronautical commissions, air taxi operators, authorized inspectors, FAA-approved repair facilities and maintenance schools. Aircraft owners and operators will have to contact one of these recipients in order to see AC 43-16.

Really dangerous flaws or problems identified by the Aircraft and Agency Section may become Airworthiness Directives mandating corrections or inspections. That action is accomplished by the region that certificated the aircraft, engine or propeller.

The Service Difficulty Program ranks as one of the most useful and least publicized activities of the FAA. Grass roots information from field mechanics, inspectors and pilots filters directly into a sophisticated data bank where it is readily available to anyone at truly nominal cost, and pilots, mechanics, inspectors, owners, operators and purchasers can all benefit from the wealth of data it makes available.

The program is as close as your telephone and nearly as quick. If you are interested in the maintenance history of a particular airplane or accessory, call the program people at (405) 686–4171/4173. The person who answers can talk your language and provide some of the most pertinent information available. If your shop does not have a supply of Malfunction or Defect Report cards, order them today and request a GADO inspector to visit your operation and explain the program.

The Service Difficulty Program is alive and well in Oklahoma City. If everyone in the industry contributed, the general aviation community could really benefit from this most useful data exchange.

POWERPLANTS: PISTON   II

They used to be called motors. Then they were engines. Now they are powerplants. As the names have become more "sophisticated", so have the propulsive systems that power airplanes. Piston engines by nature involve a propeller, so this chapter looks at the care and operation of that two-part system.

Piston engines are the backbone of the general aviation fleet. As sophistication—and prices—rise, proper maintenance becomes ever more critical. "The State of Piston Engine Maintenance" examines the best techniques for prolonged engine life, including how to select your engine maintenance or overhaul facility.

Propellers often are embraced with sublime neglect. After all, props are simple, tough and durable. Unfortunately they can self-destruct, taking the entire airplane down. Props are more than important, they are vital. "You and Your Prop" checks the common reasons for propeller failure and suggests proper procedures to avoid it. Propeller governors are small hydro-mechanical devices that control pitch as a function of commanded rpm. They are obscure and innocuous devices until they malfunction. If that happens you will need nerves of steel and perhaps some inordinate blessings to avoid an accident.

In World War II most high performance airplanes had turbocharged engines. It has taken nearly 30 years for that technology to filter down to general aviation but now it is here with a vengeance. "Turbocharging A New Generation of Aircraft" examines turbocharger design, application and operation.

Engine fire protection is as dear to the pilot as hearth and home. Surprisingly, there are no formal regulations on piston-engine fire protection systems but "Piston-Engine Fire Protection" examines the methods which have proved effective.

The State of Piston Engine Maintenance

Perhaps the pacing factor in the growth of general aviation in recent years has been the accelerated advances in propulsion system technology. Wide application of the turboprop and turbojet powered powerplants has brought about greater operational reliability, longer engine life and greatly expanded safe service time between recommended powerplant overhauls.

So beneficial have been the effects of gas turbine aircraft engines, in fact, that the end may seem near for the aircraft piston engine.

Not so. For every turbine powered aircraft in the general aviation fleet, there are more than 50 piston engine airplanes in operation.

That's the reason many informed observers are concerned that a crisis may be developing that could retard the continued growth of general aviation; the numbers of piston engine mechanics and repair facilities have not increased at anywhere near the rate pilot and airplane populations have.

While reciprocating engines have become more reliable and longer-lived over the years, that progress also is disproportionate to the number of piston powerplants presently in service in the aircraft fleet.

In its Advisory Circular 140-1J, the FAA lists some 3,300 agency-approved domestic repair stations, 346 of which are specifically certificated to perform maintenance and overhaul work on designated engine makes and models. Those are not the only sources for such services, however. Many A&P mechanics operating on or in the vicinity of the nation's 7,000 public use airports, or from other locations, can perform major engine services with impunity, even though not endowed with repair station certification. In addition, aircraft engine manufacturers compete strongly for maintenance work with entrepreneurial overhaul and repair facilities.

This apparently vast pool of piston engine maintenance support pales, however, when considered in the context of the growing demand for service. With over 175,000 piston powered general aviation aircraft flying on the order of 37 million hours annually, one can figure, conservatively, that some 30,000 engines must be overhauled or replaced each year.

Based on production rates of Avco Lycoming's Williamsport Division and Teledyne Continental Motors' Aircraft Products Division—the country's two largest producers of aircraft piston engines—the overwhelming majority of engine rejuvenations are major overhauls in the field.

Of the two companies' combined output of over 23,000 new powerplants in 254 different model lines that were produced during 1977, only about 5,500 powerplants were for worldwide aftermarkets; the remainder were consigned for installation in newly manufactured aircraft.

Additionally, the firms shipped some 3,000 "zero time" reconditioned engines (called factory remanufactured units by Avco Lycoming and factory rebuilds by Teledyne Continental) to replace time-expired or otherwise unserviceable engines in the field.

Half a dozen major engine overhaul/exchange shops accounted for about 2,000 additional field-remanufactured engines in 1977. These include Mattituck Aviation, Mattituck, New York; Piedmont Aviation, Winston-Salem, North Carolina; Sacramento Sky Ranch, California; Schneck Aviation, Rockford, Illinois, and San Antonio, Texas; T.W. Smith Engine Company, Cincinnati; and Western Skyways, Troutdale, Oregon. That indicates that about two-thirds of the major piston engine aircraft maintenance was handled via the major overhaul route.

B/CA's investigation of piston engine maintenance activities in the United States brought to light a number of interesting—as well as some surprising—bits of information. For example, some of the more sophisticated businessmen-pilots (in terms of equipment operated) interviewed were not able to differentiate between various levels of major engine services available to them, other than from the standpoint of cost.

Even a few professionally employed pilots who were responsible for ensuring the safe mechanical condition of company aircraft appeared to lack awareness of more than the basic regulatory requirements related to maintenance.

This is not intended as criticism, but it does reflect the dynamic nature of aviation as a profession and the ever-increasing amount of knowledge the airman is expected to absorb.

Deficiencies in maintenance-related matters, however, may account in part for the FAA's continuing concern over mechanically induced mishaps. During 1977, engine mechanical malfunctions (not involving fuel starvation) were cited as causal factors in 474 of 4,399 general aviation accidents. One can only speculate about the magnitude of potential engine-related incidents, but officials at the FAA Maintenance Analysis Center in Oklahoma City indicate it is disquieting.

Perhaps these statistics introduce another nub of the state of piston engine maintenance. Generally, most businessmen who fly themselves and

29

pilots who double as sales or service agents for some of the smaller companies have neither the time nor the inclination to become experts in aircraft and engine maintenance duties.

So the questions arise: How can these members of the business aviation community know, short of catastrophic failure, when major engine maintenance is required? What are the most practical and economical courses available to them? How can they be sure that they are getting the best value, in terms of reliability and operational safety, for each maintenance dollar spent?

C. Douglas Dietz, Schneck Aviation director of marketing sales, comments that the honest cost of major maintenance is not necessarily the final dollar figure, but rather how many hours of safe, reliable operation are assured and how well the overhauler stands behind his work.

"Aircraft owners who give the same kind of attention to the overhaul as they do to the selection of their airplanes," Dietz adds, "seldom seem to be unhappy with the end result."

According to experts from the FAA and the industry, operation or ownership of modern aircraft with their increasingly complex fuel injection, turbo-charged and supercharged systems, and pressurization pose new obligations in addition to the regulatory responsibilities to be thoroughly familiar with all performance and systems specifications related to one's aircraft. There is also the need for the pilot to sharpen his ability to determine when the engine is trying to tell him something and what corrective measures may be required.

This is needed to assure the most economical and practical solution to the problem at hand as well as the most effective use of the busy repair facility's manpower.

As with all things comprised of moving mechanical parts, it is inevitable that aircraft piston engines eventually must wear out. The pace at which this occurs depends on numerous factors, but technological advances over the past two decades have significantly delayed that inevitability. In the immediate post-World War II era, completion of 1,000 hours between engine overhauls was an ambitious goal. Today, TBOs of 1,500 hours are commonplace, and 2,500-hour TBOs are not regarded as unachievable.

The very nature of piston engine business aircraft operations appears to weigh against realization of optimum TBO, however. Joseph A. Diblin, Avco Lycoming customer relations manager, points out two primary factors as most injurious to a piston engine's health and longevity. One is the internal buildup of moisture and corrosive acids that occurs as a result of under-use (less than 15 hours a month). The other is abnormal engine cooling resulting from rapid descents.

The General Aviation Manufacturers Association places typical use of high performance single- and multi-engine piston powered aircraft at fewer than 200 hours a year, and a major complaint among IFR-rated business-men-pilots is that the ATC system too frequently dictates approaches that cause rapid engine temperature drops.

The secret to obtaining the longest, most trouble-free service from an aircraft engine is no jealously guarded mystery.

Aircraft and engine manufacturers are more than willing to explain it in detail at the slightest hint of interest. Briefly, listed below is a threefold formula:

• Religious adherence to preventive maintenance programs, which are dealt with in most aircraft operator's manuals;

• Adherence to recommended inspection and service schedules;

• Operation in strict compliance with procedures laid out in the opera-tor's manuals.

"Following those recommended procedures is essential," agrees J. F. Woehr of the FAA Southwest Region's Flight Standards Division. "They are based not only on rigorous ground and flight testing of each engine model, but on hundreds of thousands of hours of evaluating real-world operations. That wealth of technical data is far more reliable than the individual pilot's intuition."

Most pilots contacted by B/CA feel that manufacturer-recommended TBOs are idealistic rather than realistic, however. Eighty percent of those interviewed report maximum TBOs of 10 to 15 percent fewer hours than recommended. This finding is shared, in general, by officials of engine overhaul shops. Says one: "I'm always pleasantly surprised when an engine that comes in for overhaul has met or exceeded the maker's recommended TBO."

Repair stations and manufacturers are in agreement that the chances for catastrophic piston engine problems without some kind of forewarning are almost infinitesimal.

Abnormal or sudden variations in oil or fuel consumption may warrant a compression check and boroscope inspection of the cylinders. Noticeable changes in oil temperature or pressure, exhaust gas temperature readings or other engine instrument needle fluctuations, along with unexplainable deviations in engine power, can be signals that a landing is prudent.

Where frequent minor maintenance problems are experienced, it's al-most a certainty that total TBO life will be affected.

Perhaps the best, if the most general, guide offered was that the non-mechanically inclined pilot must learn to monitor constantly both the sound and instrument indications of his powerplants and to share any concerns with a maintenance man in whom he has confidence. In many cases the repairman can diagnose the problem expeditiously and, therefore, at mini-mal cost if he has an accurate description of the symptoms.

But how does one go about finding a repair facility in which one can have confidence? It is not always an easy task. Because of the growing demand for service, most FAA-certificated repair stations have lengthy waiting lists. The pilot who patronizes the "shade tree" mechanic for priority treatment or bargain basement rates is the one who is most apt to rue the experience at a later time.

"Most of the complaints the FAA receives," Woehr says, "are from aircraft owners who apparently believe that all A&P mechanics must be pressed from the same mold of knowledge and experience in order to earn their certificates. The agency can only assure that they meet established minimum standards. When, because of inexperience or lack of adequate equipment, an A&P does a shoddy job, the aircraft owner may find that in his attempt to save a few dollars he has had to pay more in the long run."

A list of suggestions on how to locate the repair facility that will be most appropriate to one's individual requirements was offered by manufacturing and maintenance shop managers, as well as by several business aircraft operators with broad experience.

Perhaps the most effective way to find a suitable repair shop, however, is to talk with other longtime pilots in your geographic area.

If possible, take the time to visit several of the facilities recommended. Ask the manager of each shop for a guided tour. The shop's appearance and the attitudes of its employes can be clear indications of the care and attention your engine would receive.

Selecting an Engine Maintenance Center

The following suggestions on how the aircraft owner might choose a maintenance facility were supplied primarily by officials of piston engine repair facilities:

- Get estimates from at least three engine repair facilities on what your maintenance needs will entail in both parts and labor and what the cost will be.
- Find out how long the facility has been in business and what the qualifications of its lead men are.
- Inspect each facility and its FAA certificate to insure its capability to handle your requirements.
- If possible, arrange a visit to the shop to personally examine and discuss the condition of disassembled engine parts.
- Find out how much of the work will have to be subcontracted due to equipment or personnel limitations.
- Check all warranty conditions carefully.
- Determine what the facility will do for you if problems develop away from its geographical area.
- Ask about and inspect run-in test equipment and quality control procedures.
- Specify the use of genuine factory parts where replacements are required, and make sure that repaired/reconditioned parts will meet acceptable standards.
- Find out what those factory-recommended service standards are.
- Ask about the facility's product liability insurance coverage.

It's also wise to examine the shop's recordkeeping procedures and basic service bulletin compliance sheets. Poor recordkeeping should raise a red flag. Good records, conversely, can translate into savings of time and money.

If the subject of a service bulletin subsequently gives rise to an AD note, a simple telephone call to the repair facility to find out whether the SB was complied with can be more convenient than poring over engine logs or scheduling an inspection.

One seasoned company pilot observed that he'd look askance at any overhaul shop supervisor who, in addition to responding candidly to the pilot's questions and requests, did not attempt to learn as much as possible about how the engine was operated, in what environments and for what types of missions.

Let's assume that you've found an engine repair facility at which you'll feel comfortable leaving your ailing powerplant. Considering your flight requirements (and the financial outlay, of course, which easily may be the largest single expenditure since purchase of the aircraft), will the comparatively low-cost top overhaul suffice, or is a complete disassembly and minute check of each engine part more desirable? Should you keep the old engine or replace it with a field remanufactured, new, or factory zero-timed powerplant?

There are pros and cons to each of these alternatives, and cost differences between them can be quite substantial.

As a very broad rule of thumb, a factory-rebuilt engine may cost about 25 percent less than a new unit, a field remanufacture another 25 percent less, a major overhaul still another 25 percent less, and a top overhaul only about half as much as a major. But, again generally speaking, service warranties descend proportionately.

Contrary to a commonly held misconception, a top overhaul does not constitute a major engine revitalization in the strict sense. It consists largely of correcting a low compression or high oil consumption problem by removing the pistons, reworking the cylinders and replacing rings, gaskets and other exposed, obviously unserviceable parts. While it may afford a significant performance improvement, it is not intended to establish a new TBO life. The owner of an aircraft with a recommended 1,500-hour TBO who buys a top overhaul at 800 hours should still expect to have the engine majored at 1,500 hours or sooner.

Similarly, a 1,200-hour engine that has undergone a major overhaul at the recommended TBO is not a zero-time unit, but rather a 1,200-hour powerplant that has seen no operational use since repair. Nor is an engine that has been rebuilt by one of the half-dozen better known engine overhaul exchange shops in the United States technically zero-timed. Even though all of its internal parts may be new, the serial number identifies it as an engine that may have experienced thousands of hours of previous use.

Only the original engine manufacturer is permitted by the FAA to produce a zero-time powerplant, which is assigned a new serial number even if it contains serviceable parts retrieved from dozens of other run-out engines. For that privilege the manufacturer must ensure that the zero-time unit meets the same rigid tolerances and quality control standards as an entirely new engine and that interim model improvements are incorporated into it.

Generally, the top overhaul offers advantages in both cost and downtime. Should the owner wish to restore performance of an engine prior to a major overhaul, or if he just wants to "dress it up" to sell or trade his aircraft, the top overhaul may suffice.

The major overhaul, particularly the first time around, is the next least costly alternative. But because the engine must be completely disassembled, each part cleaned and thoroughly inspected, unserviceable parts replaced and the engine tested to ensure that it has been restored to performance limits specified by the manufacturer and approved by the FAA, time out of service may be extensive. One repair facility supervisor noted that a complete overhaul may require three weeks, longer if needed replacement parts are not readily available.

The chief advantage of the factory/field rebuilt engine and a new unit is that the aircraft is out of service for a minimal time. Most shops promise installation and return to service in a week or less if proper arrangements are made sufficiently far in advance.

Most major engine overhaul shops today offer flat rates on powerplants (either your own or an exchange unit) that reportedly are restored to like-new condition. Those rates are based roughly on 25 percent for labor and 75 percent for parts replacement and may afford a handy guide for maintenance budget planning. In most cases, however, money can be saved by asking for a time and materials estimate in advance.

Among company flight department heads interviewed as a part of our investigation, the majority expressed a preference for factory rebuilt engines rather than overhauls. The rationale was that factory rebuilt units in particular are subject to rigidly controlled standards that do not necessarily apply to the independent overhaul shops. Additionally, it was felt that the minimum downtime compensated for the extra cost of those engines.

There is a vocal minority, however, that believes it is better to major your old engine since its past history is known to the operator. They argue that remanufactured engines use reconditioned parts from various sources, and that short of buying a new engine only overhauling your old powerplant provides the assurance of knowing exactly what went into the reconditioning process.

THE STATE OF PISTON ENGINE MAINTENANCE

A growing problem mentioned by both aircraft operators and repair station officials in relation to major maintenance work involves apparent inadequacies in engine parts distribution systems. Shortages of critical components from local distributors' inventories were cited by many shops as the primary reason repair facilities often underestimate the length of time to complete a job.

Cost estimates customarily have been more accurate. But "a 17 percent average increase in engine parts' costs last January has put us in a spot," says the owner of a Dallas repair station. "On work for which we had given estimates, we could not pass that increase on to the customers, so in many cases we lost money."

One exception to cost estimate accuracy that has surfaced recently is due to a surge in crankcase and crankshaft problems in both Continental and Lycoming engine models. These components can add $1,000 to $3,600 to a quoted repair bill. Thus far, engine manufacturers have not been inclined to mitigate those costs, even on comparatively new engines that have passed out of warranty.

Salaries for engine repairmen have felt the impact of inflation. While still below those of automotive, airline and company flight department mechanics, pay rates for general aviation repair facility maintenance personnel have risen by over 15 percent over past years.

Few repair stations reported severe personnel shortages, but several noted that the salaries they are able to pay do not attract mechanics of the skill levels they desire. Further, some acknowledged that expansion plans have been impeded by a dearth of A&P mechanics.

Among those pilots interviewed by B/CA the most serious complaint voiced was that downtime required for major maintenance seems to be increasing. Whether or not this trend continues into a real maintenance crisis may hinge on the general aviation industry's willingness to effectively employ existing maintenance resources and to recruit adequate numbers of technicians into the field to fully satisfy projected needs.

You and Your Prop 5

by Robert Stangarone

With all the growth and sophistication that have come to piston-powered aircraft in the seven decades since Kitty Hawk, the last element in the power chain—the propeller—has remained basically the same. Energy from the rotating machinery is converted to thrust by an "air screw" not unlike the screws used to propel ships. There have been improvements in materials, reliability, longevity, airfoils, efficiency and weight, but we're still converting engine power to thrust by using a rotating airfoil.

In a way it's surprising that we haven't sought out new methods to make this energy conversion. Compared with today's standards of technological sophistication, props remain comparatively heavy, noisy, inefficient, dangerous and simply not in line with a streamline design philosophy. But they do the job required of them.

The most significant change in props over the years, of course, has been in fabricating them from metal instead of wood. As stronger, lighter metals were developed, prop manufacturers adopted them for their products. Today, most prop blades are made of an aluminum alloy. The innards of the prop hub, and the hub itself, are made of steel, aluminum or combinations of both.

Inside the hub is a cylinder mechanism and mechanical components to vary the blade angle. Also considered part of the prop assembly is the prop governor, which directs a quantity of oil against a piston within the cylinder, which in turn positions the prop blades at the appropriate pitch.

Because props are sensitive to balance and blade angle control, and experience brute forces, they require special attention and care. Without proper maintenance, prop-induced vibration is capable of tearing an engine off its mounts and shaking an aircraft into oblivion. It happens too often.

NTSB records show that of the 99 accidents attributed to prop failure from 1973 to 1976, 10 percent were fatal. These figures do not reflect the number of prop failures that did not result in a reportable accident, which would certainly magnify the fact that proper propeller care and maintenance are critical.

An examination of the Safety Board's records shows where efforts are necessary to minimize prop accidents. "Inadequate maintenance and inspection" is a phrase frequently found in prop accident reports. Here's a sampling of prop failure incidents and some causes, as shown in NTSB reports for the past four years:

• Seven inches of blade separated in flight. Nick ⅛ inch long and 1/32 inch deep at point of separation.

• Three feet of prop blade separated. Caused damage to engine. Machine tool marks and corrosion found.

• Nicks improperly dressed.

• Prop blade failed due to fatigue induced by improper machining in balance hole cavity.

• Prop blade actuating pin failed.

• Prop unapproved for engine installation. Blade separated in flight.

• Prop hub spider failed. Blade separated and penetrated cabin.

• One blade separated from prop. Engine tore out of its mounts due to torsional vibration.

• Prop retaining nut not properly installed. Prop separated.

• Damaged blade improperly repaired.

• Prop failed two inches from clamp assembly strap. Prop and engine separated.

• Prop blade failed. Wrong crankshaft-counterweight combination installed.

• Fatigue crack originated at small stress corrosion crack. Blade separated in flight.

Before getting into exactly how we can minimize our chances of ending up on NTSB scrolls because of a prop failure, it's necessary to examine how a prop works.

The blade pitch of the propeller (the angle between the chord line and the plane of blade rotation) varies along the length of the blade, making the prop essentially a twisted wing. The twist is necessary because the blade elements near the tip move faster than those near the shank, so they require less of an angle to produce the desired amount of lift or thrust.

Note that the thrust produced must vary along the length of the blade, normally decreasing toward the tips, to keep bending moments within structural tolerances and to satisfy aerodynamic limits. Because of this, each individual prop element (or station along the length of the prop) is designed for its most effective angle.

All things being equal, the thrust a blade produces is proportional to the speed at which it is rotating. The rotational speed is limited, however, by the resultant tip speed. As blade tips approach the speed of sound there is a loss of efficiency and an induced vibration that can become quite severe.

Because of the high rate of rotation, a prop is subjected to a variety of forces and harmonic problems. Centrifugal force pulls the blades away from the hub as they spin. There's also a twisting force, which is the tendency of the blades to be turned in their sockets toward a lower angle. Additionally, bending forces are imposed on the blades due to the forward pull of the prop. But bending forces are counteracted by centrifugal force.

Vibrations attributable to the prop can vary from macrocosmic to undetectable. They are normally the result of an aerodynamic or dynamic imbalance. Aerodynamic imbalance may result from bent blades, an out-of-track condition or blade angle variation due to problems within the hub. Ice on the prop or in the spinner, or a mismatch in the weight of the blades for a variety of reasons, will result in a dynamic imbalance.

Vibration may also be the result of operating the engine in a restricted rpm range. Many prop/engine combinations have critical ranges of operation. Running the prop within this rpm range for an extended period of time may result in severe vibration and damage to both prop and engine.

Prop blade flutter is the result of an aerodynamic imbalance that causes the blade tips to twist, or change in pitch, at high frequencies. It can occur during high rpm and high disk loading situations, as in a low-speed, maximum power climb. Obviously, the twisting of the blades at the tips fatigues the metal on the outer third of the blade, so high-power, steep climbs should be avoided as much as possible.

Each prop design has its own natural frequency. To avoid resonance, engineers determine what that frequency is and retune it using various dynamic and aerodynamic tricks so the forces that cause vibration (such as engine shaft bending, torque impulses or engine movements on the mounts) do not reinforce this natural frequency. The result is a quieter prop.

Noise, vibration and other design considerations usually determine if blade tips are round or square. Rounded tips can be insignificantly more efficient than square ones, but square tips have extra material that can be removed after minor damage without reducing the overall diameter.

Three-blade props are found on both single-and multi-engine airplanes today. The advantages of the 3-bladed prop lie mainly in the areas of ground clearance, fuselage clearance (in a twin) and less vibration. An added benefit is a lower noise level because of the smaller diameter and the resultant lower tip speed. Aircraft performance is sometimes enhanced as well.

Newly designed propellers for business airplanes go through extensive testing. Blades are subjected to centrifugal forces twice those expected in normal operation, by either whirl tests or static pull demonstrations. All vibration load patterns must also be explored.

With all this testing and safeguards, how can the prop failures that result in accidents be explained? Generally, they're the fault of the operator, the overhauler or the inspection facility.

Blade failures are most often due to fatigue cracks that start at mechanically formed dents, cuts, scars and nicks or at leading edge pits due to corrosion. Many times a failure occurs where some minor form of damage was repaired because fatigue failure started before the repair took place. Often a failure occurs where an earlier repair was performed unsatisfactorily.

Lines of force in propellers normally run from the shank to the tip of the blade. When a nick penetrates the blade it diverts and converges these lines of force, concentrating them at or near the nick. This increases stress in the area that may develop into a failure. Once stress fatigue begins, it cannot be reversed. The nick itself may later be repaired, but the metal fatigue that occurred prior to the repair is permanent. That's why it's critical to have any, even the smallest, fault dressed out prior to the next flight (and an equal amount of prop material filed off the other blade or blades at the same radius to restore the balance).

When damage is repaired instantly, even the nastiest nick will do not permanent damage. One B/CA editor—who is also an A&P—picked up a large nick while taxiing in on a gravel taxiway. Because he checks his prop carefully, he spotted the damage and repaired it before the next flight. The repair left a conspicuous dip in the blade leading edge, but 1200 hours later, when the prop was overhauled, the blade was found to be still serviceable.

It cannot be emphasized enough: A thorough examination of the prop before each flight is essential. If a defect, no matter how small, is found, the engine should not be operated until the damage is looked at, and if necessary, repaired by a licensed mechanic.

What is a defect as opposed to normal wear and tear?

You'll get all kinds of opinions on that, but here's a safe rule of thumb: If the nick cannot be shaved out with the smooth edge of an auto ignition key to the point it can no longer be seen, the attention of an A&P is required. You just run the back side of the key up and down the edge of the blade a half dozen times in about six-inch strokes, being careful not to leave a new gouge where the key stops at the ends of the strokes. Any nicks left after that deep enough to snag your thumb nail are cause for concern. Call an A&P.

In event no A&P is available (the usual case on a gravel or dirt airport, where damage is most likely) you've got a problem. The FARs do not allow any sort of prop repair by a pilot/owner. *However,* we're of the opinion it's better for a *small* nick to be removed before flight by a non-A&P than for it to be smoothed down several flight hours later by an expert. "Small" means less than $\frac{1}{16}$ inch deep on a leading or trailing edge and within the outer half of the blade length. No repair should be made by an unlicensed man in the shank area of a blade. Under no circumstances should anyone other than a skilled propeller repairman touch a defect in the face of a blade, especially the rear face. Remember, natural bending places the rear face under extreme tension, so any scratch or gouge on the rear face is cause for alarm. Have it looked at instantly.

Because of all the variables, neither we nor anyone else can give the non-A&P generalized instructions on making emergency repairs. You should talk to your maintenance man and take his advice for your particular prop. He'll probably give you a small piece of semi-fine emery cloth and tell you if you can't work the nick out with the emery, using *your thumb only* for a tool, have a mechanic fly in to make the repair.

Getting back to the preflight inspection, check the external surfaces of the spinner for damage and the attachment parts for normal tightness.

You may have noticed that on some variable pitch props there is a slight wobble present when the tip is moved by hand. This is because the very small tolerances at the blade root are magnified many times when projected to the tip. This "blade shake" does not adversely affect prop strength or performance, and once the prop starts to rotate, it disappears because centrifugal force seats the blades rigidly against the retention bearing. Just because the blade shake is normal is no excuse to grab the tip and shake it vigorously on each preflight. That practice will lead to shank bearing damage.

Nor should you ever use the prop blades as a tow bar. If the aircraft must be moved using the prop or props for handles, grasp the blades as close to the spinner as possible—*but do not push on the spinner itself.* It's surprising how many mechanics and line personnel do not know the damage that can be done in heaving and shoving on props and spinners.

During the preflight inspection of the prop, observe and feel the blades in their entirety, not only the leading edges, but also the front and back surfaces of the blades and the hub area. Even though failures normally occur near the blade tips because they are under greater loads, many failures also occur around the shank.

Near the hub area, be on the lookout for oil deposits, an indication of a crack or leaking seal in the hub or dome.

Corrosion can create some unique problems in areas of the country that are polluted or near the seashore. A good practice is to wipe the blade with the same rag you use to wipe the oil dipstick, thus leaving an oil film on the blade for protection against corrosion. If you notice corrosion buildups on the prop, get out that ignition key and run it along the length of the leading edge to remove the corrosion pits.

Intergranular corrosion, sometimes referred to as delamination, occurs near salty environments. Hard alloy materials are particularly susceptible to intergranular corrosion, and props using this material require additional care. Nicks accelerate the effects of it, so that's another reason to dress them out as soon as they're discovered. Added protection can be obtained by painting the blades, a practice now being recommended by the NTSB and the FAA for conspicuity. But in areas of salt and pollution-laden air, the paint should be removed annually for a thorough inspection of the base metal. Incidentally, decals on a prop have also been known to permit the accumulation of hidden corrosion.

To protect the prop while the airplane is tied down, a prop cover is a wise, inexpensive investment. It will shield the surface of the prop from corrosion and bird calling-cards.

In cold weather operations, check the inside of the prop spinner for ice in case water was deposited, either by washing or by rain, then frozen inside. In cold weather, some pilots leave a spinner opening toward the ground when parking for the night so water will drain out the bottom instead of collecting and freezing inside the spinner. The only problem with leaving the prop vertical is that water will then run down the upper blade and collect in grooves and crannies in the hub area. In the case of an aircraft not flown often, corrosion around the shank of the blade may result. In winter, the water will freeze against the seals and bearings, which can result in damage. Also, a prop parked vertically leaves one blade pointing down where it may be damaged by a tow bar on a single. To overcome all those problems, we recommend small drain holes drilled in the spinner at appropriate spots so the prop can be parked horizontal and the spinner still drain. In the case of a three- or four-bladed prop, the only solution to all those problems is a cover.

It's important to avoid running up on loose stones and gravel, of course. When taking off from an unpaved runway, advance power slowly so the aircraft moves forward as the prop tips kick up debris, thus keeping the blades ahead of the dangerous particles.

Anytime you experience a heavy vibration in climb or cruise you should suspect that you've lost part of a blade. Immediately pull the throttle or throttles to idle and reduce airspeed to minimize windmilling as much as possible. As the prop, or props, slow down, you'll probably be able to see where the blade is missing. At night, a landing light may help; otherwise, the only option is to cut rpm on the suspected engine and if the vibration is reduced, you've probably lost a blade tip.

In a twin, of course, feather the affected prop and head for an airport. In a single, you have no choice; shut the engine down with the mixture and slow the aircraft in an effort to stop the prop rotation. Low pitch and throttle closed will sometimes help stop it. With a worn, low compression engine, the airspeed may have to be reduced to near stall to stop prop rotation.

Circumstance dictates actions, certainly, but as a rule it's foolhardy to try to nurse a bit of thrust from the engine and prop in an effort to reach an airport. The risk is that the engine will be torn from the mounts. It's obviously better to land in a cow pasture than have that happen. In the best case, the vibrations may still be so severe the aircraft and systems are damaged far more than would occur in a forced landing.

An acquaintance once nursed a Cessna Cardinal 10 miles to an airport after losing about eight inches from one blade and the vibrations totalled the airplane. The radios literally fell out in pieces, and all the rivets forward of the main gear were popped or loosened.

In IFR flying without prop de-ice you'll occasionally experience roughness due to ice building up on the blades. This is a classic case of an ounce of prevention being worth a ton of cure. The winter IFR pilot should keep his prop super clean and smooth. In fact, ice will seldom collect at all on a polished and waxed prop. Since few businessmen have the time or patience to polish the blades, an alternative that's worked well for B/CA pilots is Icex or some other such preparation applied liberally. We carry a can in the baggage compartment and any time ice is a possibility, we spray the blade leading edges and spinner until they are thoroughly soaked. It's a good idea to do that even when the aircraft is equipped with electric or alcohol prop de-icing systems.

If all else fails, there is a technique of last resort. If the airplane is nosed down slightly to pick up a little speed, then the prop control briskly pushed forward, the sudden rpm increase, and the resultant increase in centrifugal force, should cause the ice to shed. As we said, however, that's a technique of last resort.

We've had to use a similar technique with a fixed pitch prop, but simply running at maximum rpm has kept ice off the blades of airplanes with constant speed props for us on several occasions.

A good practice while aloft is to periodically feather the props on a twin (one at a time, of course). Prop-knowledgeable people say this keeps sludge "ledges" from building up inside the prop dome, and keeps the walls of the hub lubricated. Engine manufacturers agree, saying you cannot do harm to the engine with this procedure. One other reason the props should be feathered occasionally is to check their operation and confirm that blade travel is not restricted by prop boots.

Like most mechanical devices, props suffer as much from lack of use as from misuse. If your airplane has low utilization, running the engine periodically will prevent corrosion and gum from developing in many systems.

Hub friction, usually due to congealed grease in the pilot tubes, along with insufficient counterweight force, has led to several instances where the prop rpm would not reduce properly after takeoff. If the friction is consistent, it's simply a matter of replacing the grease. But if the prop functions properly intermittently, it's a good indication that the balls in the blade retention bearings are jamming, resulting in excessive friction because of the rubbing action. This condition requires the services of a prop overhaul shop.

Blade tips are frequent entrance and exit points for lightning. When it occurs, sometimes arcing is evident on the race (casing) and balls of the bearings within the hub. Also, when lightning strikes enter or exit through the prop, all steel parts become magnetized due to the flow of the current. Following a lightning strike, therefore, the thrust bearings in the engine should be replaced since they also receive damage, and all steel parts should be demagnetized. Blades should be inspected, and the shank area checked for evidence of arcing.

There have been several instances of blades slipping in the blade clamps to slightly lower angles over a period of time on certain props. This results in roughness and a tendency for the prop to windmill when in the feathered position. This can be detected on the pre-flight inspection if a strip of plastic tape is installed on the blade shank and clamp, then sprayed with a lacquer to prevent cleaning solvents from washing it off. Any slippage will be recognized by a misalignment of the tape. You may be tempted to simplify this procedure by simply scribing a line across the blade shank and clamp. Avoid doing this as it may become the start of a crack.

If the prop makes unplanned contact with the ground, resulting in curled tips, the blades are not necessarily irreparable. Curled tips, within certain limitations, can be trimmed off up to about two inches in some cases, providing the bend doesn't exceed that allowed for the particular blade. Regulations allow a 10 percent variance of performance, and shortened props generally fall within this requirement.

Since props go through a great variety of stresses and strains, depending on the particular operation, it's almost impossible to predict how long any one prop will operate properly and efficiently. There are signs of impending problems, and guidelines to minimize the possibility of prop failure.

Generally, new props and prop components are warranted for six months after delivery to the customer. If the prop is repaired or altered in any way, the manufacturer has the right to void the warranty if the alteration effects prop stability, performance or reliability. Other ways to void the warranty are excessive engine damper wear, overspeeding the prop, improper installation or using the prop under abnormal operating conditions. There usually is no warranty given for factory overhauled props, although they are generally assumed to be equal to new. Because of previous service, overhauled props may have a reduced useful life.

Inspections by a certificated mechanic are an integral part of the prop maintenance and preventive maintenance program. Preflight inspections done carefully and thoroughly will catch any obvious problems, but more subtle indications of a failure in the offing must be uncovered in periodic inspections by a trained mechanic. For instance, at 100-hour inspections, when the spinner is removed (or should be), is the time to inspect the hub for cracks or wear. The spinner itself should get a thorough going-over for cracks, and the hub should be inspected for leaks.

On a recent 100-hour inspection on our company Cessna 310, we half-expected to find a problem somewhere in the prop area because of a subtle-but-noticeable vibration under certain power conditions. Sure enough, the inspection revealed a crack across the diameter of the spinner bulkhead.

At 1000 hours time in operation, a good look should be taken at the prop and a decision made regarding overhaul. If your operation has been entirely on paved runways in erosionless, corrosionless environs, then you may decide to wait until the manufacturers' recommended overhaul period to have your prop or props overhauled. However, if your aircraft has been through some rough operations, 1000 hours is a smart time to have the overhaul done. While the manufacturers' recommended overhaul period for turboprop propellers is about 3000 hours, most props used on reciprocating engines have a recommended TBO of 1000 to 1500 hours, and in both cases the calendar year limit is four years.

Because of the catastrophic nature of a prop failure compared with a failure of any other aircraft system, we cannot recommend operation of a prop beyond recommended TBO. It's done, but it's not wise.

Several factors determine recommended overhaul periods. One is the engine used in conjunction with the prop because it is the engine/prop combination that determines the pattern of vibration or stress.

The care a prop gets while in service is a TBO limiting factor, especially if recommended procedures are not carried out properly. Manufacturers say that props not maintained according to their recommendations should be overhauled every 1000 hours, not exceeding two calendar years for recips, and every 1500 hours, not exceeding three years for turbine operators.

Prop overhauls can be done by the manufacturer or by an FAA-approved prop repair station. It's important to find a shop that has the know-how to overhaul your particular prop, one that follows manufacturers' service manual instructions, service bulletins and letters, and has the proper equipment, technical information and personnel necessary to handle your make and model. FAA-approved shops are licensed and authorized to work only on specified prop models. Major prop manufacturers have lists of authorized service centers and repair stations. All you have to do is call them.

Prop shops are a rather small fraternity; there are about 180 of them throughout the United States. The best way to choose one is to ask the advice of operators who have recently had their props overhauled. We also recommend that you work through your FBO when possible. Should a warranty or some other problem grow out of the overhaul, he will have more clout in demanding satisfaction since he controls a larger portion of the shop's customers than you. He'll be interested in seeing that you get a fair deal because he wants your other maintenance business and probably even hopes to one day sell you another aircraft.

You have a couple of alternatives to getting your prop overhauled, one being to get a new one. This is the most expensive alternative, but if your prop has gone through five or six overhauls, your blades may be reaching the limits of length and width and simply cannot be ground down anymore.

You can purchase new blades without purchasing a new hub assembly, which is probably a wise choice since hub assemblies can be overhauled virtually an unlimited number of times and are not life-limited. Incidentally, Cessna owners should investigate the possibility of exchanging old blades for new ones carefully because several years ago the designs were greatly improved. We recently exchanged blades on a Cessna 182 and picked up three knots indicated airspeed.

There is no compulsory replacement time for propellers, only limitations on how much the blades can be cut down. (One exception to this are the props for the Beech-99, which are life-limited because of shank limitations.)

The best alternative to a prop overhaul is a prop exchange, which is about the same price, but the downtime can be as little as two hours (three hours for a twin) instead of the usual overhaul downtime of three to 14 working days. When exchanging the prop, the airplane is flown to the shop and the prop is removed. Someone else's overhauled prop is then installed on your airplane on the spot. If you haven't established credit with the shop, you leave a check in the amount of 75 percent of the value of a new prop assembly. After your prop is overhauled, you are refunded the difference between your deposit and the actual cost of overhauling your old prop.

This system has both advantages and disadvantages. Operators who take pride in caring for their aircraft, including the prop, know that they've done their best to extend the life of their investment, and an exchange means giving up their well-cared-for unit in return for one with an unknown history. Prop overhaul shops say, however, that all props are brought within certain tolerances and one is as good as another.

But, the exchange can work the other way too. One B/CA editor took his airplane in for an exchange with serviceable blades and received an over-hauled prop with two new blades in exchange. You just don't know what you'll get back.

In the overhaul, after the prop is disassembled, prop boots are stripped off and all components are inspected using various sophisticated non-destructive testing methods for wear, cracks, corrosion or other abnormalities. Ball bearings and gaskets are generally discarded immediately, while other parts from within the hub are reconditioned, refinished and brought within the manufacturer's tolerances. Hardware, gaskets and 0 rings are replaced.

Blades are reconditioned as long as they can be brought to within manufacturers' tolerances for width and length. A surprising amount of metal can be removed from blades with chewed-up leading edges and tips. In the process the faces may also be ground down, resulting in a shorter, thinner blade. As a rule, this has little effect on efficiency. In some instances, performance is improved. After the grinding, the prop is repolished and the finish restored through anodizing or a paint and baking process.

After the overhaul procedure is complete, the props are balanced, either in a micropoise or a suspension balancing stand. (A dynamic balancing device is usually used in balancing turboprop propellers, particularly those for the Garrett TPE 331 engine.)

Finally, each blade gets a conformity check for face alignment.

Prop overhauls vary in price, but you should expect to pay $350 to $450 for overhaul of a typical two-bladed prop (including hardware, but not including any major parts that may need replacing) at a top prop overhaul facility. The actual bill for the recent overhaul of a McCauley prop on the B/CA Cessna 182 mentioned above was $294 for labor and $112.15 for routine parts. A three-bladed prop will cost an additional $150 to $200. About $500 to $600 will be charged for a turbine prop with full reverse capability. Boots, which are always removed for the overhaul, are usually extra.

Compliance with service letters and bulletins is a large part of proper care and maintenance for the propeller. Bulletins—which carry greater emphasis than letters—many times are developed into ADs. They deal with a variety of topics. For instance, a prop manufacturer issued a service letter recommending a fix for vibration characteristics for a particular engine-prop combination. Another manufacturer issued a service letter noting that clamp and blade cracks were showing up more on a certain engine/prop combination in which the engine was being run long periods between overhauls. The bulletin concluded that these failures were due to worn engine damper bushing and pin combinations.

We cite these examples of service bulletins to demonstrate that props need more than just physical care and periodic maintenance. Just as important is the need to keep up with these service bulletins by visiting a quality prop shop at intervals. This is the only method manufacturers have for communicating with you after their product leaves the factory.

One last word on service bulletins: Since a lot of prop operations are based on rpm, the accuracy of your tachometer is important. Several service letters point out that the tach should be checked periodically and brought within 25 rpm tolerance. It's up to the operator to check tach accuracy and it's very important, especially if there are restricted rpm ranges for the particular engine/prop combination.

In the coming years props are certain to go through some minor evolutionary changes, but the basic concept—conversion of engine power to thrust by using a rotating airfoil—will remain the same. More efficient airfoil sections and improved metals may result in somewhat thinner blades that will be lighter, stronger and less susceptible to corrosion and erosion.

Composites, such as carbon fiber and boron, will eventually find their way into prop technology. We may even see fiber props with no moving parts. The articulation may be achieved through the elasticity of the fibers, a technique already being used by helicopter manufacturers for rotors. When that day arrives, the problems of maintenance and longevity will be greatly reduced for aircraft owners.

But until then take extra good care of your prop. If you don't, that rapidly turning mass may self-destruct and that's always a big letdown in any pilot's day.

Managing Your Prop Governor

6

by Robert Stangarone

There are a number of mechanisms and systems on airplanes we don't think about much until they (1) break and scare us, (2) break and cost us a fortune or (3) both.

So it is with propeller governors, those innocuous devices that control prop pitch as a function of commanded rpm and several other parameters we'll explore momentarily.

Why talk about prop governors at all? The fact is that with proper operation, thoughtful preventive maintenance and a bit of TLC, they can last the overhaul life of the engine. But without those considerations, they can become maintenance headaches, increase overhaul bills and become downright dangerous. But before we get into specifics, let's see what they are, how they work and what they do when they're working.

Long before the Wright brothers first lifted their conglomeration of machinery skyward in 1903, governors were prevalent in industries other than aviation. As early as 1870, Amos Woodward, founder of Woodward Governors, employed a crude device consisting of two spinning iron balls —demonstrating the purest of Newtonian mechanics—to govern the rotation of waterwheels. After aircraft came into being and a need developed in the DC-2 era to keep the speed of a turning prop constant in the face of changing load circumstances, the governor proved its usefulness in this new industry.

The concept of the governor has changed little since those days. Now, instead of heavy iron balls several inches in diameter, governors use tiny flyweights. In today's governors, fluidics is as important as, if not more important than, rotational forces. But the concept is still basically the same.

The main function of the prop governor is to command propeller blade angle changes so that an engine rpm selected by the pilot is automatically maintained, regardless of the aerodynamics or engine loads imposed on the prop.

In order to maintain a constant engine speed (rpm), the prop blade angle must be varied to change the load on the engine in response to the changing conditions of flight. You've probably noticed that with a fixed pitch prop, such as on a Cessna 172, on takeoff roll there is a high load on the prop (indicated by the tach not reaching a full takeoff power indication). But as the takeoff progresses, the load is lessened and the engine comes up to a higher rpm as a result. The prop may then even overspeed if the climb is not at a high enough rate to keep sufficient air loads on the prop. By using a mechanism that changes the pitch of the prop blades, namely the governor, the prop adjusts to give full rated rpm during the takeoff run and, therefore, maximum, preselected thrust. It won't overspeed as airspeed increases because the angle of attack of the prop blade is automatically increased to maintain the selected rpm setting.

The use of the governor is obviously more essential the higher the airspeed capability of the aircraft.

The governor can be looked at as one element in the propeller system. The others—including the hub assembly, synchronizers and accumulators—combine to convert the rotation of the engine to a resultant force that pulls (or pushes) the aircraft, while meeting a variety of miscellaneous requirements.

In the hydromechanical governor, today's most popular type, the angle of the propeller blade is changed by pumping oil into a relatively simple piston/cylinder/cam assembly in the hub. Essentially, this converts the translational motion of the cylinder to a rotational motion that varies the prop blade angle. The trick is to move the cylinder the right amount to get the desired blade setting. Or, said another way, to direct the right amount of oil pressure into the cylinder.

That's what we have a governor for: to meter this flow of oil. Compared with the relative simplicity of the hub's piston/cylinder/cam arrangement, the governor itself is a can of worms—or gears, valves and springs, to be more exact.

A look at the illustration will offer a better idea of the components of the governor, which will be useful when we discuss its maintenance and operation later on. For now, remember that the actual blade angle required for a given rpm is determined by the horsepower being developed and the airspeed of the aircraft.

The pilot interfaces with his governor in the cockpit through a prop control lever or push-pull control. Through it, he tells the governor what rpm he would like the engine to maintain, depending on whether he's taking off, cruising, descending, approaching or whatever. The governor does the rest. Simple? Yes. But not trouble-free.

Under normal operating conditions and with reasonable care, the governor can be expected to last at least until engine overhaul. Governor manufacturers recommend it be overhauled when the engine is overhauled. But

49

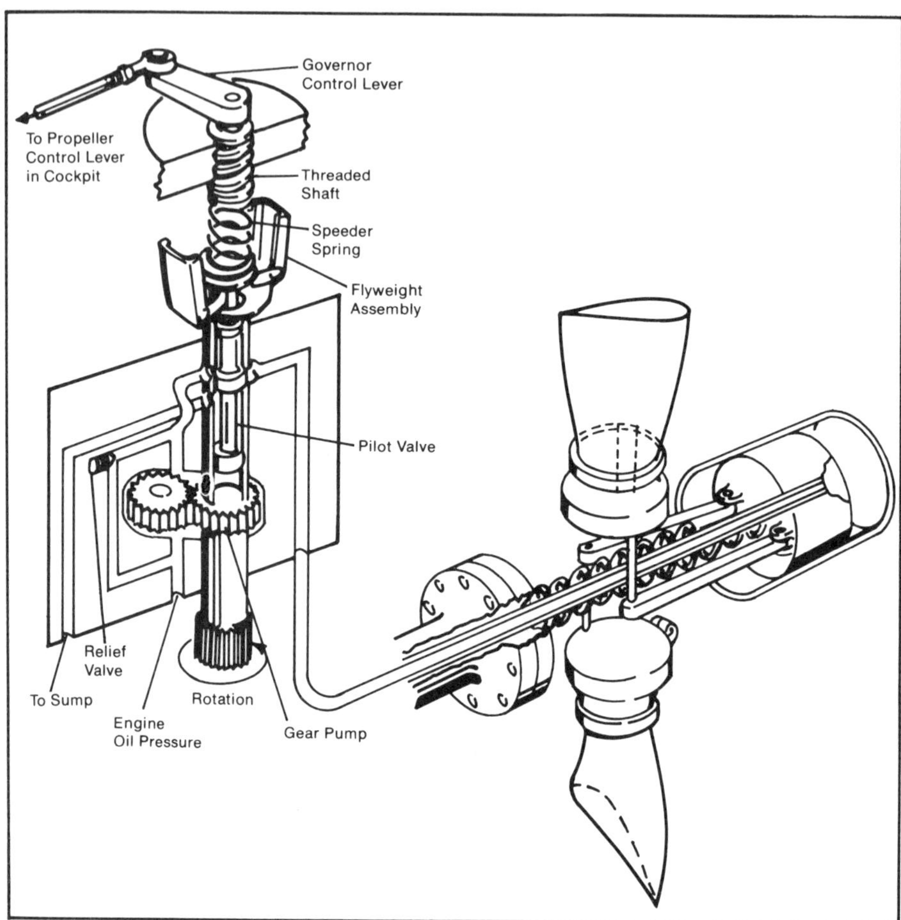

This illustration shows how one type of governor works. The rotational speed of the flyweight varies directly with engine speed. Centrifugal force, working against a spring pressure varied by the pilot, tends to tip the flyweights outward which controls the position of the pilot valve. The pilot valve directs oil to or from the propeller dome and piston which changes the blade pitch.

sometimes it just doesn't last that long for a variety of reasons.

The greatest opposing force to long governor life is dirty engine oil. Mechanics at governor overhaul shops we spoke to all agree that this is one area in which the operator can help. Since the oil used in the governor is the same oil used in the engine, it's important that it be changed at frequent intervals—about every 50 hours, most mechanics say. This will help keep the passageways free from gummy deposits caused by dirty oil. Oil additives are discouraged by governor manufacturers because they also gum up the oil lines of the governor.

Operators should be aware that in addition to extending governor life by keeping the oil clean and avoiding the use of additives, they should be on the lookout for symptoms that may indicate impending failure or problems. Sluggish response, hunting or rpm creep may indicate something in need of repair within the governor. Cold oil will sometimes be the cause, but once the engine oil is warmed up, you can eliminate that as a possibility. Most likely there are partial restrictions in the oil lines. Many times, suspected governor problems turn out to be tachometer problems. When a fix for a governor problem is being sought, don't forget to include the tach in your examination. A tach more than 25 rpm in error can be dangerous. It can result in rpm in excess of the limits, which might lead to vibrational or harmonic destruction of the powerplant or substandard power due to less than the rated rotational speed of the engine. McCauley has developed an inexpensive device that checks rpm by observing prop rotation, like a timing light.

If, on takeoff, your engine doesn't achieve takeoff rpm or exhibits surges or overspeeding tendencies, get your mechanic into the act. The governor may need a simple adjustment, or the pitch stops may need attention.

By including the governor in your preflight inspection, and certainly in the runup check, you may avoid unsafe and costly situations in the air. Check for oil leakage and cracks around the governor area. If you do find an oil leak, chances are you'll have to have a minor governor overhaul.

Be sure to observe your rpm while taxiing and at runup, since an indication of the governor losing oil pressure is a surge in rpm with power changes.

Runups in most business aircraft are done around 1700 rpm with the prop controls in the high rpm position. When the prop is cycled, prop response may be slow if the oil is cold. Governor manufacturers say it's necessary to cycle the prop only once during the runup to check for proper operation; this replaces the oil in the governor lines.

For a more thorough check in a twin-engine aircraft, run the engines up to 1800 to 2000 rpm and make sure they are synchronized. Pull both prop controls back to feather position and note the rate of rpm change. When 800 to 1000 rpm is reached, return both prop controls to the maximum rpm position and note the rate of recovery of the two props. If any significant lag is evident in either rpm decrease or increase, it's an indication of excessive friction in the propeller.

Your last chance to check the governor before you get airborne is on the takeoff roll. The tach reading should come up to within 40 rpm of the red line as soon as full power is applied, and it should stay there for the entire takeoff. If the engines of a twin do not synchronize by the time 85 knots is reached on the takeoff roll, the high-rpm stop screw of one governor is

51

probably in need of adjustment. For either single or twin aircraft, if an engine is slow in reaching the maximum rpm setting during takeoff, an adjustment of the propeller low pitch blade angle may be needed.

For a cruise check of the prop governors on a twin-engine aircraft, set up cruise power in smooth air and carefully sync the engines with the prop controls. Tighten the friction lock and give the airplane a minute or two to stabilize. Increase the airspeed by slightly lowering the nose of the aircraft. Hold the new airspeed for several minutes and observe the rpm. If the props remain synchronized at the previously set rpm setting, the governors are working properly. If the rpm of both engines increases slightly but they still remain synched, this is an indication that a considerable force is necessary to change the blade angles, and lubrication of the propellers may be needed, but they can still be considered to be operating satisfactorily. If the props go out of sync during the change in airspeed, and then resynchronize after airspeed stabilization, you've got one governor working properly and one governor that needs lubrication.

The worst condition you can have is the props going out of sync during the increase in airspeed and staying out of sync after the airspeed is stabilized, causing one prop to turn faster than the other. This is most objectionable because small changes in airspeed effect synchronization, and it's very difficult to resynchronize by adjusting the prop control. Essentially, one prop is acting as a fixed pitch prop over a narrow rpm range. Similar observations of rpm excursions in a single-engine aircraft indicate similar problems.

Modern governors have been designed with an overall safety of operation in mind. For instance, governors for single-engine aircraft are different from governors for twin-engine aircraft because a failure mode places single- and multi-engine aircraft in a different kind of jeopardy. Since governor operation is based on receiving oil from the engine, the governor ceases to function if the engine loses oil pressure or fails. Obviously, in a twin the instant need is to minimize the drag of the dead engine, and a twin governor works toward that end by automatically bringing the prop into high pitch with the help of a spring. What happens when you lose oil pressure in a single-engine aircraft depends largely on what type of governor you have. Most will go automatically to high pitch, but there are some that go to flat pitch. Check your operating manual or call the manufacturer for this information for your particular airplane.

There have been several cases of control levers of the governor vibrating off their shafts. This obviously causes loss of the ability to control the governor, but it will still govern the prop. The rpm may reduce somewhat; however, the governor will still hold a setting close to the setting selected prior to the separation of the arm. To avoid this, check all levers and accessories around the propeller and governor area at each periodic inspection.

A cable problem is another malady that is rare, but does occur. Most governor cables are of the push/pull type similar in structure to those of an automobile speedometer. There's plenty of friction built into the cable, so if it parts company with the cabin prop control, it will have a tendency to hold the governor at the same setting. If it separates at the governor control arm, the last setting will probably be retained although most governors have a weak spring to help the governor creep up slightly toward higher rpm.

We often hear about "runaway" props, even though such an occurrence is extremely rare and unlikely. When it does occur, it's usually due to a metallic chip in the governor oil line that is holding the pilot valve open, thus allowing more oil into the cylinder than is needed. This causes the prop to go into flat pitch and overspeed. Generally, when the overspeed occurs, it flushes oil through the governor, taking the metallic chip with it, thus correcting itself. A screen to filter oil before it goes to the governor makes this situation even more unlikely.

Governors are still in various stages of development. Woodward is in the process of testing a governor for future Beech aircraft that would limit takeoff power to 100 rpm below the maximum rating of the engine. The reason for this stems from new EPA regulations regarding aircraft noise. By reducing takeoff rpm by 100, the noise profile is considerably reduced. If the pilot needs the extra 100 rpm for an emergency, he can push a button on the throttle, or throttles, and the governors will automatically restore the 100 rpm and thus allow the engine to develop rated power. Such features in governors of the future are certain to become commonplace.

Governors are a relatively trouble-free, essential part of the aircraft propulsion system. When treated properly, they'll be loyal and reliable, but when subjected to neglect and abuse, inevitably they'll start acting up.

Governors have become pretty complex since those water wheel days in the 1800s, and ironically, with complexity came reliability. But they still need attention.

Be aware of Service Bulletins distributed by the manufacturer, and ask your mechanic to be sure to visually inspect your governor and prop system regularly. It's the least you can do to contribute to the safety and efficiency of your operation.

Turbocharging a New Generation of Aircraft

7

by Richard N. Aarons

Aircraft engine supercharging is hardly new; powerplant manufacturers and modifiers have been employing it for well over 50 years now. Of course, those 50 years have seen many changes. Engines that used to be vertical and round are now flat and rectangular; simple carburetors became automatic (altitude) carburetors and, ultimately, fuel injection systems; and superchargers evolved into turbosuperchargers (multi-stage devices powered by direct shafting and exhaust gas turbines) and then into turbochargers.

But the basic function of superchargers, turbosuperchargers and turbochargers—creating higher mass airflow into the engine—has not changed. As we'll see later in detail, supercharging and turbocharging devices increase mass airflow through the engine and thus enable the engine to develop higher power at sea level (ground turbocharging) or to maintain sea level power as the aircraft climbs to higher altitudes.

The ability to maintain rated climb power through the ascent makes total climb quicker. Thus mid-level icing encounters can be made relatively brief, terminal area climbs can be expedited and, when necessary, cruise can be conducted well above the 10,000-foot level to avoid weather and catch good winds. (Of course, true airspeeds are higher at the higher altitudes assuming a constant power level.) Turbocharging also substantially improves light twin, single engine cruise performance by lifting the single engine service ceiling. And, turbocharging also overcomes much of the density altitude problems at takeoff experienced on hot, humid days at high elevation fields.

Despite all that has been written about these systems, it is appropriate now to take another look at the turbo charger, not because it is in itself new, but because some of its applications are new—and quite clever.

A NEW GENERATION OF AIRCRAFT

Statistics have told the turbocharger story over the last decade. The devices, once found on only the largest engines powering the most expensive airplanes, have filtered down through the ranks to the humblest members of the business aircraft fleet.

The key to this proliferation of turbocharged light aircraft is, as you might suspect, recent reductions in the complexity (and thus cost) of turbocharger installations. Simply stated, as turbocharger systems become simpler to build, install, operate and maintain, they become feasible on more and more aircraft. And, of course, as more pilots are exposed to the operational advantages of turbocharging, the desire for these systems increases and the cost/benefit relationship appears to improve.

In any event, the turbocharger systems on today's lightest aircraft (the Cherokee Turbo Arrow III and the Rockwell 112TC, for example) are significantly different, especially in control, from those found on larger aircraft. We'll take a look at those differences here, in terms of both design and operation. Let's start, however, with a brief review of basic turbocharging principles.

First, consider the normally aspirated (nonturbocharged) reciprocating engine. It's simply a device designed to convert into mechanical energy the thermal energy generated by a burning gasoline/air mixture. All other things being equal, the amount of work done by the engine (horsepower) is directly proportional to the amount of gasoline/air mixture burned. (As you remember, the relative amounts of air and gasoline in that mixture change only within a small field.) Thus, a significant increase in gasoline requires a similar increase in the mass of air, and vice versa.

The turbocharger unit (excluding for the moment its controls) is simplicity itself (see Figure 1). The unit is powered by a turbine wheel which extracts energy from engine exhaust gases ducted into the exhaust inlet. The spinning turbine wheel is mechanically connected to the compressor wheel, which it drives. Compressed air leaves the compressor housing and is ducted into the aircraft induction system. The pressure developed by the compressor is simply a function of compressor speed, which is a function of turbine speed because the two are shafted together.

Turbocharger units, as pictured below, are manufactured primarily by Garrett AiResearch and Rayjay Industries. Teledyne Continental and Avco Lycoming use both these turbocharger vendors, depending on application. However, the origin of the system matters little to the pilot; all units function alike and have similar limitations.

The most important limitations on the turbocharger itself are shaft speed and turbine inlet temperature (TIT)—typically about 1650°F (899°C). We'll take a closer look at this temperature later. For now, suffice it to say that TIT is read directly from an EGT-like gauge in the cockpit. Design speed limit for most turbocharger units is about 100,000 rpm. System speed is not

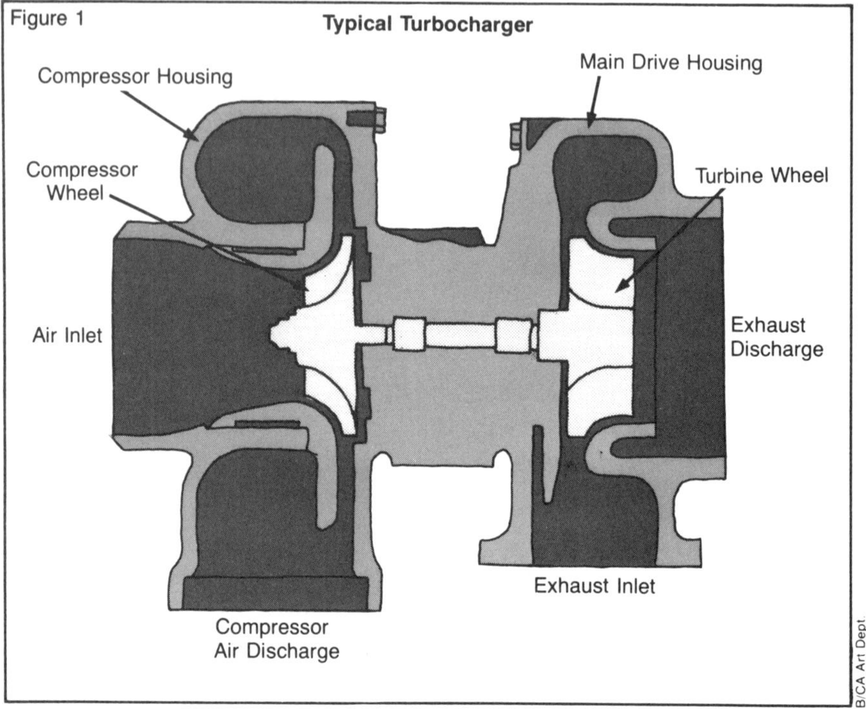

AiResearch and Rayjay Industries are the primary vendors of general aviation aircraft turbocharger units. The products of each are similar in that an exhaust-driven turbine wheel turns a compressor that increases mass airflow in the induction system.

reported to the cockpit but rather is restricted by flight manual limitations and manifold pressure as a function of altitude (more on this later, too).

The first turbochargers were simply bolted on to the side of normally aspirated engines. The output of the compressor was hooked up to the induction system, and the inlet of the turbine section was fed by the engine exhaust system. The only other element was a butterfly valve in the exhaust system upstream of the turbine inlet. The position of the valve—it's called a "waste gate"—was controlled by a cable run through the fire wall to the cockpit. Opening the valve ducted exhaust gases overboard before they reached the turbocharger, while closing the valve forced most exhaust gases through the turbine.

The waste gate, then, was a control for the system; the turbine would run at maximum speed when the gate was closed and at minimum speed when the gate was open.

In typical operation on takeoff, the waste gate would be open and the

56

compressor would therefore be contributing nothing to manifold pressure. During the climb the engine would function like any other normally aspirated engine. That is, the pilot would have to open the throttle continually as ambient air pressure dropped and manifold pressure fell. Long about 5,000 to 6,000 feet msl, the pilot would run out of throttle. The solution at that point was to begin to close the waste gate. That action would direct exhaust gases over the turbine, which would spin up the compressor, increasing manifold pressure. As the aircraft continued to climb and ambient air pressure continued to fall, the waste gate would be closed more and more to keep manifold pressure steady at the climb setting. Ultimately, however, the waste gate would be fully closed and virtually all exhaust gases would be ducted to the turbine to drive the compressor. This point was the *critical altitude* for the open throttle position. Climb above that altitude would result in a reduction of manifold pressure and loss of power.

This system, while entirely effective, had several drawbacks. One was that at any combination of throttle and waste gate settings, changes in ambient pressure or temperature or aircraft speed (ram induction pressure) brought about changes in manifold pressure. Before the system settles at a new manifold pressure, it oscillates to find a new equilibrium in a process called "bootstrapping."

Another disadvantage was that the engine could be overboosted easily. For example, if the pilot forgot to check that the waste gate was open on takeoff and it was, in fact, closed, the turbocharger would deliver full boost as soon as the throttles were fully opened. Manifold pressures then could exceed 60 inches—enough to turn most general aviation engines into junk.

A similar unpleasantness could befall the pilot who forgot to open the waste gate during descent and then attempted a full power go-around.

To solve the problems with the original manually controlled turbochargers, the engine and turbocharger manufacturers collaborated to develop fully automatic systems. (Surprisingly, they skipped enhancements to the manual systems that would appear years later to produce semi-automatic systems suitable in cost and performance for small engine applications.) The automatic systems have the same basic turbocharger unit as the manual systems, and the output of the compressor is also controlled by the amount of exhaust gases passing by the waste gate to the turbine. The difference is that while in the manual system the pilot controls the waste gate position directly by manipulating a cable-operated butterfly valve; in the automatic system oil pressure controls the waste gate position (see Figure 2). Oil pressure metering is accomplished by pressure sensing devices commonly (and collectively) called the "density controller." The details of how these clever pneumatic/hydraulic devices work are not really important to the pilot, but he should keep these basics in mind:

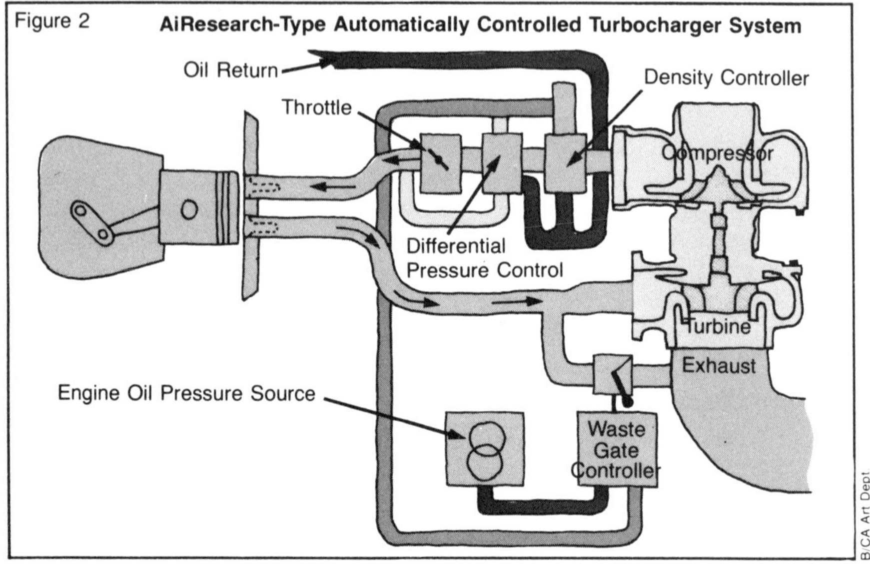

Automatically controlled turbocharger systems use engine oil pressure, metered by induction system pressure sensors, to control the exhaust waste gate position. When the waste gate closes, maximum exhaust gases are ducted to drive the turbocharger.

• A fully automatic turbocharger system maintains a pilot-selected manifold pressure regardless of changes in ambient temperature, pressure or airspeed. This situation exists until the system reaches its critical altitude, which is usually at or near 16,000 feet.

• The automatic system maintains a continuous watch on manifold pressure and throttle position and hydraulically manipulates the waste gate to control turbine speed, thus damping changes in induction pressure.

• These systems are complex and therefore relatively expensive, both at initial acquisition and in maintenance.

Turbocharging is desirable to enable operations at relatively high altitudes where the air is thinner and true airspeeds are higher, and also to provide optimum climb capability and single engine performance in the altitudes from sea level to 10,000 feet where the crews of most unpressurized aircraft prefer to operate.

Airframe manufacturers wanted to provide these operational benefits to operators of the smallest twins and the high performance singles. Once again, the engine manufacturers joined forces with the turbocharger makers, but this time with considerable input from the airframe engineers. The goal was to design a turbocharging control system less complicated than the automatics and thus less expensive to own and maintain, yet one that was reliable and relatively simple to operate.

Two systems emerged, a manually controlled, fixed waste gate system from Teledyne Continental, and a manually controlled, mechanical interconnect system from Avco Lycoming.

The fixed waste gate system is the ultimate in turbocharger control simplicity, as Figure 3 indicates. The movable waste gate (from the earlier manual and current automatic systems) has been replaced by a screw-type, ground adjustable waste gate valve. On the induction side, the complex density controller assembly of the automatic system has been replaced by a simple modulating overboost safety valve, which limits induction system manifold pressure to a predetermined value. The ground adjustable waste gate valve is preset so that full throttle critical altitude is about 12,000 feet. That is, the engine can produce full rated power at 12,000 feet with the throttle wide open, the overboost safety valve fully closed and the ground adjustable waste gate preset to keep everything in balance at the altitude.

It follows that at full throttle operation at lower altitudes, the overboost safety valve will be somewhere between fully closed and fully open.

The most significant advantage of this approach to turbocharger control is simplicity, both in fabrication and maintainability. The only moving part

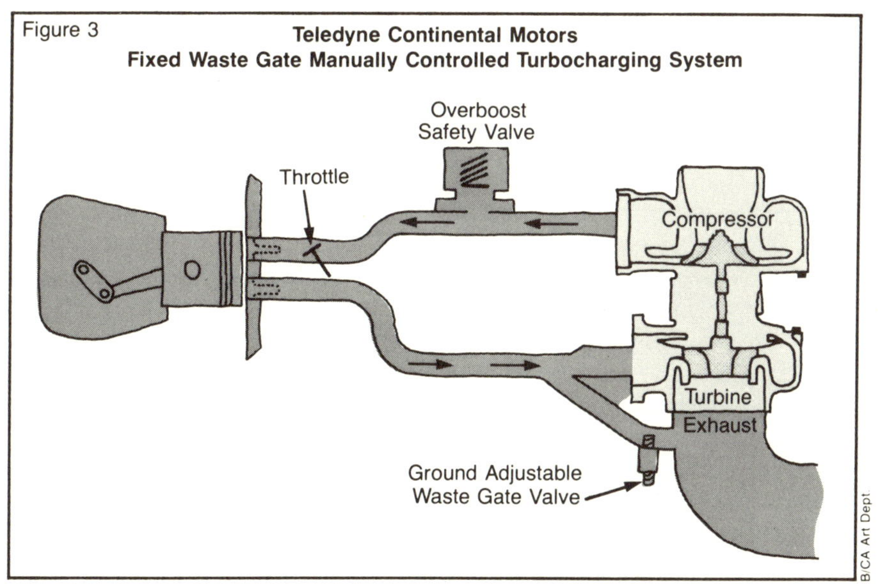

Teledyne Continental's fixed waste gate system uses only a modulating overboost safety valve and a fixed orifice in the exhaust bypass line to control system pressures.

is the poppet in the spring-loaded overboost safety valve, if indeed, that can be said to be a moving part. Operation too is simple, but the pilot *does* have to compensate manually for changes in temperature, airspeed and pressure.

The main disadvantage of the fixed waste gate system is that its full throttle critical altitude is relatively low, so the system is not really suitable for high altitude operations such as those required by the pressurized twins.

Avco Lycoming's approach to light aircraft turbocharger control consists of a mechanical interconnect between a flight-adjustable waste gate valve and the carburetor or fuel injector butterfly (Figure 4). As Lycoming explains it, the relationship of the waste gate position to butterfly position is such that at ground level the rated manifold pressure and power occur at less than full throttle. The pilot, therefore, advances the throttle control during climb to maintain rated manifold pressure. In the induction system, a pop-off type relief valve is installed between the turbocharger and carburetor (or fuel injector) to guard against overboosting from inadvertent excessive throttle opening. As is the case with the fixed waste gate system the pilot operating the engine with the mechanical interconnect system must compensate through throttle movement for changes in pressure, temperature and airspeed.

The primary advantage of the mechanically interconnected system is that its critical altitude (depending on installation) can be higher than that of a fixed waste gate system because the former's waste gate is controllable to a fully open position.

The main disadvantage is that the mechanical interconnect system has several moving parts, all with critically adjusted tolerances. The system will, in all probability, require more field adjustments and repairs than the fixed waste gate system.

Regardless of control type—automatic, manual, fixed waste gate or mechanical interconnect—turbocharged engines must be thoughtfully and carefully operated, with continuous monitoring of pressures and temperatures. Let's consider temperature first.

There are two temperatures to be monitored in any turbocharged engine —TIT (or sometimes exhaust gas temperature) and cylinder head temperature. The TIT or EGT limits are set to protect the elements in the hot section of the turbocharger, while cylinder head temperature limits protect the engine's internal parts.

Most turbocharged engine installations include cowl flaps to aid in maintaining cylinder head temperatures (CHT) below limits. In fact, engine manufacturers recommend that CHTs be kept 30° to 50° *below* the red line at all times despite the fact that the green arc on the gauge usually runs to the red line.

60

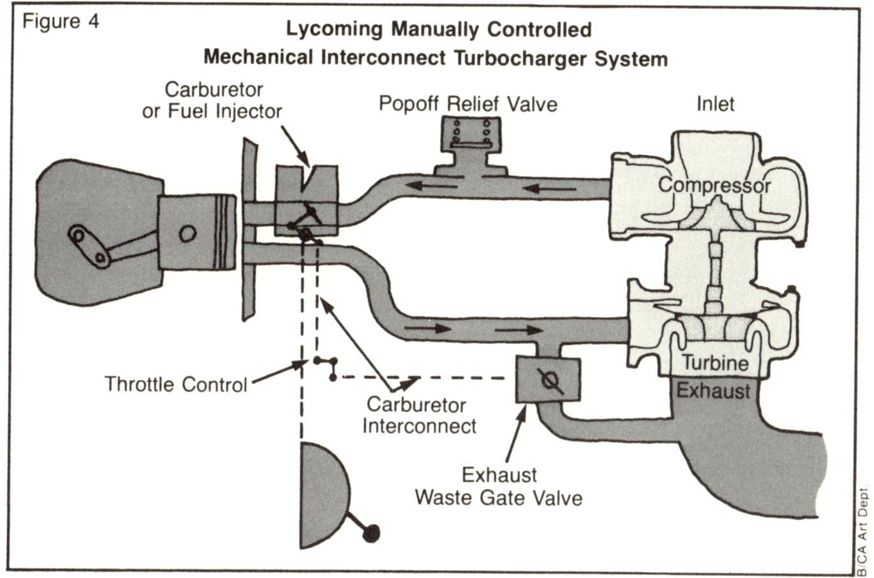

Avco Lycoming employs a mechanical interconnect between the throttle (or fuel injector) butterfly and a variable waste gate. Although this system is more complex than the fixed waste gate system, it can deliver higher critical altitudes.

Don't automatically close the cowl flaps after a relatively cool climb and forget to monitor CHT in cruise. At high altitude, where exhaust back pressure is lower, turbine speed will level off at an rpm well above the average rpm during climb. This higher speed creates a higher compression ratio in the compressor/induction system and thus a higher induction air temperature and higher CHTs. It is thus not unusual to level off at cruise, reduce to cruise power and then see CHTs continue to climb. Use cowl flap and power adjustments to keep CHTs comfortably below red line.

The TIT limit is usually about 1650°F (899°C). An EGT-type gauge is used to monitor TIT and the mixture knob to control it.

Although aircraft flight manuals often allow operation at peak TIT, such operation makes engine manufacturers nervous. "It's not that the engine can't take it," one engineer says. "It can. The problem is that the temperature gauges at best are accurate only to plus or minus six percent, and usually they are in less than best shape. The depth of the probe into the exhaust stream is absolutely critical. Too deep and it reads too hot; too shallow and it reads too cold. And here we're talking about hundredths of inches." Continental and Lycoming engineers urge all operators to have their temperature gauges and probes checked periodically. In the meantime, mistrust them and run a little on the cool side.

Pressure is what turbocharging is all about. Just enough pressure produces guaranteed performance; too much pressure creates detonation, stress failure and other unpleasantness. Overboosting in the automatic systems can be avoided simply by monitoring pressure whenever power settings are being changed, and on the three nonautomatic systems by being especially watchful on takeoff and descent.

All movements of the power controls on turbocharged engines should be slow and gentle, both to reduce bootstrapping and to prevent short-term overboosting.

Regardless of the class of piston airplane you operate, there is a turbocharger in your future if it's not already in your present. The new, low-cost, low-weight, low-maintenance systems will spread turbocharging (we think) to all but the smallest aircraft and we are sure you're going to like the change.

Operated carefully, turbocharged engines should have maintenance histories and overhaul lives similar if not identical to normally aspirated powerplants.

The new systems, while requiring a bit more pilot attention than the fully automatic systems, seem to fit a niche nicely. A friend of ours who operates a Turbo Arrow III loves his fixed waste gate system. Asked if he would spend an extra $4,000 on his $65,000 airplane for an automatic controller, he said, "Absolutely not. With four to five hours in the airplane, adjusting the throttles becomes entirely reflexive. Adjusting for ram air changes and altitude bumps becomes so second nature you don't even notice you're correcting for them."

If you're in the market for a new piston aircraft, consider the turbocharged version; it could make a heck of a change in your day-to-day operations.

Piston-Engine Fire Protection

8

by Dan Manningham

Engine fire protection is caught up in one of those unfortunate controversies. Engineers disagree with each other on basic designs; buyers and sellers weigh the technical merits against the cost penalties; operators consider the weight and maintenance factors. Only pilots are unanimous in their attitude towards this emergency equipment—they like engine fire protection to a man.

Many engine fires, other than those occurring during the starting cycle, are caused by leaking fuel or oil or by some electrical malfunction. Such fires can often be extinguished by merely shutting down the engine, which stops the source of ignition as well as the supply of fuel. Unfortunately, it is not always possible to detect a fire early enough to prevent the ignition of engine components, which may continue to burn even to the point of catastrophic failure after the engine is shut down.

Fire in a nacelle must rank as one of the most serious of all emergencies. FAA regulations mandate fire detection and extinguishers for all large and jet-powered airplanes. Similar regulations demand fire detection equipment on all turbine-powered helicopters. Ironically, piston-engine and small turboprop aircraft, which may be more susceptible to catastrophic fire, are not so covered by federal regulation, with the single exception of those aircraft used for FAR Part 121 operations and, therefore, Part 135.2 operations as well. However, there has been a Notice of Proposed Rulemaking proposing that FAR 23.1203, fire detector systems, be applicable to all small multi-engine turbine-powered aircraft and turbocharged piston-engine aircraft.

Given that regulatory vacuum, it is the piston-aircraft buyer or operator who must assume the responsibility to select the best fire protection system. In order to do that effectively, he will need to understand the technical basics of piston-engine fire protection. Fortunately the subject lends itself to four specific considerations:
- Fire detection.
- Extinguishing agents.

- Distribution systems.
- Rate and duration of agent application.

Firemen will tell you that there are three ways to stop a fire:

- Remove the fuel.
- Cool the fire below kindling temperatures, a process usually accomplished with water.
- Blanket the fuel so that the fire smothers from lack of oxygen. CO_2, dry chemicals and foam all work in this fashion.

Notice the first option. When a pilot is alerted to engine fire quickly, the simple expedient of removing the fuel by shutting off mixture and fuel selector will kill the fire. That sort of early warning can only be provided by electronic fire detection equipment.

Fire detectors in most light-piston applications are nothing more than temperature sensors in the nacelle that illuminate a cockpit warning light at some predetermined temperature. Competitive systems are very similar, but may vary in terms of threshold temperatures and number and placement of sensors. You will want to be sure there are enough sensors to cover all fire sensitive areas, but your choices may be limited. Fire detection is normally an integral part of any fire protection package offered for piston singles and twins. You may have to accept the detection and extinguishing systems as one unit.

Early engine fire extinguishers used CO_2 almost exclusively. In the 1950s several other chemicals began to replace CO_2 because that agent was comparatively heavy in the quantities required for aircraft engine fires. Some aircraft used methyl bromide, an effective extinguishant but a highly toxic chemical. Methyl bromide is so toxic, in fact, that spare containers could not be carried within the pressurized portion of the aircraft because accidental discharge would create a disaster.

In the late 50s, a unique extinguishant appeared. It was first used on the last Lockheed Constellations and Douglas DC-7s. Until recently it was simply called Freon. Although it carried that DuPont Company trade name, this product is very different from the refrigerant and so has been renamed Halon 1301.

Halon 1301 has so many desirable qualities as an extinguishing agent that the list can become cumbersome. On a weight-of-agent basis it is the most effective gaseous extinguishing agent available. It mixes very rapidly with air, is effective against all classes of fires, is colorless, odorless, nonconductive, noncorrosive, and leaves no residue. Halon 1301 is also so low in toxicity that it is the only gaseous extinguishant approved by the National Fire Protection Association (NFPA) for use in occupied areas. Underwriters Laboratories classifies Halon 1301 in toxicity group 6, the least toxic category.

Still, the unique feature of Halon 1301 is the mechanism by which it extinguishes fire. Unlike any of the more familiar agents, which smother or cool, Halon works as a physiochemical inhibitor of the actual combustion process. In some still unknown way, Halon 1301 breaks the basic chain reactions that propagate from one fuel molecule to another. In a five percent to seven percent Halon 1301 environment, the burning process simply cannot function, even though there may be plenty of fuel, oxygen and ignition. (See Figure 1.)

Since the early 1960s Halon has steadily replaced all other engine fire extinguishing agents. Older flight manuals and product literature may refer to it as Freon, Freon 13B1, Freon 1301, FE 1301 or Halon.

Halon is super stuff, and in concentrations of six percent by volume it will absolutely extinguish and/or prevent any class A, B or C fire. The real

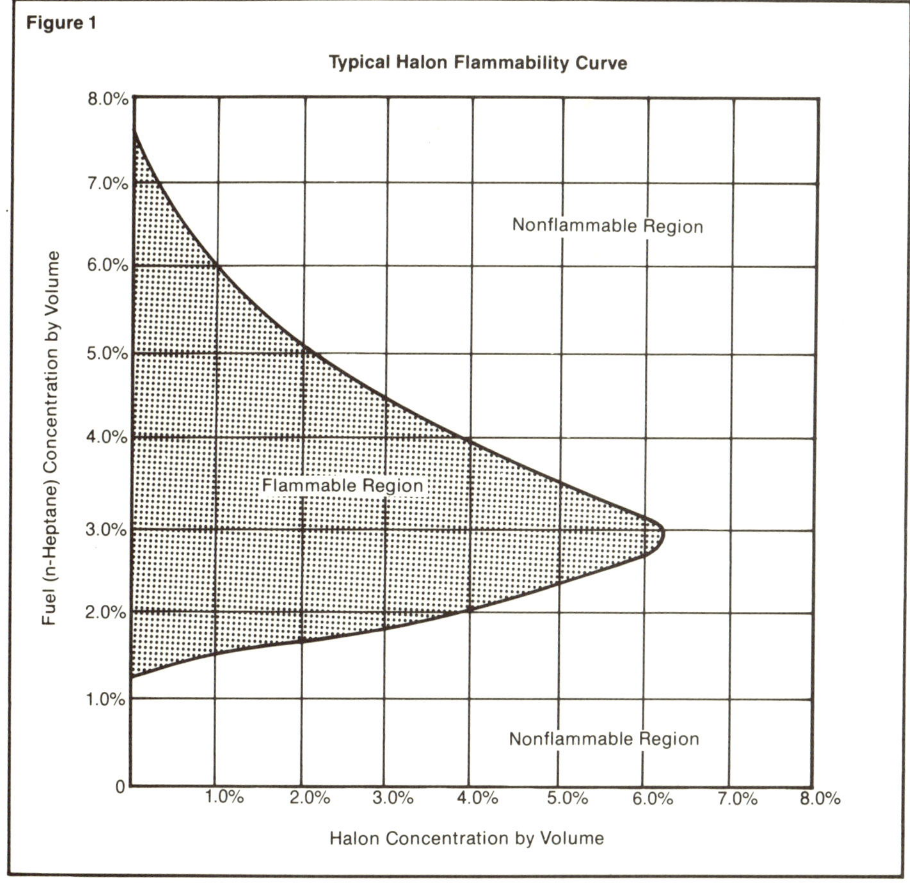

The above chart shows the flammability curve of Halon 1301.

challenge is to distribute that chemical effectively throughout the engine nacelle.

Airflow through a piston engine is so grossly contorted and chaotic that it is nearly impossible to predict its exact path with any accuracy. Early engineering work on engine fire extinguishers used the simple expedient of actually setting the engine on fire to see if the prototype extinguisher could put it out. One classic study done in 1943 by A. W. Dallas and H. L. Hansberry for the old CAA involved 1290 fire tests.

Those pioneers set two goals for their tests:

• To determine the efficiency of various agents when applied to gasoline and oil fires in both the power and accessory sections of aircraft engines inflight.

• To determine for each agent the quantity required, the rate of application necessary and the optimum methods of distribution for both the power and accessory sections.

Although Dallas and Hansberry's work was done on radial engines, with old-fashioned agents, their work was technically sound and some of their conclusions may still be valid.

They found that the nacelle area included innumerable flame holders where fire could linger to generate reignition unless the extinguishing agent was applied to all areas in sufficient quantities. Similarly, re-ignition from hot metal parts, glowing carbon or dirt particles was a significant problem if the duration of agent application was less than two seconds, even though the main fire was usually extinguished in less than one second. They also found that when the fuel was not shut off, fire tails developed behind the nacelle that could not be extinguished.

Dallas and Hansberry came to several conclusions as a result of those actual fire tests:

• Fuel must be shut off *prior* to using the extinguisher.

• The agent must be distributed to the power section, accessory section, exhaust stack wells, strainers and firewall, *simultaneously.*

• Airblast is the most serious factor to overcome in the extinguishment of engine fires and is overcome by using *high rates* of agent application.

• An extinguishing agent applied too far forward in the engine nacelle results in *spillage* and waste through the front of the cowling due to the back pressure caused by deceleration of free stream air at the front of the powerplant.

• In general, it is easy to extinguish the major body of a nacelle fire, but *re-ignition* is a very real problem.

As a result of this and other research work, it appears that your engine fire extinguisher should have separate nozzles for at least the power and accessory sections, and they must discharge simultaneously. The front nozzle should not be placed so that agent can spill forward out of the

66

nacelle at high speed. All things being equal, several well placed nozzles would seem to be better than one or two. Finally, it would seem logical to provide for a substantial agent discharge in the accessory section for effective protection in the event of a ground fire in a tailwind situation.

This particular aspect of fire extinguisher design is the most controversial. Basically, the rate of discharge must be sufficient to provide a concentration of extinguishant that will inert the atmosphere around the fire. Then that inert environment must be maintained long enough to allow complete extinguishment *and* enough cooling to prevent re-ignition from flame holders and/or hot spots. Surprisingly there is considerable disagreement on how best to accomplish this.

As Dallas and Hansberry found in the early 40s, the enormous airflow through an aircraft engine nacelle at high speeds demands a very high rate of agent discharge to assure effective concentrations. You can see by Figure 1 that a Halon 1301 concentration of six percent is sufficient to create that inert environment in which fire will die and not re-ignite. Accordingly, all extinguishing systems currently available for light piston airplanes are designed to discharge enough Halon 1301 to achieve at least that six percent concentration.

The real question becomes one of duration.

Since those early experiments, extinguishing research has been done with a device called a Statham Analyzer, a device to measure agent concentrations in the nacelle under actual conditions.

It works like this: Twelve probes are placed inside the engine nacelle and connected to a vacuum pump. The probes are designed to measure the density of a gas mixture—in this case the Halon 1301 density—by measuring the pressure drop across a porous metal plug. Those measurements are then fed to a high-rate recorder, which inscribes them for later analysis.

The actual test is performed inflight by configuring the engine and aircraft appropriately and then firing the extinguishing system. The Statham Analyzer records individual gas densities from those 12 probes, and the engineers then adjust the distribution, rate and/or duration of agent discharge as necessary. Tests usually are conducted during takeoff and normal cruise.

Unfortunately, the Statham Analyzer test is not required for light piston-engine extinguishers, and the high cost of this test has so far discouraged anyone from so testing their piston equipment. Piston-engine fire extinguishers are still designed on a "looks good" basis without any required testing.

Turbine engines typically have a very high volume of airflow, which demands a proportionately high rate of agent discharge. Turbine engines are also somewhat smoother structurally, so that they do not have the same potential for flame holders and hot spots as do their piston counterparts.

67

Since only turbine engines are required to have fire protection by the FAA, the appropriate regulations may be biased in their direction. Technical Development Report Number 403, the applicable document in this case, requires a minimum Statham Analyzer reading of 15 percent for 0.5 second at all pickups. That 15 percent equates to an actual six percent concentration in the nacelle. That concentration is provided, in turbine engines, by High Rate Discharge (HRD) systems. HRDs are designed to dump a lot of agent in a short time to overwhelm a fire before it can spread. Such systems are now the standard for turbines, but there is some question about whether that theory carries over to piston requirements.

No one will argue with the six percent concentration. It is definitely high enough to extinguish any fire, but the 0.5-second duration raises some eyebrows.

Dallas and Hansberry did their last extensive work with actual fire tests, and one of their prime conclusions was that the inerting concentration should be maintained for at least two seconds They found that two seconds allowed complete extinguishment in all potential flame holders *and* provided cooling for hot spots that might otherwise cause re-ignition. The recent emphasis on turbine equipment has obscured that particular point by presuming that anything good enough for jets is surely good enough for a light piston twin. It's an open question.

Bill Enk, president of Enk Aviation and designer of the FiQuench extinguishing system, relies heavily on Dallas and Hansberry research. Enk feels strongly that gas analysis is no substitute for actual fire tests, especially when gas analysis suggests reduced protection parameters. As a result, the FiQuench system is engineered to initiate that six percent minimum concentration instantly and maintain it for at least two seconds. Ironically, Enk, who is openly critical of Statham Analyzer data as a basis for design, has taken the time and trouble to check his system with a gas analyzer of his own making. As a result, there is *some* documented evidence that the FiQuench system may be able to extinguish fires.

HTL Industries, a major producer of fire extinguishing systems for aircraft engines, takes a different tack. HTL uses the HRD approach to flood the nacelle with 1301 in 0.8 of a second, feeling that the high concentration will knock the fire down faster and still provide adequate Halon levels for enough cooling.

The sorry fact is that piston engine fire extinguishers are largely designed by guess and by gosh. There are no absolute standards, nor absolute proof that any particular system will actually work.

Therefore, when shopping for piston-engine fire protection, don't be misled by the words "FAA Certified." There are no applicable regulations for extinguisher effectiveness. "FAA Certified" merely means that the installation does not compromise safety.

One other note for the shopper: Some systems advertise "automatic Halon release at 180°." Don't be fooled by that claim. The 180° release is just thermal protection for the Halon bottle which may accidentally dump into the distribution manifold. This type of thermal protection is certainly superior to dumping the extinguishant overboard, but it does not constitute an automatic fire protection system. In fact, any such automation would seriously compromise safety by releasing the agent before engine shutdown, which is always a futile gesture.

Fire protection systems provide two levels of protection when used properly. If the fire warning light indicates an engine compartment fire, you are faced with a dilemma. Either the engine is burning or you have received a false warning, a not uncommon occurrence, especially with thermostatic type sensors. If your airplane is configured in a way that allows you to visually check the engine, do so before wasting the single extinguisher shot. If you are not in a critical phase of flight—takeoff or go-around—shut down the engine during or before the visual inspection as a precaution. When fire is definitely indicated, be sure to accomplish at least the following steps in order:

Fuel off—Turn off all fuel boost pumps, tank selectors and crossfeeds to that engine.

Shut down engine—Close throttle and mixture, and feather if possible. Turn off magnetos and alternator, prop synchronizer, alcohol and hydraulics.

Wait—Wait 15 to 20 seconds to see if the fire will go out as evidenced by an extinguished fire warning light and a good visual check.

Fire the Halon—If the fire persists, close the cowl flaps and shoot the bottle. There is some evidence that engine fire is intensified by closing the cowl flaps, so it may be better to save that step until just prior to using the extinguishant.

Pilots have no trouble justifying fire protection systems on their aircraft. IFR weather, night operations, over water or mountainous terrain, are all good, sound reasons for having some engine fire protection aboard.

Owners may take a more fiscal approach. Most obvious, of course, is the cash outlay for the system itself. It varies from $465 for a single-engine aircraft to $3000 for a pressurized cabin twin. Carefully check installed prices because field installations may vary considerably in price, even for the same equipment. Installation times vary from 10 hours for a single-engine aircraft system to 40 hours for a pressurized cabin twin system. That figure should be tempered by the appropriate tax advantage and the residual value of the system when the aircraft is sold or traded. Aside from such direct cash accounting, there are four other minor considerations.

• Fire protection systems add some small amount of weight to the aircraft so that gross weight could be a consideration in extreme circumstances. For example, a single-engine installed weight is typically 10 to 25 pounds; a pressurized cabin twin system weighs anywhere from 22 to 50 pounds.

• If the system is not factory installed, you will have to consider the cash value of whatever ferry time and/or downtime is necessary.

• On the plus side, check with your insurance agent for any possible break in hull rates as a result of your new fire protection equipment.

• Finally, you will need to consider the undefinable value of possible increased passenger confidence.

Despite the regulatory vacuum, these systems offer some significant level of protection against the threat of a powerplant fire. You will have to carefully analyze the claims and check total installed prices, but when you do make the purchase, your aircraft will be measurably safer.

POWERPLANTS: TURBINE III

Turbine engines are the answer to aviation's dreams. They are lightweight, smooth, efficient and fantastically powerful. They are also exceedingly expensive and somewhat delicate. For those reasons, turbine-engine care and maintenance are particularly important.

There are ways to delay the need for an overhaul and to insure that you get the most for your money when overhaul is necessary. "Care and Repair of Turbine Engines" explores all the possibilities, including pilot technique, use of outside consultants, and proper maintenance. It could save you a bundle or even an engine.

Max Beitscher is a brusque, hard-nosed, and sometimes an abrasive man. This former service manager at Airwork speaks with the tangible authority that springs from years of experience in turbine engine repair and overhaul. Max's 12 tips for cutting costs and increasing safety are detailed in "Max Beitscher On Turbine Maintenance."

Ever hear of a $60 spark plug? Your turbine engine probably has at least two. They're called igniters. For a short course on turbine-engine ignition systems and those expensive igniters that can burn up like soft candles stay with this section.

Turbine-engine fuel controls are among the most complicated devices an airplane carries. Hydromechanical fuel controls, long the standard, are slowly giving way to lighter, more efficient, electronic models. "Electronic Fuel Controls" explains the background and the future of these promising gadgets.

For years the airlines have used a reduced-takeoff-power technique to extend hot-section life and conserve fuel. The so-called "assumed temperature method" (ATM) of calculating that reduced power is a straightforward procedure that does not require additional test flying or certification data. This section contains an explanation of how to apply this proven technique to any jet operation. And there is advice on avoiding foreign object damage.

Care and Repair of Turbine Engines

9

by Robert L. Parrish

What's the matter, Mr. Business Jet Pilot?

You say you're lost in the wilderness of technicalese when it comes time for a turbine engine overhaul? Feel like you're being had but you're not quite sure how? Afraid to question maintenance proposals because it might show that you're not as up on those propulsion systems as you feel you should be?

Don't assume that you're out there all alone. With the complexity and operational sensitivity of the current generation of aircraft turbine power-plants; with rapid escalation of labor and parts costs; with a limited number of fiercely competing repair shops to which your ailing engines can be taken; and with flight crews finding more of their time occupied just in keeping abreast of constantly changing regulations and procedures, the number of business pilots who share your maintenance malaise is legion.

Turbojet, turbofan, turboprop and turboshaft propulsion systems unquestionably have brought better reliability and travel efficiency to the business aviation community. But they have also brought higher initial acquisition costs, steeper maintenance and repair bills, and new learning problems that still—after nearly two decades—are not wholly resolved.

Turbine engine makers claim that their products are more economical in the long run than piston engines. While time between overhauls for the latter have remained relatively unchanged from what they were 20 years ago, almost all the turbine engines employed in the business aviation indus-try today boast minimum TBOs twice as long as those for piston engine models. On many turbine powerplants TBO has given way to on-condition maintenance that calls for periodic inspections and repair and replacement of parts only as necessary. Flight department heads find it hard to rational-ize, however, when they note that the tab for major turbine engine repairs today may exceed what they paid for an acceptable executive aircraft a few years ago.

Several reasons can be given for turbine-related price structures. Even though the turbine powered business fleet has grown by 800 percent in 10 years and continues to expand at a rate of nine percent annually, both the manufacture and repair of turbine engines are still relatively narrow-based endeavors. There are only about 8,000 turbine-driven aircraft out there, compared with a total of over 200,000 aircraft in general aviation. Consequently, engine and spares production has not yet approached a volume that will drive costs down appreciably.

In addition, heat-resistant and exotic metals used in these engines are quite costly and require special equipment for machining or repair. The FAA standards to which the engines must be built, tested and maintained also add to the bill.

These points can be easily understood. Questions to which many business aircraft operators seem to be groping for answers, however, include: How can one know with some certainty how much inspections and overhauls should cost? What should—and should not—be done to the engine during major teardown or repair? What are the exact scope and limitations of warranties? When may a worn or damaged part be repaired rather than replaced, and what are the tradeoffs? Most importantly, perhaps, how can the operator be sure that he is getting the most timely, cost-effective maintenance and overhaul services for each dollar spent, considering his individual flight missions and the environment in which he operates?

A series of B/CA interviews with turbine aircraft pilots, engine manufacturers and officials of overhaul/repair shops disclosed that there are no simple answers to these questions; only generalities are possible. For example, bargain repair work is simply not a reality, but there are ways to sustain or restore performance more economically than many operators realize. They boil down to a single truth: The better you understand your turbine engine, the more likely you will be able to optimize expenditures for both fuel and repairs.

Virtually everyone who flies a turbine powered aircraft has been exposed to at least one engine orientation school sponsored by the airframe or engine manufacturer. Many pilots also participate on occasion in seminars offered by repair and overhaul facilities. Unless they are A&P mechanics, however, many of these pilots admit that they remain mystified about other than the most general technical aspects of their engines.

An official at one overhaul shop contends that answers to all the questions posed above can be obtained through seminars held by his company or through overhaul pre-contract negotiations. But the manager of another facility acknowledged that detailed explanatory information usually is given only when specifically asked for. It appears, then, that one cause for potential misunderstanding—as in any interaction between a customer and a seller—is a lack of adequate communication between the customer and the repair facility.

The fact that operating philosophies differ slightly among the various factory and authorized repair centers could contribute to confusion.

Airwork Service Division, in Millville, New Jersey, attempts by means of a computer-centered monitoring system to provide for its customers airline-type job directives and work-scopes. While its salesmen work closely with clients to structure the exact overhaul jobs the computer tells them are needed, the salesmen concur that the ultimate determinant of what is to be done is how much the customer feels he can or wants to pay. Airwork officials are among those who believe that turbine engines can be restored to the point that they equal or exceed original specifications but admit that the bill for such service might be astronomical.

Pacific Airmotive Corporation and Aviation Power Supply, both in Burbank, California, along with Cooper Airmotive in Dallas, appear inclined to follow recommendations laid out in manufacturers' overhaul manuals. In the final analysis, however, they'll give the customer what he asks for, within airworthiness limitations.

Perhaps because it has 17 authorized overhaul facilities throughout the world, Pratt & Whitney Aircraft of Canada has become aggressive in the overhaul competition in recent years. One of the world's leading producers of turboprop engines, P&W applies a "baseline standard" to its repair and overhaul programs. For the PT6A-27, 28 and 34 models those standards include 16 mandatory modifications that apply to all repairs and 75 additional service bulletin modifications that are recommended on all overhauls. Company officials admit that they do their best to convince customers of the wisdom of incorporating all those measures when they contract for work.

P&W's baseline standard reportedly was developed from monitoring thousands of hours of operations under all conceivable conditions, and the mods cumulatively assure the customer that his overhaul includes the firm's latest technological advancements.

As have the makers of larger turbine engines, P&W recently has begun to emphasize the modular concept for repair and overhaul. Specialists there believe that within a few years that practice will be standardized throughout the industry.

Garrett AiResearch spokesmen in Phoenix claim that their turboprop overhauls are restoring engines to original performance standards or better. The rationale used here is that every overhauled TPE-331 engine goes out the door with a performance edge two percent above the standard.

Garrett's flat rate "mod standard" overhaul program, while it may penalize the operator who has pampered his engines, at least gives management a firm figure against which to budget for overhaul.

There are several ways in which the turbine engine aircraft owner can minimize operational and maintenance costs. Of course, fully understanding the powerplant is essential.

As with all aircraft engines, turbines are designed, built and certificated by the FAA to deliver specific levels of performance, efficiency and economy. These standards are derived from pressure ratio (the degree to which air molecules are compressed before reaching the combustion chamber), fuel flow rate through a series of nozzles into the combustor (expressed as specific fuel consumption, or SFC, and defined as the pounds of fuel required per hour for each pound of thrust produced) and the engine's internal heat level (ITT, or interstage turbine temperature). If any of these elements is out of predetermined balance, it will adversely affect the others and, therefore, engine performance and health.

So long as the engine is run within its prescribed limits for each of those parameters and there are no external influences such as FOD or adverse environment it may show little physical signs of wear at stipulated inspection and overhaul periods. Conversely, operating with any of these parameters above or below established limits will result in more rapid deterioration—plugged fuel nozzles, hot gas "burn-throughs" in critical areas, heat distortion blade wear, contour changes and possibly catastrophic failure.

Two examples of exceptional operational procedures are reflected by Rio Airways, a Texas commuter airline that has posted well over 11,000 hours without a major overhaul on a PT6A-28 engine; and American Airlines which, with its FAA- and manufacturer-approved "condition monitored maintenance" program, has stretched the interval between hot section overhauls on the P&W JT3 engine to over 4,000 hours. Due to the fewer hours flown per year, similar records are not found within the business aviation industry, despite strict adherence to prescribed operational procedures.

Technically, only high-speed rotating parts of turbine engines are life-limited by federal regulation and must be replaced after specific numbers of hours or cycles of use. These are limited generally to compressor discs and blades, impellers and turbine discs. But to maintain airworthy status, every part of each engine must be inspected individually and tested at given intervals and found to meet tolerances that have been established by the manufacturer and approved by the FAA. Parts that cannot meet the tolerances must be repaired or replaced.

It is not required that replacement parts be new, only that they be serviceable for a predictable period of time, such as until the next periodic inspection or overhaul. Use of reconditioned parts therefore can offer substantial economies on overhauls.

A question that frequently troubles flight department maintenance supervisors is, when do performance restoration measures cease to be cost-effective? An investigation by American Airlines sheds some light in this area.

When the price of fuel began to rise sharply in 1973, it had a marked impact on virtually every flight operation's overall operating budget, including American's. Prior to the rise, jet fuel purchases accounted for about one-sixth of the company's costs. As that ratio grew, maintenance officials set a goal of achieving a $3 fuel saving for every dollar spent on major maintenance activities. Greatly improved SFCs and reduced fuel use per aircraft mile were achieved under that program.

But as Charles Wollmershauser, director of American's powerplant engineering, pointed out, most of the engines in the airline's fleet no longer were new and to restore them to their original levels of performance would be cost-prohibitive, if not impossible. A project conducted by R.H. Wulf of General Electric Company would seem to bear out that contention.

That project involved a GE CF6 turbofan from an American DC-10 that reflected abnormal deterioration in early use. As a disinterested party, Cooper Airmotive, headquartered in Dallas, was selected to overhaul the

Turbine Overhaul Facilities

Operators of turbine engine business aircraft have a limited number of facilities through which they can obtain major overhauls. Whether arranged through the aircraft maintenance department, a fixed base operator or other medium, overhaul of turbine engines may be legally performed only by the following companies. Some of these have more than one strategically based facility.

AiResearch of Arizona Phoenix, Az.	Pacific Airmotive Corp. 2940 N. Hollywood Way Burbank, Ca.
Airwork Service Division Municipal Airport Millville, N.J.	Pratt & Whitney of Canada Longueuil, Quebec Canada
Aviation Power Supply, Inc. 3111 Kenwood St. Burbank, Ca.	Rolls-Royce, Inc. 375 Park Ave. New York, N.Y.
Cooper Airmotive, Inc. 7555 Lemon Ave. Dallas, Tx.	Teledyne Neosho Neosho, Mo.
General Electric Aircraft Engine Group 1000 Western Ave. West Lynn, Ma.	

unit and to help determine at what point the cost of restoring performance became disproportionate to the improvement gained.

Following existing airline modular work-scope procedures, the technicians achieved a restoration of 92 percent in SFC and 80 percent in EGT at a cost only nominally above that of a regular overhaul. But to obtain another few points of improvement in each area might have equaled or exceeded the cost of the gross restoration gains, project engineers found.

For business aircraft users, there are a number of such cost control guidelines in use. One overhaul facility calculates that, as a rule of thumb, a turbine engine aircraft operator can expect two-thirds of his overhaul bill to be for parts and one-third for labor. Since labor rates are relatively standard, the most significant potential savings therefore lie in parts costs. Determining when parts can be repaired or when used but serviceable items can be substituted for new parts can save considerable expense on a turbine overhaul.

Manufacturers' manuals and catalogues often contain broad schedules for maintenance or price lists from which the customer can extrapolate data, but this is a time-consuming and inexact method. By far the most ideal way to monitor both cost and quality of overhaul work is to have your own maintenance chief "live" with the engine through at least its disassembly and cleanup.

If time or economics render such monitoring unattractive, an alternative is to seek a turbine engine overhaul consultant. There really are such people, and their number appears to be growing. Consultants B/CA contacted are all engineers, technicians or marketers who were former long-time employes of turbine engine manufacturers or overhaulers. Each is familiar with the personnel, operations and procedures of major overhaul centers and each claims to be able to facilitate handling as well as to reduce repair costs for his clients. Furthermore, they are expert in regulatory requirements related to repair versus replacement, warranty policies and other matters that can make a big difference in the bottom line of overhauls.

"The airlines and engine manufacturers have always had representatives assigned to the overhaul facilities to look out for their interests," observes one consultant, "but the business aircraft operator has had no one."

Filling that gap is how this consultant serves his clients. As a contract negotiator who is intimately aware of both the repair facility's capabilities and the customer's needs and desires, he provides on-the-spot technical support and surveillance, shorter engine turnaround time and audited cost control.

On some of his accounts, this consultant receives a monthly fee. From others he gets a direct commission or a percentage of the money he saves the client. From still others he receives no remuneration at all but instead is compensated by the overhaul shop for the new business.

"I know of only a few others in this work," he says. "Each of us operates a little differently, but we all have the same objectives. The business still is too new to have any firm ground rules."

While he would not quantify the value of his service, "I tell my clients that if I can't lower by at least 10 percent the price quoted directly by an FBO or repair center, they don't really need me."

Another consultant claims he can document an instance in which a company flight department had seven jet engines in need of repair. The overhaul station's estimate, based on a fixed labor rate for each engine plus replacement of all damaged parts with new ones, came to more than $60,000 per engine. The consultant says he was able to cut the bill to $38,000 per engine by recommending ganging of some labor functions and use of repaired or reworked parts, where possible.

"At first," he recalls, "the major repair centers were reluctant to deal with us [consultants] because they apparently felt that we'd reduce their income and cause customers to feel that center personnel were inattentive to the customers' needs. But they have come to realize that we represent a source of new business; we eliminate the hassles over warranties and bills; we help to improve customer relations; and we are even of some help to them in stabilizing workloads and developing parts-pricing policies."

The greatest responsibility for realization of the benefits of turbine technology, however, still belongs to the pilot. The following engine operational tips may seem basic, but they are essential to engine longevity and health and cannot be overstressed:

• First, operate the turbines as much as possible in strict accordance with procedures set down in the manufacturers' manuals. These directions derive from expert knowledge and exhaustive testing of the airframe/engine combination, and adherence to them will help assure that warranty claims are honored should problems arise.

• Where possible, don't shut down during brief stopovers: repetitive heating and cooling of the engine components can result in premature metal fatigue and high potential for failure.

• Plan ahead for routine inspections and maintenance. When cowlings are removed for scheduled checks it may be wise to have the maintenance crew inspect all exposed components. In many cases damage or incipient failures are discovered this way, and costly repair bills thus can be avoided. Besides, the task of repeatedly removing and resecuring cowls can add up to a substantial labor bill over a period of time.

• Don't allow the engines' gas generators to bog down during low rpm operation. If damage occurs, invariably it will be to such high-cost components as turbine wheels, impellers, diffuser ducts and major bearings.

• When possible, try to cruise at slightly reduced power. Fuel savings can be substantial and wear and tear will be reduced; and 10 minutes longer en route can pay off with many additional hours of reliable service.

• If the aircraft or engine manual recommends it, have the compressor section washed, cleaned and inspected as stipulated. Cleanliness is perhaps the most vital element for maintaining engine efficiency. Additionally, the procedure will allow maintenance personnel to more readily discern indications of damage or wear.

• Don't overlook the potential value of spectrometric oil analysis as an aid to monitoring the condition of the engines. Even though there is some controversy over the efficacy of this practice, it should be noted that it is almost universally accepted by major airlines. And it is a mandatory part of the progressive maintenance program approved in lieu of TBO for the TFE-731 turbofan engine.

• Insist on detailed records of all maintenance, inspections and repairs performed on your engines. Such records are required by FARs, and they can help reveal any incipient problems and performance trends. Also, if service and routine maintenance are done by out-of-house facilities these records can serve as a "report card" on the capabilities and conscientiousness of those who work on your aircraft.

• Bear in mind that deterioration of SFC by fractional points can affect fuel consumption by as much as 50 pounds an hour. At a nominal 500 flight hours a year, that represents a needless waste of 25,000 pounds and nearly $3,000 in fuel costs.

Can't you think of better things to do with that money?

Max Beitscher On Turbine Maintenance

10

Airwork is missing a bet. Anyone who operates a turbine aircraft would pay handsomely just to sit in Max Beitscher's office and eavesdrop on his telephone conversations. Our interview with Airwork's crusty service manager was interrupted a half-dozen times by calls from concerned operators of turbine equipment, and each got infinitely more than his nickel's worth. One, a high-time pilot of King Air 100, got a crisp lecture on how to start his PT6A-28 engines. By applying what he was told he'll probably avoid a gearbox failure within the next year. Another, a Lear operator, was brusquely told that his "curmudgeonly" maintenance habits were costing him performance and hundreds of dollars in wasted fuel. Within the next year that pilot will, if he listened, save the cost of a hot section.

In his private life, Beitscher isn't at all the hard-nosed guy he must seem to those who call or stick their heads into his office during business hours. In our conversations he has always come across as a rather quiet, at times almost shy, man. When he accepted the Joe Chase Award from the Professional Aviation Maintenance Association in Washington last spring, he was genuinely humble.

But when he talks about the abuses that manufacturers and pilots heap on his engines, he's very direct and often caustic.

"Power management training is usually given by those with an obligation to see that airframe performance matches sales claims," he wrote recently. "Flight manual takeoff, climb and cruise power curves are set by airframe manufacturers. Engine performance and limits are set by engine manufacturers. But economic and safety limitation are set only by the flight crews."

Such statements probably do little to endear Max to manufacturers, but it's hard to argue with the dollars and cents.

When an operator stops and listens, he's rewarded with Max's 12 tips for cutting costs and increasing safety in the operation of a turbine engine.

1. *Start it fast*—"The guy who takes the professional approach to his equipment will monitor his starts even more than he does engine parameters at cruise. He should stopwatch each one and log the time from button to idle."

Why? There are two primary reasons. First, most engine deterioration occurs during the start cycle, and it's the time of the start cycle that counts —not the maximum temperature as most pilots are taught to think. Temperature instruments don't necessarily measure the hot spots at the igniters, nozzles and turbine wheels—and hot spots are almost certain to develop during a sluggish start. Often, in fact, the coolest start will result in the most hot spots.

To prevent that, operators should strive for the fastest starts possible— even to the point of opting for the highest-torque starters available. They spin the engine through the light-off zone quicker and prevent the accumulation of heat due to a low volume of airflow through the hot section. Certainly, the operator should keep all the items that contribute to fast starts in top condition, and that leads to the second reason for timing and logging the button-to-idle interval: it'll tell you what kind of maintenance you're getting.

"If times are growing longer, that's telling the operator he has oxidized battery leads, a deteriorating battery, corroded relay contacts, a weak exciter, improper depth of an igniter or the igniters, or an igniter going out. All of those are quality-of-maintenance items, and that's why *every* start should be timed."

2. *Unfeather it slowly*—"It's stated right in the flight manual that the PT6A-28 should be started with the prop controls forward. If that practice is followed, by the time oil pressure reaches the first and second stage reduction gears and the high-speed pinion gears, it'll be marginal because the first pressure goes to the prop to unfeather it. Start the gas generator first, establish oil pressure and oil temperature, *then* put the prop control forward. In Alaska, or anywhere it's minus seven degrees Centigrade or below, we tell operators to strap the prop down and not even permit it to turn. Light the engine, and after oil pressure and temperature are established, at idle, pull the strap off and allow the prop to turn. This will insure that gear-case parts receive proper lubrication."

(Note that this applies to the PT6 only; *don't* try it with a single-spool turboprop.)

"Conversely, when stopping a PT6, most pilots make two motions: they pull the prop into reverse and the fuel into cutoff. Again, this starves the gearbox bearings. This is the major PT6 reduction gearing failure problem. The *major.*"

3. *Don't decouple it*—"The second PT6 reduction box failure problem is decoupling the gearing. The manufacturers demonstrate to pilots that they

can come in high, pull the power off and dump the airplane 2500 or 3000 fpm for a landing. It's spectacular, but when you do that, you decouple the prop gearing. Instead of the engine driving the prop, the prop drives the engine.

"This causes the back side of the gear teeth to ride on one another, and at this point they've never met. They start shaving those square teeth off and all that metal circulates through the pinion bearings, and the pinion bearings start to fail. This is not something new. There was a minimum power requirement on old piston engines to avoid this decoupling affect, but no one ever talks about it in reference to modern engines. They should."

4. *Warm it up*—"I've seen operators repeatedly light an engine off, particularly on ground checks, and as soon as stabilized idle is achieved, throw the throttle to full takeoff power. That's the worst possible thing they can do. The engine has not expanded and contracted to the stabilized condition its heat-soaked parts require. That uneven heating is what causes turbine rub and other internal damage."

Beitscher recommends that the engines be allowed to run at or near idle for a couple of minutes before high power is applied. He cautions that even the power often used to blast off from a ramp is harmful. This, obviously, indicates that the fuel-efficient practice of starting one engine for taxi and the second one just before departure may not be economically efficient after all. It requires relatively higher power from the one engine to taxi while it is still warming up, and takeoff on another engine that is not yet heat stable.

"If you taxi out on one engine, then light the other on the blocks and take off immediately, the engine that was just started won't develop takeoff power. The power loss will be anywhere from 10 to 15 percent. When we calibrate an engine on a power run, we delay a minute and a half to three minutes so that it's heat stabilized before we take our measurements. If we didn't wait for thermal stabilization, our calibrations would be five to 10 percent in error."

5. *Coddle it*—"The guy who takes the engine up to power slowly will have the least problems."

Max is certain that the prevalent kick-the-tires-and-light-the-fires attitude is costing some operators unnecessary maintenance dollars. The reliability of turbine engines and the slow spool-up following a snap application of power has caused operators to become callous. The fact is, though, smooth throttle handling will pay off just as much today as it did back when we were all flying R-985s and 2800s.

6. *Fly it cool*—"The American jockey generally is known as a throttle-to-the-wall operator. When he buys a particular airplane, it is demonstrated to produce a certain performance, and he's going to achieve it whether it makes economic sense or not. If he'd just watch those temperatures a little

83

more than he does the performance numbers in the sales literature, he'd save many dollars.

"The recommended cruise ITT for the King Air A90 is 715 degrees. Pilots who hold ITT to 700 degrees find little change in block-to-block speed, but a big reduction in repair costs at each hot section inspection. There's a direct connection between the throttle of an engine and the engine's rate of deterioration."

In general, Beitscher recommends a two percent reduction in temperature limits, *provided* the engine gauges can be trusted. If they can't, temp limits should be reduced more like five percent (for reasons to be discussed). This reduction should be practiced at all stages of the flight in which safety is not compromised. On a hot day at gross that won't be possible. But on a cool day (which is half the time for most operators) when excess performance is available anyway, a two to five percent reduction in internal engine temp parameters will do amazing things for the maintenance budget. (It'll also produce quieter departures, we must add.)

7. *Cool it down*— "Whether you light off and immediately shove the power to take off (as discussed earlier) or pull up to the gate and snap the cock off for shutdown, the results are the same—dollars going out the window."

Not many pilots are aware of this. Long taxi at idle thrust leaves the engine full of heat that must be blown out at a slightly elevated rpm before shutdown. In addition, at idle rpm the oil scavenger pump on some engines is marginal.

"A JT-12, for example, idles at 44, 45 percent rpm. So you taxi in at Greater Pitt, and it's about five miles from the landing zone back to the terminal. If you pull the cock off when you get there, you're likely to see what appears to be a number-one bearing leak, simply because the engine has not been scavenged of oil properly. So before shutdown, cool the engines with a one-minute acceleration above idle. Pull the stopcocks off with a slow but steady motion, rather than snapping them off. This helps prevent sudden torque loads on engine mountings."

8. *Record its cycles*— "Turbine wheels are cycle-limited and so the operator should keep careful records on cycles. Why? There is no inspection procedure that allows us to look at the molecules of the metal and tell how much longer a wheel will operate safely. Therefore, the only protection the public has, the only protection the manufacturer has, the only protection the operator has is to count the number of times the wheel has been subjected to an excursion to power."

Max's point is that if the operator doesn't keep records, when the engine is torn down for overhaul, the overhauler has no choice except to base the number of cycles parts have been subjected to on total time. In the case of an operator who makes long trips, he'll replace the wheel before it's necessary because his cycles per hour will be lower than the average. In the case of the operator who makes many short trips, or a lot of touch-and-go landings, he'll end up with a wheel that has many more cycles than his records show. He thus runs the risk of a failure. Should that occur, the manufacturer, not knowing that the failed wheel had actually exceeded the current cycle limit, may be forced to set a new lower limit. Then *all* operators will suffer an unnecessary cost escalation.

9. *Customize it*— "Manufacturers produce engines *not* to fly; overhaul shops overhaul engines *not* to fly. That's a hell of a note, but it's true. Engines are produced to a manufacturer's test cell specification at sea level. If they make the listed performance, they're acceptable. But in the PT6, for example, we can take a PT6A-20 off the test cell at 1765 degrees Rankin and call it satisfactory. If we do, and mount it on the left side of an early King Air, where it has to drive a mechanical cabin supercharger, you can bet your boots it'll be temperature-limited before it reaches its rated power. On the right side, or on a Twin Otter, that same engine will not be temperature-limited, *but only up to about 10,000 feet.* Yet it's a satisfactory engine."

For competitive reasons, overhaulers have no choice but to turn out engines meeting that minimum spec. But Beitscher recommends that operators pay the extra cost (about $3,000 in the case of a PT6) for a customized overhaul. By going into the test cell and splitting the compressor case— once, twice, three times—the overhauler can produce an engine that will deliver its rated power at a much lower Rankin temperature. Airwork has customers who will accept no engine over 1730 degrees Rankin.

Operators who opt for the lower temp limit at rated power enjoy better performance, lower fuel burns and lower hot section costs. The reason is obvious. "An engine producing its rated power at a lower temperature is doing so at lower speed and lower fuel flow. Every mile it's flown, it's saving the operator dollars in fuel consumption and deterioration of hot section components."

Why don't all operators demand this economy? "They don't know. They accept what's available, then complain about it later. They should get acquainted with this service because the overhauler can deliver any customized engine the operator is willing to pay for—and it'll save him money downstream."

10. *Calibrate its instruments*— "A Sabreliner operator with only 200 hours on his airplane came to us for help. He had been experiencing high fuel consumption and short range. Investigations disclosed that the OAT gauge was inaccurate. Since EPR limits are set from the OAT curve, those engines had been operated at military power, and an expensive hot section resulted."

The lesson is clear: If your airplane is performing unnaturally well, don't accept it as pure good fortune. It may be lying gauges. "We consistently see engine instrument inaccuracies—and they're always on the *low* side. In most maintenance manuals the manufacturer recommends recalibration every 30 days. They know that's totally unrealistic. Realistically, operators should re-calibrate all the engine-parameter instruments at least once a year. They generally deteriorate, and in a year's time drift downward anywhere from five to 10 degrees. So, in fact, the pilot will pull five to 10 degrees more temperature than he is seeing on his instruments. That's another reason for *not* operating right at the temperature limits all the time."

11. *Corrosion-proof it*— "Of all the things I've said before, none is as important as *preventive* maintenance. Preventive maintenance is the avoidance of *catch-up* maintenance, and catch-up maintenance is very expensive. We get CJ610 or CF700 engines in here for overhaul and the compressor segments, which are slid into frames to make up the compressor assembly, can't be removed because they're corroded into place. In order to remove them we have to destroy them. That adds thousands to the cost of the overhaul, merely from neglecting to spray the inlet of the compressor once a week to lubricate the parts.

"One example of what fogging the inlets once a week with something like Rocket WD-40 can save occurred to a Midwest Lear operator several years ago. We convinced him to fog weekly (it only takes a couple of minutes), and at the 1800-hour TBO he went on to 2100. At 2100 hours he went on to 2400. He led the industry, and was instrumental in eventually raising the TBO to 3000 hours. At 2400 hours we tore his engines down and found them perfectly safe for continued operation to 3000 hours."

12. *Keep it clean*— "Operators don't assign nearly enough importance to the compressor wash. A turbine engine breathes a lot of air, and that air is filled with coal tars, salts and dirt of all kinds. It clings to the compressor sections and greatly affects the performance of the engine. We have yet to wash the compressor of a JT-12, on either a Sabreliner or a JetStar, and not also retrim the engine to produce the same thrust at lower rpm, lower fuel flow, lower TGT. Therefore, every mile that airplane is flown after the compressor wash, the cost is returned a thousandfold in dollar savings."

Why don't more operators take advantage of these savings?

"Operators look on preventive maintenance as an unnecessary evil. Airplanes are meant to fly. You put fuel and oil in them and hit the button and go. All the other things are just things you read about in magazines."

Turbine-Engine Igniters 11

by Richard N. Aarons

There's nothing that frustrates a pilot more than a balky onboard system over which he can exercise little or no control. Perhaps that's why most pilots cringe when ground school instructors start talking about the turbine ignition system. Why the hell spend time studying something you can't do anything about anyway?

A good question. But, as it turns out, there *are* several reasons a pilot should understand his ignition system. The biggest is money. We're sure, at one time or another, your maintenance chief has grumbled about the high cost of igniters—the spark-plug-like devices in the combustor cans of turbine engines.

Installed and operated properly, most igniters will last for several hundred hours of engine time. However, pilot abuse or careless installation can reduce igniter life to where they must be replaced at every 50-hour inspection.

To understand what happens to igniters in service, let's look first at the turbine ignition system as a whole.

Basically the turbine-engine ignition system is the match that lights the fire. Remember the old kitchen gas stoves that had to be lighted manually? First you'd turn on the gas. Then you'd place a match near the burner, and if you were lucky, the burner would light without taking your eyebrows with it. Once lighted, the gas/air mixture usually continued to burn until the gas supply was shut off.

One of the problems with the old gas stove was that the flame could be blown out by a stiff breeze coming through the kitchen window. If nobody was around when this happened, at best, the porridge was ruined; at worst, the house blew up. To correct this situation, the pilot light was invented. As you know, the pilot light is a constant source of ignition for the stove burners; should a burner blow out, it is reignited immediately.

The turbine-engine ignition system is similar in function to the gas-stove pilot light. Like the pilot light, the turbine-ignition system lights the fire initially and then stands by to relight it if it's blown out.

Lighting the turbine-engine fire is usually a one-shot deal. Once combustion begins in the cans, it is self-sustaining unless something happens to stop the fuel supply or upset the air flow.

Most manufacturers of turbine aircraft call for the ignition system to be activated for takeoff and climb and during flight through extremely turbulent air. At these times, the ignition system is providing the same safety function that the gas-stove pilot light serves—if something blows out the fire, the ignition system provides an immediate relight.

Usually the flight crew controls the operation of the ignition system, but in some installations its operation is both manual and automatic. In one turboprop installation, for example, the ignition system can be armed to come on line whenever engine torque drops below a preset value. In several pure-jet installations, the ignition systems are programmed to go to work whenever extremely high angles of attack are encountered. (High angles of attack can induce compressor stalls, which, in turn, can cause flameouts. In this case the ignition system relights the fire as soon as proper airflow is reestablished in the burner cans.)

From a design standpoint, igniters are similar to piston-engine spark plugs in that they have electrodes between which an arc is induced by high voltage. The main difference is that the turbine-igniter spark has to be hotter than the piston-engine spark because the turbine igniter is faced with a much wider range of ambients in which it must function.

Figure 1 shows two types of turbine-igniter cross-sections. However, the type in your engine is really of academic interest only because they are selected by the engine manufacturer and certificated with the engine. Unlike piston-engine spark plugs, you cannot tinker with igniter reach or gap in hopes of getting better performance.

Inducing a spark between the igniter's electrodes is the job of the ignition exciter—a capacitance or inductance circuit that generates spikes of very high voltage. Figure 2 is a simplified schematic of a typical capacitance ignition system. The circuitry enclosed in the dashed box is the exciter portion of the system.

To give you an idea of how a typical exciter functions, we'll describe what happens in this system. Remember that there are several different exciter boxes used on business aviation turbine aircraft, and yours may work differently.

Each engine has a minimum of two independent ignition systems. Battery power is routed through the ignition switching circuits to the exciter boxes. As you can see in the schematic, each exciter box contains a noise filter, a DC motor that drives two cam wheels, an autotransformer, a rectifier and a storage capacitor.

The noise filter is similar to that in an automotive ignition system; it keeps ignition noise out of the radios.

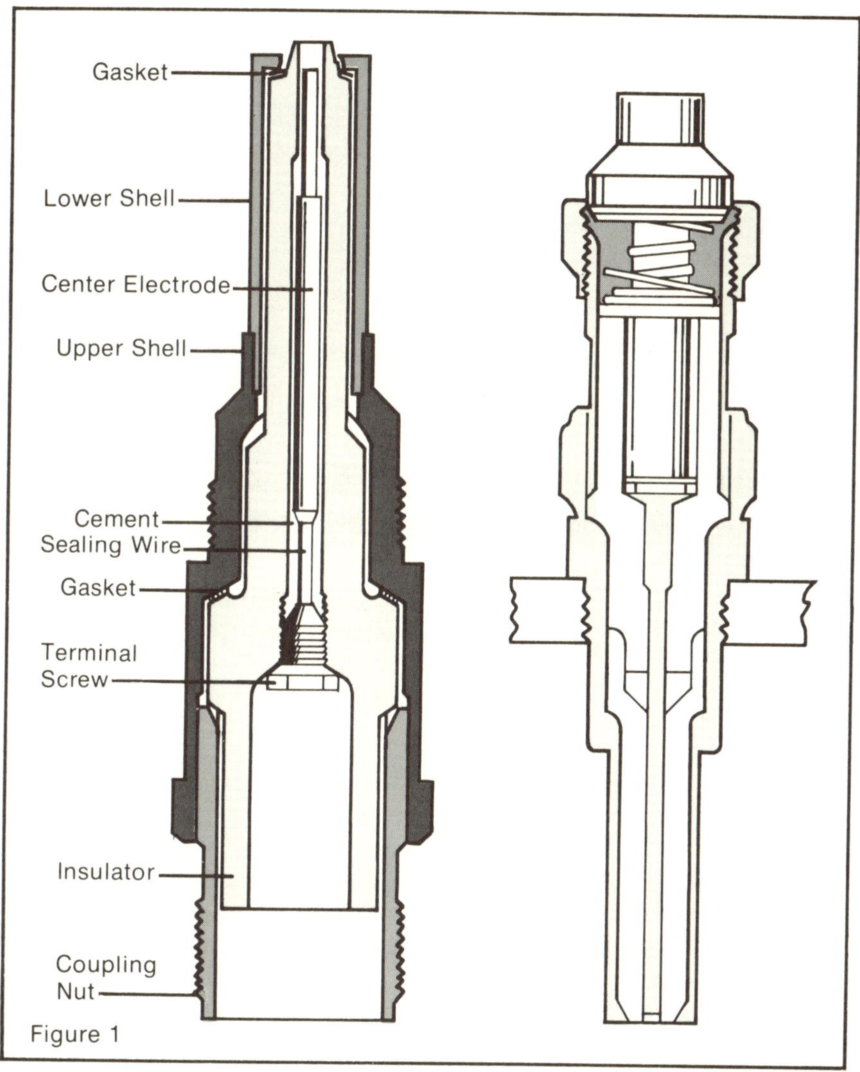

Two common igniter configurations are shown here—an annular-gap igniter plug (left) and a constrained-gap igniter plug. The hot end of the annular-gap-plug is at the top. It's sometimes called a long-reach plug because it extends into the combustion-chamber liner. The constrained-gap plug does not project into the combustion-chamber liner; however, its spark arcs away from the gap into the chamber.

Once past the filter, battery current follows two paths—one to the DC motor and the other to the breaker points, which are operated by one of the two DC-motor cams. As the breaker opens and closes, low-voltage battery

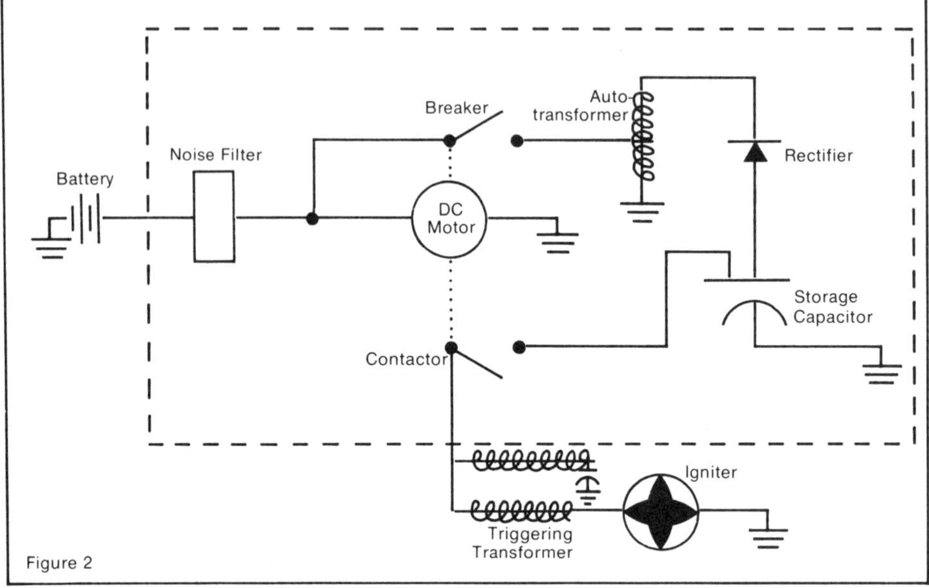

This is a simplified schematic of a capacitance-type exciter unit—the circuit that provides high-voltage electrical energy to create an arc between igniter electrodes.

current starts and stops in the primary of the autotransformer, inducing a high-voltage current in the secondary of the autotransformer.

These pulses from the secondary charge the storage capacitor through the rectifier, which assures that current flow to the capacitor is a one-way affair. The storage-capacitor output is connected to the igniter electrode through the contractor and a triggering transformer.

In operation, the capacitor is discharged into the primary of the triggering transformer each time the contractor closes. The contractor is opened and closed by a single-lobe cam driven by the DC motor.

The current pulses in the primary of the triggering transformer induce a high voltage in the secondary and across the electrodes of the igniter, thus producing a spark. Spark rate is a function of DC-motor speed, which, in turn, is a function of applied DC voltage. The breaker points and contractor are in synchronization; usually an igniter will spark eight to 10 times a second.

The function of the triggering transformer is to create the highest possible spark of the shortest possible duration. This type of high-energy spark literally vaporizes globules of fuel for even ignition.

Some newer engines have solid-state exciter boxes. The theory of their operation is similar to the electro-mechanical device described above, the only difference being that breaker and contractor switching is electrical rather than mechanical.

The voltages created in the exciter box and at the igniter electrodes are extremely high—at or above 20,000 volts. So any maintenance conducted on or near ignition system components should be accomplished with care.

To this point, we've been talking about "true" igniters—the type that produce a high-energy spark between electrodes. Most of the Pratt & Whitney PT6A-series turboprop engines have glow plugs instead of igniters. The business end of a glow-plug looks exactly like the business end of an automobile cigar lighter, and it works in roughly the same manner. When the ignition system is activated, current flows through the resistance coils of the glow plug, causing them to glow with a yellow heat. (Glow-plug temperature has to be about 1650 degrees Centigrade to assure ignition.)

Ignition system designers assert that use—and use alone—causes eventual igniter failure. This assumes that the igniter is installed properly and that the flame pattern in the burner can is correct. Therefore, the only thing the flight crew can do to increase igniter life is to keep ignition cycles and duty time to a minimum.

Obviously, the ignition system must be on for start, and, if required by the flight manual, for takeoff and climb. So, to preserve igniters, see that the ignition switch is the *last* checklist item accomplished at the start of the takeoff roll and the *first* checklist item accomplished after the aircraft is established in the climb.

The use of the ignition system to guard against flameouts in certain operational situations is certainly necessary; however, remember that continuous operation of the igniters subjects them to severe electrical stress and accelerated erosion.

In most turbine aircraft, annunciator panel lights illuminate whenever the ignition system is operating. The sole purpose of these lights is to save you money, so heed their warning.

Most King Airs have an automatic system that can be armed to activate the ignition whenever torque falls below a preset value. This system is armed by the flight crew during takeoff and in certain weather conditions. The system is a good idea. However, if the flight crew forgets to disarm the system before letdown, the ignition will come online when power is reduced for descent and the glow plugs will be subjected to unnecessary wear. A service boss we talked to recently said, "You'd be surprised how many King Air pilots forget this fact and leave the ignition system armed all the time, despite the blinking annunciator lights. Then they're surprised when they only get 50 hours out of the plugs."

The way to prevent this type of costly mistake is to understand thoroughly the ignition system on your engines. Even though pilots are rarely involved in ignition system maintenance, flight crews should be aware of some ignition system maintenance factors.

Make sure the service people working on your ignition system have the appropriate manuals and service material in hand before attempting to replace or service it. Practically speaking, there is no standardization of igniters among gas-turbine engines. Igniters are designed for a particular burner can configuration; therefore, the igniters in one type engine are rarely suitable for use in another.

Not only are designs different, but servicing techniques vary. Champion Spark Plug Company, maker of igniters for most general aviation turbine engines, uses this example in its service manual: "To illustrate a servicing difference, it is functionally desirable to clean the firing end on some igniters; on other types, cleaning the firing end will make the igniter completely unusable. Carbon deposits, which cause piston spark plugs to misfire, actually improve the firing capability of certain turbine igniter types. Consequently servicing *must* be tailored to meet the igniter configuration."

Flight crews can check the functioning of their igniters relatively easily. A properly functioning igniter emits a sharp, snapping noise when firing. The higher the energy of the ignition system, the louder the spark noise. To make this check, stand to one side of the tailpipe while an assistant in the cockpit turns the ignition switch on. Listen to this sound right after the ignition has been overhauled and you'll have a basis for comparison later. Any sound other than a steady snapping noise from each igniter is cause for concern.

Most flight manuals list limitations for ignition system duty cycles. One manufacturer, for example, limits ignition system duty time to two minutes on; two minutes off; two minutes on; 24 minutes off. These limits have nothing to do with the igniters, but rather they protect the exciter box from overheating. Be sure to observe these limits carefully.

A piston-engine spark plug tells the mechanic much about engine health. Unfortunately, turbine igniters tell little of their own history, let alone provide insight into the engine's health. However, there is one thing to watch. If the igniters are literally burning up over very short periods of time, the flame-propagation pattern in the burner cans may have been disturbed. In this case, hot spots may develop in the cans and these hot spots can actually torch the igniters into useless globs.

One final thought on igniters. As we mentioned earlier, there is no standardization in the turbine-engine industry on igniter specifications. That, in a nutshell, is why they cost so much. It would be great if engine people in the Society of Automotive Engineers were to get together and pick a half-dozen different igniters and stick with them. According to the major igniter manufacturers, that move is the only thing that could reduce igniter bills significantly.

Electronic Fuel Controls 12

by Richard N. Aarons

Turbojet fuel controls, as any harried mechanic will tell you, are the most infuriatingly complex devices hung on airplanes. On business jets they generally take up little more space than a shoe box, but that shoe box is stuffed with precision servo and metering systems, speed governors, feedback and followup devices, pilot and sleeve valves, three-dimensional cams and enough curled pipe to make a bowl of spaghetti appear ordered by comparison.

If you've been flying pistons and have yet to tangle with these hydromechanical monsters, a bit of background will help you appreciate the magnificent simplicity of the new electronic fuel controls.

You already know the basics of turbojet operation, that is, a big pipe takes air in the front, mixes it with fuel in the middle and ignites that mixture in the end. The burning fuel-air mixture expands rapidly and rushes out the back of the engine causing a pressure differential (and thus thrust) between the back and front.

The major components of a turbojet engine are (from front to back) (1) a compressor driven by the turbine wheel which gathers ambient air and compresses it to increase both its heat and pressure; (2) a combustion chamber in which the compressed air is mixed with fuel and ignited; (3) a turbine wheel which is driven by the rapidly expanding burning gases rushing from the combustion chamber, and (4) a jet nozzle which forms the escaping gases into an efficient shape.

The operation of a turbojet engine is continuous rather than broken up into discrete cycles as is the case with piston engines. Therefore, the compressor is always compressing; the fuel-air mixture in the combustor cans is always combusting, and the expanding superheated fuel-air mixture leaving the combustion chamber is always giving up power to the turbine, which in turn keeps the compressor compressing. It's a bootstrap operation.

Basically, thrust developed by a turbojet engine depends on the mass of air (and fuel) moved through the engine. And to get a greater mass moving through the engine you must spin the compressor faster, which means you must deliver more power to the turbines by putting more fuel in the combustors. But a sudden increase in fuel flow to the combustion chambers could lead to a too-rich mixture, which in turn could lead to excessive turbine temperatures, compressor stall or flameout. (Or perhaps all three.) In that the whole sequence of events is bootstrapping, too much fuel (or fuel injudiciously added) could cause surging.

Simply stated, then, it's the job of the fuel control unit to watch all the possible variables within and without the engine and to act as a go-between for the pilot and the engine. When the pilot moves the throttle of a piston engine, he is actually moving a plate in the carburetor throat that controls the amount of air entering the engine. Then the carburetor adds the appropriate amount of fuel to the air and the mixture is delivered to the cylinders for ignition. In a turbojet engine, the picture is different. When the pilot moves the thrust lever he is actually telling the fuel control what amount of thrust (as a function of maximum rated power) he wants. Then the fuel control takes over and accelerates or decelerates the engine to the level signaled by the pilot. At the same time, the fuel control monitors ambients and adjusts fuel flow to keep the present thrust level relatively constant despite changes of altitude. Also, the fuel control is always watching engine performance versus engine limits and will, when necessary, reduce fuel flow to avoid critical temperatures, pressures and speeds.

Summing up the what-does-it-do of the fuel control, it performs these major functions:

• At all times—It protects the engine from critical temperatures, pressures and speeds.

• During steady-state operations—It maintains approximate thrust levels in the face of changing ambients.

• During acceleration and deceleration—It controls the mixture in the combustion chamber to prevent extremes.

Hydromechanical fuel controls are, indeed, ingenious. They are computers that use the flow of fuel and the movement of rods and cams and wheels to calculate ratios and proportions and work out the dynamics of turbojet fuel flow on a real-time basis. Typically, the inputs to a fuel control are (1) thrust level position, (2) compressor inlet temperature or pressure or both, (3) combustion chamber pressure, (4) turbine temperature and (5) compressor speed. This raw data is processed into functions in the fuel flow equation. For example, with known compressor inlet temperature and pressure, the hydromechanical fuel control computer can calculate inlet air density, which is a factor in determining the mass of airflow into the engine. Combustion chamber pressure and compressor speed are processed in a similar manner to determine whether the engine is approaching compressor stall.

94

ELECTRONIC FUEL CONTROLS

Hydromechanical fuel controls do their job well, but there are certain problems intrinsic to the hydromechanical approach. As said before, they are vastly complex and thus require careful maintenance and adjustment. A particle of grit can bollix up the entire mechanism. And, of course, they are heavy.

As a rule of thumb, engine management cockpit workload decreases as the fuel control becomes more complex. But, as the fuel control becomes more complex, that is, as more inputs are added, its probability of failure increases.

The engine really doesn't care how the fuel management calculations are done. They can be accomplished by the familiar hydromechanical fuel control computers or by relatively dumb electronic computers. From a purely theoretical standpoint, electronic fuel controls make a lot more sense than their hydromechanical counterparts. A couple of postage stamp-size chips can do the work of 40 pounds of cams, servos, pilot valves and plumbing. The chips don't wear, nor do they get flat spots, nor will they freeze up. Electronic fuel controls just sit there and work out engine control problems so long as they've got electrical power and good inputs.

Electronic fuel controls are really not all that new to the aviation industry. They've been used for quite a while on APUs and on big military and air carrier turbine engines. But it wasn't until the introduction of Garrett's TFE 731-series engines that they filtered down into business aviation. (The TFE 731s are on the Falcon 10, Lear 35/36, TFE JetStar and JetStar II, and have been selected for the Westwind 1124 and the Falcon 50.)

Perhaps the biggest advantage of electronic fuel control (to the engine designer, at least) is its precision. Turbine engines, even the smallest designs, are becoming increasingly complex and are required to work close to their maximum limits. The precision of the electronic control is needed to enable the engine to operate safely near these limits with attendant lower margins for error.

Engineers talk of two types of electronic fuel controls—*supervisory* and *full authority.* In a *supervisory* system the pilot remains coupled to a basic hydromechanical fuel control via the thrust levers and associated linkages. The electronic element in the *supervisory* system acts in parallel to the pilot's inputs to improve system accuracy and smooth out the operation of the basic hydromechanical control. A *full authority* system is hooked up in series with the hydromechanical system and has full responsibilities for many of the basic fuel control operations.

The system used on Garrett's TFE 731 is of the full-authority variety. The computer is essentially analog and uses solid-state, monolithic, integrated circuits.

Basically there are three separate systems involved in fuel control for the TFE 731. They are (1) a hydromechanical metering section, (2) a pneumati-

95

cally operated surge bleed system and (3) the full-authority, solid-state electronic fuel control. The hydromechanical metering section and surge bleed section can control the engine by themselves to *satisfactory* performance levels. But addition of the electronic fuel control to the system brings engine performance to *optimum* levels. This distinction between *satisfactory* and *optimum* levels of performance is an important one. If the aircraft loses electrical power or the computer goes off line for some reason, the engine will still function, but at a reduced performance level with an increase in cockpit workload.

(When flying the Falcon 10 for our initial report on this aircraft, B/CA pilots failed the electronic element at cruise to test its effect on engine performance. The engine spooled down a bit and the thrust lever became very sensitive and nonlinear. Garrett engineers tell us the engine will spool up under some ambient conditions and the pilot will have to back it down immediately to avoid exceeding placarded limits.)

TFE 731 fuel control designers had four basic requirements for the system when they put it together: (1) Simple starting procedures, without the need for simultaneous actuation of switches; (2) Capability of unrestricted power lever movements; (3) Rapid thrust transient capability free

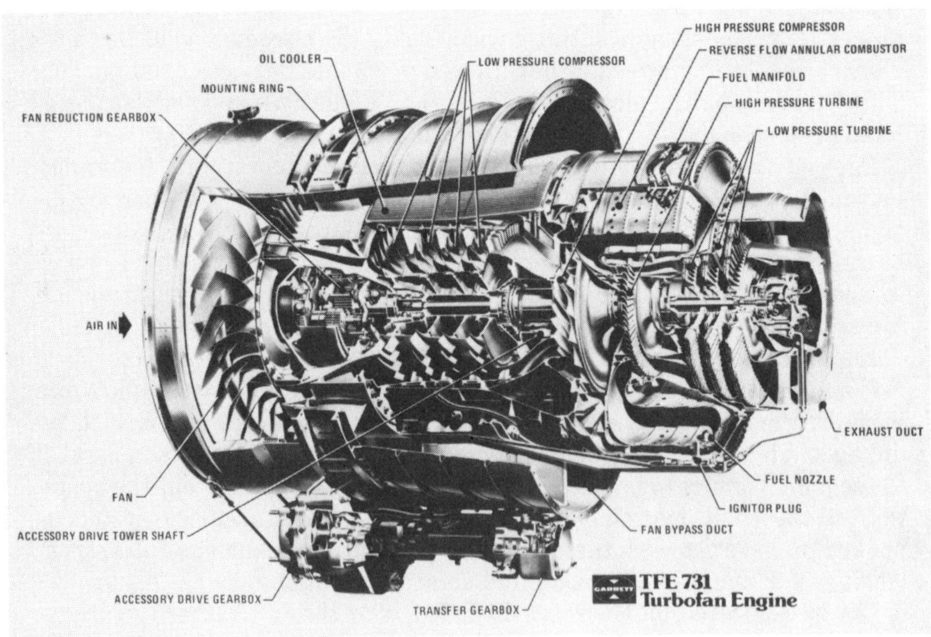

Garrett's electronic fuel control on the TFE 731 series engines takes inputs of engine parameters and power lever commands and computes proper fuel flow. The electronic fuel flow computer is housed in an avionics-type black box and mounted remote from the engine. The hydromechanical fuel controller, which serves primarily as a backup to the electronic unit, is mounted on the engine.

96

of engine surge or lean burner blowout, and (4) Engine protection functions during start and warmup.

The second item (unrestricted power lever movements) is the chief advantage of electronic fuel control from the pilot's viewpoint. The power lever moves through a 20-degree arc. At maximum condition the engine produces maximum available thrust, limited by turbine temperature or flat-rating power, whichever is most restrictive under existing ambients. The pilot merely pushes the power lever to the firewall and he's got all the thrust that the engine can give under the circumstances and he gets that power without need to compute limits or to watch the gauges for those limits. Computing those limits against real-time ambients and monitoring the engine's performance against those limits is one job of the electronic fuel control.

When the power lever is in the idle position, the engine operates at a preset minimum thrust level despite ambients. This too is a function of the electronic element.

The engine's response to power lever positions between maximum and idle is linear. The electronic element does the compensation necessary to produce this linearity. And, like other fuel controls, the electronic system maintains a power lever-commanded thrust at a constant value as ambients change. But it does so, according to its designers, much more precisely than do straight hydromechanical fuel controls.

The other functions of the electronic fuel control are primarily involved with monitoring engine performance versus engine limits. The start schedule, for example, is computed to optimize starting time and minimize turbine inlet temperature. To do this, the computer controls fuel flow as a function of high-pressure-compressor discharge pressure, corrected by engine inlet total temperature. (Starting the TFE 731 is a pretty simple affair. The pilot activates a single switch which turns on the starter and ignition. The power lever is moved to idle position to open the fuel valve. When the engine hits 50 percent high-pressure spool speed, the starter and ignition are automatically deactivated. Although the starting process is fully automatic and the electronic fuel control keeps an eye on limiting temperatures, flight manuals on aircraft equipped with TFE 731s warn that a start within temperature limits may not be possible with a deteriorated starter or battery system, so the pilot should still monitor the procedure.)

The metering section, mentioned earlier, is actually a rather crude hydromechanical fuel control. In normal operation, it handles fuel shutoff and fuel pumping requirements and provides an electromechanical interface for the entire fuel control system. If the electronic system drops off line for any reason, the metering section provides surge and blowout protection by monitoring fuel flow as a function of compressor discharge pressure. Its functioning in this respect is a bit on the crude side, but then it was designed to be an emergency backup which allows *acceptable* pilot control of thrust in the event of a computer failure.

The bleed valve system, also mentioned earlier, is normally controlled by the computer to prevent low-pressure compressor surge. During backup operation, the valve remains one-third open to prevent surge, but this constant open position reduces maximum available thrust by about five percent.

We've described what the electronic fuel control system does to directly affect cockpit workload. For the mechanics, engineers and turbine engine buffs among B/CA's readers, here's a complete list of its functions:

• Computes maximum high-pressure spool speed to provide available engine power limited by either turbine temperature, high-pressure spool speed or flat-rated power limit. This setting is a function of inlet temperature and pressure.

• Maintains high-pressure-spool speed without droop.

• Provides a deceleration schedule that avoids blowouts and a gross mismatch of the two spools.

• Provides a signal to schedule the bleed valve opening to avoid surge during acceleration or deceleration.

• Provides an idle speed schedule as a function of inlet pressure and temperature.

• Provides a topping governor for the low-pressure spool speed.

• Provides an overspeed switching action for both high- and low-pressure-spool speeds.

• Provides a 50 percent corrected speed switch to turn off the starter and ignition.

• Provides for fuel enrichment for lightoff.

• Provides a starting fuel schedule to idle.

• Provides for internal monitoring of computation and automatically switches to manual mode if the computed voltages go out of normal range.

• Provides for monitoring of all inputs and outputs.

Obviously it takes an electronic computer to provide monitoring and control to this extent and it is only the development of monolithic integrated circuitry and large-scale integration that makes it possible. The fuel control computer, housed in a black box 3.5 inches wide, 7.6 inches high and 12.5 inches deep, is remotely mounted to provide its elements protection from the heat in the nacelles. It weighs about 8.5 pounds. On the inside it looks like any other black box on the aircraft; that is, a collection of printed circuit boards stacked in neat rows.

Like any new airborne device, electronic fuel controls are suspect in some quarters, and their introduction has not been without problems. Recently a mandatory service bulletin appeared on the TFE 731 controller requiring replacement of a transistor. It seems that failure of this transistor under some circumstances could cause engine shutdown.

This bulletin didn't help solve the credibility problem. Some pilots simply don't trust any black box. They feel you can get along with a busted nav or com (and bust they will, eventually), but risking a malfunctioning fuel control is an unhappier prospect. The hydromechanical backup, of course, goes a long way to calm these worries. Will the day ever come when electrical fuel control systems are handling the entire fuel control problem without hydromechanical backups? It's possible, say the engine designers, when we develop enough confidence in aircraft electrical systems and the electronic fuel controls.

Manufacturers of piston engines have been experimenting with electronic fuel controls for years, but price and complexity still seem to be problems and manufacturers are reluctant to talk about their efforts or predict the ultimate outcome of their work. Two years ago, Jack Shaffer (FAA Administrator at that time) told a group of light aircraft manufacturers that simplifying the pilot task should be the priority goal of aircraft and powerplant engineers. Why should the light-aircraft pilot have to worry about mixture and propeller controls and rpm and manifold pressure limits? Why should he have to adjust power settings according to complex graphs and charts? Why not give him a thrust lever similar to that in turbojet cockpits? Why not indeed? The obvious answer is an electronic fuel controller that would provide a fixed thrust (percent power) in the face of changing ambients and would monitor pressure and temperature and rpm limits while providing linear response to power lever movement. The technology is unquestionably available. But the economics do not seem to be. The replacement cost of the TFE 731 fuel control computer is about half the replacement costs of some reciprocating engines. Keep an eye on electronic fuel controls for both turbine and recip engines. If the experts are right, we'll be seeing a lot more of them in the future and chances are that you'll be pushing the power lever attached to one someday.

ATM: A Technique for Extending Turbine-Engine Life

13

by Dan Manningham

There is an old chestnut about the captain who calls for takeoff power during some critical inflight emergency and his addlebrained copilot sure enough obliges by taking off all the power. Takeoff thrust—full, throttles-to-the-stops takeoff power—has historically been an inviolate institution, as sacred as reserve fuel or balanced field length. That attitude, which largely grew out of aviation's experience with reciprocating engines, is rapidly changing as engineers and operators take a more critical look at the realities of turbojet and turbofan engine management.

Maximum turbine engine power ratings are established with close regard to the metallurgical limitations of the hot section. At takeoff power, burner cans and turbine blades are operating very near their thermal limits. Since deterioration of these parts is directly related to the time/temperature exposure to those upper limits, any reduction from maximum Turbine Inlet Temperature (TIT) is desirable. In other words, when you reduce exposure to the limiting TITs associated with takeoff thrust a little bit, you increase hot section longevity a whole (Figure 1) lot. At the below maximum continuous power, TIT reductions offer less dramatic benefits because significant thermal fatigue does not occur at those reduced power settings.

Considering that even small reductions in maximum temperatures will yield a significant return in reduced engine wear, there is ample incentive to consider some program of reducing takeoff power when possible. Basically there are three methods available to derate takeoff thrust.

(1) Operate the engine at some already established lower thrust setting, such as limiting the TFE 731-3 engine to TFE 731-2 power ratings. This approach is easily applicable to older equipment that has subsequently been fitted with uprated versions of the same engine, because the performance figures are already available.

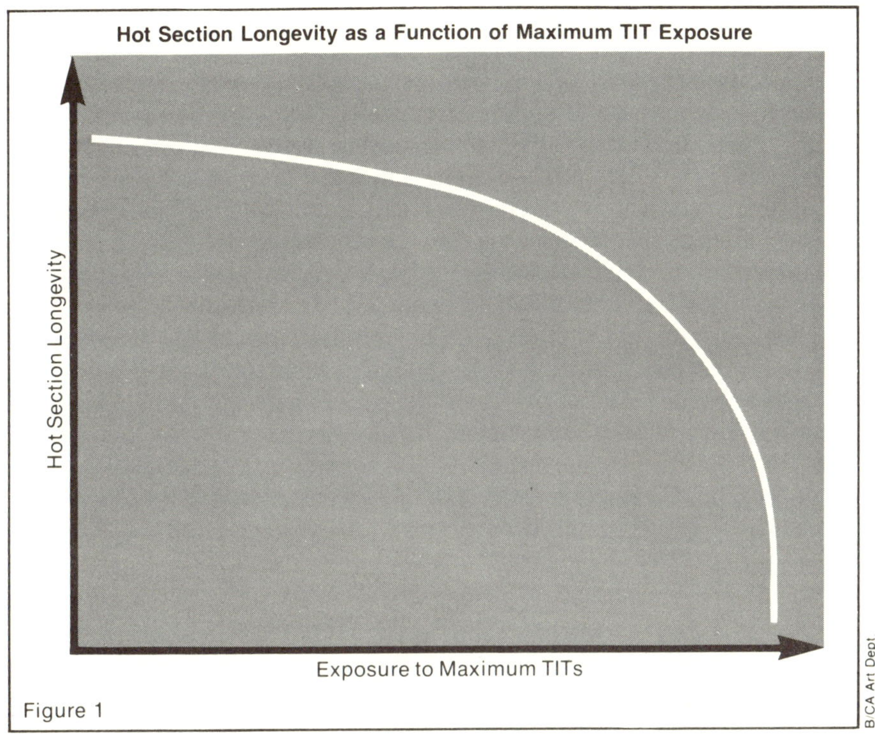

Figure 1

(2) Operate the engine at some arbitrary reduction from rated power, a procedure which, although technically very simple, requires an entire new set of takeoff certification performance tables. In addition, this choice and the one above do not allow complete flexibility through a range of power options to conform to operating conditions.

(3) Reduce engine power in proportion to actual operating circumstances using the assumed temperature method (ATM). This procedure takes into account the actual runway length and ambient temperature for that takeoff, allowing a thrust reduction appropriate to existing conditions. Of all the available options, only the assumed temperature method allows a simple and tractable approach to derating, which capitalizes on existing flight manual performance plots.

The assumed temperature method makes one logical assumption: if the flight manual charts allow this same takeoff at some higher ambient temperature, then it should be conservative to use the reduced thrust associated with that higher temperature at the actual lower ambient temperature. All calculations can be performed using the existing flight manual charts, with minor paperwork changes. For a given takeoff, the manual is consulted to establish the highest allowable ambient temperature for that particular combination of runway length and gross weight. This maximum OAT, which is the *assumed* temperature, is then used in place of *actual* OAT for thrust, speed and performance calculations. ATM thrust reductions are available anytime airplane operating weights and ambient temperatures are below certification limits for a given airport. They are also in proportion to the differential between actual and assumed conditions. In day-to-day operation it works like this.

A Learjet 35/36 (this is for example only; ATM takeoffs must be approved by application to the FAA) is scheduled from a sea-level airport with 6000 feet of runway on a four degree Centigrade day at 14,000 pounds. The pilot checks the takeoff distance (Figure 2) and finds that he will need only 3850 feet of that runway in this no wind, no gradient situation. Checking one step further, he finds that the hottest day for a legal takeoff at 14,000 pounds would be 43 degrees Centigrade. Knowing that the takeoff is legal at 43 degrees and that performance is better when *assuming* the higher temperature than when the temperature is *actually* at 43 degrees, he

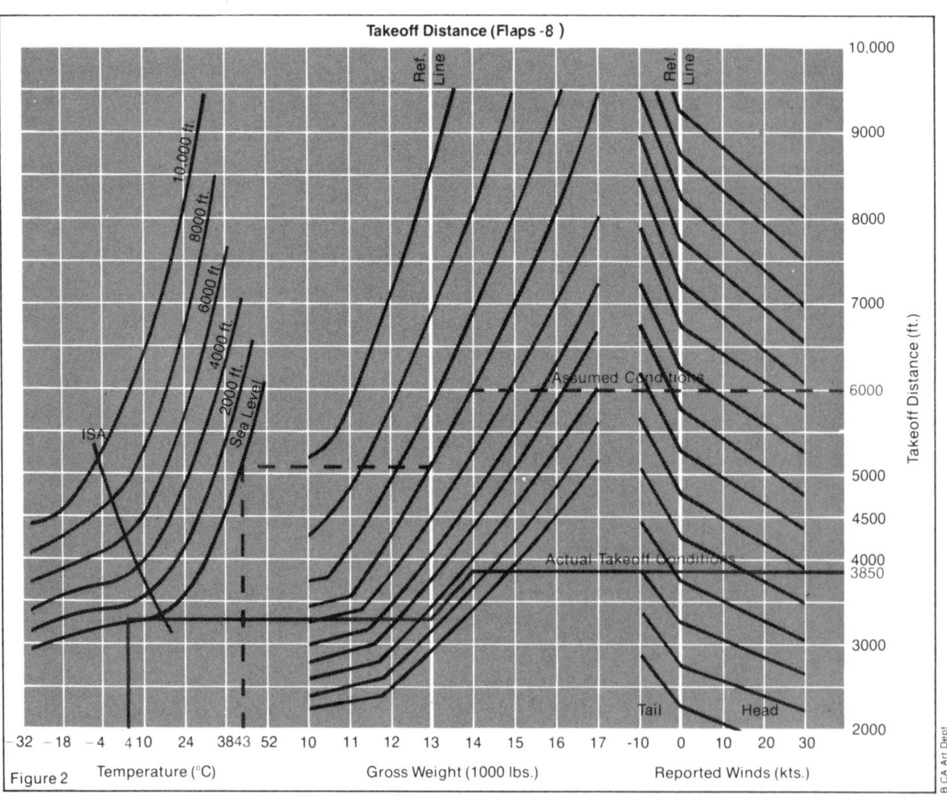

Figure 2

proceeds to compute power settings and V speeds using that higher *assumed* temperature.

The takeoff power N_1 speed is computed using that 43 degrees assumed temperature (Figure 3) found to be 92.1 N_1, a significant reduction from the 94.2 N_1 allowable at four degrees Centigrade. Likewise, the pilot calculates V_1 speed using the same 43 degrees assumed temperature and finds it to be 132 knots, about four knots faster than V_1 for four degrees. Using these numbers, he knows that takeoff performance is well within all certification standards and that he has reduced TIT and consequent engine deterioration by some undefined but significant amount. He has traded excess runway for reduced TIT.

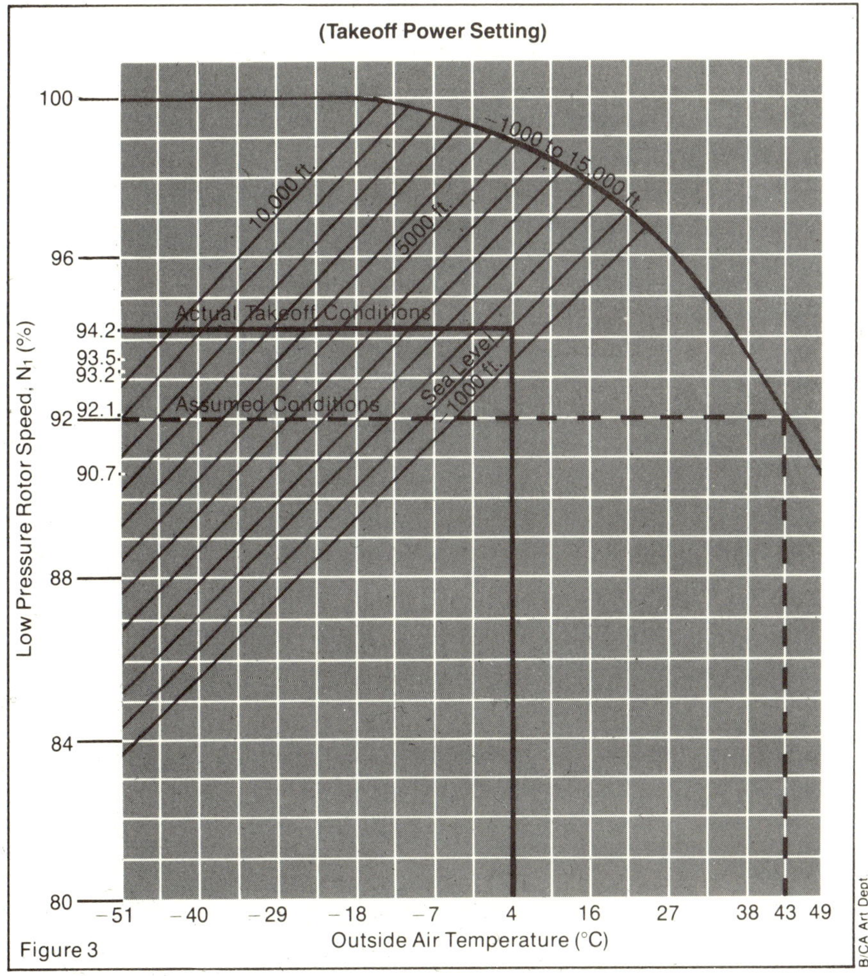

Figure 3

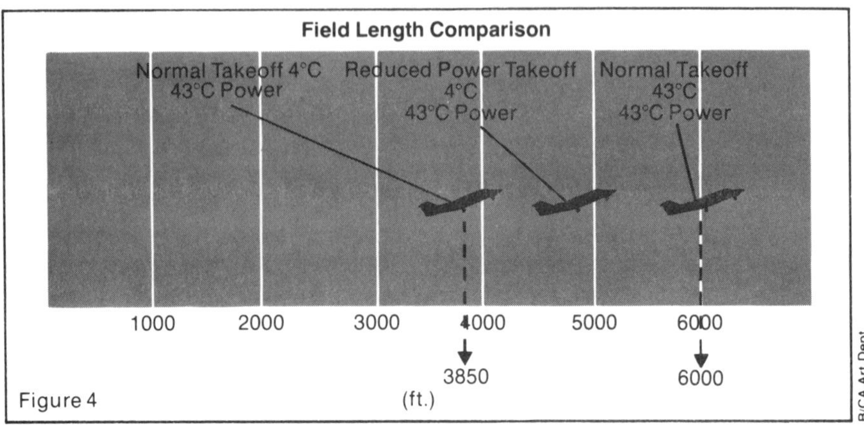

Notice in Figure 4 that even with reduced power the airplane will use less than the allowable 6000 feet of runway. If the temperature were really at 43 degrees Centigrade, all 6000 feet would be required. In this case, with the temp at four degrees Centigrade, but using a takeoff power equivalent to a 43-degree Centigrade day, field length required will be somewhat less than 6000 feet for a simple but subtle reason: True airspeed increases with temperature, in this case about nine knots. At 43 degrees Centigrade, our Lear 35/36 would have an actual speed almost nine knots faster at these critical takeoff speeds just due to that TAS increase. With the actual temperature at only four degrees Centigrade, acceleration distance is measurably shorter since TAS values are lower.

For this very reason, ATM takeoffs are always conservative. The procedure is in nearly universal use by airlines, foreign and domestic, and the FAA has finally approved guidelines for this method of thrust reduction:

• Total thrust reduction may never exceed 10 percent below the maximum takeoff thrust approved for the existing ambient conditions for that aircraft. The FAA has based this conservative limitation on a study by two major airlines. Other regulatory agencies have accepted more generous reductions. New Zealand operators are reducing takeoff thrust by the ATM method as much as 22 percent.

• V_1, V_R, V_2 may not be less than those that will comply with the required controllability margins with the maximum thrust available for the actual ambient conditions.

• Reduced thrust settings must not compromise configuration warning systems. Some combinations of temperature and field elevation could produce such minimal throttle settings, even within the 10 percent limitation, that takeoff warning horns for trim, flap selection and so on would never

104

be actuated. In those instances, power reduction would have to be limited to allow for normal configuration warnings.

• The flight manual should state that the use of reduced thrust procedures is not recommended when the runway is contaminated by water, slush, ice or snow.

• The operator must establish some means to periodically check the availability of full-rated thrust. The intent here seems to be to make certain a deteriorated engine doesn't compound a bad situation. One means the FAA considers acceptable in meeting this requirement is for the operator to require the use of full thrust at least once during each 100 hours or 100 takeoffs, whichever occurs first.

Some airlines have imposed additional restrictions to accommodate their own equipment and operating conditions. These restrictions generally preclude the use of ATM in specific circumstances such as tailwinds, barometer below 29.70, icing conditions and inoperative anti-skid.

One of the nice things about ATM is the ease with which it can be modified to accept a more conservative bias by the pilot or operator who does not wish to derate his takeoff power to the maximum allowable. There is a very simple way to buffer the derating. Some operators add an arbitrary weight increment to actual weights so that all ATM numbers are calculated for a somewhat heavier airplane than actual. In our Learjet example, 1000 pounds (or any other amount) could be added to actual takeoff weights for the ATM calculations. In that case, the charts would be entered using 15,000 pounds, and the maximum assumed temperature at which the 15,000-pound airplane could depart a 6000-foot runway would drop to 38 degrees Centigrade. Using that assumed temperature, N_1 is 93.5 percent for a total thrust reduction of less than one percent N_1. Also, remember that in the event of any kind of emergency the pilot can always go to full rated power on the engines—or remaining engine—and realize an additional performance margin.

ATM thrust reductions have been widely used by the airline industry for six years. The benefits are so well established and documented that air carriers now consider ATM to be an essential operating procedure. The JT3D-3 fan engine in wide airline service enjoys a 54-to-66 degree Centigrade TIT reduction when using 43 degrees Centigrade takeoff thrust on an ISA day. That TIT reduction is enough to provide a 50 percent increase in hot-section service life with only 50 percent implementation of the ATM procedure. Since the hot section is really the consumable portion of a jet engine, any increase in its life will yield significant savings in maintenance costs.

Aside from simple engine longevity and reduced maintenance costs, there is the even nicer prospect of improved reliability. The increased thermal fatigue resistance associated with those lower turbine inlet tempera-

105

tures provides substantial improvements in engine reliability and indications are safety is not the least compromised. In fact it may be improved. Since the introduction of ATM thrust reductions in Air Canada's fleet, there have not been any accidents during takeoff. Incidents have decreased steadily as have the numbers of inflight shutdowns and premature engine removals. In fact, reliability has been so enhanced by the airline industry's use of ATM thrust reductions, that even the most skeptical pilots must now consider the very real tradeoffs between full power and engine reliability.

Fuel conservation is another decided benefit of takeoff thrust reduction. Delta Airlines carefully documented a two percent improvement in fuel mileage on its Convair 880 fleet after 16 months of takeoff power reductions. That fuel savings probably comes for two separate reasons: During the takeoff maneuver itself, there is some immediate saving of fuel because the engine is operated closer to its design point for fuel economy. Then, in addition, there is a measurable saving attributable to lower hot-section deterioration rates because of the reduced thermal erosion at reduced TITs. In addition to fuel savings, the use of reduced thrust results in lower nitrous oxide emissions and makes us all better neighbors.

As you know, everything has its price. In the case of reduced power takeoffs, the biggest penalty may be the additional noise reaching ground level due to the lesser climb gradients associated with decreased thrust. Perceived decibel ratings (PNdB) at the surface will always be less than they would be at the actual higher temperatures. Unfortunately, they may also be somewhat more than they would be at full rated thrust or at the recommended noise-abatement thrust setting. In some localities that minor noise increase may tip the balance in favor of full power operations. But that, as is true of other takeoff options, is a matter for crew judgment.

Despite the success of ATM in airline operations, little or nothing has been done with it in smaller turbine equipment. Grumman has published the required appendix, calling it Flexible Takeoff Thrust (FTOT), but it has so far been used by only one or two flight departments. Unfortunately, there has been little pressure from operators on either jet or turboprop manufacturers to provide reduced-power takeoff procedures and capabilities. Without that pressure manufacturers have avoided producing the required flight-manual appendices even though that task is a simple paperwork process. At some point, when engine maintenance costs start to upset flight department budgets, operators will begin to demand ATM. In the meantime, individual manufacturers have a unique opportunity to grab a competitive edge in the marketplace by voluntarily offering ATM to prospective customers.

Takeoff power reductions are certain to be a controversial subject. Some pilots will feel that departure profiles afford such slender margins in the engine failure case that no reduction can be justified. Some will question the wisdom of flattened climb profiles in an increasingly noise-critical world. But most will find that considered use of the assumed temperature method (ATM) of reduced-takeoff thrust provides valuable returns in powerplant longevity, fuel conservation, minimized emissions and safety.

Foreign-Object Damage 14

by Robert L. Parrish

FOD is an acronym with which everyone who flies and maintains business jets is familiar. Each year an estimated 100 operators learn all about foreign object damage the expensive way.

Business aircraft FOD involves engine ingestion of things such as pebbles, gravel, loose bolts and birds, and is most common on turbojets. While the incidence of engine FOD apparently is stable, the price tag for FOD repairs has risen steadily over the past five years. According to aviation insurance companies, the average cost of repairing business jet engine FOD in 1978 is $22,000 per incident in labor and parts compared with $13,000 per incident in 1973.

Consequently, operators may soon have to pay substantially higher hull insurance premiums or accept policies with clauses that exempt engine damage from coverage. Some underwriters are already insisting on engine damage exemptions.

A B/CA survey of business jet operators, repair stations and insurance companies revealed that FOD can result from a variety of sources:

• A helicopter turbine engine manufacturer reported a case in which a wristwatch was literally sucked off the arm of a mechanic who was standing too close to the air inlet.

• A second engine company told of a Learjet in which the passengers were liberally sprayed with sawdust from the environmental conditioning unit blower after the plane clipped a pine grove during an encounter with wind shear. The same manufacturer also has recorded engine ingestion of a loaded garment bag, microphones, headsets, refueling mats and engine inlet covers as well as nuts, bolts, ice, rocks and runway asphalt and even some customs forms.

• Still another reported that a kite hawk with a nine-foot wing span was compressed into the two-foot diameter engine inlet of a business jet that struck the bird on takeoff.

• A major repair station said it received for overhaul a jet engine that sustained compressor damage when it gobbled up a six-foot antenna cable that broke loose from the aircraft in flight. Another business jet engine had no trouble shredding a loaded canvas mail pouch left in front of the air inlet, but the compressor wheels and stators were corncobbed by the pouch's brass lock chaser. In at least one instance, an engine sucked up a nearby maintenance worker's lunch pail. And there is the case of the engine that plucked the key from a baggage compartment lock.

Damage is frequently caused by ingestion of such objects as pipe clips and oil spouts carelessly left in the engine nacelle after maintenance or servicing. Other FOD results from rubber from blown tires or when blown tires cause aircraft to swerve into snowbanks; ice breaks loose from landing light rims; and internal rivets, blades or other engine parts separate.

The latter situation raises a knotty question for both operators and underwriters: Can material inherent to the engine be considered "foreign" when it separates and enters a part of the engine where designers didn't intend it to be?

Also controversial is the claim filed on an FOD engine that was almost due for a major overhaul involving costly replacement of life-limited components. Some insurance investigators suspect fraud or unethical practices in such cases.

Perhaps because of that suspicion and constantly rising costs of FOD repair, insurance claims investigators are inspecting engine damage more thoroughly for cause and extent.

What are the chances that the airplane you operate or fly will suffer FOD? Engine manufacturers report that only four to seven percent of all overhauls result from FOD. One manufacturer, in fact, claims that just six of 7,000 units of a particular engine series have become victims of FOD in the field. A major repair facility says about 50 to 2,000 engines it handled last year required teardown for suspected FOD. Another reports that an estimated five percent or less of its annual overhaul and repair volume involves FOD. However, an insurance firm that writes about one-third of U.S. business jet policies claims that 30 percent of claims have been for FOD. Therefore, there seems to be an inverse relationship between the percentage of reported encounters and claims.

Considering this evidence and the relatively stable number of FOD incidents reported each year, the business jet operator statistically can expect to experience significant FOD, once in every 10,175 aircraft hours—or once every 20 years for any particular aircraft, based on a 500-hour year.

The damage ingesting a foreign object causes is often unpredictable. The chief pilot of a jet charter firm was unaware that he had experienced a bird strike until preflight for a subsequent trip revealed bird residue on the air inlet lip. Cockpit instruments apparently had not detected anything amiss, but a maintenance inspection uncovered substantial compressor damage. The engine that ingested six feet of antenna cable, on the other hand, required no new parts; only minor compressor blade and stator vane dressing and straightening were necessary.

109

In engines with centrifugal compressor systems or high bypass turbofans, foreign objects that enter the air inlets are frequently thrown away from critical engine parts and are spewed out the rear of the engine without inflicting any damage at all.

There is no absolute corollary between size of a foreign object and the damage it may inflict. Large birds have been sucked through jet engines without bending a blade while small, case-hardened cotter pins have caused enough damage to require replacement of major parts.

On several engine models, compressor wheel blades of relatively soft material have broken off, found their way into the hot section and in molten form have impinged on turbine components, causing imbalance and serious damage to the engine.

Generally, ingested objects will cause the heaviest damage to fans and low- and high-pressure compressor stages. If one suspects FOD, the sooner the engine is inspected, the less likely that secondary damage will occur. An example of secondary damage is that which takes place when compressor blades weakened by primary FOD later separate.

A number of insurance companies offer a "mechanical breakdown coverage" as a separate provision—and charge a substantial premium for it. Such a policy may become popular, however, because when it comes to determining whether engine damage is the result of ingestion of a foreign object or mechanical breakdown, there is a wide divergence of opinions among experts.

Engineers at one repair facility contend there is usually enough debris or trace material remaining within the engine to ascertain what it was and what damage it may have caused. Type and location of damage, impact outline and object imprint often provide valuable clues. Impact-induced failure of blades and vanes leaves quite different separation surface indications than centrifugally induced failure. If all else fails, metallurgical analysis can afford irrefutable evidence of damage causes, according to some overhaul shops.

Insurance investigators express less certainty that the source of engine damage can be determined precisely. One investigator says his company handles three or four cases a year in which engine damage is so extensive that the primary cause cannot be ascertained. Another investigator, whose firm specifically excludes engine internal component breakdown from normal hull/engine FOD coverage, said the onus is largely on the insuring agency; if it cannot definitely establish that the cause of damage originated internally, the FOD claim is honored.

Some jet aircraft models are more prone to engine FOD than others. Air inlet diameter is a factor, as is engine location in relation to landing gear and runway surface. In general, turbofan engines, while susceptible to bent fan blades and resultant imbalance problems, sustain less serious compressor section FOD. An exception appears to be the rear-mounted fan.

Fortunately, FOD rarely causes accidents. One insurance company reports that since 1966 FOD was the cause in only five of the accidents for which it received claims. Of those five, just one resulted in fatalities. There are exceptions, however, and most involve bird strikes. Pilots recall that a Learjet crashed into a residential area in 1973 when it struck a flock of birds on takeoff from Atlanta's DeKalb-Peachtree Airport.

Jet engine manufacturers are paying increasing attention to FOD prevention. While noting that there is no instant cure in the works, some claim that the high bypass turbofan concept will make their products less susceptible to critical FOD. Several manufacturers are researching the use of new turbine wheel blade configurations and materials that reportedly will be more resistant to impact damage. Also under study is a reduction in the number of moving engine parts. The trend toward modular engine fabrication will help allay the cost and seriousness of incidents.

A builder of helicopter turboshaft engines says his firm has done extensive experimentation with easily removable and cleanable inlet screens that might be adapted to fixed-wing jets.

Until engine and airframe manufacturers devise a panacea for FOD, there are a number of procedures the business jet operator can follow to minimize the risk of foreign object ingestion.

First and most basic is good housekeeping. The ramp that is kept in good repair and swept clean of debris can't harm engines—or the appearance of the facility. Other preventative measures include:

• Use engine inlet covers whenever the aircraft is shut down for more than a few minutes. One insurance underwriter says his company soon enjoyed a drop in FOD claims after it advised its business jet operators to follow such a practice.

• Never, ever set *anything* on an aircraft engine inlet lip, and reprimand those who do.

• Avoid, if possible, taking off too closely behind heavy aircraft or in the vicinity of helicopters. It's not only the wingtip vortices of big aircraft that bite: they also throw stones.

• If your aircraft engines have thrust reversers, follow to the letter flight manual procedures for their use. Some reversers scoop up debris like a shovel when employed at low groundspeeds.

• Try to avoid landing on rough or poorly maintained airstrips. If you must use such facilities, limit ground engine running and taxiing times as much as possible.

• Be aware of the location of public dumps, wildlife conservation areas and migratory bird flyways in the vicinity of airports you use. At jet speeds there's little chance to see and avoid most birds.

• While taxiing in adverse weather, stay clear of muddy and slushy areas. Jet engines seem to have an affinity for mud and slush, as indicated by surges in ground ingestion incidents during inclement conditions.

FOD is as much a fact of life to the business aviation community as wind shear and thunderstorms—it won't go away, so it deserves at least equal attention from operators.

ELECTRICAL SYSTEMS IV

Time was when the electrical system served as a pleasant convenience for starting the engine and operating the lights. Not any more. The aircraft electrical system has become an essential part of flight and its failure or malfunction can be menacing. When the voltage drops below limits, the isolation of flight becomes very real and possibly dangerous.

In order to understand an electrical system you need first to understand the basic terminology and concepts. "An Electrical System Primer" verbally constructs that system, one component at a time. It is an essential piece for those who need to grasp the basics of that important system.

Beyond the primer stage, much of the mystery of electrical systems can be dissolved by a careful analysis of the power sources themselves. "Your Alternating or Generating System" examines each of those possible sources with a careful explanation of how it contributes to the system.

When an alternator or generator drops off the line and won't come back, you must immediately begin to shed the nonessential electrical load. "Coping With Alternator Failures" provides insights and methods to use should that problem ever happen to you.

Most turbine engines incorporate a single unique component which serves to start the engine and then to generate electricity. These aptly named starter/generators are far more complex and expensive than the basic alternator. They are a story unto themselves, which is included herewith.

An Electrical System Primer 15

by Richard N. Aarons

For many of us, the ultimate frustration in checking out in a new aircraft is attempting to understand the workings of its electrical system. Our motivation for this understanding is constantly assaulted by illogical schematic diagrams, ground school instructors who speak in the jargon of electrical engineers and an ingrained belief that anything involving electricity is by definition difficult to comprehend.

This state of affairs wouldn't be so bad were it not for the fact that airplanes can no longer get from A to B without functioning electrical systems. It used to be that the "electrical system" was a battery, a few feet of wire and light bulbs on the wing tips. Now the electrical system navigates, calculates, communicates, heats, cools, regulates cabin pressure and, on the newest turbine engines, controls fuel flow. (As one aircraft manufacturing executive put it recently, "Now we're selling avionics with an optional airplane.")

A B/CA staff member recently spent a grim afternoon sitting in a factory ground school listening to an instructor explain that the "left feeder bus is connected in series with an overload current sensor and the whole package is tied into the system with bus-tie contactors monitored by ground fault sensors." The problem was that not one student in that room had the faintest knowledge of the workings of a *feeder bus,* an *overload current sensor,* a *bus-tie* or a *ground fault sensor.* After the lecture was over they could draw a beautiful block diagram of the system, but they couldn't tell you how it functioned to save their life.

Unfortunately, you really can't find out what these things are by studying the aircraft manufacturers' publications. Their manual writers make the assumption that since you are a pilot you already know what they are. (That, of course, is absurd.) To sort out all this electrical system jargon, we roamed through a half dozen old textbooks and talked to an equal number of engineers at the various aircraft design houses. We're setting down here a few of the notes on basic electrical system components and principles that we picked up from them. Our hope is that you'll find this compilation a handy reference the next time you have to figure out the workings of a new-fangled aircraft electrical system.

If there were a way to avoid all technical talk in reference to electrical systems, we'd have no problems. But there are a few basic terms which must be understood if the rest is to make any sense.

Volts—The volt is a measure of electrical pressure, nothing else. Electrical pressure is the force that moves electric charges in a conductor. The movement of those electric charges is current. Voltage or electrical pressure is very much akin to the pressure in a water pipe before the faucet is opened—it's there, it's measurable, but it isn't doing anything. A 12-volt battery has a 12-volt electrical pressure differential between its terminals. The battery voltage is there and measurable, but doesn't do anything until a circuit is completed between its terminals.

Amps—It's voltage that forces electrical charges through a circuit. The flow of electrical charges is called *current* and it's measured in amps. Amperage is actually a flow rate. That is, one amp is the rate of flow when 6.28×10^{18} electrons move past a point in one second.

Ohms—Resistance is electrical friction and it's measured in ohms. It takes one volt to cause a current of one amp to flow through a resistance of one ohm. Double the voltage and the current doubles. Double the resistance and the current halves.

Watts—Power (in electricity) is the rate of doing work and it's measured in watts. Voltage, remember, is pressure, and amperage is the movement of charges. When a force is applied to something and it moves, work has been accomplished. The product of volts and amps (in direct current applications) is watts. For example, a 12-volt power supply causes a current flow of three amps. The power produced is 36 watts.

Watt-hour and *amp-hour*—You'll run into these terms often in electrical system studies. As the terms themselves imply, they consider not only the amount of power or current flow but also the duration of power or current flow. In theory, a 30-amp-hour battery can supply current at the rate of 30 amps for one hour or 15 amps for two hours or one amp for 30 hours. (This is important to remember when going through load shedding operations to cope with a partial electrical system failure.)

The amperage rating of aircraft engine-driven power supplies (alternators and generators) is important to know. A 60-amp alternator can supply up to 60 amps at any instant in time. However, in a well-designed system, total current draw will be significantly less than maximum output of the power supply. In the case of a twin, either engine-driven power source should be capable of handling all essential electrical equipment without help from its partner.

All twins (and larger aircraft) have ammeters which display the actual current draw at any given instant (in amps). This is an ideal setup. Some singles are equipped with ammeters of this type, but most have automotive type ammeters which show only *whether the battery is charging or discharging.* This type of meter tells you whether you've got a problem, but it doesn't help you much in solving the problem.

Automotive type ammeters won't tell you exactly how many amps the system is pulling, but they will tell you the relative power drain in the event of an engine-driven, power-source failure.

Ammeters that read out actual current load tell you exactly what's going on and therefore can be used for load shedding when an engine-driven power source fails. Suppose you're flying along under IFR conditions pulling 30 amps from the electrical system and the alternator drops off line. You go through the alternator failure emergency procedures and the thing still doesn't function. In the case of a single-engine aircraft all electrical power must now come from the battery, and the battery has a limited amount of electrical energy to offer.

The first step is to get rid of all nonessential items, remembering that heaters, motors, high-wattage lights and avionics with transmitter components have the highest power draw. After you're down to a minimum, check the ammeter to see what the load is and you can get a rough idea of your endurance (at least as far as the electrical system is concerned). For example, we'll assume that the electrical load has been reduced to 15 amps. If you've got a 30-amp-hour battery and it's in perfect condition operating under ideal ambients, you've got about two hours of electrical power. But remember, your battery isn't in perfect shape or operating under ideal ambients.

Keep in mind also that every time you transmit, the load increases significantly. The best policy, of course, is to land immediately. In a radar environment you can reduce the load to necessary cockpit lights, instruments and one transceiver. Ask ATC for vectors (instead of keeping nav receivers on line) and tell them you'll not respond verbally to instructions until you begin the approach. They'll ask you to keep your transponder on line, but see if you can get them to skin-paint you, at least during en route segments.

On a twin, the failure of one alternator is not necessarily as bad a situation as it is in a single, but it can still be a problem. De-icing equipment, especially hot props, pull a tremendous load. So it's not unusual to find that a light-twin electrical load at any given time will exceed the output of a single alternator.

If your light twin is equipped with two 100-amp alternators and your electrical appliances and avionics are pulling 120 amps total, the failure of one alternator will cause an immediate current drain on the battery and, under some circumstances, can pull the other alternator off line. The idea here is to be aware of the consequences of an alternator failure any time total load exceeds the output of a single alternator. Be ready to reduce the load to below the maximum output of the functioning alternator immediately. Once this is done, you can go through the alternator-failure emergency procedures.

Some aircraft owners compile lists of electricity-using appliances with the power requirements of each item. (This information is available from the component manufacturer on catalogue sheets or can be gleaned from the information plates affixed to the devices themselves.) A quick-and-dirty method to get this information is to check the rating of the circuit breakers used to protect these devices. This will give you numbers higher than the actual current drain of the various electrical devices, but it will tell you which to turn off first.

Some twins are equipped with multi-functional meters. One in common use displays the output of either alternator, bus voltage and battery charge-discharge condition. In flight, this type meter should be kept in the battery mode. If the needle swings to the discharge side, the output of each alternator should be examined to determine the source of the problem.

Obviously the function of the electrical system is to power various electrical appliances on the aircraft—avionics, gear and flap motors, blowers, lights and dozens of other devices. Electrical system designers attempt to keep the system as light and simple as possible; therefore they make wire-runs as short as practicable and attempt to group loads at single locations rather than scattering them throughout the aircraft. Take a look at the simple landing gear motor circuit (Figure 1).

When the gear switch is closed, the circuit from the positive battery terminal through the motor to the negative terminal is completed and the motor runs. Notice that it takes two wires to make the system operate. However, one of the wires can be eliminated if the aircraft structure itself is used as a conductor as shown in Figure 2.

This setup is called a *negative ground system* and it's used in most U.S.-manufactured aircraft. A schematic diagram of this system appears in Figure 3.

All ground symbols are considered to be connected to each other or to a common conductor such as the aircraft structure. This concept of negative ground is important to the pilot. Handbook diagrams show only one lead from each component—the other is assumed to go directly to ground.

Buses are used to further reduce wire runs. Suppose we had to hook up four lamps to the same power supply. It could look like the diagram in Figure 4. Or like the one in Figure 5.

The second scheme is much more desirable. Here only one wire runs from the power supply to the general area where the lights are installed. Then the lights are connected to a common terminal called a *bus*. These buses

ELECTRICAL SYSTEMS

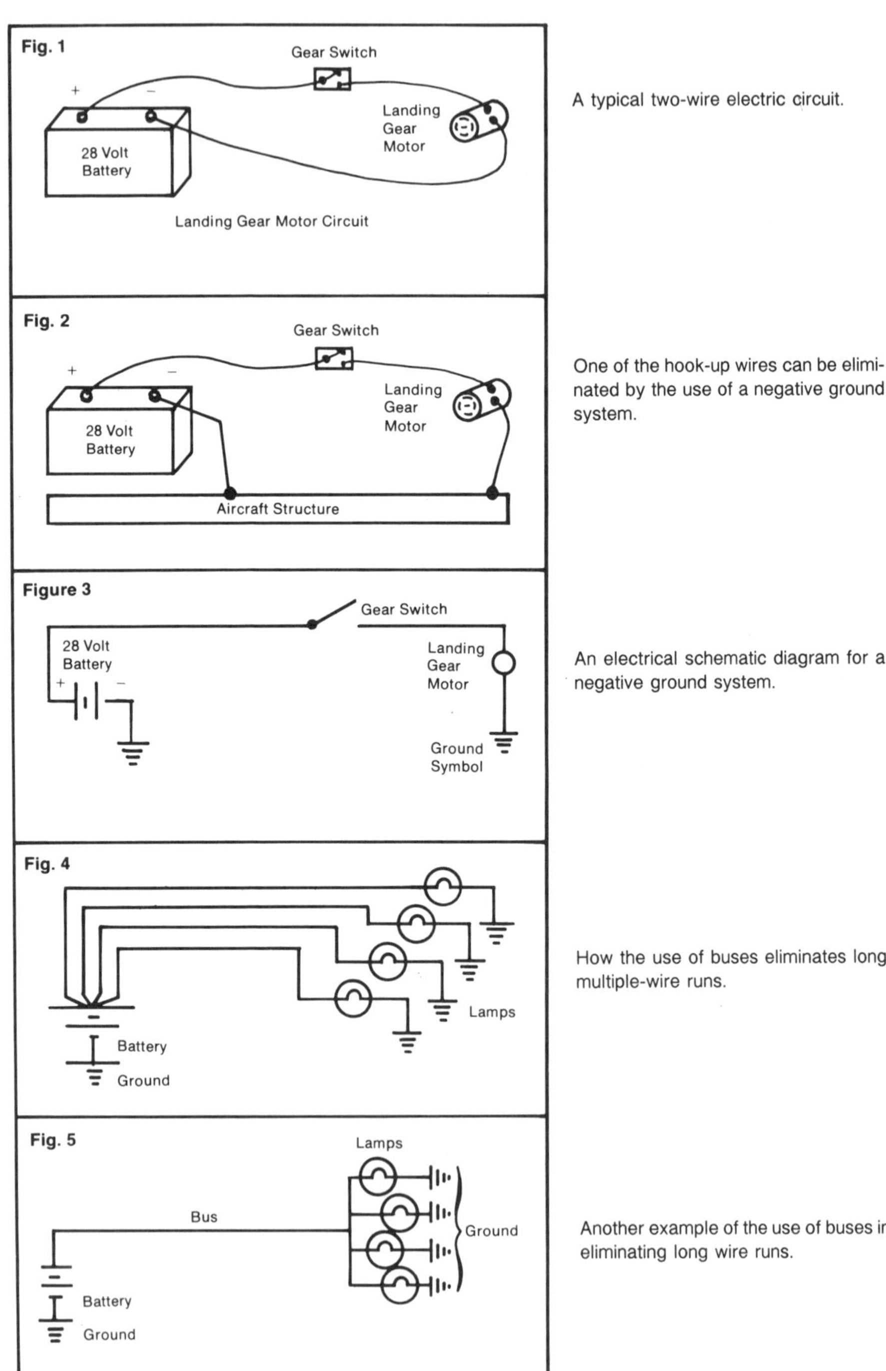

A typical two-wire electric circuit.

One of the hook-up wires can be eliminated by the use of a negative ground system.

An electrical schematic diagram for a negative ground system.

How the use of buses eliminates long multiple-wire runs.

Another example of the use of buses in eliminating long wire runs.

are named either for what they power (avionics bus, for example) or for where they get their power (right generator bus).

A simple electrical system may have only one bus. Often single-engine aircraft have an avionics bus to power the radios and a main bus to take care of all other electrical appliances. In this case the avionics bus is automatically disconnected from its power supply when the engine-starter motor is energized. This is to prevent voltage spikes from zapping the radios.

Multi-engine aircraft normally have several power sources—a battery and at least one generator (or alternator) per engine. These electrical systems are usually set up so any bus can be energized by any of the power sources. For example, a typical system might have right and left generator buses served normally by the right and left engine-driven generators. These buses will be connected by a normally open switch which isolates them from each other. If one of the generators fails, power will be lost to its bus, but power can be restored to that bus by closing a *bus-tie* switch. When this is done, the good generator powers both left and right buses. Bus-tie switches can be automatically actuated relays, standard circuit breakers or manually operated switches. In some aircraft the ties are arranged so that you have an either/or situation. That is, you can have either radar or the FD, not both, with one starter-generator or inverter off line.

The certification requirements for both large and small aircraft are pretty vague on electrical system design. The FARs only state that each essential component must be protected by a current-limiting device, and that the failure of one item shouldn't drag down the entire system.

Aircraft fuses are similar to automotive and household fuses. A fuse is simply a wire that melts and breaks when current flow through it exceeds a certain value. Circuit breakers are like fuses in that they break the circuit when current flow exceeds a certain preset value, but unlike fuses they are not damaged when tripped and are easily reset. Often circuit breakers are used to serve dual roles as manually actuated switches and circuit protectors.

Since each important appliance must be protected by a circuit breaker, you'll always see the circuit breaker symbol between the appliance and its feeder bus on a schematic. (See Figure 6.)

Overvoltage relays and ground fault sensors can be thought of as circuit breakers because they do just that. In sophisticated aircraft, these protective devices can be reset manually or will reset automatically. But remember, like the circuit breakers on the electrical system control panel, if they trip, something is wrong. Attempt to isolate the problem using handbook procedures.

Never hold a circuit breaker in if it wants to pop. If a device is drawing

ELECTRICAL SYSTEMS

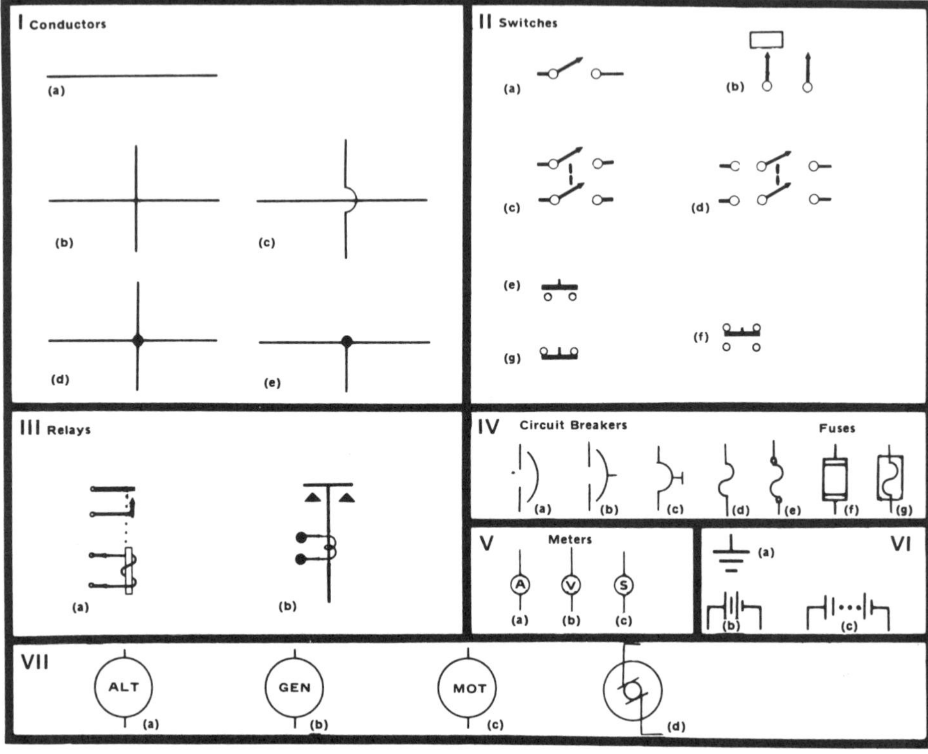

Ideally, complete schematic diagrams should be left entirely to engineers and technicians, but they show up from time to time in owner's handbooks. Happily the trend is away from these hieroglyphics and toward schematics in which the symbology takes on the appearance of actual hardware. (See Figure 7.) If however, you are stuck with a complete schematic, you will find that the symbols above (or variations of them) are used.

(I) Conductors (wires) are shown as straight lines (a). An electrical connection is present between crossing lines only if a dot appears at the intersection (d) and (e). The wires in (b) and (c) have no electrical connection at the intersection.

(II) There are literally hundreds of switch types and an equally large number of schematic symbols to represent them. A single pole, single throw (SPST) switch is shown in (a) and (b). Switch (b) is a slide type. Type (c) is a double pole, single throw (DPST) switch. The dashed line indicates that the poles move together to control two circuits. Switch (d) is a double pole, double throw (DPDT). The switches in (e), (f) and (g) are push buttons. Note that (e) is normally open and (g) is normally closed. Switch (f) momentarily opens the normally closed circuit and closes the normally open circuit, but only so long as the pushbutton is depressed.

(III) Relays are electrically controlled switches. These are often called "contactors" in aircraft electrical system diagrams.

(IV) Circuit breakers and fuses are indicated by these symbols. All essential aircraft electrical appliances are wired in series with current-limiting devices.

(V) Meters are usually indicated by a circle and a letter which identifies the function of the meter. "A" indicates that the unit is an ammeter, "V" a voltmeter and "S" a synchroscope.

(VI) Common to all schematic diagrams are the symbols for ground (a) and batteries (b). The negative terminal is always the short line in the battery symbol.

(VII) Often motors and generators are displayed as circles with an identifying abbreviation. "Alt" stands for alternator, "gen" for generator and "mot" for motor. Sometimes motors are indicated by the symbol shown in (d).

120

enough power to trip its breaker repeatedly, there's probably a short-circuit in the appliance. Holding the circuit breaker in might start a fire and it'll certainly further damage the equipment the breaker is designed to protect. If a breaker pops, wait at least two minutes for it to cool before attempting to reset it. If it pops again, leave it out and squawk the system.

Relays are electrically controlled switches and you'll find them in all aircraft electrical systems. The master (or battery) switch actually activates a relay which connects the battery to various buses. The starter switch controls a relay which connects the battery to the starter motor. You'll often see the term *contactor* on schematic diagrams. This is a relay.

Understanding electrical distribution is a must for any pilot. Electrical system failure modes range from annoying to catastrophic and in any case they must be dealt with immediately.

The airplane, during an actual electrical system emergency, obviously is the wrong place to start learning about power distribution. The pilot must know to which bus each essential item is hooked and in addition how to isolate that bus or feed it from other power supplies.

In a single-engine aircraft—especially older models—you should begin your studies with an analysis of what *can* happen. For example, the Cessna 182 has a relatively simple electrical system with two buses (avionics and main) supplied by a battery and alternator. Avionics and other appliances are protected by flush-mounted circuit breakers which cannot be tripped manually. This setup is easy to understand, but its simplicity is not necessarily good. Remedies for system failures are practically nil. Any alternator failure other than one which takes out the main 60-amp alternator circuit breaker will require the pilot to turn off the master switch and therefore turn off all electrical appliances. If you've got to get the alternator off line, there's no way to do it manually without taking the battery off too. Similarly, if the battery has to go for some reason, you can't get rid of it without taking the alternator down. Newer 182s are equipped with a split master switch which enables the pilot to isolate either the battery or the alternator.

(If you study the old 182 system long enough, you'll find at least seven malfunctions which could lead to total electrical power loss. Installation of a push-pull type alternator circuit breaker in place of the flush breaker will eliminate some of the catastrophic potential. Installation of a double-switched hot line from the battery to the avionics bus will provide a good standby source. This installation, however, is a major system modification and requires FAA approval.)

The point here is not so much that you should re-engineer your electrical system, but rather you must understand its limitations.

When checking out in a new type aircraft, study the manual, then sit in the cockpit and play with the electrical system. Decide on a list of *essential* electrical equipment and figure out how that equipment gets its power. A typical list would include avionics, attitude and engine instruments, gear and flap motors and, perhaps, basic environmental system appliances. Study the circuit breaker panel itself. It's often marked with a schematic (of sorts) showing at least how the various appliances are grouped and how the buses are (or can be) tied. Then pose a set of operational problems for yourself.

Turn off portions of the power supply and see what happens. Attempt to re-establish circuit paths by using the bus-ties. Buses are like branches on a tree, often with one feeding another, and each protected by its own circuit breakers. Understand how the various buses interface and be able to use the interconnect system to its maximum capability.

Just about the kindest thing you can say about existing handbook electrical system schematics is that they are inconsistent. Some manufacturers use true schematic diagrams which show all circuit components with electronic symbology. If you fall victim to this abuse of pilot time, Figure 6 may be helpful. It's a compilation of the most frequently used electrical symbols.

Other manufacturers present what can only be described as bastardized electronic schematics. These scribbles use standard electronic symbols, but only portions of the circuitry are shown. Any attempt to trace the circuits (normally a good method to reinforce system concepts) leads to confusion. Only a working knowledge of the components themselves can help the pilot faced with these references.

Happily, the trend in schematic representation is to use block diagrams in which each component is represented by a symbol that has the same basic appearance as the actual hardware. (See Figure 7.)

(GAMA has recommended a standardization of electrical system diagrams within the framework of its *Specifications for Pilot Operating Handbooks.* In the future, GAMA members—and that means virtually all airframe makers—when drafting illustrations for their handbooks will remember that the "user of the schematic diagram is a person of undefined background. The schematic diagram shall not be created for primary use by a mechanic or technician. The schematic diagram shall tend to deal with overall systems rather than with sub-systems. For example, the air conditioning system rather than a compressor or blower within the air conditioning system." In GAMA's words, "to the maximum extent possible, each symbol shall physically resemble the actual system component." GAMA says pilots should not be required to learn intermediate symbology made up of abstractions. "If an abstraction must be used, it shall be selected from a recognized national standard or it shall be simply a box with a title inside." A portion of a GAMA-recommended schematic is reproduced in Figure 7.)

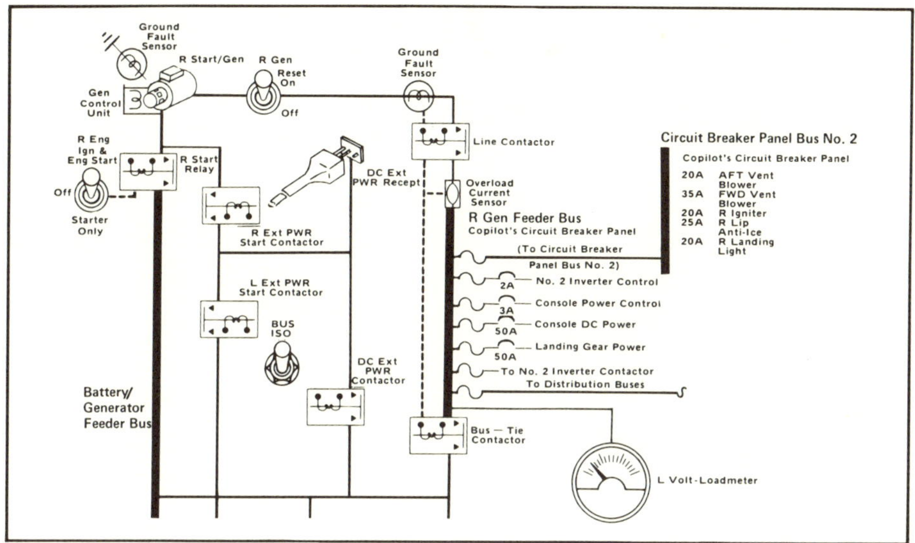

Fig. 7: Industry handbook writers have agreed to simplify electrical system schematics in owner's manuals. Shown here is a portion of one such simplified schematic. Notice that the components are drawn to resemble the actual electrical system appliance. The thick lines are buses, the normal lines are power circuits and the dash lines are control circuits.

Your Alternating or Generating System

16

by William J. Kendall

The electrical system of modern day business aircraft is probably the most perplexing of all. Concepts such as voltage and amperage are simply too intangible to be easily understood. However, if we examine the primary electrical power sources we can get a foothold on understanding the electrical system as a whole.

This chapter will discuss only primary power sources, but it puts things into perspective to say that aircraft electrical power sources fall into three general categories: *primary, secondary* and *standby.* The primary power source, which is engine-driven, can be an alternator (AC generator), DC generator or a DC starter-generator. Secondary sources, which are driven by the primary source, include rotary and static DC-to-400-cycle-AC inverters and 12-volts-DC-to-24-volts-DC static converters. The standby source is, of course, a battery.

From the system designer's standpoint, the primary power source should be capable of supplying all the aircraft's maximum electrical needs. As long as the primary source is operating properly, the battery's only function is to remain fully charged.

Turbojet and turboprop systems designers always do a pretty good job in meeting this goal, but their task is easier than that of their counterparts in the piston aircraft business. For example, as soon as a turbine engine is started, the electrical generating machine is spinning fast enough to produce maximum power. That is not so for the piston-engine system.

In piston-engine aircraft, for a number of reasons, the primary power source is not always capable of meeting combined electrical loads. This is especially true of older aircraft equipped with DC generators, which usually do not cut in until the engine reaches 1400 rpm. Below 1400 rpm, the battery has to handle the load. This problem was solved in the mid-60s by switching from DC generators to alternators in most aircraft. Alternators can be run at higher rotational speeds and are more efficient than DC generators in that they cut in at a lower engine rpm. The 12-volt, 60-amp

Prestolite alternator (Figure 1) used on Lycoming engines, for example, comes up to voltage at about 460 engine rpm (1500 alternator rpm). When the engine is running at 600 rpm, the alternator (running 2000 rpm) is putting out 20 amps. With the engine at 1000 rpm, the alternator (at 3500 rpm) is putting out 50 amps.

Modern piston twins generally use alternators with outputs ranging from 60 to 200 amps. When both alternators are operable, they are capable of supplying the maximum normal electrical loads, except at very low engine idling speeds. However, the same cannot be said for well equipped single-engine aircraft, which use a single 60-amp alternator as primary power source.

On a single-engine aircraft with a lot of avionics onboard, a regular inflight current load could be as high as 30 amps. If you then turn on pitot heat (10 amps), nav, instrument and landing lights (13 amps), rotating beacon (seven amps) and an auxiliary fuel pump (seven amps), you have already exceeded the alternator's 60-amp maximum. Now, if you lower the gear (10 amps) and run the flaps down (10 amps) simultaneously, you are forcing the battery to supply the additional current.

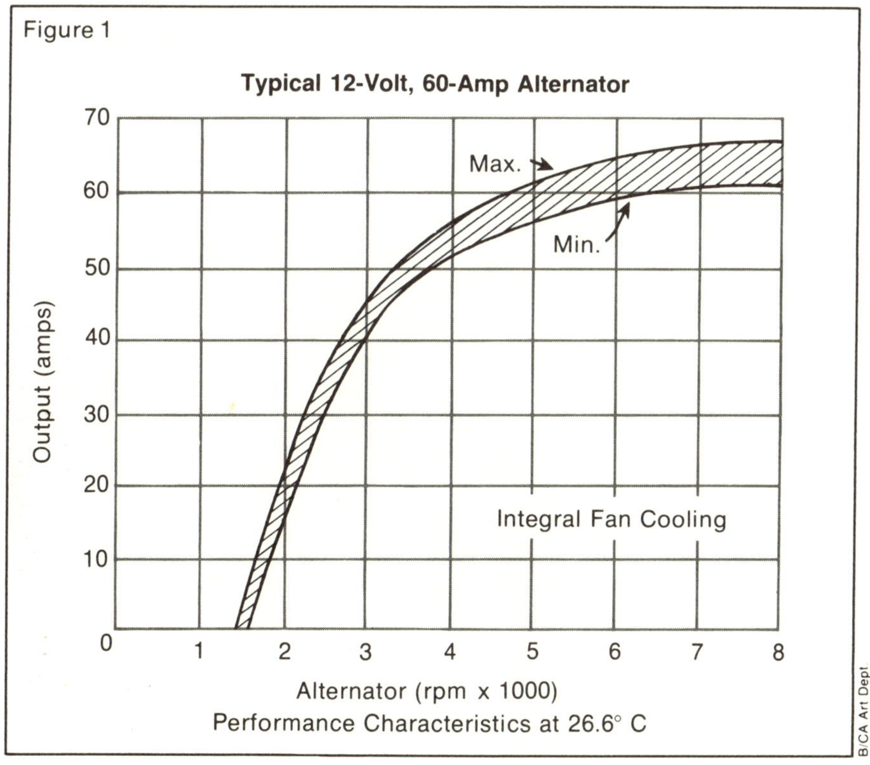

Pilots of single-engine aircraft should turn off what they don't need. Batteries will last much longer when they are not discharged, and equipment will be protected from under-voltage operation. (When the alternator is supplying the load, operating voltage is 14 volts. As the battery starts to assume the load, voltage drops to around 12.5 volts or lower, depending upon the discharge rate and the health of the battery. While this lower voltage is not supposed to affect critical instruments and avionics, it can do so.)

Direct-current generators produce electrical energy by moving coils of insulated wire (wound on a rotating armature) past magnetic fields of stationary electromagnets. The coils of insulated wire used in the stationary electromagnets are called *field windings.* Electrical energy is induced in the armature coils when current is passed through the field coils (they become excited) and the armature is mechanically rotated. The value of the voltage induced in the armature coils depends upon the speed of rotation and the amount of current exciting the field coils.

The alternator (or AC generator) also produces electricity by electromagnetic induction. Unlike a DC generator, however, the electromagnetic field rotates while the armature coils are stationary. The rotating electromagnet is called the rotor. Carbon brushes riding on two conducting slip rings on the rotor shaft are used to feed the excitation current. Like a DC generator, the voltage induced in the armature coils is both positive and negative. This produces an alternating current output across the ends of the armature coils.

On large jets with AC primary power sources, the alternator output is fed directly into the electrical system. Most other aircraft, however, have direct current primary-power sources—either 12 volts (single-engine and small twins) or 28 volts (larger twins, turboprops and smaller jets). In these cases, the AC output at the armature coils must be converted into direct current before it can be used. This is done by solid-state rectifier diodes that allow current to flow in only one direction. On 60-amp automotive-type alternators, these diodes are usually encapsulated and mounted directly on the alternator. On bigger units, the diodes are contained in a separate rectifier unit.

Aircraft alternators have a three-phase output. Simply stated, this means that three separate AC currents are generated across three isolated armature windings. While the AC output of each winding is individually rectified, a combined direct current output is obtained. Consequently, it is possible to have a partial alternator failure. If you notice that the current being produced at idle power is not up to par, chances are you've got a partial failure of some sort. If one phase goes out because of a bad winding or diode, the alternator would continue to function, but with a reduced output.

Alternator failures are indicated by a failure warning light or a discharge indication on the amp meter or meters. The correcting procedure usually calls for reducing the load on the alternator to zero, shutting it off, resetting the alternator circuit breaker and then bringing the alternator back on the line. If the circuit breaker pops again, turn the alternator off and leave it off. Then reduce the electrical load as much as possible and get on the ground before the battery runs down.

The length of operation of an alternator between overhauls varies according to whether it's new or rebuilt. In the case of a rebuilt one, the service life depends on how well it was rebuilt.

Noise in the radio on certain frequencies may indicate alternator problems in the offing. Pulsating DC due to defective components in the alternator will contribute to what technicians call "high ripple content" in the radio. When this occurs, the alternator should, of course, be checked. That may not always solve the problem. It may be necessary to, in addition, install a new or modified filter in the circuit to eliminate the noise.

There's really not much the operator can do to make his alternator last longer between overhauls. To insure peak performance, be sure to use it often. Idleness breeds service problems far more than usage. The belt should be at the proper tension. A loose belt may reduce the alternator potential by one volt; it doesn't sound like much, but it may mean the difference between charging and not charging the battery. Also, have the mounting bolts checked. A&Ps find broken ones on periodic inspections.

Most technicians agree that keeping the electrical load on the alternator low doesn't add to its life expectancy.

Age has more of an effect on the alternator than operating hours. Deterioration due to time, such as cracking insulation and brittle field wires, are real culprits.

There are no regulations requiring overhaul or replacement of alternators, so it's mainly up to the pilot to make sure his alternator is in good operating condition through preventive maintenance and frequent monitoring of all the indicators available.

Because the voltage output of both alternators and DC generators is a function of their rotational speed, which, in turn, varies with engine rpm, some means must be provided for obtaining the constant 14 or 28 volts needed as primary power. Regulating the voltage value is accomplished by varying the amount of excitation applied to the field windings. In Figure 2, the regulator is represented by a variable resistor, which is basically what it is. As alternator or DC generator speed decreases, the regulator's effective resistance decreases, allowing more excitation current to pass through the field windings. As the speed increases, the regulator's resistance also increases to reduce the excitation current. The end result is a constant voltage.

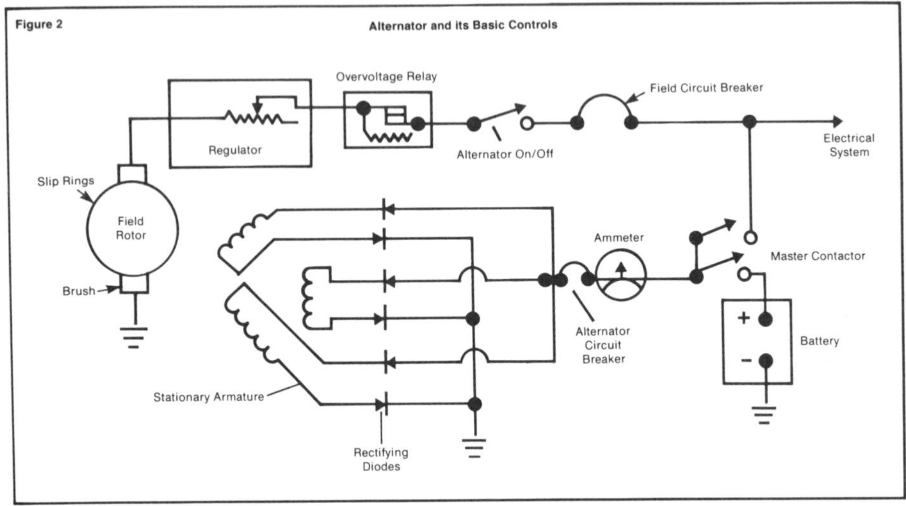

Solid-state regulators have made older types obsolete from a technical standpoint. Their design is really quite simple. No mechanical elements are involved, and unlike vibrating contact units, field excitation variations are uninterrupted and precise.

The residual magnetism in the field of a DC generator supplies the start-up excitation until the reverse current relay closes and applies regular excitation current. Sometimes a generator will lose its residual magnetism or become incorrectly polarized because of heat, shock or a momentary reverse current. When this occurs, the residual magnetism must be re-established by momentarily applying voltage to the field ("flashing the field"). In sophisticated DC generator systems, provision is made for applying battery voltage through a limiting resistor directly to the field windings by a reset switch.

Start-up excitation current is usually supplied to the field rotor of an alternator from the battery when the master contactor is energized and the alternator on/off switch is closed. In aircraft where a separate contactor is provided to isolate the battery from the electrical system, an emergency alternator excitation switch is usually provided for connecting the field directly to the battery or to a separate emergency excitation source.

Until the mid-60s the DC generator was virtually the only primary direct-current power source for aircraft. However, thanks to the development of high-current solid-state diodes and control devices, it has been widely replaced by the alternator.

Alternators are lighter, simpler, less expensive and inherently more reliable than DC generators. The use of slip rings in place of segmented commutators is the big plus. Brushes last longer and are less prone to arcing. Alternators can also run at higher maximum rotational speed than DC generators. As a result, higher pulley ratios can be used with piston engines for more output at lower engine speeds.

Characteristically, a 50-amp DC generator cuts in with a 25-amp output when its rotation speed reaches 3500 rpm. Its rated 50-amp output is available from 4000 to 8500 rpm. If it were driven with a three-to-one pulley ratio, the generator would cut in when the engine reached 1170 rpm and deliver its rated 50 amps at 1330 rpm.

Compare this with the characteristics of the alternator plotted in Figure 1. Notice the alternator comes up to voltage when it's turning at only 1500 rpm. At 3400 rpm when the DC generator has just cut in, the alternator is capable of delivering 50 amps, or almost all its rated capacity. Moreover, since it can be run as high as 10,000 rpm with a 3.25-to-1 pulley ratio, the alternator starts delivering at lower engine rpm.

As mentioned above, alternators are less expensive than DC generators. This is especially true for the 60- and 100-amp units that were initially designed for the automotive industry. Compare them with their automotive brothers, and you're hard put to see any significant difference other than the price tag. However, there are some important differences in internal construction. Aircraft units are designed to operate in harsher environments and at higher altitudes. Their carbon brushes are made harder to last longer and minimize arcing at high altitudes. Tougher insulation and potting compounds are used for the windings.

A variety of alternators with outputs of 200 amps and more are made for aircraft. While some of these units have 24-volt outputs, most produce 115 volts. The 20-KVA alternators used on G-IIs have a primary output of approximately 180 amps at 115 volts wild frequency AC. Some of this primary output is used directly to power 115-volt equipment that is not frequency-sensitive. Most of the alternator output, however, is transformed down to 28 volts and rectified to drive inverters with outputs of 115-volt, three-phase, 400-cycle AC.

While alternators have been coming on strong in recent years, the DC generator is far from obsolete and will be flying for some time to come. The G-II, for example, uses two 288-volt, 300-amp DC generators along with its two 20-KVA alternators. Beech also reports that some of its Queen Air customers have requested GE 200-amp DC generators in place of the GE 200-amp alternators, usually installed. However, the biggest factor in the continued use of DC generators is that they can double as starter motors for turboprops and turbojets. Take a DC generator, excite its field, apply a DC voltage to its armature and it will rotate. Hence, the DC starter-generator.

Unlike the slow-cranking, high-current DC motors used to start piston engines, those used to wind up turbines have operating characteristics similar to aircraft DC generators.

All DC starter motors have limits with regard to how long they can be energized and to what degree they can be loaded. With starter-generators, the limits are particularly critical. On the Swearingen Merlin IV, for example, maximum starting duration is 10 seconds. Maximum loading is 20 percent engine rpm. If these prescribed limits are exceeded, the system can be damaged.

The best way to get long life and reliability from your primary power sources is to understand their limitations and plan never to exceed those limits. Toward that end, climb into your aircraft flight and maintenance manuals for a bit of home study.

Coping with Alternator Failures

17

by Gerard M. Bruder, Jr

Electricity makes life easier and more efficient, so it is not surprising that aerospace technology has incorporated electricity into the operation of dozens of important aircraft components: landing gear, flaps, de-icing boots, encoding altimeters, strobe lights and weather radars, and communications and navigational equipment, to name just a few. Electricity even controls the meters that monitor the health of the electrical system.

One or more generators or alternators serve as primary electrical energy sources on aircraft, and usually these sources are reliable. Generators and related components can malfunction, however, so aircraft electrical systems include a standby power source—the battery. Of course, the battery also is used to supply power for engine starts.

In its standby capacity, the battery unfortunately offers limited insurance because its output duration is finite. As with bank accounts and fuel supplies, battery usefulness depends on what is available and what is taken out. If you're operating IFR at night, several hundred miles from the nearest usable airport, your electrical power insurance may not provide adequate coverage.

An inflight failure of the primary electrical power source or sources, therefore, can be a serious development. As a pilot, you should be prepared for such a development and know how to apportion the available battery energy to assure a safe termination of your flight. The purpose of this chapter is to suggest ways in which you can increase that preparation. (For convenience, we will refer to battery in the singular even though larger aircraft often employ dual batteries in a single unit setup.)

Pilots of multi-engine airplanes, particularly the newer jets, are unlikely to experience electrical system problems so devastating that they must resort to battery energy for further electrical requirements. These aircraft have a primary electrical power unit on each engine and enough fail-safe systems to preclude all but the most bizarre applications of Murphy's Law.

Yet, the bizarre *can* happen; in 1972, a thermal runaway in the number-two battery of a Grumman G-II caused a fire that destroyed the battery relay panels, knocking out the *entire* electrical system except for the emergency power packs. Luckily, the weather was VFR (though at night) and the jet made a safe emergency landing at Kennedy Airport.

(Thermal runaway refers to overheating of a nickel-cadmium battery—the type used by most transport category aircraft—after failure of one or more cells, polarity reversal and overcharging. In 1971 and 1972 the FAA issued ADs requiring that battery temperature monitoring equipment and a method of isolating the battery from the rest of the electrical system be available on aircraft with nickel-cadmium batteries capable of starting an engine or an APU.)

Electrical emergency situations are more common on single-engine aircraft because usually there is only one primary electrical source—and a limited number of problem-solving options available.

Regardless of what you fly, however, preparation is the key to surviving inflight electrical emergencies.

Fundamental to such preparation is an understanding of basic electricity, just as an understanding of aerodynamics can help you recover from a stall.

What should a review of basic electricity cover? Amps, volts, ohms, DC and AC are pertinent, as are the functions of buses, relays, feeders, circuit breakers, fuses and sensors. Then there are generators, alternators, regulators, inverters, converters—and batteries. Don't be content with merely memorizing definitions; *understand* these electrical components and the interactions they have with other parts of the total system.

A thorough familiarity with the electrical system is very important. Be sure you know where the battery is and what its voltage and amperage ratings are. Learn the location of the various buses and which equipment they serve. If some circuit breakers are not within cockpit view, find out where they are. Learn what is automatic and what is manual in the system. Know how the system manifests problems and potential problems. Make a list of all electrical equipment that can be shut down in flight and note the power requirement of each item. (See the checklist.) Then memorize those items that need the most power. Of course, also memorize procedures for electrical system trouble.

In general, be versed enough with the electrical system in your aircraft to give a ground school lecture on it. (You can neglect brushing up on your public speaking techniques, however.)

The flight manual will provide much of the data you should know, but if some is omitted or the detail is insufficient, fill in via your mechanic, airplane manufacturer, component manufacturer or other source. Make sure your source is reliable, however. A fellow pilot doesn't necessarily qualify, even if he flies the same type of plane.

The maintenance people and battery manufacturer representatives we interviewed were almost unanimous in their criticism of pilots (private to corporate) for shallowness of knowledge of both basic electricity and aircraft electrical systems. One battery repairman said he'd be out of business if pilots were competent in these areas, and a mechanic we talked with claims he knows several commercial pilots who think the engine will quit if the master switch is turned off.

There is some basis for such cynicism; according to NTSB accident briefs, pilot negligence or ignorance was a factor in practically all of the 18 crashes of business or corporate aircraft involving electrical failures from 1972 through 1975.

The actual number of incidents related to electrical failure is undoubtedly higher since causes and contributing factors are not always established. Nor do the NTSB figures reveal the number of times electrical power problems produced emergencies, aborted flights and trickles of perspiration.

A background in electricity and a knowledge of the electrical system you fly with are important not only to help you respond effectively when a system failure occurs, but also to discourage that failure in the first place. For instance, you should know that overloading the system is asking for trouble, that it is unwise to reset a circuit breaker more than once after it pops and that on a light twin one generator or alternator may not be able to carry the entire electrical load if the other fails.

An electrical overload does not always break something; more often it simply pops a circuit breaker. The failure of an electrical power source may be temporary or partial. So if a system warning light activates, don't assume you've lost the system. Instead, follow the appropriate flight manual procedures and try to correct the problem.

For example, after an alternator annunciator light comes on in a Piper Seneca II, the first step is to look at the ammeters to determine which alternator is inoperative. Then the appropriate alternator switch is cycled, and the circuit breaker panel is checked. If the alternator does not come back on line, all avionics are turned off except for one navcom and transponder. To maintain an electrical load of less than 65 amps, the windshield heat is switched off.

If both ammeters indicate zero output, the load is reduced to a minimum and the alternator switches are cycled one at a time; the alternator showing the *least* (but not zero) current is left on and the other remains off. The electrical load now may be reinstated up to a maximum of 60 amps.

The Piper Seneca II flight manual notes that compass error may be more than 10° with both alternators shut down.

Some maintenance people say that the immediate reaction to an electrical system warning light should be to turn off all nonessential equipment to conserve battery output in case a failure has taken place that cannot be corrected inflight. Then and only then, they say, should you investigate the situation.

A pilot told us his policy is to turn off everything except the autopilot (and necessary related components) so he can direct his full attention to whatever problem has arisen. A co-pilot, of course, provides the same freedom with no battery power expenditure.

In any event, follow your manual procedures unless you receive manufacturer or FAA authorization to revise those procedures.

If you do shut everything off and it's nighttime, a flashlight will make it unnecessary to turn on the cockpit lights to locate the manual or go through troubleshooting procedures.

A note on resetting circuit breakers: Since overheating is frequently the reason for a popped breaker, try to wait a couple of minutes before you reset it to give the appliance a chance to cool. This will help prevent damage and decrease the likelihood that the breaker will pop again.

If a serious electrical failure is evident, land at the nearest usable airport, even if that field has no maintenance facilities. Most manuals recommend such action, and the rationale is that a fire or other complication can develop after electrical trouble occurs. The urgency of a landing is in inverse ratio to how well you know your airplane, how certain you are of what happened, the potential for repairs at the nearest airport and the weather.

If your passengers are insistent on reaching their destination, tell them an emergency exists (or that you want to prevent one).

Whether you should squawk 7700 on the transponder and transmit your situation verbally during a battery power situation depends on the weather, the availability of an airport, traffic, the condition of the battery and other factors that may be relevant. Generally, the best policy is to use as little electrical equipment as is feasible (which means as little as is safe).

Remember that transmitters, especially on radios with tubes rather than solid-state components, drain more current than do receivers; you might need the power you save by not making an unnecessary transmission for an unexpected development while you're making an approach. Sometimes it is possible to obtain the advisories you need simply by listening to transmissions from ATC and other aircraft.

As with any emergency, the FARs are secondary to safety when an electrical failure occurs. You may have to file a few reports afterwards, but that's less painful than running out of battery current at the wrong moment and not having an afterwards.

If an airport is not at hand or you cannot for some reason make a landing soon, hoarding battery power becomes especially important. Unfortunately, it is difficult to determine exactly how much power you have, and thus how much you can count on. A battery that is rated at 30 amps theoretically means you can pull 30 amps for one hour, 15 amps for two hours or 7.5 amps for three hours.

But you probably won't start off with 30 amps. If the battery is old, if it hasn't been properly maintained or if the system was under a heavy load when the failure took place, you can't rely on full battery capacity. Voltmeters are helpful, but remember that volts and amps do not dissipate at a linear rate and that it is possible for a battery to have almost no usable amperage while maintaining enough voltage to keep the battery relay switch closed. Ammeters, of course, tell you what is being drained from the battery, not how much is available.

Some pilots get themselves into trouble in a battery-power-only operation by complacency. Presuming the battery to be fully charged, they need ETA, battery amperage and electrical component power requirements to calculate how much equipment they can leave on and how many amps must be conserved for landing.

If conditions are ideal, you can get away with that—just as you can land with fumes in the fuel tanks if you know exactly how much fuel you have, exactly how much fuel the engines are using and exactly what time you'll touch down.

But if you're an advocate of defensive flying, we suggest you leave on only what equipment is absolutely necessary and take what action you can to render that equipment less necessary. One mechanic put it this way:

"The unknown factor is too great to play around with numbers; always assume the worst and turn off everything, then get the hell on the ground."

The point he was making is that you have no way of knowing how much power remains in the battery when you noticed that the generator or alternator dropped off line, nor how fast that remaining power is being depleted.

If the battery is old, its capacity may be off as much as 30 percent. Moreover, the drain from your battery may be greater than indicated on the ammeter for a number of reasons ranging from an inaccurate meter to a short in a system that does not report to the ammeter.

How quickly you turn off everything after a failure of the primary power source can make a significant difference in battery usefulness, especially if you're operating at system capacity. In fact, in some cases you can squander 50 percent of that usefulness by not knowing your airplane and fumbling around with the flight manual for several minutes to find out what that red light means.

Whether you hit the master switch, component switches, circuit breakers or bus switches depends on the aircraft you fly and its electrical system. The point is to know what to do and to do it quickly.

One pilot told B/CA his company has installed red colored circuit breakers for equipment that should be shed immediately and green breakers for less critical items.

Although we recommend proceeding with as little equipment in use as possible, a list of electrical equipment and individual power requirements can help you decide whether it is relatively safe to bring a certain appliance back on line. For instance, if you note that the landing lights draw nine amps you'll probably keep them off until just before touchdown. And if you see that the de-icing equipment requires 17 amps, you'll probably change altitude or take a chance on picking up ice.

On the other hand, you might decide to leave a navcom receiver on after reading that it uses only an amp or so. Naturally, you'll want to lower the gear by cranking, free-fall or other nonelectric method, if possible.

Again, what you can do without is a matter of circumstance and pilot judgment.

Some flight manuals, especially those for most light aircraft, do not provide lists of electrical equipment and power needs. You can compile your own, however, from data stamped on component information plates or component literature. Keep a list handy (a good place is with other printed emergency materials) and remember to update it as you add equipment.

If you don't like lists, you might consider individual component placards, but it's more convenient to have the information together. Of course, if you left the list in the flight operations office or can't locate it in the cockpit, placards will make guessing unnecessary (so will memorizing the highest drain items).

Circuit breaker ratings and ammeters that display actual current draw can also be used to find out which items need the most power. With an ammeter, for instance, you would note the difference in indications with an appliance on and off.

There will be some electrical items you won't be able to turn off, such as the clock, fuel gauges and other instruments. However, the drain from these items is negligible in most cases.

One thing you must thoroughly understand throughout this process, however, is what happens when certain electrical switches and appliances are turned off. For example, if you fly a Cessna Cardinal RG, a Piper Seneca, a Rockwell 112, or any of several other retractable singles and twins, are you aware that the gear will bleed down if electrical power to the hydraulic power pack is interrupted for any reason? In some situations the speed loss from dangling gear might be crucial.

You should also know what happens to various instrument indications when power to them is off. In some aircraft, an interruption of power results in the oil temperature indication going up into the red. In some, oil pressure goes to zero. Fuel gauges normally go to zero and in some cases fuel pressure and fuel flow may also go to zero. Those indications may give you quite a start if you aren't prepared for them.

Also consider what may occur within your fuel system when the power is off. You may not be able to transfer fuel from certain tanks with the power down. In some instances, fuel valves will not open and close and in still others automatic transfer functions do not occur which could result in electrical problems being compounded by loss of an engine or engines.

In that respect, certain emergency situations beyond the electrical failures will demand a change in your thinking in reference to which systems can be shed. Smoke in the cockpit from the electrical failure itself may demand that you bring the environmental blower back on line. An engine failure may require activation of certain circuits necessary to close firewall shutoff valves or to crossfeed fuel. If a collison threat is high, you may even be forced to bring up certain external lighting.

Those surprises can be avoided only by studying thoroughly the flight manual and systems descriptions for your aircraft.

You won't turn off anything if you aren't aware that a failure has occurred. Many aircraft don't have warning lights. But those that do aren't oversight-proof. Warning lights are supposed to activate when the electrical power falters and the load automatically (and quietly) switches to the battery, but bulbs can burn out and lights can be dimmed by a coating of dust or tars from cigarette smoke. Also, you may not notice a warning light if the sun is in your eyes or you're watching out for traffic.

In any event, as a hedge against failing to notice that an alternator has dropped off line, get into the habit of including electrical power meters in your routine instrument scan; even the simple automotive type ammeter, which shows only whether the battery is charging or discharging, will at least alert you if the system has begun drawing energy from the battery. Since with a full battery these simple amp meters tend to set at zero, we've made it a practice to switch on a landing light or the pitot heat at odd intervals during the flight to make certain the meter isn't stuck at zero. We also make it a practice to look before starting the engines, to note whether the generator or alternator lights come on when we flip the master switches on. Double-check the lights before takeoff if there are "push to test" buttons.

Jets and large piston planes have an elaborate network of warning lights and caution bells so that if something in the system develops trouble, it practically screams for attention.

Since the battery is your aircraft's standby power source, it should be capable of serving in that capacity at any time. Battery maintenance, therefore, is imperative.

Procedures vary with the type of battery, the aircraft it's installed on and

ELECTRICAL SYSTEMS

<table>
<tr><td colspan="5" align="center">Business and Commercial Aviation
ELECTRICAL FAILURE DATA SHEET</td></tr>
<tr><td colspan="5">Aircraft_________________________________</td></tr>
<tr><td rowspan="4">POWER CAPACITY</td><td>Bat. volt</td><td></td><td colspan="2" align="center">LIMITATIONS/NOTES</td></tr>
<tr><td>Bat. amp/hr.</td><td></td><td colspan="2"></td></tr>
<tr><td>Alt. or gen. amp/hr.
(total if twin)</td><td></td><td colspan="2"></td></tr>
<tr><td>Alt. or gen. amp/hr.
with 1 inoperative
(twins only)</td><td></td><td colspan="2"></td></tr>
<tr><td rowspan="22">POWER DRAW</td><td align="center">EQUIPMENT</td><td align="center">Amp/hr.
require-
ment</td><td align="center">Bat. de-
pletion,
30 min.
descent/
landing
(amps)</td><td align="center">Remarks</td></tr>
<tr><td></td><td></td><td></td><td></td></tr>
<tr><td></td><td></td><td></td><td></td></tr>
<tr><td></td><td></td><td></td><td></td></tr>
<tr><td></td><td></td><td></td><td></td></tr>
<tr><td></td><td></td><td></td><td></td></tr>
<tr><td></td><td></td><td></td><td></td></tr>
<tr><td></td><td></td><td></td><td></td></tr>
<tr><td></td><td></td><td></td><td></td></tr>
<tr><td></td><td></td><td></td><td></td></tr>
<tr><td></td><td></td><td></td><td></td></tr>
<tr><td></td><td></td><td></td><td></td></tr>
<tr><td></td><td></td><td></td><td></td></tr>
<tr><td></td><td></td><td></td><td></td></tr>
<tr><td></td><td></td><td></td><td></td></tr>
<tr><td></td><td></td><td></td><td></td></tr>
<tr><td></td><td></td><td></td><td></td></tr>
<tr><td></td><td></td><td></td><td></td></tr>
<tr><td></td><td></td><td></td><td></td></tr>
<tr><td></td><td></td><td></td><td></td></tr>
<tr><td></td><td></td><td></td><td></td></tr>
<tr><td></td><td align="center">Total</td><td align="center">Total</td><td></td></tr>
</table>

the frequency of use of that aircraft, but every operation should include some sort of routine for battery maintenance. Manufacturers can suggest specific steps and furnish you with maintenance booklets.

Insufficient maintenance is one of the major causes of battery failure. Also high on the list is abuse, such as making several engine starts in rapid succession without giving the generator or alternator time to replenish the battery and turning on lots of equipment immediately after starting the engines. Heat is a perennial battery enemy, and it can be produced not only by heavy electrical loads but also by tightly enclosed battery compartments that provide no vents for protection from ambient temperatures.

Aircraft that require large amounts of power for engine starts have battery temperature sensors and warning lights, and the battery should be removed from the plane and checked after a flight on which overheating occurred.

The use of ground starting units will help promote long battery life, especially if flight legs are too short to allow proper cooling and recharging of the battery.

Of course, batteries can be damaged by faulty electrical equipment itself, so regular maintenance of the system will help protect the battery—and discourage the development of a situation in which the battery is needed.

Faulty electrical equipment can damage more than the battery. The NTSB reports that a corroded bus bar panel was responsible for an electrical failure in a Beech 55 that subsequently suffered substantial damage because the pilot failed to properly lower the landing gear by emergency means and it collapsed.

Large aircraft often have, as standard equipment, auxiliary battery power packs that are independent of the main batteries and provide emergency power to some avionics and gyros.

In fact, FAR 121.305(j) airline regulations requires that large jets used

---

(1) Under POWER CAPACITY list the appropriate rating of the variable installed electrical generating and storage devices.

(2) Under LIMITATIONS/NOTES, list any restrictions or procedures applicable after an electrical failure, such as "Gear must be lowered manually," "Set transponder to 7700," or "Limit load to 90 amps with 1 alt. out."

(3) List electrically operated equipment that can be turned off in flight and individual amp/hr. requirements *in descending order* of power drain. We suggest that you list items that *must not* be shed in IFR conditions in red. You may also want to color code items that should be left on in various kinds of weather; the radar for instance in a thunderstorm situation.

(4) List the amps each item would deplete from the battery during an emergency 30-minute descent and landing. Notations will be one-half of figures under "Amp/hr. requirement" column.

(5) Under REMARKS, note any special equipment conditions or considerations. For landing lights, as an example, you might note "assume 3-min. use"; for flaps, "assume 30, no cycle"; or "If hydraulic pump is turned off, the gear may bleed down."

as air carriers have an attitude indicator that can be operated for at least 30 minutes on a source independent of the electrical generating system. Such equipment can also be installed on lighter aircraft.

As with any addition to your aircraft, check with the airplane manufacturer to determine if installation of a power pack is permissible.

Here is a summary of suggestions on how to prepare for a possible battery power situation:

• Review the principles of electricity and electricity producing appliances relevant to airplanes.

• Study the electrical system on your airplane and make a list of equipment that can be turned off in flight. Memorize flight manual procedures for coping with electrical problems.

• Make sure you know how electrical problems are manifested on your airplane and be on the alert for signs of trouble.

• If an electrical problem develops, try to correct it before resorting to battery operation.

• Land at the nearest airport if you can't correct the problem.

• While you're en route, use as little electrical equipment as possible—but don't turn off items that are essential to safety.

• Provide regular maintenance on the battery and electrical system in your aircraft.

How to Increase Starter/Generator Life   18

The principle of the starter/generator is almost as old as electricity itself. An electric motor is simply a loop of wire suspended between the poles of a magnet. When current is passed through that loop in the proper direction, the magnetic field is warped and the loop will turn 90 degrees. If the direction of current flow is then reversed, the loop will turn another 90 degrees in the same direction. If the power source is direct current, as it is from a battery, the current flow reversal is achieved with sliding contacts (brushes) on a split ring (the commutator).

By coincidence (courtesy of Mother Nature) a generator is also a loop of wire suspended between the poles of a magnet, and that loop and magnet are exactly like the one in the electric motor. If that loop is rotated by some outside means (such as being connected to the engine), current is induced in the loop each time it turns through the magnetic field. The only problem is, as the loop is rotated, the induced current keeps reversing and alternating current is produced. Guess what? To resolve that and produce direct current for compatibility with a storage battery, the induced current is picked off the loop with sliding contacts (brushes) on a split ring (the commutator).

It doesn't take a Thomas Edison to comprehend that the two machines just described are identical except for the way the current flows. Thus one machine will do both jobs if current from the battery is simply directed to the loop for starting, then a lesser amount to field windings (to reinforce the magnet) for generating current in flight.

Of course, this explanation is oversimplified—starter/generator engineers will cringe—but in a nutshell, that's how it's done. The advantages are obvious. One machine will do two jobs. That saves weight, cost and a drive pad on the accessory section of the engine. It also should save maintenance hours because there's only one machine to fail. But that doesn't work out in real life; more in regard to that later.

Although the basic principle of the starter/generator is simple, the engineer who designs one must know his business well. First, he has to somehow achieve a balance between starter torque and generator output. He can design in as much of either as is necessary, but the penalties for higher performance are weight and size. Weights vary from 16 or 17 pounds for a unit with a 100-amp generator output up through 35 to 40 pounds for a 400-amp machine. Starter/generators are from 5.25 to 6.5 inches in diameter and 8.0 to 12.5 inches in overall length.

The rotational speed also affects the maximum generating output. Earlier starter/generators in the 100- to 200-amp class turned at 7000 to 8000 rpm with the engine itself turning at normal cruise rpm. The modern trend is to turn the units at 10,000 to 12,000 rpm. It's harder on bearings and brush life, but higher rpm allows the engineer to achieve outputs of 400 to 600 amps while keeping the weight down to a reasonable level.

The starter/generator is connected to the engine with a splined shaft. Behind the splines, next to the mounting flange or face, the shaft is turned down—grooved—purposely to create a weak point, a fuse. If in the starting mode the machine applies more torque to the engine than the fuse limit, it snaps to protect the accessory case and internal gearing. Likewise, if in the generating mode the unit should hang up or begin to drag beyond the fuse limit, it snaps.

Normally, this fused spline end is separate from the primary shaft so it can be changed easily.

Internally, that loop of wire described above is multiplied many times to form the armature. The ends of the loops are connected to a segmented slip ring, the commutator. Carbon contactors (called brushes) ride on the slip rings to transfer current to and from the armature loops.

The armature shaft turns on bearings at either end of the starter/generator case. To cool the unit a fan is bolted directly to the shaft, normally at the commutator end. Since it turns at up to 12,000 rpm, the fan must be carefully designed, fabricated and balanced. In most cases it's a solid die-cast unit. Air is ducted, usually from outside the nacelle, to the fan, which then blows it through the unit and out exhaust ports at the other end. The air inlet and exit screens, as well as the splined shaft and fuse, can be seen in the photograph.

Starter/generator engineers design to a TBO of 1000 hours, with a brush replacement at about 500 hours. Manufacturers say their units routinely go to the 1000 hours with no attention other than one or two brush changes. That's quite at odds with what mechanics on business aircraft say. They're happy to get 300 hours between removals for some repair or other.

With older designs, the most frequent problem was—and is—a sheared shaft. Operators of older equipment have changed so many shafts they automatically assume that's the problem whenever they push the start button and nothing happens. In fact, however, the shaft problem is rare on new designs. Today, the problem is more often at the brush holder.

Interestingly, the cause of the problem is probably the same, but the effect has jumped from the front end to the rear of the machine. After talking with engineers and mechanics, we're convinced the problem all along has been excess current in the starting mode.

Figure 2 gives a clue as to what is often the cause of a sheared shaft. Most older starter/generators were rated at 1000 to 1100 amps maximum. But much higher currents are often pushed through them. There is a tendency to think that the more amperage the better, so ground APUs are set up a smidgen sometimes. Cross starts using power from the generator on the first engine started are common, and sometimes the pilot will even nudge the rpm up a bit over ground-idle to make certain he has plenty of current flowing.

The result is excess current to the starter. APUs putting out 1500 amps aren't uncommon. Nor is 1500 amps to the second, third or fourth engine started. In that event, as Figure 2 indicates, the torque applied to the engine may increase 60 percent and the fuse may let go.

To combat that, starter/generator manufacturers optimized their fuses to more closely match the structural capacity of the engines they start. On small capacity starter/generators, that was the end of the problem. Small capacity units are self-limiting on current flow. But on larger units, when the fuses stopped breaking (which unloads the unit electrically as well as mechanically) the problem jumped to the brush holder. As the high current flow pushed against the high torque, it would begin arcing from the brush to the brush holder. The brush (or brushes) float in the holder so they will stay tightly in contact with the commutator. The arcing would melt portions of the holder, resulting in the brush becoming wedged. With contact on the commutator broken, the starter/generator would cease to function.

Lear Siegler, which manufactures starter/generators for most turbine-powered business aircraft, including helicopters, first encountered this problem on the Citation. The fix then was a current limiter installed on the aircraft by Cessna.

When the problem popped up again, this time in spades on the 731 JetStar, Lear Siegler itself tackled the problem. Its engineers isolated the brush holder from the direct current flow. We're not sure just why that works, but in Lear Siegler's labs we've seen a demonstration to 1700 amps with no sign of arcing. The new units are in fact rated to 1700 amps. (Operators of 731 JetStars who want to incorporate this fix on their present starter/generators should contact AiResearch or Lear Siegler and ask about service bulletin 23065-01.)

Eventually, this approach will no doubt be taken with all starter/genera-

143

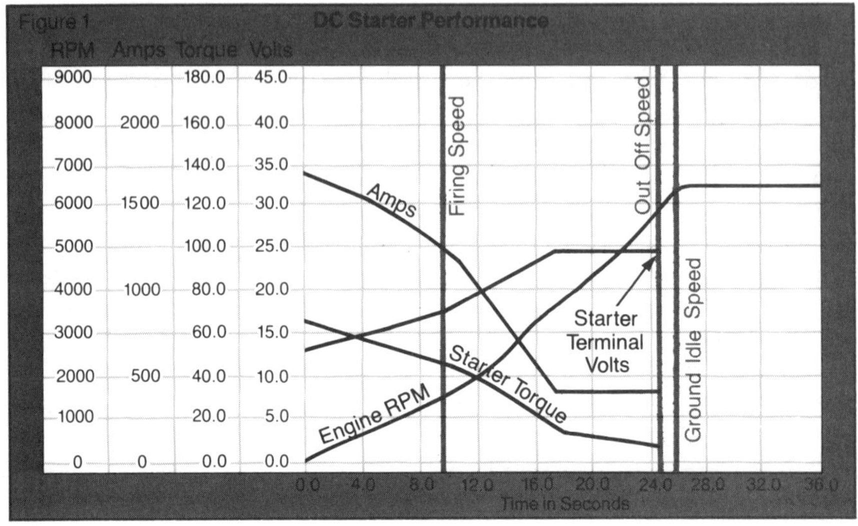

This graph shows what's going on inside a starter/generator in terms of current flow, voltage and torque during a cold-day start.

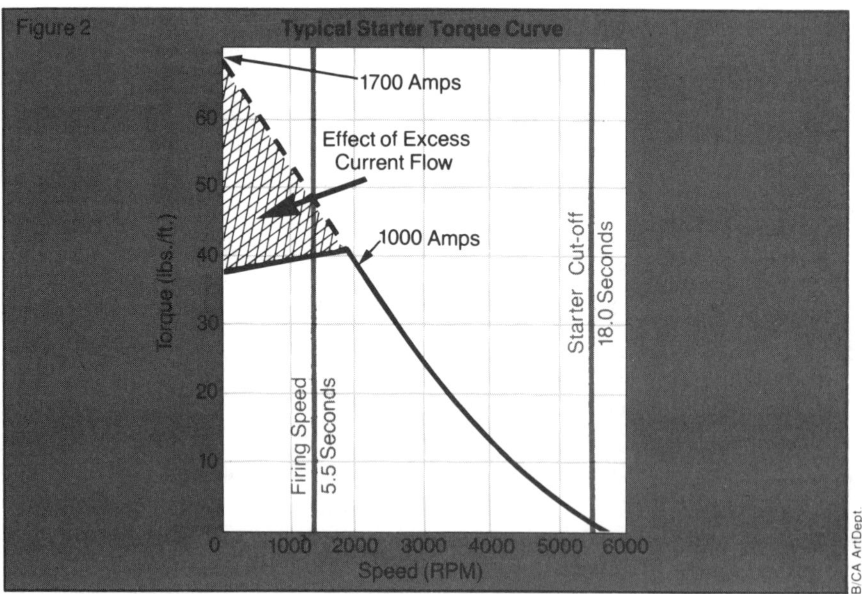

If too much current is supplied during the start cycle, torque may be increased 80 percent or more. This may cause a snapped shaft, brush arcing or even damage to the engine itself.

tors. In the meantime, operators can save themselves a lot of headaches by being more cautious about starting current flows.

Careful operators will not use ground power unit starts. They should at least insure that GPUs used are properly limited to 1000 amps. Cross starts should be conducted with caution. The rpm on the running engine(s) should be low. That varies with the aircraft, but Figure 3 illustrates what can happen. The current flow from generators and battery is cumulative in the start mode.

Of course, you do need enough current to get a cool start. But the point is, 1000 amps is enough. As Figure 1 shows, the current flow is down by the time the engine lights off anyway. So an extraordinarily high current doesn't help that much during the period when high torque is needed to hurry the engine through the hottest part of the start cycle.

After tending to the starting current, operators can further increase starter/generator time between overhauls with common sense and good maintenance practices. Contrary to what many think, virtually all the brush wear occurs in the generating mode, not in the start cycle. And brushes wear more as altitude increases. Certain contaminants in the air may also increase brush wear.

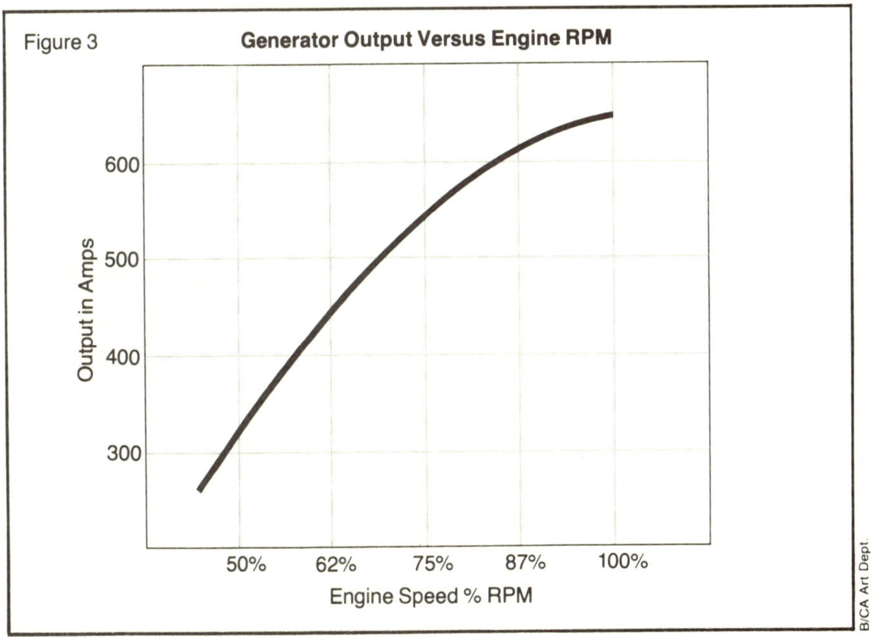

When engine speed is increased, the current output of a starter/generator increases quite rapidly. Thus, running the first engine up to get a better start on the second can result in excess current flow and starter/generator damage.

Wise maintenance people, and pilots, will watch those things. Brushes should be checked carefully at no more than 100-hour intervals.

At the same time, bearings should be carefully checked. The cooling system should receive special attention. The ducting is critical. If air can't reach the machine freely, overheating may result. This can affect the internal insulation. In extreme cases it can cause a breakup of the wire loops in the armature.

It evidently occurs rarely—we've never talked directly to a pilot who has experienced it—but a breakup of the armature can lead to an unbalance and, at 12,000 rpm the vibration could force a shutdown of the engine. An object in the ducting, perhaps resulting from a breakdown of the ducting itself, can also be sucked into the fan and unbalance it. Again, if the fuse on the drive shaft doesn't let go, the vibration might force an engine shutdown.

Finally, keep the generating load down as much as feasible. At an output of 300 amps in the generating mode, the unit may pull as much as 15 hp from the engine. That much work takes its toll on the machinery.

Starter/generators would probably be more reliable than they are now were it not for two factors.

First, manufacturers seem to get little direct feedback on problems encountered by their business aviation customers. The field service picture gets through to them somewhat distorted because it must often first bounce off the engine and/or airframe manufacturer. Also, problems often aren't the fault of the machine itself. If the starter/generator control unit malfunctions, the starter/generator itself may be damaged and get the total blame. With every starter/generator failure, the mechanic should check the control unit for proper operation.

Second, too often field service problems develop because the starter/generator manufacturer was not consulted when the airframe manufacturer wrote the starting procedure. As discussed above, engine rpm during a cross-start procedure is critical. But engine and airframe manufacturers want cool starts so they sometimes call for more rpm than really necessary to doubly insure an adequate current flow.

The basic starter/generator problem then is the age-old one of communications. Starter/generator manufacturers would do themselves and business aviation a favor if they would open direct lines of informational flow.

INTERIORS V

Aircraft interiors are not normally considered as a system and yet, to the occupants, they are the most obvious if not the most important part of the machine. A shabby cabin detracts from value, comfort and personal efficiency.

The business aircraft interior must be a pleasant combination of efficiency and elegance. Its design and installation requires the melding of several talents. Whether you are outfitting a new aircraft or refurbishing an older one, "The Inside Story" tells what you should know about where to go and what to get. This selection includes an interior checklist for coordinating each step of that operation.

Lightplane interiors take a terrible beating. Seats are routinely stepped on, food is spilled, and dirt accumulates in obvious but inaccessible places. In too short a time that new-plane-look gives way to the charm of a New York taxi. "Refurbishing a Small Aircraft Interior" covers the entire subject and considers several options.

Executive Aircraft Interiors: The Inside Story

19

by Gordon Gilbert

The business aircraft interior must be more than purely cosmetic. It has to be a combination office, den and conference room in the sky. Corporate aircraft interior design is no longer a matter of selecting a few fabrics or asking the opinion of the nearest secretary as to her color preference.

Far beyond eye appeal, a well-crafted, properly-installed and well-maintained interior involves considerations of soundproofing; weight and balance; comfort; utility, FAA regulations; care and maintenance, and maximum utilization of space.

Whether you operate the largest corporate jet or the smallest owner-flown business aircraft, selecting the right shop to do the installation, choosing the appropriate design consultant, deciding upon the kind of interior and following up on the actual work requires quite a lot of prior knowledge or experience in some of the facets of aircraft interior design and installation.

It all starts, of course, when the boss or aircraft owners decide to do a partial or complete refurbishment. When or how do you decide it's the right time for major cabin interior work to be done? Aside from the obvious requirement to do it when purchasing a new aircraft, there are several conditions that might call for major interior work.

For instance, the need to repair some minor fabric damage many times leads to a complete or partial interior replacement because it may require little or no more downtime, and thus the relatively small additional cost may make it more convenient and economical to do a refurbishment at the same time. In addition, when the operator/owner talks with an FBO about a repair, he may be getting exposed for the first time to what's really available in total interior designs. This leads many times to a refurbishment. Also, many corporate operators *continually* update their aircraft.

One G-II interior was redone after only five years because the owners wanted the advantage of new techniques and improved materials to insure that the cabin interior, like the cockpit avionics, reflected the latest in state-of-the-art.

On the other hand, an F-27 interior installed in 1958 remained unchanged until 1971. Then the only thing done was some minor upholstery replacement. Often, long-time ownership of an aircraft by one operator will lead to a new interior simply because the boss wants a change. Additionally, when there's an owner change, it's common to change the interior. Finally, operators anticipating sale of their aircraft may refurbish the interior to enhance resale value.

Let's suppose the owners have decided to do a partial or complete face-lifting on the inside of the cabin. The "inside" information follows.

Selecting and installing interiors for larger corporate aircraft (from the Sabre 60 up) is much more complex and costly than for smaller, owner-flown business aircraft. The larger plane has to be considered from a variety of quick-change utilization standpoints which can be anything from holding conferences to individual deskwork in the same cabin, and the additional equipment and safety regulations of FAR Parts 25 and 135.2.

Whether refurbishing or outfitting for the first time, there are three main ways to go: (1) let the aircraft manufacturer put in the interior, (2) have an FBO do the entire job or (3) hire an interior design consultant to create the plan and oversee the actual installation by second party specialists in interior furbishing.

B/CA doesn't recommend any one of these methods over the other. But one or another may be more suitable for your operation. For example, an independent design consultant will not only find the qualified FBO to do the work, he will also assign one of his staff to the project. This may be the preferred choice if yours is an operation which can't afford to spare a man or the time to find a qualified FBO and oversee the work. On the other hand, a flight department that has gone through an interior design project previously or that can spare a man to oversee the work, usually knows or can find a qualified FBO.

Once the decision is made as to the FBO or consultant to be used, *your* first step is to get the boss involved, if he's not already. After all, the interior must be designed and installed to meet *his* requirements, and it will save lots of time and money if his input is fed into the process right from the start.

The *designer's* first step is to ascertain the present and future uses of the aircraft. This is done at the initial conference with the company executives and the aviation department. This phase establishes basic requirements and gives the designer a mental picture of the aircraft's general flying and usage patterns.

There are certain things that must be known and specific questions to be asked by the designer if he is to develop a preliminary interior concept. In order for you to be prepared with answers and comments during the first sessions with him, here are most of the items owner and flight department should be agreed upon:

(1) *Average stage length.* The normal (not exceptional) stage length and the usual airports of operation will determine the need for extensive or modest lavatory, galley and sleeping provisions. If stage lengths include overseas flights, you'll have to think about life raft and survival kit storage space. If trips are commonly made to the northern latitudes, storage areas for cold weather survival gear must be considered.

(2) *Onboard activity.* This refers to the primary pastime when flying from point A to B. This is especially important because it determines the basic scheme of the main cabin: what kind and how many tables, seats, divans and cabinets, as well as the extent of bar, galley and entertainment provisions. The owners should mutually decide which of the following activities the aircraft will be (or is) *primarily* used for: conferences (with company personnel, customers or business acquaintances); individual desk work; leisure (cards, chess or other games); quiet; relaxation (with stereo); sleep; thinking and planning; phone calls (airborne telephone); reading; entertainment; dictation and typing (consideration for secretarial accommodations).

(3) *Desired impression of interior.* The interior can be custom designed to give a desired impression of the business of the company, the personality of the owner, or one of leisure and relaxation. Most corporate interiors are basically conservative with a tendency to get the office or living room up in the sky. Interiors have been done in exotic and even erotic style, but in that case the aircraft has obviously ceased to be a true business machine and so is outside the scope of this article.

Having the office or living room atmosphere "is all right because familiar surroundings make passengers feel better," says Dave Ellies, president of Dave Ellies Industrial Design. "But, avoid the tendency to put too much into the cabin and be open to innovative suggestions by the designer."

(4) *Number and type of passengers.* The flying executives should ask themselves: is the aircraft hauling a lot of people around and being used strictly as a mini-airliner, or is it transporting a few executives at a time? Is it the same group of passengers or constantly different persons? Are the passengers customers, company personnel or business acquaintances? Is the primary passenger an especially large or small person, physically handicapped or fearful of flying, thus requiring special design considerations? Are female passengers routine? Will pets or animals be transported regularly?

(5) *Basic materials and trim.* The design consultant or experienced FBO

will provide choices on color and material of carpets, seat upholstery, accessories and trim and will recommend what's best for your type of operation. You should listen to him.

The aircraft owner should be aware that the highest quality interiors consist of natural materials—wool, linen, mohair, leather, calfskin—and that it is uneconomical to hedge here. First off, since the labor of upholstering a chair or laying a carpet remains about the same regardless of what material is used, choosing the best is really only the difference between the per-yard costs of the various fabrics and materials. Second, a better-quality material is not only easier to install, but wears better and therefore lasts longer. Third, most high-quality fabrics are naturally fire-resistant and thus meet or exceed appropriate FARs without requiring fire-resistant treatments.

After the designer clearly establishes what type of trips you'll be taking, how often, how long, who the passengers are, what business activity will be conducted onboard and design preferences, he can prepare preliminary floor plans and rough sketches.

The professional consultant insures that the design concept reflects what the boss really wants and needs. In the case of Ellies Industries, for example, design consultants will visit your boss' offices to note its decor and the way he and his top executives dress. From this mental picture, Ellies can determine if the aircraft interior should reflect a corporate personality or an individual personality, a liberal theme or (most common) a conservative theme. The staff interior designer of the larger FBOs will provide this service also.

Through further discussion and consultation, a detailed floor plan is drawn with particular attention given to all furnishings and customer requirements. At this step in the process, company executives, flight crew and design team must be sure that all the interior items have been considered and decided upon.

In some special situations, like an original installation or a bunch of unique features, a full-scale interior mockup will be built.

In order to prevent oversights of essential items, a checklist/worksheet should be used. We have designed one that can be used ahead of time to give a thorough idea of everything you should be thinking about during the interior design stage *before* installation work starts. Our checklist/worksheet can also be used after the interior is completed to account for each item's proper installation. (It is also a valuable help in coordinating your exterior paint and trim design plans with the interior design.)

The smaller-aircraft operator and the businessmen pilot who flies his own aircraft should also use our interior design checklist/worksheet, although he faces a somewhat different set of problems than the owner of larger aircraft. First, a modest budget and cabinsize minimizes selection of materials and accessories. Second, the smaller business-aircraft operator usually resorts to the advice or service of an FBO who is not exclusively an interior specialist. Third, all too often, an FBO who also offers interior work may simply ask "What do you want?" and not ask the next crucial question: "What do you need?" Sometimes, getting what you asked for isn't necessarily what you need or what you *really* wanted after you see the finished aircraft. The result is aggravation, expense and wasted time.

We talked with several specialists in smaller aircraft interiors, including Jim Gionola, co-owner of Westair Interiors, Jefferson County Airport, Broomfield, Colorado. Realizing the problems that face the smaller and medium-size business aircraft owner in attempting to select an interior shop, we have these suggestions.

(1) *The facility.* Use *only* an approved aviation service center, either an FAA-certified repair station or at least a facility with licensed A&P mechanics. Believe it or not, some pilots have had furniture or auto upholsterers do an interior simply because it was cheaper and convenient. This is not only illegal, it can be dangerous. We know of an incident where carpeting was laid down in a single-engine business plane by a furniture upholsterer unfamiliar with aircraft. A hole was drilled that penetrated the floorboards *and* the elevator pushrod. A self-tapping screw was driven in and the elevator locked during takeoff rotation. It was only by brute strength that the pilot was allowed a more or less normal landing.

(2) *Material.* Since the smaller aircraft spends most of its life exposed to the elements, selection of the proper material is of critical importance to the life of the interior. A quality interior should last at least five years, depending on the amount of use and care.

Some of the olefins (herculon and vectra, for example) are susceptible to sun rot. In addition, these (and other synthetics) must be processed to meet FAR fireproofing standards. The chemical process of fireproofing not only accelerates sun rot, but creates corrosion where the material comes into contact with aluminum. We've also seen a once beautiful and expensive interior completely ruined by fireproofing treatment.

(3) *Soundproofing.* While your aircraft is "stripped" for interior installation, you should consider additional soundproofing. The most effective sound-deadening materials, like medicine, are hardest to take. These materials employ lead—lead vinyl and lead foam.

A severe weight penalty results when they are used extensively. When used only in the most critical areas, in concert with lighter materials, sound level decreases can be dramatic.

One highly effective method of reducing noise with minimum weight penalty is *vibration dampening.* The owner of a Cessna 320, for example, reports about the same noise level at takeoff power after his interior work as had been experienced at 68 percent cruise power. "Of course, in cruise it's now a dream," he says. Cost of soundproofing is about 10 to 20 percent of the complete interior cost.

Manufacturer's soundproofing methods on aircraft coming off the assembly line have improved greatly over the last few years. Some time ago, the Big Three, for example, began using more stringers, stiffeners, honeycomb panels glued in place and "monkey-skin" glued into critical areas. Some of these advances can be incorporated in your new interior.

(4) *Seats*. Seats are one of the most important items in an interior on any size business aircraft, but they are the real heart of the interior in a smaller aircraft in which occupants must remain seated throughout the flight.

Initially, seats should be completely stripped; mechanisms repaired; frames painted, and the foundation rebuilt to a bucket configuration using

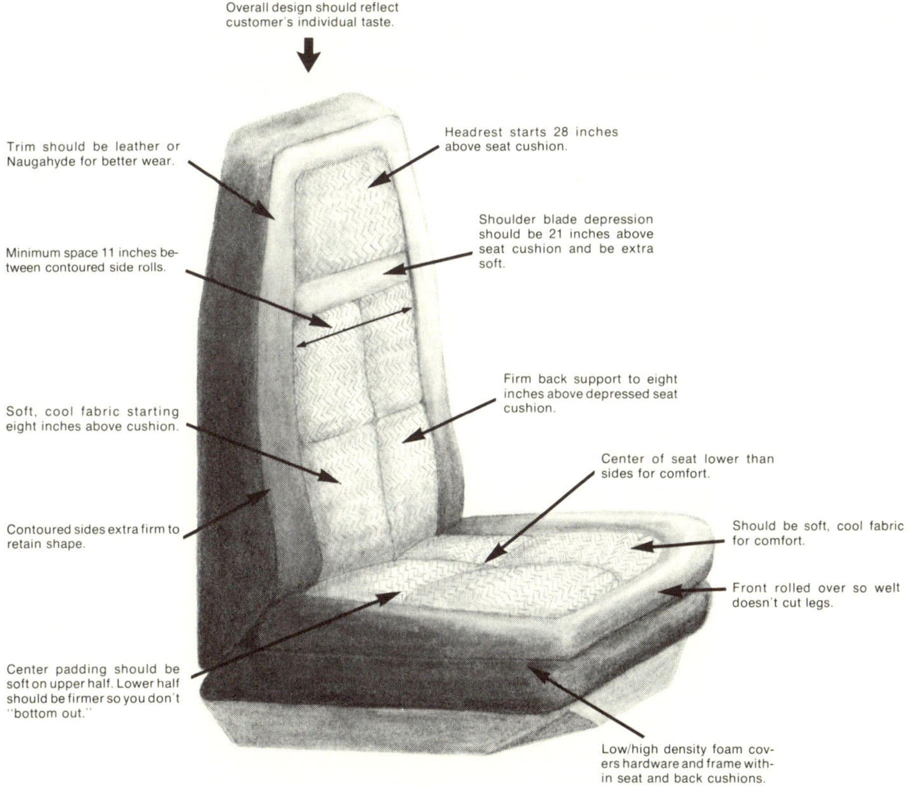

The seats, of course, are the focal point in any interior. Properly built, they not only provide increased comfort and beauty, but enhance durability as well. The principles illustrated above are generally the same for rebuilding a chair in a smaller aircraft as well as a larger one. However, smaller aircraft in which the occupants remain seated should have smaller and firmer chairs, contoured to the body. In larger aircraft, the seats should be larger and softer allowing the body to contour it. The same rules apply for smaller versus larger couches.

low and high density foam. The covering should then be made from quality and durable fabrics secured to the padding or foundation.

(5) *Interior design.* This is the most individual portion of the interior. After choosing the proper fabrics, material, texture and color, the *good* shop will sit down with you and design seat patterns and sidepanels to your individual taste. Even the standard black glareshield can be color-coordinated with a simulated suede material.

(6) *Interior paint.* There are only two basic rules regarding interior paint. First, below the bottom window line the paint should be somewhat darker. From the window line up to the headliner, the paint should be an off-white "leaning very subtly towards the darker color below." The secret is to avoid darker colors above the bottom window line. They tend to make the cabin "close in" and give a top-heavy effect.

The second rule of interior painting is that paints should be custom mixed to coordinate unobstrusively with the fabric colors selected.

You can expect your aircraft to be down at least two weeks for a complete interior redesign or refurbishment. For the same reasons mentioned in regards to larger aircraft—economy and convenience—the smaller aircraft operator should consider what other work might be done at the same time, such as rewiring, seats completely changed for a newer design or better articulation, vents revamped or relocated.

If the shop you go to gives careful consideration to at least the six points described above, you can be pretty certain you've found a reputable aircraft interior service center.

The traditional philosophy is to try and make the cabin look larger by making it look longer. This is wrong, says Ellies. All you get is a tube effect. The interior should be designed to make the cabin look *wider.* If this is done properly, the entire cabin looks larger. The wide look can be accomplished by a *lateral* treatment of the headliner. Since it has been easier to work designs longitudinally rather than laterally, the wide-bodied concept is catching on only slowly, but it's something operators should think about.

We warn against trying to shrink down an airline-type design scheme to make smaller cabins appear larger. This has been tried in not only custom interiors but also by one business jet manufacturer. The result is the cabin looks too busy and no larger. The design imperfections that are unobserved in an airliner are noticed in a corporate aircraft because it's like looking at the airline scheme through a microscope.

As for color, the key to making a smaller jet appear larger is "hue harmony." Lighter monochromatic colors are recommended. There should be little contrast and no very bright colors because "they tend to advance towards you" as Ellies puts it, "setting up uncomfortable eye vibrations."

Texture and subtle color changes can accomplish a lot. Patterns must be used carefully. Overhead and hidden areas should have a minimum of contrast and be uncluttered.

Since the seats are usually smaller than on a larger jet and are occupied for most of the flight, they don't need to be a flashy color. In smaller airplanes, Ellies says, "the passengers are the color. They fill up the interior and hide the seats when sitting down. Their different modes of dress provide all the color and contrast that accessories, decorations and pillows provide in larger aircraft."

So, now it's 30 to 90 days later and you're standing in the cabin admiring a brand new interior wondering how long it's going to look that sharp. The greatest threat to the appearance of a quality interior are punctures and stains. Punctures in fabric are normally caused by penetration from the following: silverware, mechanic's tools and shoe heels.

Maintenance personnel working in the cabin should be careful that tools are not protruding from back pockets and crewmembers should see that silverware is collected and stowed as soon as possible. Shoes should be removed if a seat must be used for a step ladder.

Stains are a more common malady, but easier to repair. The trick is to take care of them immediately after landing. The longer you wait, the harder they are to remove. Different stains require different treatments and cleaners.

There are several dependable stain removing products on the market (Servicemaster Equipment and Materials Co., Downers Grove, Illinois, offer a good selection) and even a special air-sickness cleanup and deodorizing kit from Sherwood Products, San Antonio Texas.

In the absence of these products, any mild detergent and a sponge will do. We wouldn't recommend this, but one operator we know discovered accidentally that a concoction of Duz dishwashing detergent plus 7-Up was a dandy spot remover.

In any case, for best results, treat stains promptly. First, a hidden part of the fabric should be tested to insure that the stain remover and method of removal is effective and not harmful. Second, stains should be lifted out by absorption rather than excessive rubbing. Third, several light spongings are better than saturation, which might cause another stain.

In addition to guarding against punctures and stains, occasional polishing of furniture and fabric with approved waxes gives added protection.

The carpet should be vacuumed regularly. Ellies suggests that when possible, an extra standby carpet be purchased at the same time if a removable carpet is installed. This allows the standby carpet to be put down if the original carpet must be removed for cleaning or repairing. (Buying both carpets at the same time insures they are identical in pattern, texture and color.)

155

	C	FC	MC	E	AC	B	G	L	BA
AIR CONDITIONING				■					■
VENTS AND AIR DUCTS				■					
CHART HOLDERS		■	■	■	■	■	■	■	■
MANUAL HOLDERS		■	■	■	■	■	■	■	■
FLASHLIGHT HOLDERS		■	■	■	■	■	■	■	■
PENCIL POUCHES		■	■	■	■	■	■	■	■
MICROPHONE HOOKS		■	■	■	■	■	■	■	■
CHECKLISTS		■	■	■	■	■	■	■	■
GLARESHIELD		■	■	■	■	■	■	■	■
OXYGEN STORAGE				■		■	■		■
FIRE EXTINGUISHERS				■		■	■		■
OBSERVER'S SEAT			■	■					
CREW PLAQUE				■	■				
CABIN INSTRUMENTS				■					
CALL BUTTONS				■					
INTERCOM				■					
TELEPHONE				■					
ENTERTAINMENT CENTER				■					
REMOTE ENTERTAINMENT SWITCHES				■					
CAUTION PLACARDS									
DOORS									
DIVIDERS				■					
LIGHTS									
CHAIRS				■					■
DIVAN	■					■	■	■	■
DESKS	■			■		■	■		■
CONFERENCE TABLES	■					■	■	■	■
GAME TABLES	■			■		■	■		■
TABLE COVERS	■					■	■	■	■
ASH TRAYS									
BLANKET/PILLOW STORAGE	■							■	
BULKHEADS									
CABINETS	■			■					
SHELFS	■			■					
CARPETS									
CUP HOLDERS									■
CUP DISPENSERS									■
WINDOWS									
CURTAINS	■								
DECORATIVE ACCESSORIES									
DECORATIVE PLACARDS									
TRIM									
SIDE PANELS									
MIRRORS	■								■
PROTECTIVE COVERS									
MAGAZINE RACKS	■					■	■		
HEADLINER									
BAR TOOLS	■	■	■	■	■			■	■
DECANTERS	■	■	■	■	■			■	■
ICE CONTAINER	■	■	■	■	■			■	■
SMOKE DETECTORS									
SURVIVAL GEAR STORAGE						■	■		
THERMOUS STORAGE				■					
COLD STORAGE	■	■	■	■	■			■	■
FOOD/CONDIMENT CONTAINERS	■	■	■	■	■			■	■
FOOD TRAY STORAGE	■	■	■	■	■			■	■
DISHES/SILVER/GLASS CONTAINERS	■	■	■	■	■				■
OVEN	■	■	■	■	■				■
COUNTER SPACE	■	■	■	■	■				■
FAUCET	■	■	■	■					■
TOILET	■	■	■	■			■		■
SINKS	■	■	■	■					■
SOAP DISPENSERS	■	■	■	■					■
KLEENEX/NAPKIN DISPENSERS	■	■	■	■					■
WATER HEATER	■	■							■
WATER TANK	■								■
ELECTRIC OUTLETS									■
COAT HANGERS						■	■		

156

EXECUTIVE AIRCRAFT INTERIORS

How long can you expect your interior to hold up? That depends on quality, use and care, of course. But under normal use and maintenance, a quality interior in a larger corporate aircraft should last at least seven years without noticeable deterioration.

Unfortunately, you cannot expect that same interior to last as long in a smaller aircraft. It simply wears out faster and requires more attention because passengers sit in the seats longer, walk over the same narrow track in the carpet and constantly rub against side-walls.

It's obvious that next to avionics, the cabin interior is the most important and costly consideration. You won't go wrong—or steer the boss wrong—as long as you remember that the cabin interior setup is as important to him as the cockpit setup is to you.

INTERIOR CHECKLIST. This checklist, or one like it, is designed to be used by the flight department, designer and executives throughout the refurbishing process. Ahead of time, it will help determine all the items you should be thinking about before installation work begins. During installation, it will help account for each item's proper installation. When considering each item, you should not only be thinking about its desired location, but also about its color, material, function and method of installation. For some items, we've colored-in those locations where you wouldn't normally need to consider an installation.

C—Cockpit	B—Bar
FC—Forward Cabin	G—Galley
MC—Main Cabin	L—Lavatory
E—Entrance	BA—Baggage Area
AC—Aft Cabin	

157

Refurbishing a Small-Aircraft Interior

20

by David N. Vine

The light plane is a marvelous and comfortable business tool that carries with it a lot of pride in ownership. But what happens when the assembly line spit and polish wears off? Frequent inspections and meticulous maintenance will keep your aircraft aloft, but periodically the interior will have to be ripped out and completely replaced.

Not surprisingly, there aren't too many facts around for the owner of single-engine and light-twin aircraft to consider after he's decided to refurbish his well-worn interior. Aside from doing all the work himself, there are only two possibilities. Although the most expensive of the two alternatives, the custom interior shop refurbish will result in your having exactly what you want in the way of color schemes and special attention. The other route is to order the needed components from a mail-order house and have your FBO install them.

There are various levels of quality in the custom job, usually directly related to the shop hours you're willing to pay for, but also contingent on the materials selected. On the other hand, a good interior refurbish can be done by many FBOs at rates for labor plus those mail-order parts.

The first thing you must do when the old, store-bought interior begins to look shabby is decide what you *really* want to do about it. If you just want it to look nice again, that's one thing. If you want a new interior that will reflect your personality or the nature of your business, that's something else. Or you may want to upgrade the comfort and quietness of your airplane.

Finally, you may wish to customize your aircraft. Perhaps you need more luggage area to carry around all those sample cases. Or perhaps you want an interior that's quieter and conducive to soothing clients' apprehensions about flying.

Each of those desires will require a different approach to the refurbishing adventure. So in the beginning, spend a lot of time thinking about just what your ideal interior would be like and how the current one should be altered to fit that ideal.

Don't give up any part of that ideal too easily. It's surprising what can be done in a small aircraft if you want it badly enough. We've seen a club seating arrangement on the right side of a Cessna 182, a wet bar in a Bonanza, a hidabed in a Cherokee Six and chemical toilets in several singles and light twins. We've seen special ashtrays for a pipe smoker, every conceivable sort of camera hatch, his-and-her suits that match the interior fabrics and we've ridden in several airplanes that were half as noisy after a custom interior job.

The limits seem not to exist.

When should the interior of a small aircraft be refurbished?

The answer would seem simple. When the fabrics have faded and begun to fray, replace. That answer overlooks a number of factors, however.

For example, if only the businessman owner and his immediate associates occupy the airplane, the interior can be allowed to run down a lot more than if customers or clients are often onboard. So, from that standpoint, the answer to when depends purely on the judgment of the owner. When he begins to feel uncomfortable with the appearance of the interior, it's time to refurbish it.

But another factor enters in. An interior renewal is an act of maintenance. It involves taking the seats and sidewalls out, carpet up and the headliner down. In a small airplane, it's an opportunity to inspect and repair parts of the structure and systems far more thoroughly and easily than during any other maintenance program.

That puts a different perspective on the "when" question. Considering the importance of this maintenance activity, we feel that the entire interior should come out at no more than eight-year or 2000-hour intervals.

Obviously, when it comes out, you'll want to have a really top flight inspection team go over the exposed areas. In every case, a critical area will have been laid bare. Wing carrythrough structure is in the cabin area and so are primary control cables or torque tubes, electrical wiring and environmental ducting. It must all be minutely inspected and even minor discrepancies should be corrected. It'll be far less costly in terms of shop hours to replace that aged wiring now compared to taking down the interior to get at it later.

Replace critical bolts in the area and search thoroughly for corrosion so it can be effectively treated when access is most conducive to doing it right.

Finally, this is the time to replace all the environmental ducting or hoses in the area that are subject to age deterioration.

Of course, from this maintenance standpoint, it makes little difference whether an interior kit or custom shop is used for the refurbish. But other considerations enter in. Let's examine them.

Several companies sell complete kits to replace seat upholstery, carpeting, side panels and headliners. One advantage to buying a mail-order kit is low downtime. Once the kit arrives, your FBO installs it after stripping out the old interior. A skilled man can do the job in a few days, particularly when the job coincides with other scheduled maintenance.

You *can* do some of the work yourself and it is a good opportunity to get familiar with your plane if you are the handyman type. But don't underestimate the downtime if you elect to do it personally. As a safe estimate, multiply the time the kit salesman claims by four.

You don't want to get involved in time overruns because once the job goes beyond the period you have put aside for it, business and family pressures may stretch it out to months. You can't have your business machine out of service that long.

When ordering a ready-made interior, it's essential that you give all the details including aircraft type, model, serial number, year of manufacture and any optional or non-standard seating arrangements. Don't forget to list optional headrests, armrests or third windows. It's not uncommon to find that a previous owner has replaced the seats with those from another type or model, so you'll have to fully identify the new seat.

Also, mid-year changes are sometimes made by airplane manufacturers that are hard to pinpoint by serial numbers. Never remove or destroy the old interior before all parts of the new one has arrived and proper fit is insured.

If in doubt when ordering, send a picture along to show the part in question. In case of a misfit, a reputable mail-order firm will exchange the affected parts.

To assure a good match, all parts of the kit should be ordered at the same time. And in the event something must be exchanged, do so quickly. The same batch of fabric may not be available at a later date.

Here are some other things to watch out for when ordering a mail-order kit are:

Headliners—Be sure you're getting all the inspection-opening zippers, attaching strips and bow channels as in the original. Also, headliner material should be a fire resistant vinyl or other man-made fabric. Natural fibers may not meet FAA fire resistance requirements.

Wall panels—Make sure these are genuinely new, not just recovered units. If they are on aluminum panels, be sure the old upholstery is removed; if the base panels are fiberboard, insist on new fiberboard. Panels should be padded to mask any surface irregularities and thus give a more luxurious finish. If the originals had armrests, check to be sure these are included.

A well-designed wall panel set will include kick panels of carpeting along the lower edges so the panels will not be defaced by hard wear. Map and certificate pockets are desirable.

Chair upholstery—Be sure your order is not for a simple set of seat covers. This is particularly important if your chairs are the contoured bucket type. Slip covers will not follow the contours. A well designed set will include more than just the seat fabric. The outer panels should be padded with foam and lined with dacron. This provides a surface that fills out any irregularities. The lining adds strength and provides a slippery inner surface so the assembly can be drawn easily over the cushioning.

Seat surfaces should be finished in a woven, breathable fabric. All-vinyl seats can be uncomfortable in direct sunlight—especially in low-wing aircraft.

Carpets—Carpeting should be supple enough to conform to tunnels, housings and other areas of irregular shape. Avoid thick shag carpeting because it can foul seat rollers and tracks. Heel scuff pads—preferably aluminum ones because plastic may break—near the rudder pedals are desirable.

In many instances, carpeting should not extend to the firewall under the rudder pedals. For one thing, it could come loose and foul the pedals. In other cases it will be subjected to leaking hydraulic fluid from the brake master cylinders. Check that out carefully. A good carpet set will extend the full length of the cabin, including the baggage compartment area. All track slots should be bound and all snap buttons should be identical to the original. A pure nylon rug is said to be the most durable and easiest to keep clean.

The big advantage to a custom job is that you get exactly what you want. You deal face to face with craftsmen, or a craftsman, willing to accommodate your design whims. It's your money, so they'll do anything you wish as long as you authorize the shop time.

Custom interior prices begin at about $1500 for a simple spruce up and clean up and range to the-sky-is-the-limit. For a four-place single or light twin, figure on $3000, minimum, for a first-class job. (1978 dollars)

The price will be lowest—and the downtime used most efficiently—if the interior work is combined with new exterior paint by the same shop.

While he may not charge you $3000 to $4000 for a custom interior, watch out for the fellow who works out of his van on the ramp. He may well be a skilled craftsman turned maverick, but let the buyer beware. On the other hand, there are many small, sometimes one-person aircraft interior shops around the country that do excellent work at reasonable prices. Often these shops will install a combination custom/mail-order interior at a very reasonable cost. Or they will do partial jobs for you, perhaps redoing the chairs, but only touching up wall panels and trim.

161

In the executive world, personal style is important. It's reflected in many ways and is an individual thing. Style can reflect leadership and a taste for elegance. But factory interiors are mass produced in all but the most expensive aircraft models. They are stamped out of plastic, using bland colors that will not offend any buyer and are designed mostly for utility. That's the attraction of a custom refurbish; you can express yourself and tell a lot about your life and business style by selecting the right colors and features.

Custom shops like to feel out the customer for his color preferences. Occasionally, a company color scheme is used, but most often interior colors are chosen with regard to the exterior color. Though they don't necessarily have to match, the colors should not clash. Loud combinations such as red and blue or red and green are usually in poor taste. The best selection is often a base and trim in the same color, but not necessarily in the same shade. This provides the popular "two-tone" effect.

An owner's mood and personality can be woven into the interior color scheme. But think carefully before selecting something wild and outlandish. When the novelty wears off, it can be very disappointing. Also, if you decide to sell the aircraft for any reason, your entire refurbishing investment may be lost. You might even be forced to unload it. Few people want to be the *second* owner of a jazzy, talked-about airplane. Relaxing, warm interiors are considered best for business aircraft. Earth tones such as golds and beiges often work well.

The custom shop will have styling expertise to help you. "When an individual brings in a plane, we sit down and show him pictures of interiors similar to his that we've done," says Jack Palmer of Palmer Airmotive, Wellsville, New York, a well known northeastern interior and paint shop. "We pick out a fabric that has the colors he likes. Everything is then built around that fabric."

"Occasionally we'll sketch a design on paper," says Palmer. "We'll draw the side panels and give the customer an idea of the perspective lines and whether he wants buttons. We make rectangular buttons, square buttons, round buttons and the size and shape of those selected has an effect on the overall job." Use of buttons in the design depends on how busy the fabric pattern is. Plain fabrics may need buttons to set them off while busy designs need none.

"We normally ask the client if he would like a sports-car type atmosphere, or office or business type. Conservative or sporty would sum it up," says Palmer, adding "What is difficult is conveying to the customer how the finished product will look. This is where I have to guide the customer carefully, so he gets a picture in his mind of the way it's going to look when it's done."

Palmer suggests light-colored headliners. Drapes should be a solid color and must blend and transition from the headliner to the normally darker sidepanels.

Color choice is not entirely an esthetic matter. Climatic considerations may influence it. "Take the south Florida area for example," Palmer explains, "where an airplane sits out a majority of the time. In that case, one thing you have to take into consideration in fabric selection is that it may fade, so it has to be sun resistant. Also, you must lean toward a lighter color interior because of the heat. If you choose a black vinyl seat, you get into the airplane down there and you'll fry before your body temperature cools down the fabric," Palmer adds, "I'd rather have a cloth seat because cloth does not hold the heat like vinyl."

Vinyl would be preferred over leather in tropical areas since leather may rot. Vinyl, unlike leathers, is resistant to abrasive action. It has color throughout where leather is surface dyed. Scratches on leather will show. Also, it must be periodically cleaned with saddle soap or it will dry out and crack. However, there is nothing so luxurious as the feel of softworn leather.

If you choose leather, insist on seeing an interior that the shop has done that is at least two years old. Some shops have a way of making new leather look like last year's vinyl. Other shops turn out leatherwork that wears poorly. After a couple of years it looks like 10 years later.

Some of the better quality vinyls, on the other hand, look and feel like leather. Quality materials can be expected to last eight to 10 years, given reasonable care. This includes cleaning and conditioning vinyl with any one of the numerous vinyl conditioner/waxes. The household cleaner Fantastic is recommended for cleaning.

A custom shop will pay particular attention to the seats, stripping the chair right down to the metal frame. They'll sand and repaint the seat frame and replace any broken parts.

It is possible for a custom shop to consult with the doctor of a person who has back problems before building up the cushioning. Extra padding can be added to give support to critical areas in an effort to relieve some stress a person with back problems might encounter.

Short pilots can get a boost from a custom redo of the interior. The type of foam rubber used in the seat can be selected to raise the pilot up several inches. High-density foam may be used in this case. It has less compressibility. Or more low-density foam may be used to jack up a short pilot who also demands a soft seat.

On occasion, two pilots of radically different heights may use the same plane. Removable wedge-shaped cushions can be made for the shorter pilot to use when he flies.

Everyone agrees that the addition of a shoulder harness to the seat belt system will give the occupants of a light plane a much better chance for survival. Of course, it's a good idea to have them added along with the new interior.

They cost as little as $200 if done during an interior refinish—and it's a wise investment. It's possible that the FAA may eventually require a retrofit no matter how old the aircraft.

Many airplanes have wasted space under the seats that can become handy for storage with the addition of aluminum compartments with drawers. The cost for this extra is about $50 per seat. Usually there isn't much room for the addition of cabinets or writing desks in the single or light twin, though if an owner insists, a light-weight structure can be fabricated of honeycomb aluminum covered with leather or wood veneer.

But extras need not be so elaborate. While the interior is out, a number of relatively inexpensive little extras can be applied here and there that will increase comfort greatly.

First is the environmental system. Unfortunately, the airframe manufacturers are very backwards about offering upgrading kits, but before the refurbishing begins you should check—or have your shop check—with the factory customer service department to find out what's available.

If the airplane is more than five years old, chances are the heating and ventilation systems on newer models have been improved. In some instances, a few parts and a good sheet metal mechanic will make your old airplane as good as a new one from the ventilation standpoint.

Don't overlook the possibility of a field modification—thought up by you or your mechanic—that will improve the environmental systems. That can be as simple as straightening out kinks in the flexible ducting and taping joints to improve the airflow.

Also, tell your mechanic to look for airleaks in the airframe itself that can be easily stopped up. This is the time to replace boots, seals and whatever where control rods, gear actuators and so on pass through the cabin area.

Next, you and your mechanic should study the noise situation. Perhaps the things you did to the environmental systems helped. Air moves through those environmental ducts and air is noisy. Study that and you may decide to wrap some sound-deadening material around the ducts in your noise-abatement efforts.

But the more productive thing to do is study the latest model of your aircraft type. Manufacturers have lately been taking a hard look at interior noise and they've found it to be a black art. Things that should make an interior quieter don't; things that should have no effect, do. Try to cash in on their trial-and-error research. If you or your mechanics possibly can, get a look at a new model with the interior out. If the opportunity arises, drop by the factory.

Examine the new acoustical materials used and how they're laid. Remember, it's not how much, but where, sound deadeners are used. Look also for skin stiffeners not on older airplanes in the series. Often an entire interior noise reduction program reduces to a stiffener that stops the drumming in one skin panel. If you can discover and adopt it, it will give you double value on your new interior.

Again, look carefully at openings in the firewall, the rear bulkhead, in the floorboards and between the cabin area and the wing roots. A lot of cabin noise is amplified forward from the tail cone or the wing. Sometimes just sealing openings—especially openings around stringers and other structures that pass from the tail or wings into the cabin—with several layers of tape will quieten the cabin of an older airplane greatly.

Some of this, of course, is blue-skying. But the whole idea of an interior refurbish is to increase comfort and pride of ownership. Therefore, think of all the angles carefully before committing to this $1500 to $5000 investment.

The value you receive will increase almost linearly with the amount of creative thinking you do before the job actually begins.

AVIONICS: GENERAL

VI

In recent years avionics have expanded enormously in application, complexity, variety, and cost. Even a modest installation may include a dozen components. More elaborate systems may cost as much as the basic air frame in which they are installed. Perhaps even more important, avionics have become absolutely essential for safe, efficient flight. In years to come these electronic components will continue to proliferate as electrical magic assumes more and more authority in the airplane.

It is a measure of the impact of avionics that this volume contains three separate sections devoted to that subject. We begin with the selection, installation and appreciation of those mysterious black boxes, move on to individual avionics components then provide tips for proper avionics operation and care.

When the time comes to replace your airplane's avionics you may find a bewildering number of options. There are no simple answers, only questions. "The Avionics Replacement Decision" can help you find the right answers for your operation.

Owners of cabin-class airplanes must decide between avionics components which mount directly in the instrument panel or the larger units which are remotely mounted. It can be a tough decision. "Panel Versus Remote-Mounted Avionics" compares those two options.

Sometimes it is possible to modify existing avionics components and bring them up to the latest state-of-the-art performance. "Update Your Avionics" will show you how to dig out the manufacturer's modification bulletins, which are a gold mine of data on repairing and preventing problems as well as enhancing performance. You may not need new avionics after all.

Just when you think you understand avionics, we will get to autopilots. Those electro-mechanical robots have grown so complicated that the nomenclature alone is intimidating. "Autopilot Watchamacallit" opens up the whole subject.

The Avionics Replacement Decision

21

by J. Mac McClellan

The avionics replacement decision is one of the most difficult facing an aircraft operator. The problem is that several choices are involved.

The first, and often the most difficult, decision is when to replace. Next, you must determine which elements require replacement. And, finally, there is the task of choosing a replacement brand of avionics.

We expend a great deal of effort informing you of new products and developments in avionics but little has been done to help an operator decide when to purchase this new equipment. That's because there are no hard and fast answers. Avionics replacement requirements depend on so many factors that no fixed set of criteria can provide an answer.

But a review of these factors will help you reach a correct decision.

Avionics should be replaced for several reasons, including: to satisfy new regulations, to increase reliability, to add new capability, to save space and weight and, finally, to take advantage of new features that can ease pilot workload.

The most obvious replacement decisions will involve regulations. Transponders have gone through mandatory changes as the Air Traffic Control Radar Beacon System (ATCRBS) has developed. Mode C altitude reporting became a requirement for admission to more and more airspace. But if your transponder satisfies the present rules it should continue to do so for the rest of its life.

The so-called split channels that make up the 720-channel com system are being implemented for high altitude enroute communications, however, so it would be worthwhile to update to 720-channel com capability if you operate in the flight levels.

Another regulatory change that could impact avionics is possible revisions in DME requirements along with the proposed drop in the floor of positive control airspace.

Probably the most common reason for replacing your avionics is increased reliability. Ten-year-old avionics are generally full of components like tubes and mechanical movements for crystal switching, and these have limited life cycles.

Current production avionics avoid many of the problems that made older equipment unreliable. No tubes are used except in the final transmitter stages of transponders, radars and some DMEs. Single-crystal synthesizers really simplify the mechanics involved in frequency selection. In addition, solid-state components operate at low voltages, reducing heat problems, and integrated components have reduced the parts count.

Airlines are experiencing mean times between failures (MTBF) of up to 4,000 hours, even on DMEs. That represents many years of typical business or corporate flying time. But modern avionics seem to be as susceptible to calendar time as to operational time so business operators won't enjoy 4,000 hours MTBF unless that much can be flown in two or three years. But new avionics are capable of incredible reliability.

Taking advantage of the potential reliability of new generation equipment is not without risk, however. A significant percentage of all avionics problems, maybe half, are installation related. New avionics mean a new installation and the threat of new installation problems.

Another consideration to be dealt with before replacing for reliability is deciding when your present avionics are unreliable. How many failures can you tolerate? We can't answer that, but major factors in your decision should include downtime and dispatch reliability. If downtime and lack of dispatch reliability are especially costly for you, avionics updating becomes more attractive. If you can afford downtime for repair without a great deal of inconvenience, old avionics can be nursed along indefinitely before the repair bill adds up to the price of a new system.

But as avionics age, expect the downtime for each failure to increase. Components will become more difficult to find; factory support will diminish after a time and technicians will be less familiar with older units.

The trade-in value of your old avionics also should be considered as part of the equation. If you wait too long, the value of your present avionics will be negligible. Trading in old equipment while it is still in good condition and only one generation old increases its value and can help lower the cost of a new system.

The desire to add new capability is another reason for replacement. For example, if you want to add RNAV it may be necessary to replace your old DME. Adding an RMI will involve the nav receiver and compass system and some changes may be required. The thing to remember when you consider adding new capability is to take into account all elements involved in the avionics system, not just the price of the RNAV or whatever.

If your avionics are at least 10 years old, weight and space saving are factors in the replacement decision. A decade ago most panel-mounted navcoms required a remote power supply. Panel-mounted transponders were uncommon as were high performance panel-mounted DMEs.

But no current panel-mounted avionics require a remote power supply, and the transponder has become small and relatively inexpensive. Panel-mounted DMEs perform virtually on a par with remote units.

If you operate a turbine airplane with old Arinc format equipment, the change to new non-Arinc remote equipment could reduce space and weight requirements by more than half. For example, a Wulfsberg WT-200 com for general aviation is less than half the size and weight of the WT-2000 Arinc com, though both have very similar performance specifications. The Collins Pro Line and King Gold Crown avionics lines weren't available 10 years ago and either system can save more than half the space required for Arinc avionics with nearly identical performance.

Finally, your decision to replace can be based on new features that help ease pilot workload. Frequency preselect features, frequency memories, digital RMI features and automatic squelches all can help you do your job better. Are they worth the cost of a new avionics system? Only you can say.

You've considered all the factors and reached a decision to update your avionics. Now, which units should you replace?

We can find no convenient answer to that question but there is general agreement that if you're going to tear up the airplane for an avionics installation you should do as much work as possible at one time. If you replace equipment on a piece-by-piece basis, the installation simply can't be as clean and effective as is possible otherwise.

Downtime enters the picture again because installation of a completely new panel will require far less time than the sum of time for piecemeal avionics replacement. Wear and tear on the aircraft also is saved if the interior and panel are disassembled only once.

Moreover, selecting a completely new panel will enable you to take advantage of integrated systems such as the KNS 80. In one navcom-size box the KNS 80 provides VOR/LOC, glideslope, DME and RNAV functions. Another example of integration is the Narco Nav 122, which contains the VOR/LOC and glideslope receivers in a three-inch diameter unit that also includes indicator, marker lights and frequency selector. Such integrated systems save weight, space and a great deal of money but offer no direct replacement of a single older unit.

Remote avionics, however, can be updated one unit at a time. There exist adapter mounts and connectors that allow a new com or nav to be slipped into the old Arinc-size mount without any wiring changes. In any case, control heads of the avionics usually can be changed without a total rewiring in between.

In general, however, we recommend that once you send your airplane into the shop for avionics replacement you go for as much as the budget will possibly allow. You'll get a better deal on the avionics, a more effective installation and the airplane will be more attractive at resale time with a logical avionics package rather than a hodgepodge of equipment.

Updating weather radar or flight control systems involves considerations beyond those for the nav/com/transponder package.

Weather radar is an independent system that is in no way connected with other avionics systems. Also, it's a field of avionics experiencing very rapid development. Updating your radar can mean changing from a daylight storage tube (DST) to digital indicators but retaining other major system components, or it can mean changing your monochrome digital indicator for a color indicator. Or it can mean getting rid of an older, heavy system in favor of one of the new light, digital products.

The important thing to remember about radar is that the basic receiver-transmitter hasn't changed much recently with virtually all major improvements coming in the indicator. Bendix and RCA have offered kits to update a DST system to digital and may have such an option for your system. If so, that is an effective way to modernize your radar.

Whether and how to update your flight control system is the most complex of all decisions because of the certifications involved. Each flight control system must be granted a supplementary type certificate (STC) for every type of aircraft in which it is to be installed. The larger your aircraft the fewer systems that will be certificated for it, until you reach the G-II that so far has had only one autopilot throughout its production.

Piston aircraft operators will have the largest selection of flight control systems but the newest systems may not be certificated for older aircraft. The point is to be certain to investigate fully.

Typically, however, an HSI can be changed without involving the autopilot. Adding an HSI should have little impact on the overall avionics system except that in some cases a VOR/LOC converter must be added.

If your avionics are troublesome or you need additional capabilities, keep the overall picture in mind. Consider the trade-in value of your old equipment, the availability of new integrated equipment and the weight and space saving factors. The price of the new equipment and the value of your trade-in are going to be better if you buy an entire system.

By taking advantage of the new integrated avionics units, you may be able to upgrade several functions for little more than it costs to replace one unit that is giving you problems.

A new avionics system won't mean an end to avionics failures but when problems do occur, having current equipment with a coherent installation will shorten downtime and lower repair costs. Finally, consider your airplane's value, which will be increased by the new avionics system.

If you do replace equipment one piece at a time, have an idea of what your final avionics system will be because your overall plan will affect early decisions. This approach is vital for complex integrated systems like the Bendix BX 2000 and Narco E-Line, which offer features like keyboard tuning but must be packaged as a complete system to provide their full potential.

Panel Versus Remote-Mounted Avionics $\qquad$ 22

by J. Mac McClellan

Selecting avionics is a hassle for every aircraft operator. There are so many competing systems with so many features one can hardly keep track of them all. But the cabin-class piston or turboprop operator faces a tough additional choice deciding between remote-mounted or panel-mounted equipment.

We say this is a problem for the cabin-class operator because the decision comes quite easily for operators of smaller aircraft to go with panel-mounted, while jet operators automatically opt for remote-mounted equipment.

As little as a decade ago the choice didn't exist. Full capability avionics for cabin-class aircraft came only in remote-mounted packages. But electronic development has made it possible to put all functions in a panel-mounted box.

In general, panel-mounted equipment is lighter and less costly than equivalent-purpose equipment in remote-mounted form. Some may argue that remote-mounted equipment is built to a high standard of quality and performance, and that is true. But the fact remains panel-mounted equipment is doing the job well in smaller aircraft and that won't change when it's in a bigger airplane at a higher altitude.

If reliability is your only concern you could buy two of everything in the panel-mounted form for about the price of a single remote-mounted system and increase your total reliability as well as redundancy. But we don't think reliability is an issue in this decision because either type can be reliable.

You don't have to be a 30,000-hour captain to remember the days when a broom handle was an essential avionics massaging tool. A good swat was often required to get sticky resolvers and gears moving inside a nav receiver or to encourage a com transceiver to re-channel.

The first automatically tuned transceiver was developed by Collins during World War II. The "Autotune," as it was called, gave the Allies a leg up on the competition because frequencies could be quickly rechanneled in flight.

The Autotune unit used moving gears to change crystals and match coils to tune the transmitter and receiver. Moving synchros and gears remained a part of remote-mounted avionics until the current generation, which uses electronic frequency synthesizers capable of generating all frequencies in the band from a single or few crystals.

With the original maze of mechanics as well as large vacuum tubes and transformers, it's not hard to see why avionics wouldn't fit in the panel.

This is a short history of how avionics developed and why large aircraft became committed to remote mounting of avionics.

During avionics development the one thing that hasn't changed is the control head. The heads, often called Gables heads for the company that has made most of them, generally come in a single 2.5-inch width or a 5.75-inch double width. This small size enables the control head to fit in panel or pedestal locations not large enough to accommodate panel-mounted radios.

The flexibility of the control head may be the single most important reason for selecting remote-mounted radios for the cabin-class aircraft. Because quality, full-performance, panel-mounted radios are typically much newer than the design of cabin-class aircraft panels, no provision has been made for mounting panel-mounted avionics in many aircraft. Rather, aircraft designers have only been able to fit remote-mounted avionics control heads into whatever space was left over after other aircraft controls and instruments have been installed.

A King Air panel provides an excellent example of the flexibility control heads offer. A radar, eight or more control heads plus audio controls all fit neatly in the center panel. Installing the equivalent panel-mounted avionics in the same space would be difficult because of the 6.25-inch standard width of most units.

Many of the cabin-class airplanes have customized instrument panels with the heads mounted in odd patterns to take advantage of any unused space on the panel. Installing equivalent panel-mounted avionics in that same space is going to be tough.

The bottom line is that control heads give you nearly total freedom to use whatever space the airframe designer has left over. (Some cabin-class airplanes, such as the Piper Navajo, have made reasonable provisions for installing panel-mounted avionics, however.)

Another major advantage of remote-mounted avionics is the easier capability to cool them, especially in a pressurized airplane. Excess heat may be the biggest reliability problem for all avionics and it is generally easier to cool avionics outside the pressure vessel than behind the panel.

Mounted in the nose or other areas outside the cabin, avionics can be cooled with outside air. Inside the pressure vessel the best that can be done is to circulate cabin air behind the panel with a blower. Nonpressurized airplanes can use outside ram air to provide cooling just like most lighter airplanes do.

Remote-mounted avionics are not immune to heat problems, however. Often the remote boxes are packed in around other heat generating devices, like gyros, that can contribute to the problem. Cool air must be directed to the units themselves.

A final advantage of the remote-mounted avionics is their flexibility in systems integration. For example, automatic navigational systems from Collins, Garrett, Sperry and others can automatically tune standard remote avionics but would not work with panel-mounted equipment.

Remote-mounted systems also offer the flexibility of manual or electronic tuning heads or keyboard schemes. Also, system features like manual or automatic nav receiver outputs are available for RMI use with either sine-cosine or three-wire schemes. DMEs have the standard outputs to drive flight director displays. The important factor is that advanced flight control systems were designed to interface with remote-mounted avionics and a change to panel-mounted equipment can cause interface problems.

Advantages of panel-mounted equipment are that they are more compact, lighter, less costly and offer a greater number of features from more manufacturers. Panel-mounted avionics have progressed so much in the past decade that few actual performance differences remain between top-line, panel-mounted avionics and remote-mounted equipment.

For the most part, panel-mounted equipment costs half or less as much as remote-mounted equipment. Panel-mounted avionics are generally less costly to install because the control head is self-contained, eliminating necessary wiring by more than half.

Virtually all panel-mounted avionics manufacturers now offer higher power transmitter options which would be helpful to higher altitude operations. The higher power does have a drawback in that it creates more heat.

Because of the lower initial cost of panel-mounted equiment it would be economically feasible to maintain spare units either in the aircraft or at home base.

Panel-mounted avionics are shrinking in size and may soon be small enough to provide the mounting flexibility of control heads. The new Silver Crown units from King are the smallest overall, but the Collins Micro Line offers a little extra flexibility because the coms and navs may be mounted in separate units.

It will soon be possible (if it isn't already) to build a panel-mounted avionics unit the same size as a control head, for remote-mounted avionics, but the panel-mounted unit would be deeper.

Perhaps the largest edge panel-mounted avionics now have is additional features for the price. Frequency memories, electronic readouts and digital RMI functions are all very popular. Collins is offering electronic control heads for remote-mounted avionics, but that will be much more costly than the panel-mounted systems.

If you're specing out avionics for a cabin class aircraft the first thing to consider is the panel itself. Will the panel-mounted avionics you want fit neatly in the available space? If so, we would choose panel mounted.

The next consideration is system integration. Does your choice of flight control, displays and navigational equipment interface with panel-mounted equipment? If so, we would choose panel mounted.

If the panel-mounted avionics fit neatly without extensive panel modification and interface with other system components we would go that route and make sure everything is cooled to the maximum extent possible, and save from 25 to 50 percent in cost.

The decision is no longer automatically in favor of remote-mounted avionics and if you don't need the unique capabilities they provide, panel-mounted equipment can get the job done for less.

Planning an Add-On Radio Package 23

by Richard N. Aarons

For corporations operating multimillion-dollar turbines, cost is rarely a determining factor in the selection and installation of avionics equipment —at least when standard IFR avionics packages are considered.

However, operators of smaller business aircraft—especially singles and light twins—are acutely aware of the cost factor in their avionics purchases. It's not unusual, for example, to see an avionics package in a sophisticated single that exceeds the cost of the airframe itself.

It's probably inconceivable to some large-aircraft operators that many light business aircraft are purchased with minimum IFR packages that are improved upon as "flight department" budgets allow and operational requirements dictate. Add-on avionics buying sounds like something done only by recreational pilots with limited resources, but the truth is that many businesses with clearly definable requirements for small aircraft simply don't have the big bucks necessary to equip their aircraft the way they'd like at the onset.

(There are also a lot of big-airplane operators who would be surprised to know how many small business aircraft regularly fly in the meanest of weather *without* autopilots, flight directors, RNAVs, HSIs, RMIs, radio altimeters and the rest of the equipment considered "absolutely essential" by those who fly turbine aircraft.)

An add-on avionics package properly planned and installed can be every bit as good in terms of performance, reliability and ultimate cost as a one-time factory-installed package. However, an improperly planned add-on package can become a nightmare. Costs of installation and maintenance can add hundreds if not thousands of dollars to the owner's operational budget, and poor dispatch reliability caused by unreliable avionics can ultimately overcome all the positive benefits of aircraft ownership.

There are four elements involved in making an add-on avionics scheme work:

• Selecting the airframe.

- Drafting a purchase and installation plan.
- Selecting the basic avionics family.
- Selecting a partner (a good avionics shop).

It's important that the businessman or company contemplating the purchase of a light aircraft understands that an airplane is a device for hauling things through the air—specifically, people, baggage, cargo *and avionics.* Too often, the aircraft purchaser forgets about the avionics part of that list. He purchases an aircraft large enough to meet his people, baggage and cargo requirements and then discovers too late that there's no space in his new airplane to install the avionics necessary to meet his operational needs.

For example, to overstate the case, the Mooney is a marvelous business aircraft. It's fast, easy to fly and economical. A Mooney owner can usually get all the IFR avionics aboard he wants if the components are carefully selected and installed. However, if the pilot-owner decides he *must* have weather radar to alert him to thunderstorms in IFR weather, he's not going to make it with the Mooney—there's simply no place for a radar antenna or panel space for the display.

In the case of the Mooney, it wouldn't make much difference what brand of avionics were considered. However, in some cases, avionics brand selection becomes important. For example, the Cessna 310 has one of the better-designed instrument panels in the industry. There's plenty of room for radar, IFR radios, area navigation equipment, digital fuel-flow computers and a full flight director system, but only if the avionics package is selected carefully. For example, factory-installed Cessna (ARC) panel-mounted 300- and 400-series radios take up too much space to allow for the addition of a full autopilot/flight director system, RMI, altitude alerter, radar altimeter, RNAV and weather radar. But Cessna (ARC) 800-series remote equipment or panel-mounted avionics made by Narco, King or Collins could do the job. The important thing is that the aircraft you buy should have enough room, weight-carrying capability and physical characteristics to accommodate the avionics you plan to install. Conversely, if the airplane you want doesn't have much room for avionics, make sure that the avionics you select at the beginning of your add-on package are part of a family of low-cube, low-weight radios.

While we're on the subject of airframes, remember that the aircraft electrical system is just about the most important element in the avionics system, though it is rarely considered by the purchaser of a light aircraft. Generally it's best to opt for the most alternator or generator capacity the air frame manufacturer offers. In single-engine aircraft you'll want at least 60 to 100 amps output. On twins, especially those with hot props and radar, you'll want at least 200 amps. There's probably nothing as frustrating as installing the last element of your add-on avionics package and discovering that the full load of the completed package knocks line voltage down so far that the transmitter won't work.

For a given power output capability, 28-volt electrical systems are generally lighter and more efficient than 14-volt systems. All panel-mounted radios operate on 14 volts, but most can also operate on 28. However, some of the least expensive panel-mounted radios require converters to run on 28 volts and range in price from $50 to $150 each.

Good businessmen do not begin a project without a plan. In its simplest form, a plan is a statement of goals relative to the present situation, with an outline of how to get there from here.

The necessity of a plan in the creation of an add-on avionics package can not be overstated. The fruits of an ill-planned avionics add-on package can range from simple frustration to economic disaster. For example, in the last year, we've seen:

- RNAVs purchased that didn't work with the installed DME.
- Indicators added that could not be driven by the installed nav radios.
- Antennas installed in such a manner that their radiation interfered with other avionics.
- A VNAV computer installed that misaligned an RNAV computer.
- An HSI installed that only worked backwards because of interface problems.
- A DME purchased that didn't fit anywhere in view of the flight crew.
- A telephone installed that could not be reached by any crewmember.

In the mid-60s, an avionics failure was as likely to be caused by a failure in the black box itself as it was by the installation. Today, black box dependability is way up. Failures are likely to be tied directly or indirectly to the installation.

A typical navcom installation has about 50 pin-to-pin connections; an ADF has 30; a DME has 70 to 80, as does an RNAV. Thus a high-performance, single-engine business aircraft equipped with a rather straightforward IFR avionics package will have at least 200 pin-to-pin connections— 200 places where the installer can make a mistake, where solder joints can age and fail, where corrosion can build up high-resistance connections and where shorts can develop.

These 200 pin-to-pin connections represent at least 100 lengths of conductor—wire that can become brittle and break and insulation that can chafe, causing shorts.

The avionics master plan we're talking about is designed, among other things, to bring some degree of organization to the mind-boggling complexity of even the simplest of avionics installations.

To start your plan, first list every piece of avionics equipment you'll eventually want in your airplane. Then inspect the interfaces that your equipment list dictates. (We'll discuss this in detail in a moment.) Finally, work up your installation timetable. What avionics will you begin with? When will you add a DME? A second transponder? A horizontal situation indicator? An RNAV?

The single most important element in the successful construction of an add-on avionics package is the installer; he can make it or break it. The installer is both architect and contractor in the creation of your custom package, so choose him with care.

Your installation plan will be finalized during your conferences with the chief designer in the avionics shop. It's important that at this very early stage both you and the shop know exactly what the installation will and will not include. Most shops quote flat rates for installation, some quote time and materials. In either event, know exactly what you're going to get up front.

It'll be to your advantage to have the basic package harness—all the wires used to connect the individual system elements—assembled and installed at one time. Doing so will keep installation costs and weight down and system reliability up. If a complete harness is not installed at the beginning, the shop will have to design another one and stuff a new bundle of wires under the panel each time a new avionics element is installed. Avionics elements already installed (and working) will be manipulated. Often previously installed elements will have to be removed entirely and rewired into a new harness, and too often they are not. If old harnesses are left in place (but disconnected), they add unnecessary weight to the aircraft and create disorder behind the panel. (Imagine the problem an avionics technician has troubleshooting an installation when a third of the wires behind the panel don't do anything.)

Before the first wire is installed, make sure you and the avionics shop have a complete understanding of the following elements:

• All components of the eventual completed system.

• A harnessing scheme that will allow elements to be added in a piecemeal fashion with the least rework or addition to behind-the-panel wires.

• An installation scheme that provides at least the minimum behind-the-panel cooling of each avionics element as specified by the avionics manufacturer. If this will require special ventilation provisions or blowers, the work should be accomplished during the initial installation.

In addition, make sure the avionics installer is willing to provide you with:

• A complete wiring diagram of the installation.

• A guarantee that the installed equipment will be free of electrical noise and that each of the elements specified will function without interfering with other elements.

• All paper work, including FAA licensing and new weight and balance, and compass calibration forms.

• An estimate prior to the initial phase of the job of all costs for the initial phase and anticipated costs as the add-on installation grows.

Obviously, by the time you complete negotiations with your avionics shop, you will have selected the types and brands of avionics for the installation. We've saved discussion of these decisions until last because of their complexity. To begin, we'll look at a few concepts of avionics interface.

It's generally better to stick with one manufacturer as your panel grows rather than to mix brands. When we're talking about panel-mounted avionics, this statement is true. Much of the extra cost of remote-mounted radios designed to Arinc specs is involved in making Arinc radios fully interchangeable. An Arinc nav receiver of a certain specification will drive an Arinc HSI of a certain specification. It makes absolutely no difference whether one manufacturer makes both the nav receiver and HSI or two manufacturers are involved. Conversely, much of the cost savings in non-Arinc panel-mounted radios is found in the fact that these systems do not have to be designed to the electronic tolerances involved in full-system interchangeability. The manufacturer can take shortcuts. His nav receiver will operate his HSI but will not necessarily drive the competition's HSI unless some kind of converter is placed between the two components.

To be fair to the manufacturers of panel-mounted equipment, it should be stated that they are all making sincere attempts to improve compatibility. King *wants* its radios to work with Collins cockpit displays. Narco *wants* its navs to interface with Bendix RNAVs. Cessna (ARC) *wants* its autopilots to work with nav signals from any other manufacturer's radios. In a very real way, much has been accomplished in the last five years toward this end. However, the fact remains that while a Narco nav may drive a King HSI, the King nav will probably do it a little better. The reason is that each large avionics manufacturer has designed groups or families of avionics to work together.

For example, let's suppose Manufacturer A designs a nav receiver and converter in a panel-mounted box that sends a standard left-right deviation signal to an indicator. When the engineers get the unit onto a test bench, they discover that their indicator is very sensitive to noisy signals and that their nav receiver is, in fact, sending the instrument noisy signals. To fix the situation, the design group goes back into the receiver/converter and filters out most of the noise, and the system plays beautifully.

Meanwhile, Manufacturer B designs a similar system and its engineers discover a similar problem. But they solve the problem by doing the filtering in the instrument rather than in the receiver/converter box.

Finally, let's suppose later on, both systems are on the market. We like the indicator made by Manufacturer A because it's pretty, and we like the receiver/converter manufactured by B because it's less expensive. We look at the electrical spec sheet and discover happily that the same signal format is used by both manufacturers between the receiver/converter and the indicator. Therefore we assume that they'll play together.

Sure enough, we install the mismatched pair and they do play together within acceptable tolerances, but we notice that the needle is a little shakey. Because of the difference in filtering techniques, we would have gotten better needle performance by using all A or all B equipment.

With panel-mounted avionics, anybody's anything can be made to play with anybody else's anything. This statement, too, is true. But, and it's a big *but,* such cobbled-up installations always cost extra money and often cost in system performance and reliability. Recently, an acquaintance decided to retrofit his Aztec with a customized "dream" avionics package. The package had a little from the Bendix family, some from King, several Collins indicators, a little bit from Narco and even some wayout elements made by basement manufacturers. An avionics shop tackled the initial

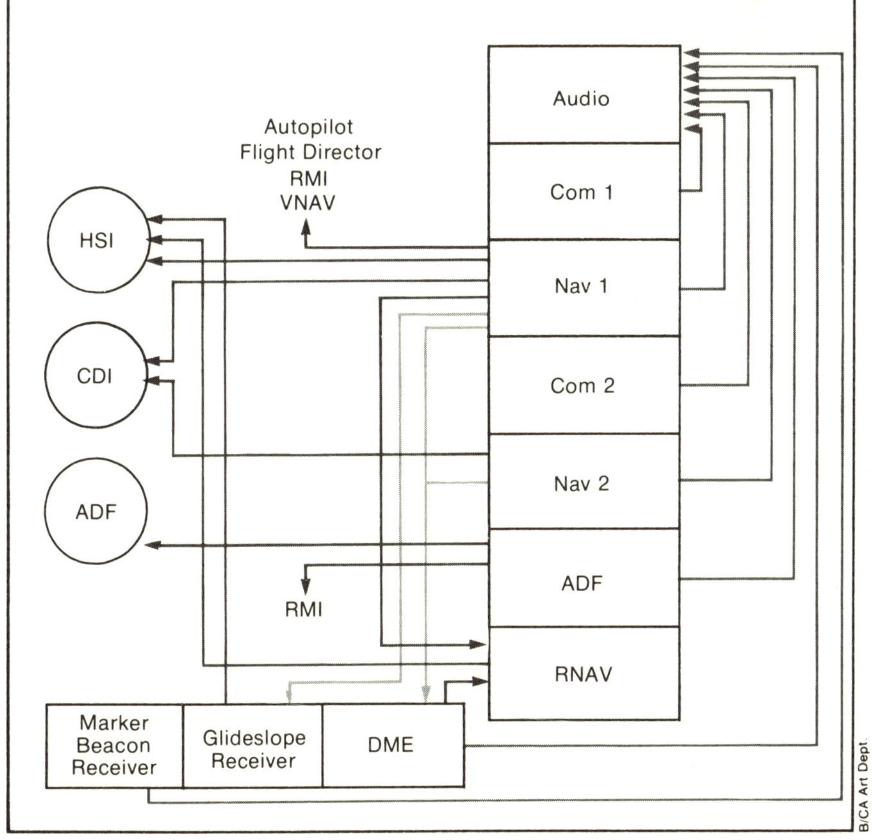

This illustration shows the points of interface in a typical family of panel-mounted avionics.

design work for him. When all was said and done, it was apparent that the converters, relays and harnessing necessary for all this equipment to play together would add thousands of dollars to the cost of the boxes.

It is true that each manufacturer of panel-mounted equipment tends to have a reputation for building one type box or another extremely well. Bendix, for example, has always had the reputation of building fine ADFs. So, for that matter, has Cessna (ARC). Narco has built a reputation for making reliable communications equipment. King has a reputation for building good basic RNAV equipment. Edo has a reputation for good indicators and autopilots. Mixing these black boxes is the stuff that dream panels are made of, but, in the end, most owners find that *money* is also the stuff dream panels are made of.

Even if you try to stick with one manufacturer's family, often you'll have to cross family lines simply because the manufacturer you've selected doesn't make a particular gadget you want to install. If the new device doesn't have to interface with anything else in the panel, you've got no problems. However, if interface is necessary, you'd best find out beforehand what it's going to cost.

One of the subtle benefits of staying within a single manufacturer's product line until you're forced out of it becomes apparent when your avionics installer needs technical help from factory engineers with an interface problem. Suppose you've specified a nav receiver from Company A, a DME from Company B and an RNAV computer from Company C. The only factory that really cares whether you get the three-component system playing is Company C. However, if you buy both the nav and DME from Company A and the RNAV from C (because A doesn't make one), your avionics technician will have two outfits caring. Company C cares because it's their RNAV, and Company A cares because you've spent a lot of money with it.

The first item listed when we were talking about building an add-on avionics plan was the list of all the equipment ultimately required. This list, considered in its entirety, will probably determine the brand of avionics you buy and the family line within that brand. Most of your decision will be based on your selection of VHF nav equipment and its outputs. The VHF nav receiver has to do more than any other box in the panel. Consider this list of cockpit instruments and systems that require input from the VHF nav receiver.

- Course deviation indicators
- Horizontal situation indicators (HSIs)
- Radio magnetic indicators (RMIs)
- Digital bearing readouts
- Area navigation computers
- Vertical navigation computers

- Autopilot computers
- Flight director computers
- Various flags

In addition to these navigation signals, the VHF nav equipment is usually called upon to channel DME and glideslope receivers.

Some VHF nav receivers simply are incapable of performing all the tasks listed here. For example, "automatic omni" and "automatic VOR" are the terms used to describe the capability to drive an RMI pointer or a digital bearing readout. Some systems have it, some don't. DME and glideslope channeling is a separate feature. Some systems can; some can't.

In addition, the number of needle movements and flags a VHF nav system can drive is limited. A typical VHF nav system might be able to drive three needles and four flags. Or maybe it will drive five needles and five flags. The point is that a panel-mounted VHF nav system can drive only so many needles and flags. (The same is true for a glideslope receiver.)

The number of needles and flags a system can drive often is not listed in advertisements or even on catalog sheets. Your avionics shop will have that information in its library.

All the other components of a full-IFR avionics package have lists of "optional features" (for lack of a better description) that you should discuss with the installer before settling on a package. We've already presented a list for VHF nav receivers. Here are some items that are often "optional" in other system elements. Many of these items are optional with the installation rather than the factory-supplied equipment.

Glideslope receiver—Does it have an on/off switch and a separate circuit breaker, or could a catastrophic failure in the glideslope receiver take a VHF receiver with it? Does it have its own antenna or will it use something else? Does it use the same channeling code that the VHF nav puts out?

DME—Will the audio be brought out to the audio panel? Did you know that DME has its own ident and that it should be checked just as the VOR ident is? Many installers don't bother to hook up the DME audio. What channeling code does the DME use? Does the DME output match that required by the RNAV you expect to install?

Transponder—Any new transponder will work with any new encoding altimeter, but you must make sure that the transponder and DME will work together. That is, be sure that you've got proper DME-transponder suppression.

Marker beacon receiver—Does it have its own on/off switch and fuse? How about a high-low switch? Does it have its own audio amplifier or must it work through the system audio amplifier? How about a volume control?

Audio/switching systems deserve special attention as you construct your add-on avionics blueprint. As a general rule, buy the very best audio/switching system available from the manufacturer you have selected for the rest of your gear. A poorly engineered audio/switching system can, in certain failure modes, disable *both* com receivers and *both* transmitters. Systems without isolation amplifiers rob your com sets of audio power; so do overloaded, inexpensive speakers. As part of the avionics installation, we recommend that you also specify an additional cabin speaker—one for the number-one navcom and the second for everything else with an audio output—and emergency audio jacks that bypass the audio/switching system entirely.

Recently, a friend, who operates a well-equipped airplane, decided to install a rather sophisticated glidepath computer to work in conjunction with his IFR-approved RNAV system. As it turned out, the installation got expensive when the installer discovered that the nav signal required by the VNAV wasn't available at a pin and had to be dug out of the innards of the VHF nav system. Avoiding such problems is difficult. When our friend first designed his avionics package, there was no such thing as a glidepath computer for use in conjunction with an RNAV system. The technology simply hadn't surfaced. When the system finally did surface, the manufacturer decided (correctly, we think) to design it around Arinc interfaces. So, his glidepath computer works great with any expensive Arinc nav system, but requires a bit of engineering to work with a name-brand panel-mounted avionics package.

Just about the only thing our friend could have done to avoid this situation—Monday morning quarterbacking, to be sure—was to select an avionics package initially with totally discrete, easily accessible components. Maybe we can make that concept a little clearer.

The manufacturers of panel-mounted equipment all have three basic design goals: (1) they want their equipment to be reliable; (2) they want it to be price competitive; and (3) they want it to be as compact as possible. The last goal—low cube—is the main reason panel-mounted equipment exists in the first place. If all aircraft had plenty of room for big black boxes, panel-mounted equipment would not be necessary.

The panel-mounted avionics manufacturer has only two places to work on cube—in the stack or behind the instrument faces. For example, a VHF nav system has three elements: nav receiver, omni converter and navigation indicator. The omni converter takes the signals received by the nav receiver and turns them into left/right signals for the indicator. In terms of cubic inches, the components of the omni converter take up about the same space as a coffee cup. The manufacturer can opt to combine the receiver and converter in one box or he can put the converter in the indicator. Localizer signals received by the nav receiver are processed in a manner different from the VOR signals. The LOC converter is therefore, a separate device, and it, too, can be located in the receiver box or behind the indicator. Some manufacturers put the glideslope receiver in the can behind

186

the instrument; others house it in its own black box. Some manufacturers build marker beacon receivers in their own remote boxes; others build them into the audio/switching unit.

The advantages and disadvantages of these arrangements can be debated endlessly. All combining schemes have their merits. However, they all have at least two drawbacks. One is maintainability. Consider, for a moment, a combination indicator/omni converter. The omni converter is often the culprit when something goes wrong with a VHF nav system. The meter movement itself is rarely the cause of problems unless it's been subjected to mechanical trauma. Pulling the indicator/converter to troubleshoot a VHF nav system subjects the meter movement to unnecessary trauma.

The second drawback of tightly integrated systems is that it often takes an electronics engineer to find a source for a signal required later on by a piece of new equipment.

So if you think you'll be making many changes and additions to your avionics package as new technologies develop, you might benefit by selecting your avionics from the family that has the highest number of discrete components. For most of us, though, this precaution should not be necessary.

Pulling it all together then, we have these general suggestions for designing your own avionics package. Although we have been discussing add-on avionics packages, these suggestions are just as applicable to one-shot installations.

(1) Plan your installation. Look ahead to your anticipated operational requirements and budget.

(2) Select a good avionics shop and make the shop installation designer a full partner in the planning task.

(3) Make sure the initial installation includes a good audio/switching system, an additional cabin speaker and harnessing to accept the rest of your package as additional boxes are purchased.

(4) Select a family of avionics that most nearly meets your individual requirements, then urge the avionics shop to take full advantage of that factory's technical services.

(5) Make sure that any component you select for your system has the signal output capability to meet all future requirements.

(6) Start with a good wiring diagram and keep it up to date. This suggestion can save you hundreds of dollars in subsequent maintenance bills.

(7) In later stages of your package's growth, make sure unused harnesses are removed.

(8) If you decide to add a component that was not included in the original plan, sit down again with the wiring diagram and the installation designer to work out the best possible system interface. Light bulb manufacturers

urge us to resist the temptation to be a "bulb snatcher" on the basis that sooner or later you'll run out of light bulbs when you really need one. For the same reason, don't let avionics technicians succumb to the temptation to become wire snatchers. If a component is to be added to the package—one for which no harnessing was done—don't rob wires intended for still later components. To do so defeats the original purpose of pre-harnessing.

(9) If a piece of new equipment is to be connected to existing components, make sure the technician checks out (and peaks) the existing equipment. There's no practical way to troubleshoot a complex new installation unless you know the points from which you've started. Do these things, and you'll have the best possible panel-mounted avionics package.

Update Your Avionics 24

by J. Mac McClellan

Avionics failures. We've all had them and always will. Avionics are getting better. But, as any operator is quick to point out, usually with a great deal of emotion and colorful comment, they are far from perfect.

Every coin has two sides, however. In many instances an avionics failure offers the informed operator an opportunity to not only repair the unit, but to bring it up to a higher level of performance and reliability—if one takes advantage of the continuing research and development the avionics manufacturers put into their equipment.

Manufacturers and repair shops are in unanimous agreement when it comes to advice on stretching the working life of a piece of avionics gear. If the unit seems to be working, leave it alone. There is nothing to be gained by removing a unit from the aircraft merely to test it and confirm your belief that it is working. Almost anything can happen, and often does, when a unit is removed from the aircraft.

But when a box does break down and must be removed, sit down with your avionics shop people and discuss service bulletins and modifications. Instead of simply repairing the unit, you may be able to bring it up to the performance and reliability level of current production equipment.

A major portion of a manufacturer's avionics support is generation of technical information that tells the shop how to repair, correct *and modify* a unit. Engineers constantly work to solve problems that are discovered during field operations and to improve the product while it is in production. That engineering data is transformed into either a repair or modification and published in service letters or bulletins and sent to all service shops and dealers. When your unit goes in for repair, those service bulletins give you the option of having your avionics not just repaired, but renewed.

There are other names for a service bulletin such as service letter, information letter or modification bulletin. But if you just refer to service bulletins, everyone in the industry will understand what you mean.

After being mailed to all dealers, repair shops, service centers and aircraft manufacturers, the bulletin becomes part of the maintenance manual for that particular product.

In rare cases, a *mandatory* service bulletin is mailed directly to the equipment operator. That brings up the compliance issue. A service bulletin falls into three basic categories—mandatory, customer option or repair.

The mandatory bulletin is just what the term implies. Compliance is mandatory. However, a mandatory service bulletin is not to be confused with an Airworthiness Directive note. In a few cases, a service bulletin can be an AD note also, but that is extremely rare. All the major avionics makers combined have not had more than a half-dozen AD notes issued against all of their products.

A mandatory bulletin will not become an AD note unless the malfunction or design flaw it corrects could be an impairment to safety of flight. A flight control problem or a navigation instrument that might provide erroneous information without warning are about the only problems that warrant issuance of an avionics AD. If an AD note is issued against a piece of avionics equipment, it carries the force of law, specifically FAR 39, just as an AD does for any other part of the aircraft or its equipment. Owners are notified of every AD, if possible, and a time limit is specified in which the modification must be made.

But, in avionics, not all mandatory service bulletins are really mandatory in the sense of an AD. Rather, the mandatory nature applies to the warranty of the unit. A mandatory service bulletin must be complied with whenever the unit comes into an approved repair station, but the owner or operator is not required to comply with it so long as his unit is operating normally. For example, perhaps there has been a problem in the field with a needle that tends to stick. A mandatory bulletin may be issued calling for replacement of the needle stops with a new design. As long as you have no problem of any sort with the unit, nothing is required. But if, say, the receiver quits and the unit has to be pulled for *that* repair, the shop will at that time change the stops whether there has been a needle sticking problem or not.

The second type of compliance is by customer option. This type of bulletin offers either improved performance or correction of a general problem in that particular unit. The customer has the option of having the change or repair made. For example, perhaps a knob keeps falling off. If you don't mind tightening the set screw once in a while, you can ignore it. But if you tire of that, a modified knob is available and can be installed on the next shop visit. Or perhaps a particular unit requires modification to interface with some other piece of equipment, or to perform properly in a particular aircraft. Those kinds of fixes are at the optin of the owner as well. Finally, there is the bulletin that simply describes the repair. It says that if the symptoms are this, do that. Change wire P from pin Q to pin R, or replace resistor S with a type T.

As we've noted, unless the service bulletin is a mandatory fix to insure safety of flight, it's best to not disturb a unit that's working properly simply to perform a modification. However, there is an exception to that rule and that is when the unit is still under warranty.

Many times service bulletins that must be paid for by the customer after the equipment is out of warranty will be paid for by the manufacturer while the unit is *in* warranty. Therefore, shortly before a warranty expires it's wise to sit down with your avionics service technician to discuss all the outstanding bulletins. Possibly a problem has been discovered and a modification devised to resolve it since your box left the factory. Compliance with that service bulletin modification could prevent the defect from afflicting your avionics unit.

But the key factor here is to thoroughly discuss the bulletin, what it covers, how major the problem is and what it can do for you. Don't have the avionics removed and bench-checked simply to be sure they're working. That may create more problems than it solves and those problems may not crop up until a few months go by, just enough to put the box out of warranty coverage.

The service bulletin will spell out the problems it is designed to solve or the performance increase that will result. Be certain you get a good explanation of those factors and rely on the advice of your shop. Problems covered in a service bulletin may not affect your equipment and the last thing you want is somebody probing around in your equipment needlessly.

Another consideration when you're thinking about compliance with a service bulletin simply because it will be paid for by warranty is the potential for future problems greater than those the bulletin is designed to prevent. In electronics, every component has at least an indirect relationship to every other component in the unit. If the shop makes a mistake, it may be difficult and expensive to uncover the problem later. The point is, don't jump for every service bulletin simply because it will be paid for under the warranty.

Of course, once a unit goes out of warranty your attitude toward compliance with a service bulletin will change. Now it's *your* money.

When your equipment breaks, don't just take it out, slap a tag on it and send it off to the shop. Take the time to get together with the shop people for a talk about what can be done not only to fix the unit, but to improve it.

Many service bulletins are going to have virtually no value to you. Simply telling the shop to comply with all outstanding service bulletins may be a waste of money. Often a modification won't buy you any greater performance or reliability because it rectifies an isolated problem. For example, Bendix once issued a service bulletin because an airplane being operated in South America experienced autopilot pitch changes when the HF transmitter was activated. After researching the problem, the engineers found how RF interference from the high-frequency transmitter was getting into the pitch channel of the autopilot and issued a service bulletin to correct it. Those with no HF onboard could not benefit at all from that service bulletin on their autopilots.

In most cases, however, there's a very good chance that whatever is ailing your equipment is covered by an existing service bulletin. Of course, you'll want that particular one complied with. Since the unit is going to come out anyway, ask your avionics repairman about the outstanding optional and repair bulletins applicable to your equipment. This discussion with him will serve two purposes. First, if the shop people are up to speed on the bulletins and what they mean, there's a very good chance they'll be able to troubleshoot your problem of the moment quicker and thus keep labor costs down. Several avionics manufacturers' service managers have told us that they often get calls from shops describing a problem the shop can't solve. The factory will ask if they've checked bulletin such and such which covers the problem. Obviously, the people in that shop don't stay abreast of advances in the state of the art relative to your avionics. So, if nothing else, a discussion of service bulletins before work begins will at least cause shop personnel to begin thinking about them and maybe that will save you time and money.

A second reason for the discussion is so you can decide which reliability and performance-improvement modifications should be incorporated while the unit is out of the aircraft. The majority of service bulletins are issued to solve a problem that was not anticipated by the design engineering team. Every manufacturer goes through extensive testing of a design, but there is no way to duplicate actual operation. Some top-line equipment is even put through AGREE testing, a procedure developed by the military to simulate hundreds of hours of in-the-field use. But the bugs just can't all be anticipated or uncovered at the factory.

When reports of field service problems start coming back to engineering, the design is modified to correct the fault or weakness. Those design changes are normally incorporated in production models and a service bulletin is issued describing the fix.

To keep track of which units have the new design feature and which don't, virtually all avionics equipment carries a modification status tag. The tag is usually made of metal with a series of numbers that can be either punched out or stamped to indicate that modification number such and such has been complied with. In this way, the shop knows what service bulletin to follow in making a repair and where to look for a problem if a likely modification isn't indicated. Narco is the only major manufacturer that doesn't use a status plate. Instead, it changes the unit chassis identification number to indicate the modification status.

Because of this ongoing modification program even at the factory on the production line, you'll often notice that a brand new unit has several modifications stamped on the plate even though it just came out of the shipping box. These indicate corrections and improvements that have taken place during the production life of that model. The box is that many modifications better than the first unit in the model series.

Examination of the modification status plate will reveal exactly what has been done to your unit, both during manufacturing and since, and what is required to bring it up to the very latest in performance. The mod plate is the first thing a good shop will look at and that's where your questioning and discussion of the available modifications should begin.

The problem-solving bulletin, as well as all other service bulletins, will spell out the units affected, the reason for the bulletin, description of the work, the compliance requirement—either optional or mandatory—and labor and parts required.

You'll want to discuss with your shop all the problem-solving bulletins that may be out on your unit. Even if you haven't had any of the problems those bulletins were issued to correct, it may be wise to have certain or all of them complied with while the unit is down for repair. Again, you'll need good advice from your shop in deciding if the potential problem is great enough to warrant compliance with the bulletin.

One spokesman for a major avionics maker told us they have trouble selling modifications that do nothing but enhance reliability. The only service bulletins that seem to win wide acceptance, he said, are the kind that add a new indicator, or knob. The problem is every operator thinks his avionics should play forever, or close to it. If the box should last forever, why spend more money on it to make it last a little longer?

Approaching the service bulletin question with an objective attitude will help you make a better decision in that regard. Instead of taking the attitude that it shouldn't have quit in the first place, examine the modifications that might be available to make your avionics unit last longer next time. Avionics maintenance remains a mystery for most operators because they don't take time to discuss problems with their shops. Service bulletins are a virtual gold mine of data on repairing and preventing problems as well as enhancing performance. But a carte blanche attitude toward service bulletins is little better than total ignorance. Several manufacturers told us units are often sent to their service centers with instructions to bring them up to new standards—put in every modification there is.

If you've got money to burn, that may not be a bad idea, but a large number of the service bulletins may do you virtually no good. Most manufacturers' service centers or factory repair centers will tell you there is a service bulletin out that could benefit your unit, if your repairman will only call and ask. Request that he do that.

During the life cycle of an avionics unit minor—and sometimes major—improvements in performance and perhaps even an increase in the number of operating modes are continually being designed into the box by the engineering department. Those improvements, of course, go into the production models and they often can also go into your existing equipment if you want to pick up the tab.

Again, it's not likely an improvement bulletin will be issued that is of enough value to cause you to remove a working unit from the aircraft. After all, if the box is still playing, how much improvement does it need? But when it does break, maybe a new cooling system, or improved final cavity or some other component may make it work better and last longer. There's always the risk that in performing a modification the technician will create a problem elsewhere in the unit, but in many cases it's worth the chance.

For example, King issued a service bulletin to modify the KN 65 DME to provide quicker groundspeed readout stabilization. The fix involves installation of a variable resistor that sets the groundspeed at a target value close to normal cruise speed of the aircraft. With this modification the DME groundspeed comes up to within a few knots of the actual groundspeed when it's turned on and so has only to adjust a little either up or down instead of always counting up from zero.

This modification requires only one hour of labor and a part kit from King.

That type of improved-performance modification is constantly coming out of the engineering departments of manufacturers. Most can be done in the field.

Another, usually more major kind of modification, is one that can be conducted only at the factory. Normally this is an entire modification program incorporating several major changes.

The reason certain modifications can be done only at the factory is economics. Assembly-line procedures performed by avionics factory workers makes a lot more economic sense than modifying individual units one at a time in a shop employing highly skilled and higher-paid technicians. These factory modification programs always improve performance and usually solve some of the problems experienced in the field. However, the factory modification can seldom be customized. It's a package deal. You get all or nothing for the price.

Incidentally, factory service centers or repair shops are an excellent place to have service bulletins complied with because they're staffed with specialists who concentrate on just a small family of units and become very proficient on those types. We're not knocking your local repair shop. Many do excellent work, but when it comes to an extensive modification, the factory center simply has more experience, better equipment and less distraction.

Manufacturers will continue to issue service bulletins and modifications

194

throughout the useful life of a product, In many cases this is more than a dozen years. In later avionics life, the service bulletin becomes even more vital. The continual development of the design and components often obsoletes certain circuits or components. Sometimes you can't even buy replacement parts, such as tubes or other old-style components. To get around this problem, manufacturers are constantly redesigning current components, to keep the box in service.

If you have purchased a used aircraft and have no history on maintenance on the avionics, the modification status plate will be vital. You should discuss with your shop any bulletins that may update performance and, certainly, when a unit breaks, you should find out exactly what improvements are possible and what has already been done. Modifications may be available to bring the older avionics up to current spec, or a factory modification program may be available. Most factory modification programs also have the added benefit of renewing the warranty for some period.

The key to taking advantage of the service bulletin support program is to take the time to develop a rapport with your shop. Service bulletins are technical documents that will have little meaning to the average operator, so you must rely on shop personnel for interpretation and advice.

When you do decide to comply with a bulletin for any reason, get a parts and labor estimate from the shop. If the shop representative is reluctant to commit to the published figures, or to even tell you what the figures are, the rapport may be jeopardized—we suggest you call the factory service department. But remember, the labor allowance published in a service bulletin is an average. If the shop hasn't done that particular job before, it may take two or three times as long. If they've done several of the same modifications recently, it may take only half as much time. Obviously, you should look for a shop that *does* have experience. It's the old learning curve problem, but you shouldn't have to foot the bill for a technician's training.

An exception to that, of course, will arise when there is some factor other than economy involved. We do recommend that you patronize one shop as much as possible and preferably it should be one where the aircraft is based. Using one shop will by itself save you money because the technicians will know the quirks of your particular installation. If the shop is close by, the expense of ferry flights is saved and ferrying to a maintenance facility can be very pennywise and pound foolish.

Finally, it's frustrating for an avionics manufacturer to hear complaints about a problem it solved with a service bulletin modification some time ago, but that happens continually. It should also be frustrating for every efficient and responsible operator who's not taking advantage of all the aids offered to him.

195

Digital Electronics 25

by Richard N. Aarons

Take a moment and leaf through some avionics ads—everything's *digital.* Weather radars are *digital;* autopilots are *digital;* RNAVs are *digital;* DMEs are *digital;* air data systems are *digital.*

The ads all claim "digital is better." As an avionics buyer, sooner or later you're going to have to ask, "Better than what?"

Don't run away yet. We're not going to make you experts on digital electronics. Half the technicians who fix digital electronic devices really don't understand how they work. Nor do you as an avionics buyer have to be able to design a digital circuit or feel comfortable in the exercise of Boolean algebra. But you should have an understanding of the basic concepts of computer theory as applied to the operation and navigation of your aircraft.

First, let's take a closer look at what the ads mean when they say "digital." This can be sorted out easily if you remember that there are three separate types of *digital* in reference to avionics equipment: (1) digital displays, (2) digital circuitry and (3) general purpose automatic digital computers.

Digital displays need little explanation. They are simply devices that present their information in digital form. For example, the DME readouts on most five-inch HSIs are digital. The numbers representing frequency on radio control heads—whether electronic or mechanical—are digital. Digital displays need no interpretation. In the case of the HSI, on the DME display, the pilot need only glance at the numbers to determine his DME distance from the station. If the thing says 053 miles, that's what it means—not 052 or 054.

The other type display—analog—always uses a pointer and a scale of some sort, leaving it up to the pilot to interpret the reading. Analog readouts include the faces of airspeed/Mach indicators, vertical rate indicators and, in fact, just about all cockpit indicators other than those displaying discrete digits.

Sometimes it's hard to tell whether an indicator is analog or digital, but the presence of a pointer is a dead giveaway. Consider, for a moment, the popular electro-mechanical DME indicators. Typically these devices have a drum on the right that displays miles, with 10ths of miles graduated between the one-mile digits. When this drum makes a complete revolution—moving from zero to nine miles—the drum to its left moves one position to display a one. Now the display reads 10. In the strictest sense the units drum is an analog device and the 10s drum is a digital device in that it counts (digitally) the revolutions of the ones drum. But, so we don't cloud the discussion, basically these electro-mechanical displays are analog-type devices.

Any avionics device that has in its innards *digital circuitry* at one point or another manipulates electronic pulses arithmetically to produce a desired result. That's all there is to it. Instead of measuring continuously changing voltages and currents, a digital device chops up voltages and currents into pulses and handles them in that form.

In most general aviation avionics these digital circuits are dedicated to a specific operation. For example, the digital circuitry in a medium-cost digital DME system—we're talking about the black box as well as the display now—can be used only in that black box for a specific operation. However, the navigation computer units in some of the more expensive automatic RNAV systems—Garrett AiRNAV 100 and Collins ANS-71, for example—are actually general purpose digital computers that happen to have been programmed for the solution of area navigation problems. These computers could just as easily have been programmed to handle the payroll for a large company or to operate an automated assembly line.

The high-speed electronic digital computer is a relative newcomer to civil aviation. In fact, digital devices have been in our cockpits for only about five years. But in five years, the proliferation of this equipment has brought about changes every bit as important as those that accompanied the switch from vacuum tubes to transistors in avionics a decade and a half ago.

Just as the pilot had to learn basic solid-state electronic theory—if for no other reason than to understand what his avionics repairman was talking about—he now has to brush up on basic computer theory.

Digital computation itself is nothing new. We've been using digital techniques since the first caveman realized he had more than one wife. He assigned each a finger, and when asked by a buddy how many wives he had, he merely held up the appropriate number of fingers.

Anyway, the important thing to remember here is that when we're talking about digital techniques (whether applied by cavemen or Collins), we're really talking about the arithmetical solution of problems—counting wives and sabertooth tigers for the caveman and counting discrete electrical pulses in the case of Collins.

Let's consider how someone might go about determining the number of marbles in a small box. He can solve this problem using either digital or analog methods. If he's going to use a digital method, he can dump the marbles out on the floor and count them as he returns them to the box. Eventually, he'll arrive at the total.

If he uses an analog method, he'll need a measuring tape, pencil and paper. To begin, he'll measure the box and calculate its volume, then he'll measure a marble and calculate its volume. Now he has a mathematical model (or analog) describing the number of marbles in the box as a function of the volume of the box. By dividing the unit volume into the volume of the box, he has the answer.

The analog system probably isn't very practical if a single small box is involved; however, if a person is trying to determine the number of marbles in a freight car, the analog solution certainly would require less time than the digital method. The problem with using an analog system in the solution of the marble problem is that it's not really as accurate as the digital solution. Our mathematical model, or analog (so many marbles per unit volume), was only approximate because we were talking about round objects in a rectangular box.

As the number of boxes increases, the error increases. It would seem then that digital techniques are better, at least in terms of accuracy, when we're dealing with problems involving discrete elements—marbles, wives, tigers or whatever.

Let's take another problem—determining the rate of rotation of a buddy who is spinning round and round on a stool. In this case, both the analog and digital solutions involve a bit of hardware. We'll look at the analog solution first.

Remembering that analog means model, we will have to build a model of rotation that we can interpret. The model will have to perform as a function of stool rotation (analogous, in fact). One way to do this is to gear a small DC generator to the stool so its shaft rotates as it does. With this setup, the generator output will be proportional to the speed of the stool. Now we can wire the generator to a volt-meter and calibrate the meter's card in terms of rpm (rather than volts). This device—the stool tachometer —is a real, honest-to-goodness analog computer. (Meter deflection is proportional to generator voltage which is proportional to stool rpm.) Note— and this is important—that the stool analog computer is solving the problem in *real time.*

Solving the problem digitally will take a little more effort. First, we need that box of marbles, a clock and a pencil and paper. We'll have to give the marbles to the friend spinning on the stool and instruct him to drop a marble in the box each time he rotates past it. Now we're all set. We start the clock and the friend starts plunking marbles in the box each time he rotates past it. Every once in a while we must stop the clock and count the number of marbles in the box. Then, using the pencil and paper, we solve the equation: rpm $= \frac{\text{marbles}}{\text{minutes}}$ and get an answer.

But wait. While we're counting the marbles and doing that paperwork, the friend is still spinning and there is no new data coming in. What's worse, the answer we get represents only the *average* speed during the period between the start and finish of the timing sequence. That is to say, the answer is history and rather rough history at that.

Obviously, our answers would be more accurate were the sampling periods shorter in duration and increased in frequency. But they can never quite be called real-time answers.

The problems involving the marbles and the stool demonstrate several important characteristics of digital and analog computers. For example, you'll remember that the analog solution to the stool problem provided answers in real time while the digital one did not.

When you think about it for a moment, you'll realize that the analog solution to the revolving stool problem works only for solving the variable in rotation and rate problems (something has to turn the generator shaft) while the digital solution to the stool problem (clock and marbles) can be used for any number of different type calculations and measurements. Thus it is clear that one of the basic differences between analog and digital computers is that the analog computer is usually limited to the solution of the specific problem for which it was designed, while a digital computer can usually handle any problem for which it's been programmed.

We've already decided that digital computers are simply high-speed counting (digit-manipulating) devices. The *high-speed* part of that definition is extremely important. Remember in both the marble and stool problems that the largest drawback of the digital solution was the time required for the calculations.

It's equally true that digital computers wouldn't be very useful if they weren't quick. Just how quick is quick? Well, typically, a high-speed digital computer can make a million additions in one second.

At this point it would be fair to ask just what it is that computers add and how they do it. This is also as good a place as any to get into some of the computer jargon that you'll be seeing on the back of avionics spec sheets.

We'll start with the concept of *state*. (By the way, if you have problems with what follows, ask your fifth grader for help. Kids today are learning computer logic—truth tables, Venn diagrams and Boolean algebra—from the third grade on.)

State is mathematics talk for the condition of something. Take a wall switch, for example. It has two states—on and off. It can't be anything else. A wire in an electric circuit has two states—either current is flowing through it, or it isn't. A piece of ferrous metal has two states—magnetized or unmagnetized. We could go on with several other examples of bistable devices, but the point has probably been made. We can use any of these

199

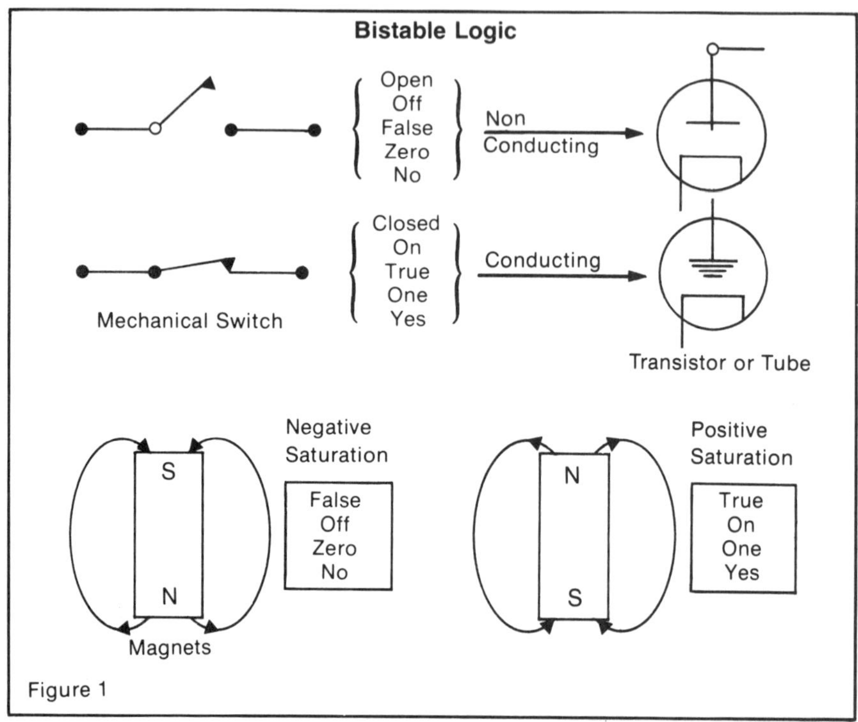

The arithmetic devices in a digital computer are basically switches that have two possible states — open and closed. Many other devices including vacuum tubes, transistors and magnets exhibit these bistable states. Because of the nature of these devices, computers must work with a number system based on one and zero. However, the bistable states can be used to identify other opposite conditions such as true/false and yes/no.

devices to build an important part of the digital computer.

The two states of the wall switch—on or off—could just as easily represent yes and no, or true and false. Or the two states could represent the digits one and zero—one for on, zero for off.

It becomes obvious that we could build a counting machine that would do a pretty credible job if we got a couple of thousand switches and wired them up in an appropriate manner. (How we wire the switches is the *program*, which we'll talk about later.)

If we were interested in making a counting machine, we'd let the on/off positions of the switch stand for one and zero. Then, of course, we'd have to devise a number system based only on one and zero for the counting machine to work. The number system most commonly used is called the "binary" number system.

On the other hand, if we wanted a logic machine, we'd assign yes/no and

Computer Number Systems

Decimal	Binary
1	0001
2	0010
3	0011
4	0100
5	0101
6	0110
7	0111
8	1000
9	1001
10	1010
11	1011
12	1100
13	1101
14	1110
15	1111
16	10,000

Digital	532
Binary	101101110
BCD*	1000 0110 0101

*Binary Coded Decimal

Figure 2

Most digital computers use a form of the binary number system shown here. The decimal system used in everyday computation is based on powers of 10, and works great for people with 10 fingers. But a digital computer has only two fingers labeled one and zero. As you can see from the example here, binary numbers can get quite long. One way to get around this problem is to assign each decimal digit a discrete four-digit code. There are several schemes for the codes, but all are called binary coded decimals. These codes are used in aircraft multiplex tuning circuits. Numbers to the base are sometimes used by computers when binary numbers get too unwieldy.

true/false labels to the on/off positions of the switches. By combining yes/no and true/false switches in various configurations, we can get ANDs and ORs and NOTs and combinations of them. As you've guessed, large general purpose digital computers use all these labels.

We've used switches to define the term state and, in fact, the first digital computers were built up of bank upon bank of electro-mechanical switches (relays). Later, space was saved and speed increased by replacing the relays with vacuum tubes, and then the vacuum tubes were replaced by transistors; finally the transistors were replaced by integrated circuitry. However, the theory of operation hasn't changed at all.

We've described the bistable (on/off) states of switches, relays, tubes, transistors and magnets. In today's high-speed digital computers two other elements are used—pulse signals and signal levels. As you can see in Figure 3, a pulse is a sharp-edge, short-duration direct current. Each pulse

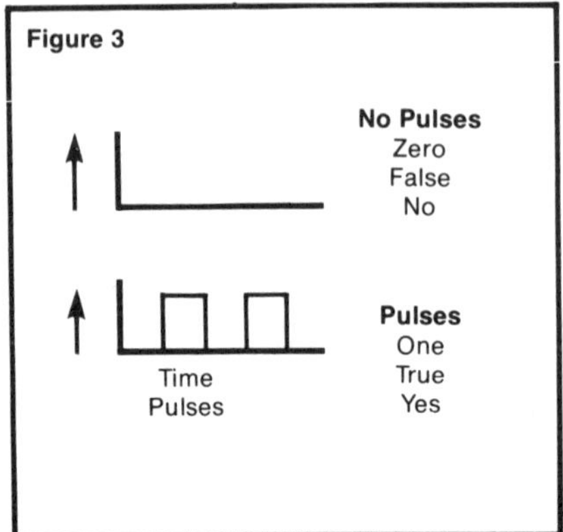

Pulses are the most common switch devices used in avionics digital circuitry. The absence or presence of pulses is used to define the bistable state.

represents a one (or yes or true), and the absence of pulses in a given time interval represents zero (or no or false). The voltage level in a circuit can also be used to represent one (high-voltage level) and zero (low-voltage level).

Pulses are the most common *switch devices* used in avionics digital circuitry. They can be stored in things called *registers,* manipulated arithmetically in things called *counters* and used in any number of ways to signal various operations.

You've run into pulses before in discussions of airborne weather radar, DME and transponders. As you can guess, these devices lend themselves most to improvement with digital circuitry.

Weather radar presents a good example. Radio pulses are transmitted from the antenna, and their round trip time from the antenna to a target and back to the antenna is measured. With conventional weather radar the returns (actually digital in nature) are displayed in an analog (continuous) manner on a bright display tube. In newer digital weather radars, the distance and azimuth data, already basically digital, are completely digitized and stored before presentation on the display. A digital computer, then, goes to work on the stored information. First it culls all the stored data for stuff that shouldn't be there—signals from other airborne radar units (rabbit tracks) and miscellaneous radio junk (noise). Intensity levels are assigned and a digital picture is generated on the screen. (It's the digital nature of the data that lends a blocky appearance to digital weather radar displays.)

The important thing to remember here is that digital techniques enable the data to be manipulated before it's displayed.

In a digital circuit, whether part of a radar display or part of an automatic computer, a single pulse represents one piece of information. Engineers call it a *bit.* Several bits combined and acted upon as a unit are called a *computer word.* You'll run into both these expressions in digital avionics spec sheets. You need only remember that bits and words are the computer's vocabulary. The greater the computer's capability to handle bits and words, both in terms of capacity and speed, the smarter the computer.

Digital DMEs are beginning to show up in medium-priced avionics lines. The advantages of digital DME accrue from the fact that DME is basically a digital device to start with. Pulses go out and trigger a ground transmitter, which sends pulses back to the aircraft. Round trip times are measured and displayed as distance. In conventional DMEs, everything is digital until the ground station pulses arrive. Then these pulses are analyzed using analog methods to make sure they are indeed meant for the aircraft that dispatched them. In our discussion of determining the number of marbles in a box, we discovered that analyzing digital data with analog techniques generates error. The same is true with conventional DMEs. On the other hand, analyzing ground station returns with digital techniques improves accuracy, and that's what happens in a digital DME.

The transponder, as you know, is a pulse device and, in a way, it works like reversed DME. A ground station sends out an interrogation (Where are you?) and the transponder replies (Here I am.). Now transponders are also sending back altitude information, but there's a snag. Altitude information is basically analog (continuous) in nature and transponder conversation is basically digital. The problem is solved, as your accountant learned a couple of years ago, by an encoder—a device that transforms analog altitude data into digital (pulse) altitude data. This is pointed out only to demonstrate that analog data can be converted to digital data and digital data can be converted to analog. Two more terms you'll see on digital avionics spec sheets are *A-to-D converter* and *D-to-A converter.* You guessed it—A-to-D means analog to digital and D-to-A means digital to analog. You've also guessed correctly that engineers try to avoid unnecessary conversions in either direction because something is always lost in the transaction.

Figure 4 shows the *interface*—that's a computer word meaning hookup —between the five major elements of a modern automatic digital computer, the kind used in sophisticated RNAV systems.

It makes no difference who makes the computer or what it does—it'll have an *arithmetic unit* where all the calculations and manipulations are done, a *storage unit* (or memory) where instructions for working the problem (program) and data necessary for its solution are stored, an *input* and *output,* and a *control unit.*

In sophisticated RNAV systems, the arithmetic unit, storage unit and part of the control unit are typically housed in an ATR-type box mounted in the radio rack. The input, output and a portion of the control unit are mounted in the cockpit. Input typically is via keyboard or card reader, output is via alphanumeric light elements or CRT (cathode ray tube) displays. Most of these digital navigation computers also provide input to the autopilot, HSI and flight director through a D-to-A conversion.

Most spec sheet data you'll run into has to do with the storage (or memory) unit. Computers are like people and have both short- and long-term memories. In the case of a computer, the long-term memory is its *program,* a set of instructions that tells the arithmetic unit step-by-step how to solve a given problem. In avionics applications this long-term memory (program) cannot be erased nor will it be lost if the unit is disconnected from its power supply.

Data in the short-term memory—waypoint coordinates, for example— can be added and removed from the memory at will. Often the storage unit requires power to retain the items stored in the short-term memory; if so, the memory is said to be *volatile.* Bendix Avionics recently introduced a digital RNAV with a nonvolatile memory. This means that waypoints are not lost when the system is powered down.

The thing that most boggles the mind about modern digital computers is their speed. Earlier we said that a digital approach to problem solving

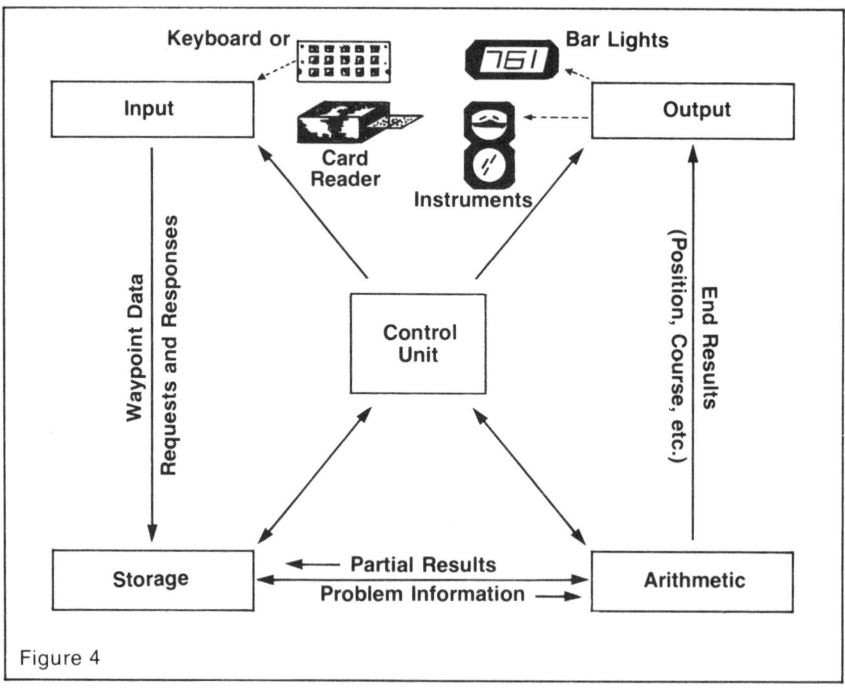

Figure 4

All automatic digital computers have at least the five major components shown here—input, storage, arithmetic, output and control. In this case, the computer is part of a sophisticated RNAV system. Note that the control unit is the boss and as such interfaces with all other components.

is often a lengthy process and is made practical only by the tremendous speed of electronic computers. This speed requirement becomes clearer when you consider that the arithmetic unit really knows how to perform only one mathematical operation—addition. Subtraction is performed by adding the complements of numbers, multiplication is merely repeated addition and division is repeated subtraction.

Obviously, then, the first thing a computer must do is convert a given problem—a differential equation, for example—into a series of addition operations. To handle all these additions, the computer needs fantastic numbers of counting devices. If you open up any digital computer, you'll find rows upon rows of identical circuit components. These are the adding devices hooked up to each other much in the same manner that the drums of the odometer in an automobile speedometer are connected.

Were you to handle a typical navigational problem involving speeds, winds and positions, but first had to reduce all mathematical operations to additions, you'd need years to complete the calculations. The high-speed digital computer handles these problems in fractions of seconds.

The advent of digital circuitry and computers in our cockpits has brought tremendous new capability. But it's also brought problems.

We've only touched here the barest tip of the digital iceberg, looking at a few of the words and concepts you'll be talking about with avionics marketers. However, the marketers themselves and the technicians who work on digital equipment are for the most part awed and in some cases buried by digital technology. The discipline is tricky. Troubleshooting a printed circuit (PC) board from the arithmetic unit of a small digital computer can be a nightmare of complexity, and the unhappy truth is that most avionics technicians are having a tough time keeping up with digital techniques and changes.

Most field repairs are carried down to the board level only. The technicians are leaving it to the factories to trace out failures in individual components.

For the pilot this is both good and bad news. The good news is simply that repairs limited to replacing an offending PC board usually mean quicker turnarounds. The bad news is that this repair technique depersonalizes your avionics. Gone are the days when good old Joe, the avionics technician, knew all the wires and components of your radio.

It wasn't too long ago that most pilots were having problems with the complexities of VOR hardware. Today the pilot, like any other businessman, must learn to live with the computer and to understand its capabilities and its faults.

Airborne computers aren't a fad. They're here now and they're here to stay. Next time you're in the neighborhood bookstore, pick up any one of the fine paperbacks designed to introduce the layman to the world of digital technology. Time spent here will pay dividends in your day-to-day operations and when you're faced with a purchase decision.

The Avionics Test Button

26

by J. Mac McClellan

What do the test buttons on your avionics really test? Are avionics test functions valid checks of a large number of system components and circuits or only a false security blanket, a placebo, for the pilot?

Most current production avionics have some type of function labeled *TEST*. You press the button or twist a knob and lights illuminate or a pointer moves in the prescribed manner. But can you be certain that everything is working properly just because your system passed its self test? The simplistic answer is no, but don't write off test functions altogether because there is much to be learned from them.

While the test functions on most avionics are billed as *self test,* implying that the black box does all the work and provides a yes or no answer, that isn't really the case. The information provided by the test is seldom of the yes/no variety. More commonly it is only an *indication* of yes/no that demands understanding and interpretation by the pilot. In order to understand what the test function is telling you, it's necessary to understand exactly what functions are being tested.

There are two popular schools of thought on the self-test issue and most manufacturers come down someplace in the middle. Test functions are not defined or required by TSO or any other regulations, although the extent of the test may be limited by regulation if a manufacturer chooses to include one in its design. Since test functions are not required, the type and extent of the test functions included in a piece of avionics may be only what the manufacturer believes is necessary to give him a competitive edge.

At one point the airlines were very interested in self-test and monitoring capability. Makers of Arinc specification equipment spent as much or more time talking about their failure detection circuits as they did discussing the actual performance of the box. Although many airlines have now drifted away from that position, Arinc format equipment still tends to contain more in the way of testing and monitoring functions than other business aviation equipment.

The reasons for the drift away from extensive testing and on-line monitoring of most equipment are cost and reliability. Self-test functions require more circuitry, circuitry that is dedicated to the self-test feature alone. The more extensive the testing or monitoring, the more circuitry required to perform the task. As the parts mount and complexity rises, so does the mathematical probability of failure. A piece of equipment with 500 parts is five times as likely to fail as a box with 100 components.

Extensive self-test and monitoring circuitry leads to another problem. Suppose activating the test function does result in a no-go indication. The question then becomes, has the test circuitry or the primary function failed? You almost need a test for the tester. If you could have a complete, 100 percent test system built-in, it would require as much or more circuitry as the primary function itself. If that were the case, a failure indication by the self-test feature would mean only that a 50/50 chance existed that the failure was in the primary function, rather than the self-test circuitry.

The next time you're in an avionics shop look at the tremendous amount of equipment required to test the various kinds of avionics. If it takes rooms full of equipment, plus hours of a skilled technician's time to thoroughly check out avionics, what are the odds that a bit of built-in circuitry can do the job?

The point is, self test is not a panacea. A point of diminishing returns is reached at which test functions can create problems as often as detect them. But test functions can alert you to many factors that affect avionics performance if you understand and know how to use the test mode. Let's discuss in general some of the ways in which manufacturers have designed self-test functions.

Probably the most basic avionics test is found in those VHF com transceivers that have a test feature. Invariably this *TEST* is simply a squelch bypass on the receiver and tests absolutely nothing in the transmitter. All it does is confirm that the transceiver is turned on, the volume is up and the right combination of switches on the audio control panel has been selected.

But there are some things you can learn from the com test. The static sound you hear in the test position is radio frequency noise coming through the receiver. When you hear static, you know the intermediate frequency is working. Also, you can detect a drop in the volume of the noise if the mixer or frequency synthesizer has failed. However, you aren't testing the receiver's front end, the frequency accuracy or many other possible failure points. As an aside, on some transceivers the test function can be used to override squelch so you can receive weak signals. This is of assistance many times when you're trying to get ATIS from far out or contact a Unicom.

The Collins Micro Line and ARC 800 and 1000 transceivers have a transmit monitor light that is activated by the final stage of the transmitter. The flicker of the light in the Micro Line indicates the signal is being modulated as you speak. This feature provides assurance that a signal is being generated and sent to the antenna connection. But the light in no way assures you that the antenna lead isn't broken or, for that matter, that the antenna hasn't fallen off. If you see the transmit monitor light flicker on, but nobody answers, you can be rather certain that the fault is in the antenna or its cable.

Narco and others use a transmit monitor light that flickers to show modulation and that power is going to the final transmitter stages, even if nothing is coming out of the transmitter.

One of the best performance and quality tests of a transmitter is to listen to the sidetones with a headphone. A garbled transmission can indicate improper mike gain adjustment or poor mike technique. If you know exactly what your radio is doing wrong, it will save you money when you take it in for repair by narrowing down the number of places the shop must check to locate the fault. Many installations are wired to feed sidetones back through the aircraft speaker so you can monitor your transmissions without wearing headphones. Speaker sidetone capability, however, is determined by the installation, not by the transceiver itself.

Another unit that virtually always contains a test function is the transponder. Even the lowest cost panel-mounted units have a selector position labeled *TEST* and the reply light glows when the switch is held in this position. As you might imagine, a $595 transponder cannot include a lot of extra circuitry just to test its function. Most transponder tests will tell you only that the unit is receiving power and that current is flowing through at least a portion of the circuitry. The test function on panel-mounted transponders normally either opens the gain to maximum or injects a signal into a portion of the circuitry to confirm that power is flowing through the encoder, the decoder and to the transmit tube. However, the receiver and intermediate frequency isn't tested and neither is the transmitter output. Encoder or decoder functions can be misaligned and the test will only detect that they are working but not necessarily working properly. The mode C function is not tested at all, so you have no assurance of an altitude report.

Arinc specification transponders costing 10 times as much as an average panel-mounted unit do a rather good job of following a test signal through the entire receiver section, encoder and decoder. They even reply to a test interrogation. Because a transponder performs computations, it lends itself to testing more readily than some other types of equipment. It can be given a sample interrogation and its response can be monitored and flagged if it's incorrect. But generating an L-band test signal is difficult and requires considerable circuitry, resulting in much higher costs and the possibility of failures in the testing circuits. This is why a thorough test is confined to the higher priced Arinc equipment.

So, when you flip over to the transponder test position before takeoff and get a reply light, the meaning of that indication depends on the type of transponder being tested. If it's a higher priced Arinc unit, it's probable that the entire system down to the antenna is working. If no reply light appears, there's a 50/50 chance the transponder is working, but the test circuit isn't.

If the test is of a panel-mounted unit, the reply light says only that you can be sure power is getting through about half the system. If you check to see that the antenna is in place during preflight, you can be rather certain that some kind of signal will go out. ATC will let you know in a hurry if the performance isn't up to par and, in that case, the best thing is to have a spare somewhere in the panel.

Nav receiver test features aren't as common as test functions on most other types of avionics. One reason for that lack of nav receiver self test is that the FARs require you to test the accuracy of each nav receiver to be used under IFR in the last 10 days or 10 hours of flight time whether you have a test function or not. Therefore, if you're flying by the book and using an approved test method at the specified intervals, there isn't as great a need for nav self test.

But there are some rather good nav system test functions available. Narco used a self-test system on its older VOA 8 and VOA 9 omni heads which is incorporated into its new Centerline nav receivers. Others have also used a similar procedure. This test requires that a valid VOR signal be within range. The nav receiver processes the VOR signal and when the self test is selected, it compares the 30 Hz variable and reference signals. If the two signals line up, the needle will center on 0° with a TO indication or 180° with a FROM indication. This test method assures that the receiver is working because it received the signal; that it is accurate because the needle centered on the appropriate OBS setting; that the meters and flags work; and that the audio is being received (because you can hear the ident).

The disadvantage of this test system is that you must be within range of a usable VOR signal, which isn't always the case on the ground before takeoff. Also, the self-test procedure is not approved for meeting the 10-day/10-hour requirement.

The best self test for VOR receivers is an authorized VOT (VHF omni test) signal which is broadcast at many major airports. Airports that have VOTs and their frequencies are listed in AIM Part 3. In flight you can get a pretty good idea of the quality of your VOR reading by measuring the course width with the OBS. To measure the course width, center the needle, note the course setting and then move that setting 10° in either direction with the course selector knob. The needle should show full deflection, representing 10° off course. Any other indication will tell you the signal is too weak to be usable or there is a fault in the VOR system, either your airborne one or the FAA's on the ground.

The marker beacon display almost always includes a self-test feature. Virtually all popular panel-mounted marker beacon receivers have a high sense, low sense and test position. Selecting the test position will light the three marker indicators, but in most receivers does little else.

But the marker beacon test, simple though it may be, is very useful. Primarily it assures that all three lights work. Also, you can manually dim the indication to suit cockpit ambient light conditions or, if the display is dimmed automatically, you can cover the photocell to be certain the sensor is working properly.

The marker beacon receiver is a prime example of a unit that could actually be *less* reliable if it had an extensive self test. The marker receiver is the most simple of all receivers, detecting only one frequency, 75 MHz. Any extensive test circuitry would only increase the parts count and the probability of failure.

The ADF indicator test function may be one of the most used self tests in an aircraft. There's really no need to complicate this feature, although some makers do. All you really need is a method of slewing the needle to a different position so you can watch its reaction. If the needle rotates back to the appropriate bearing, you can be relatively certain that the receiver and ADF system are providing a good, steady point. After using the ADF for a few hours you'll be able to determine which indications are usable. What if the needle doesn't swing back to an appropriate direction after the test? That *could* be due to a fault in your ADF system, but it might also indicate an interfering "noise" from some other source. We once had an electronic clock in one of our aircraft that would command the ADF in certain frequency ranges. Some alternator faults will also override the proper signal. In any event, the ADF system is rendered inop unless you can locate the cause of the interference and turn the offending system off.

While the simple needle displacement is the most popular form of ADF testing, other manufacturers will artificially rotate the signal inside the receiver, which in turn causes the needle to displace a predetermined amount. This type of testing doesn't really seem necessary to us because if you have a good, clear audio ident and a solid point, there's little else a self-test system can tell you about the performance or accuracy of the ADF. The ADF is subject to many errors but understanding the source of those errors will help you live with them a lot more than a test or monitoring function.

DME self test deals primarily with the display lights in most general aviation units. With many systems using seven-segment electronic digits to display DME information, it's important to check that all the segments

211

light with a test mode. If one or more doesn't, the system may be misread.

Some of the new digital DMEs will test the timing circuits as well as the display. More expensive DMEs, particularly those meeting Arinc specifications, have test functions capable of checking about 80 percent of the components. These systems generate a test signal, inject it into the front of the receiver and then monitor it as it passes through the circuitry. Such a test function provides a rather good self test prior to takeoff, but will drive up the cost of the unit considerably. For example, the Collins DME 40, which does contain a comprehensive self-test feature, lists for $2000 to $3000 more than competitive DMEs from Bendix, Edo, King or Narco. Not all of that cost can be attributed to the self-test function, but it is an important factor in the price.

In flight a DME is not really in need of a lot of testing or monitoring because of the nature of its design. Being a closed-loop computation device, the DME is most likely to quit totally rather than provide an erroneous reading. In many digital DMEs, the timing circuits control the frequency selection as well as distance computation. If that timing circuit fails, most likely the frequency will be lost as well, so there's little need to monitor the performance.

King DMEs have a patented decision-making-monitoring scheme that constantly monitors the yes/no choices the system makes in locking onto a station. King's engineers have worked out the probability factors of each possible decision and if the DME locks onto what could be a bad signal, the loop will be broken and the search resumed.

The engineers we questioned agreed that a modern DME is most likely to either work properly and present an output that is within the system's tolerance limits or not work at all. No engineer is ever going to give you that kind of a *guarantee*, but in general terms, that's how it usually works out with a DME. If you don't lock onto a station that is within range, listen to the ident before squawking the DME. If there's no ident, try another station or call an FSS to see if the VORTAC you've tuned is off the air.

Incidentally, even if you do hear a DME ident, it's not absolute assurance that the ground station is broadcasting a proper interrogation signal. Several times we have been able to receive the identifier even when an FSS has confirmed that the station is down.

RNAV is a computed function and by its very nature is compatible with a high degree of self-test confidence. Most RNAVs will work a sample problem and provide a specified answer to make certain the computer is working. Display and annunciator lights are also tested, which can be important with the usual seven-segment electronic numbers.

Many popular RNAVs in the self-test mode display the selected offset distance in the distance window and center the CDI when the OBS is set on the programmed offset radial. In this way you are assured that the system is receiving power, valid inputs from the DME and VOR receivers and is driving the displays properly.

Many sophisticated keyboard-style RNAVs have extensive self-test procedures that can be accomplished on the ramp. In most cases the owner's manual explains the procedure, which usually includes making specific entries and watching for a specific response from the computer. If the system works these self-test problems perfectly, you can have a very high degree of confidence in its performance.

Flight control systems are another area ripe for self tests and monitors. Nearly every sophisticated integrated system has some form of on-line monitoring that will detect faults that can lead to a dramatic failure such as a hardover. The King IFCS-300 even will induce faults into the system to be certain they are detected and appropriate action is taken during the self test. ARC's 400 and 800 IFCS systems check the disconnect circuitry that disables the servos in the event of a hardover. Others have similar features and virtually all will illuminate annunciator lights, bring power flags into view and assure that power is reaching the system.

Several engineers we consulted indicated that the biggest weakness in autopilot self test is the pilot, who often fails to read the self-test section of the operator's manual.

Radio and servoed altimeters both incorporate self-test functions and, in the case of these two instruments, it can be very helpful. On the ramp a radio altimeter self-tests itself. You can ascertain if the unit is operating by simply turning it on. The off flag should pull and the indicator should point to zero, or whatever its lowest reading may be in the case of less sophisticated systems. However, in flight above the maximum range of the altimeter, which is usually no more than 2500 feet, the needle usually parks behind a screen and you have no indication that the system even has power. By pressing the test button, the needle will be driven to a specific altitude indication, the off flag will appear and you at least know the system is capable of doing something. The more expensive radio altimeter systems are capable of self-testing about 80 percent of the components and their functions. That's nice to know before you start the approach.

The servoed encoding altimeter test is not so reassuring in flight, but it can at least satisfy you that power is reaching the system, the servo motor is working, the meter isn't stuck and the warning flag works. However, the self test doesn't guarantee accuracy or proper encoding for mode C operation.

In both types of altimeter systems a complete self test would require so many additional components it would be as likely for the self test to break as for the primary function to fail. A minimal self test can give you a degree of confidence that the system isn't just stuck or completely dead.

213

Weather radar is another system that demands a self test. You don't want to test it by transmitting radar pulses while on the ground for fear of injuring someone with the microwave energy or damaging your radar with a reflection from a building or another airplane—or damaging the radar in some other aircraft by transmitting a pulse directly onto its antenna. For these reasons, weather radars have self-test systems that will warm up the transmitter, display a test pattern on the indicator and start the antenna in motion. Sophisticated systems like the RCA Primus 40 and 400 inject a test noise signal far up into the receiver section and display it as a band of light on the indicator. With this test you have good assurance the radar is working without the risks inherent in transmitting a pulse on the ground. For many flight departments, weather radar is a go/no-go item, so it is important that the system give a reasonable assurance that it will perform in the air.

Another important factor of radar self test, of course, is that it provides the means for adjusting the system in preparation for flight. With the test pattern displayed on the scope it's possible to adjust the brightness to match ambient light conditions and to make certain all levels of intensity can be distinguished. With the newer digital radars that feature alphanumerics, the test mode provides an opportunity to scan the various numbers and letters on the display, in some instances, insure that the weather alert and contour features are operating.

Radar self test is of little value once the aircraft is in the air because the tilt can always be turned down for a check of the ground return. If the ground target display isn't up to par, the performance of the system in weather detection must be suspect.

The future of avionics self test seems assured, at least from the standpoint of testing the display. Lighting the numbers and annunciator lights is simple but important. Imagine a situation in which you lower the landing gear and get only two instead of three green lights. Is the bulb burned out or is the gear not down and locked? With a self-test button to light the lights, you will be able to eliminate one of these possibilities.

But more sophisticated self-test systems seem to be on the way out. In general, reliability is up on all avionics and a major reason for that reliability increase is a reduction in parts count. Self-test functions add to the parts count and, in a mathematical sense, reduce reliability. Self test also adds size, weight and cost. Modern solid-state integrated components tend to wipe out all or a large share of the system functions when they fail instead of simply degrading performance or accuracy, so a test is less necessary in this case.

Returning to our original question, can you sit on the ramp before takeoff and with self-test functions be certain that all your avionics are working before takeoff? The answer is no, but you can gain a lot of important information from even the most simple test functions if you understand and use them properly.

When it comes to selecting avionics equipment, you should certainly consider the self-test function, but be sure you understand it. Don't choose one system over the other because of a self-test feature unless you understand exactly what is being tested, why you need to have that feature and how you will use it. If the salesman can't explain *exactly* what is being tested in a system, talk to a technician or an expert who can answer your questions. If you can't grade the self-test feature of equipment you expect to purchase, you'll never know if it falls short of your requirements.

27

Autopilot Watchamacallit

by Richard N. Aarons

It used to be that autopilots were pretty simple devices—you turned them on, then tried to figure out why they weren't working. Even when they did work, they weren't too difficult to program and command. They usually came with on/off switches, pitch-and roll-command knobs and a placard which suggested that to use them within a mile of the ground was courting disaster. There are some folks who argue that things haven't changed much. "Never flew one of those damn things yet that didn't try to kill me," mumbled one senior pilot when I mentioned that I was working up this article on autopilot terminology. Personally, I think he was exaggerating a bit, but autopilot reliability and maintainability are subjects for another time. Here we're going to talk about autopilot nomenclature.

If anything has changed in the business of nonhuman flight control, it's been the sophistication of these devices. Along with that change came a whole new lexicon. Today's autopilots with all their new modes (things like "climb profile") and their super features (like "pitch integration," whatever the hell that is) boggle the mind. So even my friend who mistrusts autopilots is going to have to pay attention to this chapter so he can learn enough to tell when his autopilot tries to do him dirty. I mean, if nothing else, some of this information might help him carry on an intelligent argument with his avionics-shop foreman if the man lays something on him like: "Sorry, Jack, it looks like the attitude comparitor is shot."

Anyway, a quick scan of the ads in aviation magazines introduces us immediately to the first three terms which need, I think, a bit of explanation —*autopilot, flight-control system* and *integrated flight-control system.*

An *autopilot* is what we were flying 10 years ago. A device the primary (and often, only) function of which was to keep the aircraft right side up. And autopilot *is* the proper term to use when referring to the relatively simple one- and two-axis machines used on singles and light twins. (Engineers use the term autopilot only when referring to the muscles of the flight-control system—servos and the like.) The disagreement on autopilot terminology begins right here. Some manufacturers referring to a three-axis autopilot mean one that exercises control over all three axes—roll, pitch and yaw. Other manufacturers use the same term to describe an autopilot which has servos to move the ailerons (roll), elevators (pitch) and elevator trim (pitch again). Still others use the term to describe an autopilot with roll and pitch control and an altitude-hold feature. So when you are shopping for an autopilot, before any money changes hands, be certain you and the salesman are speaking the same language.

The major elements of a basic autopilot system are the attitude-sensing devices, servo computer/amplifiers and the servos themselves. Most low-cost autopilots sense aircraft attitude through the same panel-mounted gyros that the human pilot uses for attitude information. The pick-offs are electromagnetic in modern devices so there's no friction between the gyro assembly and the sensors. The pick-offs send signals defining displacement and rate of displacement to the autopilot computer/amplifier which processes them (more on this later) and amplifies them before sending them along to the servos. Most modern autopilot systems use electric servos which are continuously running DC motors located near the appropriate control surfaces. These motors drive capstans which, in turn, drive cables attached to the control surfaces. (Servo motors are unidirectional, but are equipped with two magnetic clutches which rotate the capstans in different directions depending on the polarity of the signal from the computer/amplifier.)

The best way to describe a computer/amplifier is to say simply that it's the black box located between all the inputs (gyro, VOR receiver, air-data computer and so on) and the outputs (servo drives). Manufacturers have different terminologies for the computer and amplifier components of their autopilots, but certain general concepts hold true for all of them.

Electronic autopilots have one *servo amplifier* for each axis to be controlled. The servo amplifier's prime task is to take the tiny electronic signals from the sensing element in the gyros and convert them to more powerful signals which operate clutches on the primary servos. But a lot happens to the signals between the time they leave the gyro sensors and enter the servo clutches.

To get a handle on what happens in the servo amplifier, let's build a simple single-axis autopilot step by step. Suppose we wanted to control the roll axis and use the attitude gyro for basic attitude information. Next assume that we simply took the signals from the gyro, amplified them and routed them directly to the aileron servo. Now as the aircraft falls off into a bank, the gyro pick-offs send a signal to the servos and the ailerons are displaced to counteract the bank. In our simple device, the control deflection will be retained until the aircraft is in a level attitude (when the gyro signal ceases). But by that time the aircraft will have developed a rolling momen-

217

tum and it will roll right through the level attitude at which time the gyro sensors will order aileron displacement in the opposite direction.

If this is allowed to go on unchecked, the aircraft will rock back and forth violently as the ailerons fight a losing battle to right it.

Obviously, we need some way to tell the autopilot when its original correction has done sufficient work and thus order it to return the controls to a neutral position before the aircraft is fully level. This is accomplished by using control surface *follow-up devices* and *rate networks* in the servo amplifiers. The follow-up devices are linked mechanically to the control surfaces (or servos) and signal the displacement of the controls back to the servo amplifier. The rate network is a simple resistance/capacitance circuit which looks at the relationship of the signals coming from the attitude sensing elements and compares them with the signals going to the control surfaces. It functions as a valve, increasing control-surface deflection as variation from the desired attitude increases and then decreasing control-surface deflection as the correction is made.

Next time you get a chance to look at a disassembled autopilot system (most manufacturers display them at the big conventions) ask the man at the booth to open up a computer-amplifier box and show you its innards. Modern designers have put each control surface's servo amplifier on an individual printed circuit board which plugs into a rack in the box. The other boards in the box are used for navigation computing and vertical modes. And at least one of those boards is an electronic device which matches the general characteristics of the autopilot to the specific needs of your aircraft. (Keep in mind while you're looking at these boxes that troubleshooting problems—and therefore shop costs—are in inverse proportion to the number of autopilot functions controlled by any single PC board. An increase in the number of discrete-function boards usually produces a decrease in troubleshooting. Of course, an unreasonable increase in the number of discrete boards would increase failure probability.)

The *autopilot* as described is a component *part* of a *flight-control system*. An example here will probably save a lot of words. I was flying an MU-2 a while back equipped with a Collins FD-109 flight director, a PN-101 compass system and a Bendix M4-C autopilot. Together they function as a *flight-control system* and are properly called that. One disadvantage of this system is that the flight director and autopilot each has its own mode selector and mode annunciator. So it's possible (and, indeed probable until you learn the system) that you'll end up flying the flight director in one mode and the autopilot in another, getting somewhat confused in the process.

An *integrated* flight-control system is one in which the components are designed to play together, and often share circuitry. The flight director and autopilot, for example, will share the same mode selector and annunciator

218

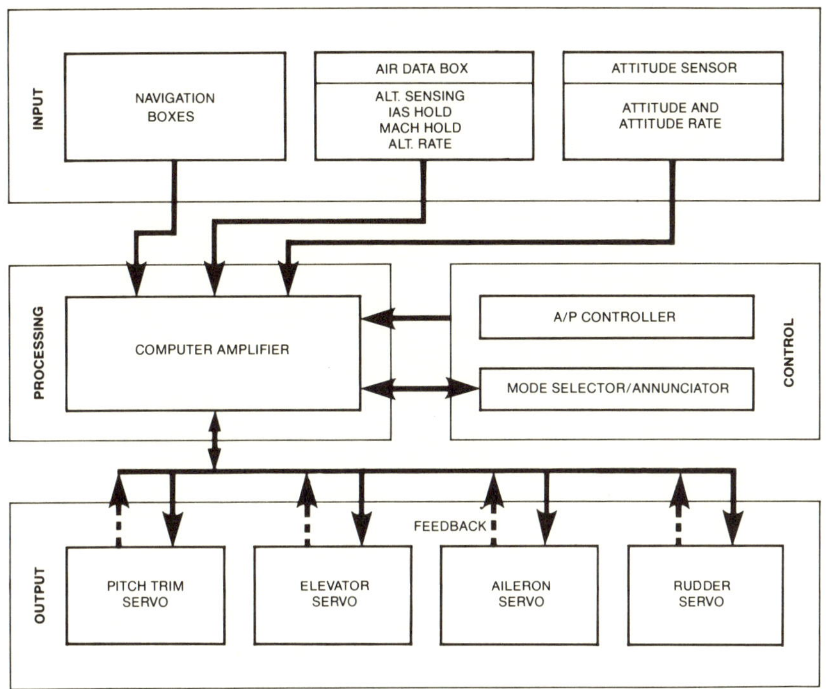

Diagram of a typical autopilot system

in an integrated system. The heading reference will be designed as a part of the flight-director system; thus the horizontal-situation indicator will be purchased with the system rather than separately.

With this background then, let's get into some autopilot/flight-control-system terminology and see if we can sort some of it out.

Automatic pitch trim—This feature enables the autopilot computer to keep an eye on the elevator servo and retrim the aircraft to reduce elevator loads when necessary. For example, the automatic pitch trim goes into operation when, while maintaining level flight, you lower the gear or change power setting. The elevator servos catch the change first, then the automatic pitch trim adjusts for the long-term situation.

Pitch integration—With this feature the autopilot, from the human pilot's viewpoint, "follows" his actions when he has control of the aircraft then takes over without a bump when ordered to do so. For example, if the pilot establishes a climb manually then engages the autopilot, the aircraft will continue the climb at the pitch which the pilot had established. Some flight-control systems have roll and yaw integration so the aircraft can be

219

handed to the autopilot in any attitude and the autopilot will maintain that attitude.

Pitch synchronization—This term is usually applied to flight directors and refers to the ability of the flight-director command bars to acquire the pitch attitude that the pilot has maneuvered the aircraft to. For example, you might want an initial five-degree rotation at takeoff followed by a rotation to 16 degrees after takeoff. On a flight director with pitch sync, you manually set in the five-degree command before takeoff. Once off the ground, you'd rotate the aircraft to 16 degrees on the horizon indicator, then push the pitch-sync button. The pitch bars will then move to the 16-degree position and command that pitch until changed. This works as a poor-man's airspeed-hold system. In this case, you establish the pitch attitude for the appropriate climb speed then hit the pitch-sync button. All you need do then is follow the pitch-command bars to maintain that speed. Of course the pitch bars would have to be reset as the climb continued.

Vertical modes—For our purposes, we'll use this term in reference to those modes which rely on pitot/static source information. The simplest of the vertical modes, then, is *altitude hold.* Altitude-hold systems in the less sophisticated autopilots consist of self-contained baro-sensing systems. The system doesn't know or care whether the airplane is at 2,000 feet or 10,000 feet. What it does do is remember the *pressure* altitude it was at when altitude-hold mode was selected. Any deviation from that altitude sends a signal to the elevator servo. On more sophisticated systems, altitude-hold signals come from the air-data box, as do *altitude-rate, IAS-hold* and *Mach-hold* signals. Some of the newer flight-control systems include VNAV systems which provide *altitude alerting* and enable the pilot (or autopilot) to reference vertical maneuvers to horizontal positions.

Rate control and *displacement control*—You hear much of these two terms from avionics salesmen. About half the manufacturers think rate control is better, the other half favors displacement control. But in any event, both terms refer to the autopilot controller knobs (usually mounted on the control pedestal). In a *displacement*-control system, the amount of pitch or bank (turn) obtained depends on the distance that the control knob (or wheel) is displaced. Usually these controls are set up nonlinearly so that movements near the center position cause relatively small control-surface deflections and movements at the end of the knobs' range cause larger flight-control displacements. A displacement-type turn-control knob will allow the aircraft to turn only while it is out of the centered position. Once the knob returns to the center position the aircraft stops turning. A *rate*-type turn-command knob works somewhat like the aircraft controls themselves. Moving the knob in one direction establishes a bank and thus a turn. The bank angle will continue to increase (up to the autopilot limits) so long as the command knob is out of its center position. When the knob is returned to center (usually via a centering spring), the roll stops and the airplane continues to turn at the commanded bank angle. To stop the turn, the knob must be moved in the opposite direction and then returned to the center position as the turn stops. The system you select is strictly a matter of personal preference—but be sure you fly both systems before making a final decision. The differences are striking.

Control-wheel synchronization and *control-wheel steering*—Control-wheel *synchronization* is similar to the pitch, yaw and roll integration discussed earlier. Basically, it's a button on the control wheel which enables the pilot to take over manual control (while the autopilot follows through) to make minor attitude changes. He relinquishes control to the autopilot by releasing the control-wheel-sync button. The autopilot then latches on calmly because it's been "flying" right along with the pilot. Some manufacturers have been using the term "control-wheel steering" in reference to control-wheel synchronization, but purists say control-wheel steering should be reserved for schemes in which the pilot flies the aircraft with the control wheel acting through the autopilot servos as he does when he uses the controller knobs on the pedestal.

Gyro platform—All of the smaller autopilots and many of the sophisticated flight-control systems use panel-mounted gyros for basic reference. But panel-mounted gyros by their very nature are restricted in size. And it's an unhappy physical fact that a gyro's stability is directly proportional to its size. Thus some flight-control-system manufacturers offer gyro systems which serve only the flight-control system. They are remotely located somewhere in the avionics rack, but because they're out of the panel they can be much larger and thus provide the autopilot with better attitude information.

Some of the supersophisticated new-generation flight-control systems have additional gyro packages (attitude comparitors) used by the computer as a reference in watching the normal gyro system's operation.

In putting this very short list of autopilot/flight-control-system terms together I talked with half a dozen engineers. The one point that each stressed was that while the industry's engineers have pretty well standardized their terminology the industry's sales and marketing types have not.

An autopilot, no matter what size it is, is a hell of a big investment. And at the same time, exactly what you're getting for your dollars is sometimes difficult to determine because of the complexity of the systems and terms used in the literature. The terms I've presented here are only to help you wade through the brochures and ads. If you're in the market, sit down with sales engineers from the various manufacturers and make up your own apples-to-apples comparison chart. Then, and this is most important, fly the systems you are interested in, paying special attention to those areas of major difference such as rate control versus displacement control.

221

AVIONICS: COMPONENTS

VII

It's good to have the big picture. That keeps things in the proper perspective. It's also good to understand the details and see how they fit into the whole scheme. This section examines several individual avionics components with appropriate tips for selection, maintenance and use.

Aircraft antennas are the first line in reception, and the final gate in transmission. Well designed, thoughtfully maintained antennas can help you get the most out of your expensive avionics.

If you are an average pilot, you take microphones for granted. When you think about it, those little handsets are your only means of using that costly transmitter. Your multi-thousand dollar radio is totally dependent on that inexpensive accessory. "Microphones" takes a quick look and offers some useful suggestions.

The instrument pilot depends on his gyros even more than his radio components. Ironically, those critical gyro instruments are often the most neglected. "Air-Driven Gyros: How To Keep Them Spinning" details the care and feeding of these sensitive creatures.

The Horizontal Situation Indicator, or HSI, is the next step up from a simple directional gyro. When properly interpreted, this distinctive instrument can greatly simplify instrument flight. Area Navigation, or RNAV, is a child of the 70s which will grow to maturity in a few short years. If you haven't flown RNAV yet, you will soon. When you do use this delightful navigation aid, be aware of it's accuracy limitations. And before purchasing a radio altimeter be sure you understand what it can do.

These avionics components are discussed in detail. They are designed for navigation, communications, or convenience. Just one device, radar, is solely dedicated to flight safety. Weather radar interpretation has so many variables that any change in the system itself can seriously compromise its usefulness. Two selections, "Radar Maintenance" and "Maintaining Your Radome" outline the procedures for optimizing that important and expensive piece of equipment.

Now you have the big picture and the smaller components. Keep going for some vital operating tips.

Antennas? Who Cares?

28

by Richard N. Aarons

What do you know about antennas?

Sure, you count them before takeoff, but do you know that some antennas are more susceptible to icing than others, or that two seemingly identical antennas may have different electrical properties and therefore perform differently when attached to the same radio? How do you select a replacement antenna for your com set if the original equipment falls victim to hangar rash or vandalism? Where should antennas be mounted to get optimum performance?

Don't feel bad if you can't answer those questions. Few pilots can. In fact, very few pilots ever think about antennas. And that list included at least one B/CA staffer until he met Marshal Sawyer, president of Comant Industries.

Just about a year ago, our staffer was roaming the exhibit floor of the Aviation Electronics Association convention when he spied Sawyer standing behind a card table heaped with antennas of various descriptions. He looked very lonely. Avionics guys and pilots were busily examining all the new black boxes, stacked up on tables around his, but nobody seemed to care about Sawyer's rods and blades.

"That's the problem with the antenna business," he sighed when asked why his exhibit attracted so little notice. "Nobody cares about antennas, but they should. The best black box in the world won't perform to its capabilities unless it's matched to the proper antenna. And, you don't automatically get a good antenna just because you order an expensive radio. Some less-than-scrupulous avionics shops install inexpensive awfuls to cut corners and pick up a few extra bucks on the installation. Even some airframe manufacturers have been known to cut corners when installing antennas on little airplanes and sometimes a pilot ends up spending a bunch of money with an avionics shop to cure a radio problem that he could cure himself with a wet rag."

It seemed incredible that a hunk of wire could be all that complicated and important. Since that meeting we've talked to antenna manufacturers, air-frame makers, avionics repairmen and pilots in an attempt to comprise a list of important things every pilot should know (even if he doesn't want to) about his antennas. The list is incomplete primarily because antenna making is still a black art. But some of the data which came our way should be helpful to you, if you're ever in the market for a new antenna. The place to start is with a description of what an antenna is.

In its simplest form an antenna is a piece of conducting wire which radiates or receives radio energy. When attached to a transmitter, radio frequency electrical energy surges back and forth along the length of the antenna creating alternating electric and magnetic fields around it. Some of the energy in these fields collapses back into the antenna, but much of it radiates out into space. The better the antenna design, the larger the portion of radiated energy.

The same antenna attached to a receiver *catches* the spillover from the transmitting antenna and sends it off to the receiver circuitry for detection and amplification. Actually, the alternating electric and magnetic fields radiating from the transmitter antenna induce a radio frequency alternating current in the receiving antenna.

One way of identifying the function of various antennas on an aircraft is to examine their relative sizes because they are sized in proportion to the wavelengths of the frequencies they are designed to receive. Low frequencies have long wavelengths, so low frequency antennas such as ADF-sense antennas are several feet in length. Higher frequencies have shorter wavelengths and therefore require physically smaller antennas for radio energy transmission and reception. The smallest ones are the 2.5-inch stubs used for ultrahigh-frequency (UHF) DMEs and transponders. Mid-size antennas are used for VHF com and nav. (Com antennas are vertically polarized and mounted vertically. Nav antennas are horizontally polarized and, therefore, mounted horizontally.)

The complexity involved in selecting the appropriate antenna for both aircraft and radio is considerable. There are literally dozens of possible combinations, but only one is best for a given aircraft/avionics setup. Finding that combination can be quite involved and, surprisingly, it's the airplane itself that presents most of the problems.

Consider a vertically polarized VHF com antenna sitting out in the middle of a field. The antenna is omnidirectional. If we were to carry a field strength meter around it at a constant radius (any radius), the reading on the instrument would be constant. That is because the ground plane is uniform and constant. Of course, this omni-directional characteristic is important for good communication.

If we had to provide VHF com for a flying saucer, we'd have no problems. We'd simply mount the vertical com antenna on the belly of the saucer (no sense in putting it on top where the saucer structure itself would be between the antenna and the ground com station). The flat, constant diameter of the saucer would be just like the flat field (ground plane) in our initial experiment and the radiation pattern would be omnidirectional.

Unhappily, we don't pilot flying saucers, but rather ungainly (electronically) airplanes with wings and tails and other things sticking out all over. All this aluminum in the way of the antenna distorts the radiation pattern. If a com antenna is too close to the vertical tail structure, for example, communication with a ground station to the rear of the aircraft might be impossible. Then too, the various antennas themselves can cause problems. For example, if the DME and transponder antennas are too close to each other, cross talk is possible. That is, the radiations of the antennas interfere with each other.

To minimize these problems, antenna manufacturers, working with airframe designers in many cases, test antenna-airframe combinations with 10th-scale models. By scaling down the aircraft and antenna by a factor of 10 (and increasing the frequency by a factor of 10) the propagation pattern of each antenna can be measured accurately. The model's antennas are jockeyed around until the optimum pattern is developed and then these experimentally determined "best" locations are used as antenna mounting points on all production aircraft.

These studies are made on all turbine aircraft, all Beech aircraft and the twins manufactured by Piper and Cessna. This basic research in antenna location is a big sales point for factory-installed avionics systems. Chances are that the factory has learned either from experimentation or experience the best location for the various com and nav antennas on each aircraft in its model line.

Ideally, all antennas should be belly mounted, but in the real world this is not always possible. VHF nav antennas, for example, fare well on the vertical tail. Glideslope antennas are usually mounted behind the radome of twins or on the windshield of singles.

Most good avionics shops collect data on proper antenna placement and are able to optimize the installation. Some shops, however, pay little attention to antenna placement and thus rob your avionics system of its full capability.

After installation you can check for proper nav and com antenna placement by flying a test pattern. First, read the literature about your avionics box to determine what its line-of-sight range is supposed to be. (A typical general aviation VHF transceiver, for instance, should operate to a range of at least 70 miles at 8,000 feet.) Second, check the antenna radiation pattern by going down range at least 70 miles at 8,000 feet and initiate a slow, flat turn.

Check your ability to transmit and receive every 10 degrees of the turn.

You'll notice that the transmission is loud and clear on some headings and a little less than five-square on others, but what you're really looking for is full 360-degree coverage. If you detect blind spots during the turn, the antenna may be improperly located or poorly mounted. The check for VHF nav antennas (VOR, ADF and DME) is made in the same manner, except you watch for nav flags instead of listening for fades.

Ideally, you shouldn't have to worry about antenna radiation patterns after the fact of installation—that's the wrong (and expensive) time. Rule one in smart antenna buying, therefore, is to let the airframe manufacturer install the antennas unless you are absolutely sure the avionics shop has enough experience and data to work out placement problems. (The airframe manufacturer will install antennas for you even if you're having the black boxes installed elsewhere.)

Suppose, however, for some reason you are starting from scratch with antenna selection and installation.

To start with, it's a good idea to ask the black box manufacturer for a list of antennas "approved" for operation with his radios. Most avionics manufacturers do not make antennas for their own radios. As one radio manufacturer told us, "It's just too damn much trouble to make antennas unless you're making them in the thousands. We only make antennas for special applications when they are simply not available from vendors."

Obviously, if you have TSOd black boxes, you'll want TSOd antennas, but TSO isn't everything. The antenna must be electrically matched to the radio and must meet airframe requirements for structure and aesthetics.

If your avionics installer gives you a catalogue from which to make your antenna selection, you'll notice that each entry includes these technical parameters: (1) frequency range, (2) impedance, (3) weight, (4) speed and (5) VSWR. There are usually other parameters, but these are the most important.

Frequency range: Obviously each radio requires an antenna capable of providing maximum performance over its full frequency range. Antennas capable of handling a wide spectrum of frequencies are described as "broad band." Those designed for use with a single frequency (or very narrow portion of the frequency spectrum) are called "narrow band." If you have 360-channel com onboard and are upgrading to 720, you'll probably need new com antennas to cover the wider band. The same goes for nav-channel expansion. The frequency range of the antenna must match (or exceed) the frequency range of the radio.

Impedance: Impedance is to avionics installers what pipe size is to plumbers. The impedance of the antenna must match the impedance of the radio. Your avionics shop will worry about this.

Weight: Weight is important in antenna selection just as it is in selecting black boxes. The lighter the better, as long as structural requirements are met.

Speed: Because externally mounted antennas stick out into the airstream they are speed rated. Wire antennas are structurally acceptable on only the slowest (VFR) aircraft. Rods (bare or coated) are usually designed for speed ranges up to 261 knots. Blade and flush antennas are rated for speeds normally considered in terms of Mach. You don't want your antenna to blow away, so make sure you've got a comfortable margin between aircraft speed and antenna speed capabilities.

VSWR: This term stands for voltage standing wave ratio and its precise definition is best left to the engineers. But it is important to the antenna purchaser as a measure of antenna efficiency. The lower the ratio the better.

Okay—you've decided to go with a light weight, strong, low-VSWR antenna. Which is best?

Obviously, external antennas cause drag—the bigger the antenna, the more the drag. Flush-mounted antennas in small piston-engine aircraft are pretty tough. Cessna has done a nice job with its twins by imbedding antennas in plastic fairings, but in most piston twins of other manufacturers and all singles, antennas are still exposed.

Here's the consensus of the airframe and antenna manufacturers on the ills and virtues of the various antenna types.

Straight or bent wire: Nobody likes them much. They are susceptible to corrosion and fatigue and have a characteristically high VSWR. They cannot withstand icing loads and are apt to depart the aircraft when most needed.

Uncoated straight or bent rods: A structural improvement over the wire types. Fatigue and icing problems are less and the VSWR curve is usually better (flatter). Corrosion can still be a problem, however.

Coated straight or bent rods: A good bet for high performance singles and light twins. These antennas have the strength and performance of bare rods with the added protection of fiberglass or epoxy sheathings which prevent corrosion and FOD. They are relatively light weight.

Aerodynamically faired rods: These antennas look like tapering airfoil shapes and provide greater strength and less drag than the coated straight or bent rods. Their aerodynamic shapes usually reduce icing loads, but weight is slightly higher.

Blades: These are stubbier versions of the aerodynamically faired rods. They provide the least drag and greatest structural strength. However, they are also the most expensive. The imbedded elements in blade antennas are physically shorter than the optimum length for the appropriate frequencies; therefore they are "loaded" with an inductance which makes the antenna "think" it's long enough to do the job. This too is better left to the

229

engineers, other than to point out that the added sophistication means added cost.

Of course, you want to consider appearance in antenna selection too. There's no reason why you can't mount a sexy blade antenna on the smallest single-engine aircraft, but, on the other hand, you certainly wouldn't want your brand new turboprop bristling with straight rods.

How about the care and feeding of your aircraft's antennas? Can you really do anything more than count them during the preflight?

Most experts we've talked to agree that a little preventive maintenance can save money and problems.

First, make sure all antennas are clean. An accumulation of grease and grime can actually detune an antenna and reduce its efficiency.

Next, inspect the seals around the base of the antenna where it meets the fuselage for proper bonding, leaks and corrosion. If the antenna is imbedded in fiberglass or epoxy, look for chips in the coating. Any break in the surface can allow water contamination, which detunes the antenna. Chips can be repaired with non-metallic base paint or other fillers. But check with your avionics shop first.

Bare metal antennas (wires or rods) should be inspected for corrosion and hairline fatigue cracks, especially near the base. They should always be painted with a non-metallic paint recommended by your avionics shop.

While you're counting antennas, make sure your ELT antenna is in place. ELTs in smaller aircraft are equipped with flimsy wire antennas which often fall victim to ice and sometimes to vandalism.

Microphones 29

by Richard N. Aarons

The guys who make their livings peddling aircraft components often mumble the old saw . . . "Nothing happens 'til somebody sells something." And from the standpoint of the economy, that's probably true.

In communications there's an analogy in the statement, "Nothing happens until the microphone does its thing." Or said another way, you can have $200,000 worth of communications equipment onboard, but it isn't worth a nickel unless the microphone works.

Microphones are like antennas: they are taken for granted. They hang on their hooks or on their headset mounts and do nothing until the pilot wants to talk. Then he pushes a button and starts yakking. If for some reason he suspects his words are not reaching the folks on the ground, or in another aircraft, the pilot kicks his radios and notes a squawk in the avionics log. Rarely does it occur to him that the culprit just might be his microphone.

Of course, this situation is actually a testimonial to the microphone. The fact is they work so well and so unobtrusively that they don't beg the pilot's attention and are thus ignored. But just as avionic black boxes have changed in sophistication and complexity over the years, so have microphones. Carbon mikes have been around since radio signals were first modulated with voice and probably comprise the majority of general aviation microphones in existence. In more recent years, the people who manufacture aircraft microphones have been touting *dynamic, magnetic* and *electret* mikes for general aviation applications. In a moment, we'll talk about each type and outline some of their good and bad characteristics. But first, here are a couple of general considerations in microphone design.

It's no secret that the cockpit is a lousy environment for conversation—especially in the smaller business aircraft most of us fly. It's simply a noisy place. The situation represents the single biggest problem in microphone design. The designer must work out a scheme to capture the pilot's voice with clarity and strength while at the same time canceling or rejecting the roar of engines and slipstream noise.

As if the audio frequency noise problems were not bad enough, the cockpit is full of stray radio frequency energy that must be rejected or canceled as well. Further complicating things is interference from 400 Hz AC cockpit equipment.

Carbon microphones: Carbon mikes are the apple pie and motherhood of voice communications. You use them every day in your telephone receiver and chances are good that the primary mike in your aircraft is of the carbon variety. (If not the primary mike, at least the standby mike stuffed under the rear seat with the tow bar.)

All microphones function by transforming the mechanical energy of sound waves into varying electrical energy to modulate the transmitter signal. A carbon mike contains a can of carbon granules hooked up to the circuit in such a way that an electric current flows through the carbon. When the granules are loosely packed little current flows, but when the granules are compressed the current flow increases. The diaphragm of the carbon mike forms one end of the carbon granule can. As sound waves strike the diaphragm, it moves alternately to increase and decrease pressure on the carbon granules, thus varying the current flow through the mike. The alternating current is amplified and then used to modulate the transmitted signal.

As you can imagine, the carbon microphone is rugged. But the simplicity that gives it its mechanical strength makes it rather cloddish electronically. Its frequency response is narrow (thus everybody sounds pretty much the same when using a carbon mike) and, like humans, it is susceptible to the vagaries of age. Its granules get sluggish as it gets older and its ability to modulate the transmitted signal wanes.

Carbon mikes are not susceptible to radio frequency interference or to the electromagnetic fields set up by 400 Hz AC appliances such as heated windshields. They are, however, highly vulnerable to ambient noise. Noise cancellation is accomplished by applying ambient noise to both sides of the diaphragm while the pilot's voice is applied to only one side.

Carbon mikes are the least expensive.

Dynamic microphones: This term is used variously by the manufacturers to describe a class of microphones that *generate* an electric current rather than simply alter one. Consider the carbon mike again. It varies a DC current flowing through it by using sound waves to alter the electrical resistance of the carbon element.

Dynamic microphones do not alter an electric current, but rather produce their own by causing relative movement between a conductor and magnetic field. In its simplest form, a dynamic mike consists of a coil attached to a diaphragm. The coil floats between the poles of a permanent magnet. Sound waves cause the diaphragm (and thus the coil) to vibrate. As the coil moves in the magnet's field, a small alternating current is produced in the winding of the coil. This current is amplified and sent off to the transmitter for further amplification before it is used to modulate the transmitted

232

signal. The dynamic mike described here uses a plastic diaphragm.

The *magnetic* mike is a mirror image of the dynamic microphone with a slight variation. In the case of a magnetic microphone, the permanent magnet is attached to the diaphragm (usually metal) and it floats in a coil. The magnetic microphone is intended to be mechanically stronger than the standard dynamic mike.

Since dynamic mikes work on the principles of interaction between fields (electric and magnetic) they are susceptible to interference from ambient electric and magnetic fields. Thus their designers have to be clever in isolating circuitry, especially in the microphone's amplifier, from these outside disturbances.

Generally speaking, dynamic microphones are preferred over carbon types because of their excellent noise canceling characteristics. Noise canceling is accomplished in dynamic mikes just as it is in their carbon-element counterparts. The ambient noise is applied to both sides of the diaphragm while the pilot's voice is applied to only one side. However, the physical characteristics of the dynamic mike are better suited to this noise canceling technique, thus a greater part of the electric signal sent to the transmitter for amplification is useful energy. (The signal to noise ratio is better.) Dynamic microphones have none of the aging problems that plague carbon mikes, but they are a bit more fragile.

As a rule of thumb, dynamic microphones are 50 to 75 percent more expensive than carbon mikes.

Electret mikes: These relatively new designs are showing up in the most sophisticated headsets. Electrically, they are similar in function to the old condenser mikes. The diaphragm of an electret mike is actually the plate of a capacitor. In condenser (or electret) mikes, sound waves move the diaphragm, thus changing the capacitance of a circuit. This signal is used to modulate a second signal, which is amplified and sent off to the transmitter. The electret microphone is light weight, has good noise canceling characteristics, and per unit weight, size and dollar, probably delivers the most useful signal to the transmitter. It is especially susceptible to 400 Hz AC interference, so make sure you check with the manufacturers before using one if you suspect a bunch of ambient 400 Hz electrical noise in your cockpit. Electret mikes are available only as elements in bow headsets.

To stay out of trouble, follow these rules.

(1) Make sure the unit has been designed for use in aircraft cockpits. Some microphones peddled in the business aviation marketplace were not designed for aircraft operations and tend to send out more aircraft engine rumbling than pilot talk. As in other avionics equipment, an FAA TSO tells you the equipment has been designed for aircraft operation and that it at least meets aircraft environmental standards.

(2) Make sure the literature on the unit specifically calls out the micro-

phone's noise "canceling" or noise "rejecting" properties. If the unit is designed for aircraft installation, the literature will use one of these terms in describing it.

(3) Buy the best microphone you can afford. It's silly to buy expensive transceivers and feed them crummy voice signals through a cut-rate mike.

(4) Dynamic mikes have internal amplifiers which should be peaked for optimum operation with your transceivers. While it is not absolutely necessary to have this peaking done, it'll get you the best possible performance from your equipment. Ask your avionics shop to check this adjustment next time your aircraft is in for black box maintenance or repair.

(5) Treat your microphones with care. They are, after all, relatively delicate electronic instruments.

Microphones are pretty reliable avionics components, but they can and do fail. Keep these points in mind.

(1) Experts agree most "microphone" failures occur in the cord, not the microphone itself. The cord is stretched and joggled thousands of times through the microphone's life and its conductors break once in a while. Reports from the ground that your signal is strong but intermittent is a good clue that the cord is broken or breaking.

(2) Carbon mikes deteriorate with age. Recurring reports of "weak" transmission might well be caused by a tired carbon element. Some oldtimers recommend a sharp rap to shake up the carbon granules as a *temporary* fix for this problem. But *temporary* must be stressed. When a carbon mike starts to die of old age, it should be replaced. Reports from the ground that your transmissions are "scratchy" are also good indications that your carbon mike is letting you down. (Make sure you've got a carbon mike rather than a dynamic mike before you try the rap treatment. A good jolt to a dynamic mike can separate the coil from the diaphragm.)

(3) Dynamic mikes don't age, but they can develop ills in their amplifier circuits and in the electromagnetic sense element. Reports from the ground that your transmission is weak and garbled can mean that your dynamic mike is on the way out. There is no cockpit check for this condition.

It should go without saying that the first rule of avionics redundancy is to have at least two microphones onboard. But we'll say it anyway just for the record. Can you imagine letting ATC catch you as a norad when you've got two $3000 transceivers aboard, but only one $30-mike?

Air-Driven Gyros: How To Keep Them Spinning

30

by Robert Stangarone

In a way it is ironic that the two instruments that are the focal points for instrument flying are also the least understood—and frequently most neglected—pieces of equipment on the panel. The attitude indicator, or gyro horizon, and heading indicator, or directional gyro, represent two of the six primary flight instruments. (The third gyro instrument in the group—the turn and slip indicator—will not be considered here since most of them are electrically driven.)

In a recent five-year period, the NTSB has listed gyro failures as a cause in 15 accidents. It doesn't sound too bad until you look a little deeper and find that 10 of those accidents were fatal. If you do have a gyro failure that results in an accident, the odds indicate it's probably going to be a fatal one. There's no way of telling how many gyro failures occurred during that period since a gyro failure in visual meteorological conditions (VMC) is usually nothing more than a casual nuisance. But the lesson to be learned is that gyro failures in instrument meteorological conditions (IMC)—as few and far between as they may seem—can be downright dangerous. So it behooves us to know how we can minimize the possibility of failures. It's important that we recognize impending failures before we launch into the soup, and that we know what to do if we have a failure while we're in it. This all leads to how we treat our gyros and how we preventively maintain them.

Review for a second what you know about attitude and heading indicators. Chances are it won't take very long to cover all the points you think you should know. But do you know the signs that indicate a failure in the offing? Do you know how to make gyros last longer, or run better? Do you know where to take your problems when you have them? And how much it's going to cost you? You should.

There are two basic power sources for gyros: electricity and air. The same basic gyroscopic principles apply to both. The growing popularity of electric gyros in recent years is due mainly to their capabilities in higher flight regimes. Vacuum gyros "run out of air" above 18,000 feet and become unreliable. Electric gyros, with their higher rotation speed, have better weight efficiency and better system reliability.

Here we want to concentrate on air-driven gyros. The aircraft gyro has been around almost since day one. Elmer Sperry (from whom sprang Sperry Avionics) is the father of the aircraft gyro. He began flying behind them in 1915 and in 1916 was awarded the Collier Trophy for his work.

Air gyros developed first primarily because air was the most available source of power in the early days. A vacuum source could be created simply by having a venturi on the side of the aircraft for each instrument installed. Those devices worked well, provided no ice was encountered.

Of course, a gyro really doesn't care where the airflow comes from, so they work equally well on pressure. With the advent of the dry pump a decade or so ago, which solved the problem of blowing oil into the instruments, pressure gyros returned to popularity, notably on Beech aircraft.

The gyroscopic instruments in today's aircraft are generally not expensive, at least not until you get into the very sophisticated gyros used in top-of-the-line business, airline or military aircraft. Typically, you purchase a new air-driven, panel-mounted attitude or heading indicator for a single-engine aircraft for a few hundred dollars. The reason for the low cost is the high volume at which they're produced, the stiff competition in the marketplace and the standardized specs of the gyros. Particularly because of the high demand of the airframe manufacturers, prices have been reduced by half in the past 10 years. Currently there are only a handful of major companies producing vacuum gyros, the most popular in this country being Aviation Instrument Manufacturing (a division of Narco), Aerosonic and Edo-Aire.

Most gyros are surprisingly similar in both theory and construction, but the higher quality ones are the result of manufacturers paying particular attention to hardware such as screws, balancing devices and adhesives. Less expensive gyros may be put together with some "rough edges" in these areas. Higher quality gyros are also designed to spin faster for better rigidity, resulting in better accuracy.

When you purchase a new aircraft, you may get gyros produced by any of the several gyro vendors. If you're interested, you can discover who produced yours by looking on the casing. The TSO specifies that the gyro manufacturer must identify his product by placing the company's name on the outside of the housing. The reason manufacturers purchase gyros from several sources is to protect themselves from one company's problems such

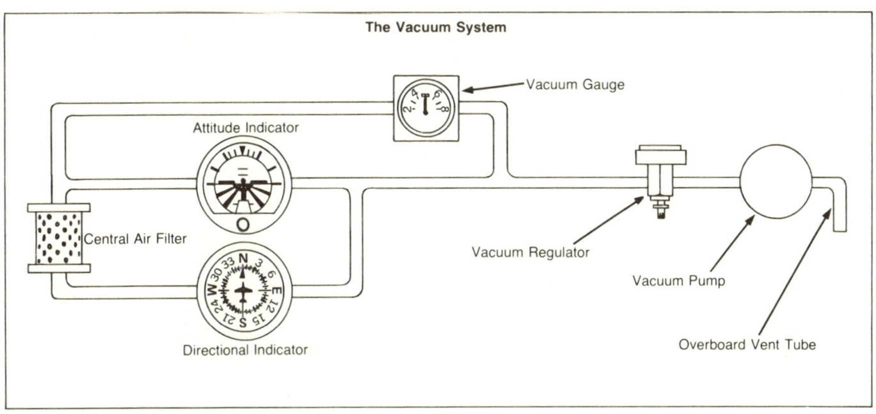

The power source for air-driven gyros is relatively simple. In most instances, air is pulled across the buckets on the gyro rotors by an engine-driven vacuum pump. En route the vacuum pressure is regulated by a spring loaded relief valve.

as strikes, or situations that may result in quality problems and higher prices.

Instruments operating under gyroscopic principles are not as durable as you may have assumed. Gyro instruments are extremely sensitive to physical and atmospheric abuse. Aerosonic has made efforts to minimize the effects of physical abuse to its instruments by devising "cushion cone" suspension and "tandem thrust" gimbals for extra support against G loads.

One of the greatest limitations gyros have is the sensitivity of the bearings, which join the fixed and rotating parts of the unit. These half-dozen or so tiny (1/16- to 1/4-inch) ball bearings are where much of the abuse to the gyro focuses. When a gyro is placed on a hard surface, subjected to short-term, high-load shocks, the bearings may develop microscopic flat spots which render them ineffective.

That explains why Aviation Instrument Manufacturing is so interested in shipping cartons. Shipping and handling shocks almost always exceed the 1.5 Gs required to meet the TSO. As a result, most gyro manufacturers produce units that far exceed the TSO (some go as high as 10 Gs) to deal better with rough treatment.

But physical shock is not the only culprit in gyro bearing failures. Poor filters, either in the vacuum system or the one built into the gyro itself, may cause smoke and pollution particles to enter the instrument and increase the friction on the bearings. This increase in friction contributes to precession. Heavy smoking in the cockpit, for this reason, has a marked effect on the gyros. Minute smoke particles in the cockpit have more of an effect on the life of the gyros than on the life of the pilot. (One gyro overhaul shop representative told us, "If they ever stopped smoking them big cigars in the cockpit, we'd go out of business.")

The physical gyro limitations of yesteryear, specifically pitch and bank limitations, are fast disappearing from the scene. Most of today's gyros are of the nontumbling variety that provide full 360° freedom in pitch, roll and azimuth. Gyros that tumble, many of which are still in operation, require extra care to avoid bearing damage. Aerobatics and roll maneuvers exceeding 55° should be avoided. Tumbled gyros can be unreliable after such maneuvers and can even be permanently damaged by aerobatic maneuvers as the gimbals hit stops resulting in damage to the bearings. Gyros subject to tumbling should be caged prior to any such maneuver. One of the drawbacks of the old five-inch gyros is that they are limited to 55° roll.

A relatively rare situation occurs when a rotor gets out of balance. This slows the speed of the rotor and causes an increase in erection time. It may also show faulty indications. If the rotation slows to 15,000 in rotors that normally spin at 25,000 to 30,000 rpm, precession will result; at around 10,000 rpm the gyro will appear to have quit.

An imbalance of the rotor and friction in the bearings are the two main causes of precession. Precession is the actual movement of a gyro spin axis from its initial alignment in space. Of course, in situations where the autopilot interfaces with the heading or attitude indicator, if the gyro precesses, it causes the aircraft to change heading or attitude by an equal amount, providing the autopilot is getting its information from these instruments. Precession has been minimized in recent years thanks to the high quality of manufacturing techniques.

A hint of something amiss usually shows up as a discrepancy between the attitude indicator, the heading indicator and the rate-of-turn indicator. If, for instance, the heading indicator shows that your heading is changing, but the attitude indicator shows that your wings are level, you should check with your rate-of-turn indicator to get its vote. If it shows a turn, your attitude gyro is most likely the culprit, but if it doesn't indicate a turn, the heading indicator is probably telling you lies.

There's not much you can do when an attitude indicator tumbles, but when a DG tumbles because its pitch or roll limitations have been exceeded, it can usually be reset after several minutes.

Following a gyro failure, especially if it's the attitude indicator, it's not a bad idea to cover it up to prevent distraction. Some pilots have reported a strong tendency to vertigo when flying with a dead or dying gyro on the panel.

Because of inaccuracies in the wet compass in a turn, it is recommended that the heading indicator be reset only while in straight and level, unaccelerated flight. It should be reset at least every 15 minutes. When you do reset it, the knob should be held in momentarily to allow the gyro to stabilize.

Acceleration error is usually associated with the wet compass, but attitude indicators are susceptible to acceleration error as well. On takeoff in high-thrust aircraft the pendulum of the attitude gyro is displaced toward the back of the aircraft as it accelerates down the runway. As the pendulum is displaced, it applies a force on the gyro that acts as if it were applied on a plane 90° to that of the actual force. This ultimately results in a false roll indication on the attitude indicator. This can occur in any aircraft. Even in the Cessna 182 operated by B/CA, a "lean" of three to five degrees is routine in the takeoff roll. On a tight departure, that must be compensated for just after rotation. On low-visibility takeoffs the heading indicator and rate-of-turn indicator should be used for roll reference until aircraft acceleration subsides.

Long-term turns also lead gyro instruments into giving erroneous information. In a prolonged turn, the gyro erection vanes are given a false sense of gravity which may cause the attitude indicator to partially erect during the turn. On rollout it will be momentarily leaning to the side opposite to the turn. Calibrations are made in each gyro for a particular airspeed at a particular bank angle, so any turn not within the limitations of those two parameters will result in some error in the display.

You should note the characteristics of your particular gyros carefully on a VFR day so you won't be momentarily confused in IMC situations. In our experience, once those characteristics are understood, they can be counted on. We've been flying behind one attitude indicator for five years and 1500 hours, and it always leans a bit on takeoff and after a 360° turn. We've found that by using the DG as primary during accelerations and for stopping turns, everything sorts itself out quickly.

Gyro drift specs—which are calibrated into the gyros at the factory—vary as distance from the equator varies. Drift can vary from 0° at the equator to 15° per hour at the poles. A gyro calibrated to operate at the North Pole will drift 30° per hour at the South Pole. Keep this possibility in mind if you notice excessive drift while operating across any significant number of latitude lines. And if you plan on using an aircraft out of a particular latitude area, you may have to have your gyros recalibrated.

The TSO for the heading indicator requires that the precession be no more than four degrees per 10 minutes. Most gyros exceed this, with three degrees per 15 minutes being typical.

Gyros being operated in extremely low temperatures may take an extra few minutes to get up to speed since the cold cabin air has a negative effect on rotor spinup time.

Gyros take a couple of minutes to stabilize, but if you recognize any significant drift after about six minutes, you may have a problem.

239

If, while resetting the heading indicator, you bend the shaft or the shaft gets caught in the panel overlay, you may think you have a bigger problem than you really do. At the first indication of a gyro going beserk in flight, check the freedom of the knob.

As mentioned previously, gyros are sensitive creatures. Anything spinning in excess of 25,000 rpm better be well oiled and well balanced. Look at the oscillation setup in your automobile due to out-of-balance tires turning at a fraction of the speed of gyros. Gyro manufacturers make certain that rotors, when they leave the factory, are balanced to incredible tolerances. Oscilloscope devices are used to insure the quality of each and every rotor.

On the gyro the points where the rotor meets the stationary part of the instrument—the bearings—require the most attention. Bearings wear, and as they do they introduce friction into the system. Smoke particles and the like that tend to accelerate wear must be kept out of the gyro. For this reason the filters, both the central filter in the vacuum system, the vacuum pump filter, and the gyro's own self-contained filter must be effective. A good central air filter changed regularly—about every 200 to 500 hours most manufacturers say (depending on cockpit air quality)—will minimize the affects of atmospheric and tobacco particles and will give gyros a new lease on life. The efficiency of such filters is about 99.97 percent on 0.3 micron particles. Filter replacements cost a few dollars, which is very reasonable considering the benefits. It's a good idea to change the filter once a year if you don't fly the 200 to 500 hours during that time, especially if you fly through areas where the air quality leaves much to be desired, and you smoke a lot. If you're operating an older aircraft that doesn't have a central filter, with minor modification your system can probably be made to accommodate one.

If you do smoke in the cockpit, it may be a good idea to keep the vents open and get the smoke out as soon as possible. You may even want to consider flight planning around pollution-enveloped cities if it's not far out of the way. But the best way to insure proper operation of your vacuum gyro system is to change the filter frequently.

A central filter that is dirty, wet or otherwise plugged up can result in the pump producing a higher vacuum pressure, which increases wear on the pump. If the gyros are being operated by a pressure system, instead of a vacuum system, poor filters allow carbon particles from normal pump wear to clog the system to a point where the pump is pushing air against a closed system. In either case, it's much less expensive to replace filters periodically than to replace the pump. The average vacuum pump should last about 1000 hours. Old age is considered the greatest threat to pump life.

Vacuum pumps on most of today's aircraft are highly reliable and, generally, if they're going to operate, they operate properly or not at all. Vacuum pump performance is displayed on the suction gauge, which should certainly be part of the pretakeoff checklist, especially for flights into IMC. A slight increase in the suction may be an indication that the filters are becoming clogged.

Careful handling of the gyros does much to keep the bearing from developing flat spots. If you're going to have a gyro removed, you may want to ask the technician who removes it to be especially gentle with it. Anyone not familiar with the sensitivity a gyro requires is sure to handle it without proper care. Making sure panel shock mounts are in good condition will also add to the life of your gyros.

Because it is linked to the sensitive inner workings of the gyro, the heading selector knob of the heading indicator is a means of abuse to the instrument. The knob shouldn't be used as a place to hang various cockpit sundries, and care should be taken not to bang it.

If for any reason you plan to store a gyro for any length of time, it should be pulled out of storage and run periodically. When you change gyros, you should check your vacuum system for readjustment. And any time a gyro is to be removed from the panel, be sure it spins down before the work begins.

Periodically, you should check the pneumatic tubing of the air (vacuum or pressure) for any unusual signs of wear or corrosion, or for any evidence of overheating due to clogged filters. Pressure increases due to clogged filters result in higher temperatures because of increased friction, similar to the heat build-up in a bicycle pump.

The symptoms of impending problems in the gyro system are usually subtle ones. The key to early recognition is to look for something unusual starting to happen. It may be a higher or lower suction than normal, or excessive precession taking place.

Noise is probably one of the most obvious signs of something amiss; it's not the normal gyro whine that you should be concerned with, but rather a grinding metal-on-metal sound or a loud buzz indicating a loss of lubrication. If the noise gets louder with every trip, you've got a sure sign of something about to fail.

You've probably noticed, more than once, a certain "jiggling" in the gyro instruments immediately following engine start. As long as it lasts for only a short time, it is nothing to be concerned about, and is, as a matter of fact, a sign indicating that the bearings have satisfactory freedom. But if you notice the oscillation when the gyro should be stabilized, chances are that a guide pin inside the gyro has play in it due to wear.

During the preflight, it's smart to check for any physical damage to the gyros and make sure all the knobs and pointers are where they're supposed to be.

241

The time it takes for the gyros to erect is also a clue to their health. It shouldn't be excessive, and it shouldn't increase with every flight. Also, during preflight inspection after startup, check to see that the caging functions are normal.

When taxiing out for takeoff, you can tell if your gyro instruments are working properly by making turns and braking sufficiently to change the heading and pitch of the airplane. The instruments should respond accordingly. If the attitude indicator leans when the nose is swung back and forth during the taxiout, be forewarned. This may indicate a substandard rotor span.

The best flight test you can run is on a clear day. Simply check the instruments in relation to your visual cues. This can be a part of every clear-day flight. You can only roughly estimate bank and pitch angle, but you should check to be sure the gyro instruments move in the direction they're supposed to move to correspond to the maneuver, and with no lag. The heading indicator can be checked by timing a standard-rate turn at 90° points through the turn. You should be at each cardinal heading every 30 seconds. You can double-check your progress by using predetermined outside references at the cardinal points.

The guidelines for gyro inspection and overhaul are nowhere to be found. There are no regs governing how often the gyros must be overhauled, inspected or replaced, and there's a varied difference of opinion among manufacturers and overhaul shops as to how often these activities should take place. The most conservative suggestion we received for time between overhauls for the gyro instruments was 600 hours of operation; the most liberal, 2000 hours. Much depends on the quality of air entering the instruments and the effectiveness of the filters. A lot of start and stop cycles, hard landings, rough-field operations and the quality of the panel shock mounts will all dictate how many hours you should let lapse between overhauls. One school of thought is to let the gyros run until signs of failure appear. While this may be economical if the odds are with you, it can cost plenty if the odds are against you.

Idleness is a major factor in how long and how well a gyro operates. The lubricant congeals in idle gyros, increasing friction and reducing performance.

For gyros under warranty, the manufacturer will be happy to tell you where to take them for repair or overhaul. But assuming the gyro is no longer under warranty, there are a number of certified gyro repair shops around the country. To minimize downtime, many shops offer exchange programs and can have you back in operation in a number of hours. Your other options are to purchase a new instrument, or send your old gyro in for overhaul, if you've got time to wait. The latter could run into several weeks downtime. A good overhaul shop will replace all the bearings, balance the rotor, check for corrosion and clean any contamination from the instrument. If you have an old five-inch gyro, overhaul time is a good opportunity to exchange it for a newer, nontumbling three-inch gyro. An adapter plate is available.

The best place to get your gyros overhauled is an FAA certified gyro overhaul facility near you. If your local FBO is not so authorized, he can lead you in the right direction. If not, a phone call to the manufacturer of your gyro will help in finding an overhaul shop.

Gyro overhaul time is a good time to consider updating your gyros instead of just overhauling them. The benefits of buying a new one include getting a nontumbling, more reliable (because of modern technology) instrument with better bearings and better shock absorption. It's worth considering.

Not too far off is a TSO that may require all gyros to be equipped with failure warning devices consisting of internal sensors that measure airflow with flags to indicate impending failure. This type of evolution is part of the normal progression in many of our instruments.

Further down the road things get much more interesting. "Gyro" instruments, sans gyros, seem to be the wave of tomorrow. Already in the works is a solid-state rate transducer. By taking a solid-state rate sensor in combination with an operational amplifier, Humphrey, Incorporated of San Diego has developed an angular position, rate or acceleration transducer. The system uses a crystal oscillator circuit inside a hermetically sealed gas-filled pump. Mechanical vibration of the crystal forces a stream of gas molecules through a network of chambers and wires. The differential temperature change across the wires indicates the degree of deflection. We have flown this device extensively, and it really works.

Another promising innovation in gyros—the laser beam—is certain to show up soon in the evolutionary cycle. NASA is now in the process of developing such a device.

It may be that one of our simplest, least changed instruments is destined to become one of the most exotic devices on the instrument panel in coming years. Only time will tell.

The HSI—A Poor Man's 31
Flight Director

by Richard N. Aarons

So you've always wanted a flight director system for your high performance single or light twin—a great big fancy flight director with all the bars and needles and stuff, plus that sexy yellow delta airplane in the middle of the display. It sure would be nice.

Combing the literature, you've probably discovered these magnificent devices have but two drawbacks—(1) they're kind of big for most singles and light twins, and (2) they're really expensive—up to $100,000 and more.

Now suppose a guy were to come up with a flight director in the $1500 to $5000 range. Would you be interested? You bet you would. And that's just what's happening with the proliferation of low-cost, three-inch horizontal situation indicator (HSI) systems.

But wait, you argue. A horizontal situation indicator is only *half* a flight director—and at that, the half without the command bars. On the surface you're right, but only so far as the hardware itself is concerned. From a human factors standpoint, the HSI is a lot more than half a flight director. If you had to come up with a number, it would be at least *two-thirds*.

B/CA reached this conclusion after considering the results of a quick-and-dirty poll of a couple of dozen business and corporate pilots with a smattering of airline pilots thrown in for variety. In each case, the interviewee used highly sophisticated flight directors in his day-to-day cockpit activities. Here's what we found out.

(1) The command function is rarely used other than on approach.

(2) The HSI is considered "primary" for lateral information even when the command bars are showing roll information.

(3) The HSI is the most watched instrument in the cockpit.

(4) Experiments have shown that a pilot only vaguely familiar with the HSI can use the instrument as sole source for *both* attitude and navigation. (More on this experiment in a moment.)

To appreciate what the HSI does, take a look at the drawing on page 246.

THE HSI—A POOR MAN'S FLIGHT DIRECTOR

This is a Collins PN-101, the granddaddy of all three-inch HSIs, but it's representative of all available systems.

The compass card provides stabilized azimuth information with the present heading shown under the lubber line at the 12 o'clock position. The least expensive HSIs have internal electric or vacuum gyros which must be reset during flight like any other DG. (These must be reset during flight to correct for precession, the bugaboo of all "free" gyros.) However, most HSIs are "slaved," which means that the compass card is set automatically and rarely needs inflight adjustment. In a typical slaved system, the gyro is remotely mounted in a black box and the indicator's compass card is servo driven.

Affixed to the aircraft in an area free from magnetic disturbance is a "flux detector" (sometimes called "flux gate" or "magnetic azimuth transmitter") which senses the alignment of the aircraft with respect to the earth's magnetic field and sends that data off to the gyro. A simple matching circuit uses the magnetic information to align the gyro to magnetic north (and to keep it aligned by continually making minute corrections whenever precession introduces an error into the gyro position.) Simply stated, the flux gate tells the gyro where north is, and whenever it forgets, the flux gate reminds it again.

Often you'll find a "slaving meter" associated with the HSI. (Some manufacturers offer it as standard equipment, others as an option.) The tiny slaving meter has a "plus" sign on one side and a "minus" sign on the other. Typically, the needle bounces back and forth between the plus and minus signs, indicating that the flux detector is making corrections.

Some systems allow the pilot to turn off the slaving feature and use the compass system in the free-gyro mode. In this mode, the pilot must correct for precession with periodic inflight adjustments. Most HSI compass systems include a fast-slave switch which is used at startup to slew the card quickly to the appropriate initial heading. Once that's accomplished, the normal slaving circuitry takes over with its continuous small adjustments.

Before going any further, we should make a distinction here in nomenclature. We tend to think of HSIs as entire systems, but actually they are composed of two separate systems—the indicator system and compass system—each of which is offered independently by most manufacturers. In the case of the Collins PN-101 seen on page 246, the drawing actually shows a Collins 331 A-3G course indicator which can be driven by any Arinc compass system. But for the purposes of this article, we'll use the term "HSI" to represent *both* the compass system and the indicator except in the case of non-slaved systems which will be identified as such.

Back to the elements of the HSI indicator as pictured on page 246. The HDG knob on the lower left moves the orange heading bug which functions

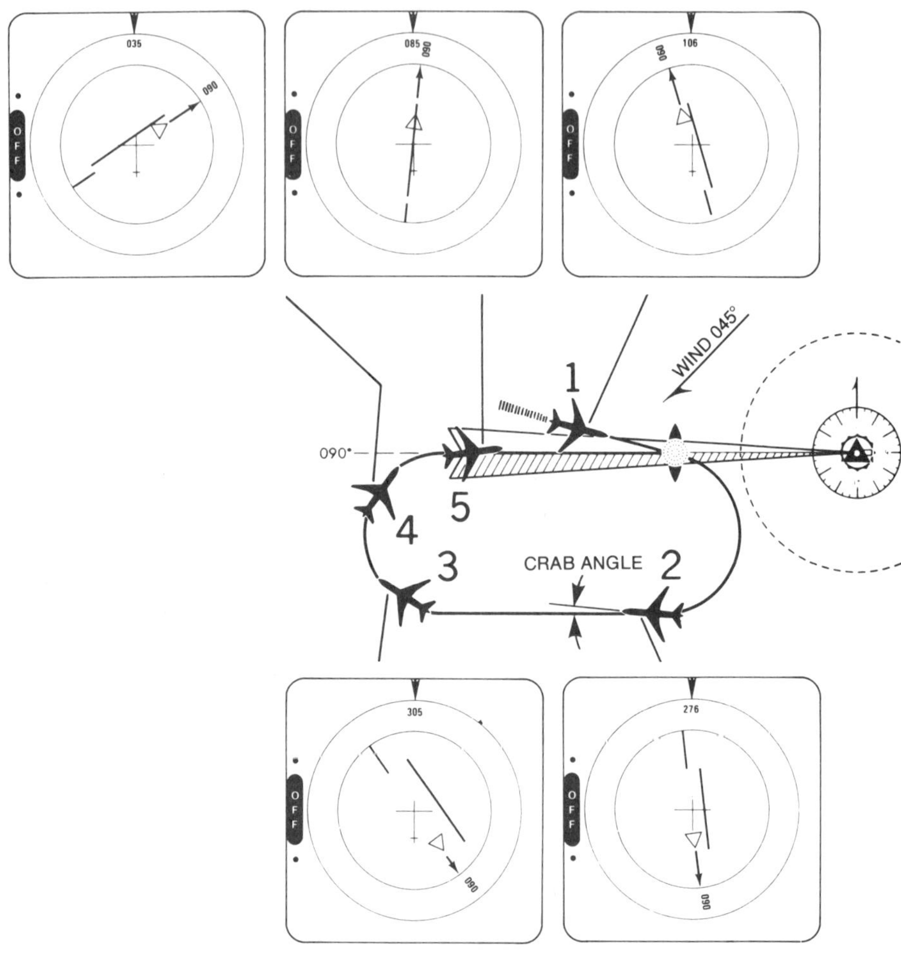

At first glance the HSI can be a bit intimidating with all its pointers and dials, but it's really quite an easy instrument to interpret. Here we've isolated the "active" components of the instrument face to demonstrate how the HSI is used in two common situations—a simple hold and a radar vectored ILS approach.

An HSI takes the sweat out of entering and executing a holding pattern. At position No. 1, the aircraft is approaching the holding course from the northwest. The course-bar had been set to represent the inbound holding radial. The "picture" presented by the HSI is identical to the overhead diagrammatic view. Notice that the mid-section of the course deviation bar is to the right of the symbolic aircraft indicating that the flight is still to the north of the radial (a localizer in this case). The convergence of the symbolic aircraft and the course-bar indicates that the appropriate intercept has been established. Follow the aircraft through the procedure and you'll get a feel for how the HSI eliminates orientation problems in the holding manuever. At position No. 2, for example, notice that the wind correction angle is shown visually and quantitatively, the latter through the difference between heading (276 degrees) and the outbound course to be made good (270 degrees). At position No. 4, the aircraft is intercepting the inbound radial. Using an HSI, the pilot can tell at a glance his precise postition in the holding pattern.

246

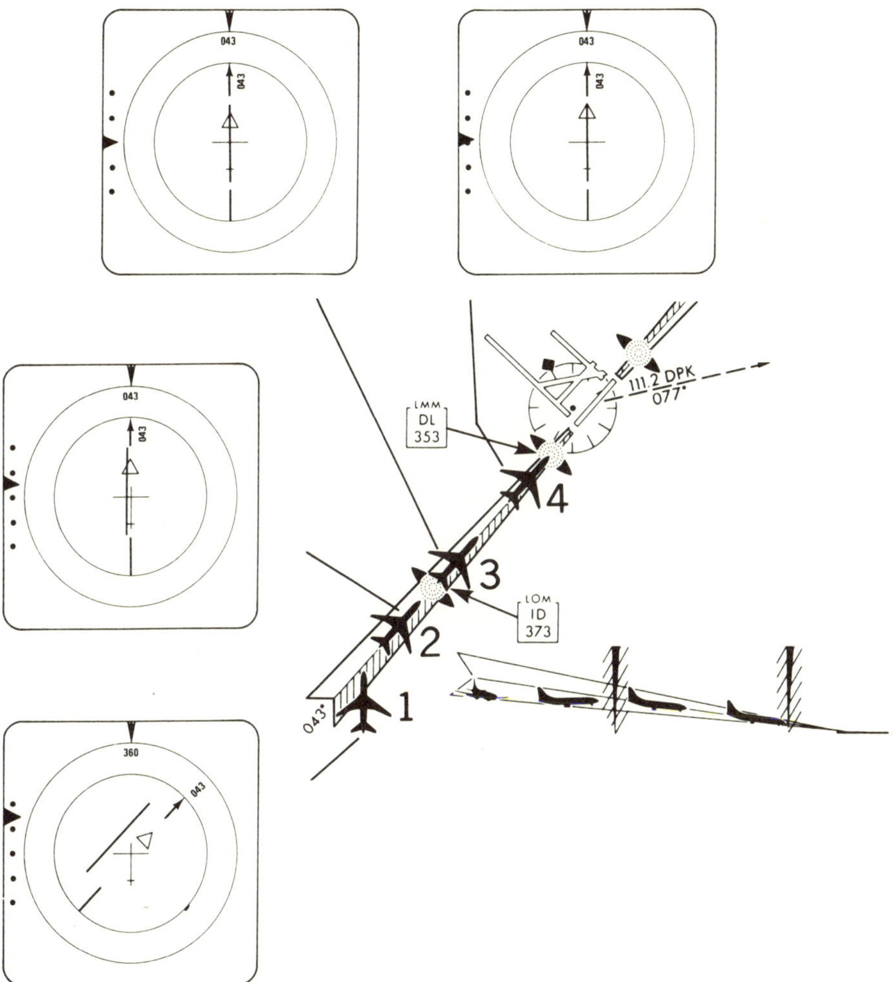

The HSI is worth its weight in gold on a sticky ILS approach. With an HSI, the pilot intuitively keeps his correction turns small because he can tell at a glance his heading relative to the ILS course and his position on the course. The rate of movement of the mid-section of the course-bar tells the pilot instantly whether his corrections are working. The result is a much smoother approach than those flown on DG and raw ILS data alone.

The aircraft depicted here is being vectored onto the final approach course. Notice in the HSI presentation for position No. 1 that at all times during the vectoring the pilot sees his position relative to the ILS course. As soon as the course-bar begins to move, the pilot knows he'd best position his aircraft for an intercept. Once on course, minor adjustments to heading keep the course-bar centered. Glideslope information is presented by the triangle shown on the left side of the instrument face. When the glideslope is out of commission, a flag blocks the indicator from view. Some HSIs have dual glideslope indicators—one on each side of the instrument face. Others have pointers similar to glideslope indicators which display angle of attack or Vnav data.

to remind the human pilot or the autopilot of a preselected heading. The COURSE knob moves the green course arrow which, with its movable center portion, provides course deviation information to the human pilot or autopilot. The white triangle at the 270-degree position moves vertically up and down the instrument face. It provides glideslope information. It's pictured here in an on-glideslope configuration. The pilot flies towards the triangle.

The orange airplane symbol orientates the aircraft in the navigation picture. Place your thumb over the heading bug in the PN-101 illustration. The position of the compass card tells you the aircraft is on a 360-degree heading. The nose of the symbolic aircraft always points at the 12 o'clock position. Now look at the course arrow—its head is pointing at the 327-degree position where it was set to indicate (in this case) a 327-degree course *to* a VOR station. (This, of course, means that the inbound course would lie on the 147-degree radial which is shown by the tail of the course arrow.) We know that it's an inbound setup because the white triangle in the center of the instrument points at the arrowhead. If the white triangle pointed at the course arrow tail, the course setup would be outbound.

The center section of the course arrow moves back and forth to show the aircraft's position relative to the preselected course. In the illustrated case, the aircraft is flying away from the preselected radial and, in fact, has already moved about seven degrees off the radial's centerline. (Count the dots.) The pilot watching an HSI is in the position of an observer in space directly above the aircraft. He looks down and sees that the aircraft is flying a magnetic heading of 360 degrees and, in doing so, is flying away from a preselected track. The observer in space can see that the quickest way back to the desired track would be a turn to the left. (A turn to 327 degrees would parallel the desired track—assuming no wind. A further left turn to 307 degrees would set up the intercept.) It may be easier to visualize the function of the HSI if you keep in mind that the compass card, course arrow and heading bug all move together as the aircraft's magnetic heading changes. While these elements are moving together, the center section of the course arrow, which is actually a course deviation indicator (CDI), moves to show an unambiguous picture of the aircraft's position relative to a preselected airway or radial.

All these words make the HSI's action appear pretty complicated, but that's really not the case. You'll find that it takes all of five minutes to get used to the picture, and once you do, you'll be hooked. The HSI takes all the work out of complicated orientation procedures.

The reason we say the HSI is two-thirds of a flight director system (at a much smaller fraction of the cost) is that it relieves the pilot of nav orientation problems and allows him to spend more time on attitude control and altitude awareness. This is especially important during departures and approaches. Consider the case of standard instrumentation—all the pilot gets are a bunch of numbers he's got to sort out and act upon. The DG presents a number (heading); the omni-bearing selector (OBS) presents another (selected radial); and the to/from and left/right needles present displays that can only be interpreted in light of the numbers displayed by the DG and OBS. The HSI, on the other hand, presents a picture which can be interpreted instantly and wholly without numbers. The pilot gets an immediate picture of the navigation situation and trends. He knows instantly the aircraft's position relative to a desired radial or airway; he knows intuitively which way corrections are to be made, and there are no heading/OBS ambiguity questions to sort out. That's done automatically by the display. Wind correction angles are displayed (when the aircraft is stabilized on-course) by the difference between the heading and the course-arrow setting. Minute corrections can be made by moving the heading bug a degree at a time and watching the trend of the course arrow's CDI. (Actually engineers can wire the HSI to display any type of nav track—VOR, INS, VLF or Doppler—but the three-inch instruments under discussion are sold exclusively for VOR and VOR-RNAV use.)

B/CA's experiment to evaluate the HSI as an attitude control device and generally to collect pilot comments on these systems was conducted in two phases. First, an instrument pilot was shown a simple VOR intercept. Then he was placed under the hood and all instruments but the airspeed indicator, altimeter and HSI were covered. Next he was given vectors for a full ILS approach. As soon as the glideslope needle activated, the altimeter and airspeed indicator were also covered leaving only the HSI for attitude control and navigation.

In two tests, pilots not familiar with HSIs shot these ILS approaches to 200 feet without ever getting the aircraft into an unusual attitude. To be sure, the approaches were rough, but certainly safe. Pitch attitude was dictated by the glideslope. Roll attitude was dictated by movement of the compass card. The picture presented by the symbolic aircraft superimposed over the course arrow represents the localizer.

As a final step in the experiment, we put a nonpilot behind the controls, explained the function of the HSI and asked this person to perform a VOR intercept. The intercept was flawless. We asked the same person to attempt an intercept using a DG and raw VOR data. After 20 minutes, we gave up. The intercept was beyond his ability.

Neither of these tests is conclusive proof of anything, but they do tend to support the opinion of the pilots questioned that the HSI makes cockpit workload a lot easier. As a poor man's flight director, it cannot be beat.

RNAV Accuracy

32

by Richard N. Aarons

If you've flown much RNAV, its accuracy has probably left you both impressed and puzzled. Some days your single-waypoint RNAV machine brings you right down the center line and zeroes out as the wheels cross the threshold. Other days, the RNAV seems hard put to get you within a quarter mile of the touchdown zone. You have probably also discovered that on some published approaches you end up consistently to the left of center line; on other published approaches, you always seem to end up to the right of center line. And how about those rare days when the RNAV doesn't seem to be making any sense at all?

B/CA's editors talked with operators of all kinds of RNAVs—from simple single-waypoint, analog, course-line computers to the most complex and expensive digital area navigation systems. Most RNAVers seem to share a conviction that RNAV is extraordinary, and that it eventually will be the salvation of an overworked, heretofore unimaginative airspace-utilization plan. Another thing RNAVers share is confusion over just what RNAV electronics are capable of and how to find out when their RNAV systems are lying—or, at least, how to tell when they're not telling the whole truth.

Quite frankly, B/CA's editors shared this optimism and confusion. We operate two IFR-approved RNAV systems in light aircraft, and we've run into the same perplexing accuracy variations that other RNAVers see daily. This study began merely as an in-house project to learn a little more about the systems in our own aircraft. But in the end, we decided to pass along to you our findings, especially suggestions from the manufacturers on inflight testing of RNAV equipment and a few notes on error sources in the complete air-ground area navigation system.

If you're serious about IFR RNAVing, you need copies of two government publications—AC 90–63, "Air Traffic Control Procedures for Random Area Navigation Routes" and AC 90-45A, "Approval of Area Navigation Systems for Use in the U.S. National Airspace System." Both sound like pretty grim reading, but they are useful to the RNAVer if for no other reason than that they give insight into what the ATC planners *think* RNAV can do. And that's what we're going to look at now. We'll confine our discussion to Rho-Theta RNAV systems—the type that seem to displace VORTACs from their actual geographical location to some other spot within their service volume area.

As shown in Figure 1, waypoints are defined in terms of bearing and distance from the reference VORTAC. Figure 1 shows an RNAV course (D-E) predicated on a waypoint (B) that is 20 miles out on the 045 degree radial of the reference VORTAC (A). Input to the onboard RNAV computer is DME (Rho) and azimuth (Theta) from the reference facility. Other input is made by the pilot, that is, waypoint definition (distance/bearing) and RNAV course. The RNAV system continuously, sequentially solves trigonometrically, the triangle ABC, ABC′, ABC″, where C, C′ and C″ represent positions of the aircraft at the instant of calculation.

There are five error sources in Rho/Theta, VORTAC-based area navigation—the ground VOR and DME radiated signals, airborne VOR/DME equipment, airborne area navigation equipment, pilotage (flight technical) and slant-range error. We'll explore each in detail before looking at their cumulative effect.

Ground VOR and DME radiated signals—You can't fly VOR very long before you discover that VOR radials aren't always where they're supposed to be. In theory, a VOR radial should be like a taut rope defining an

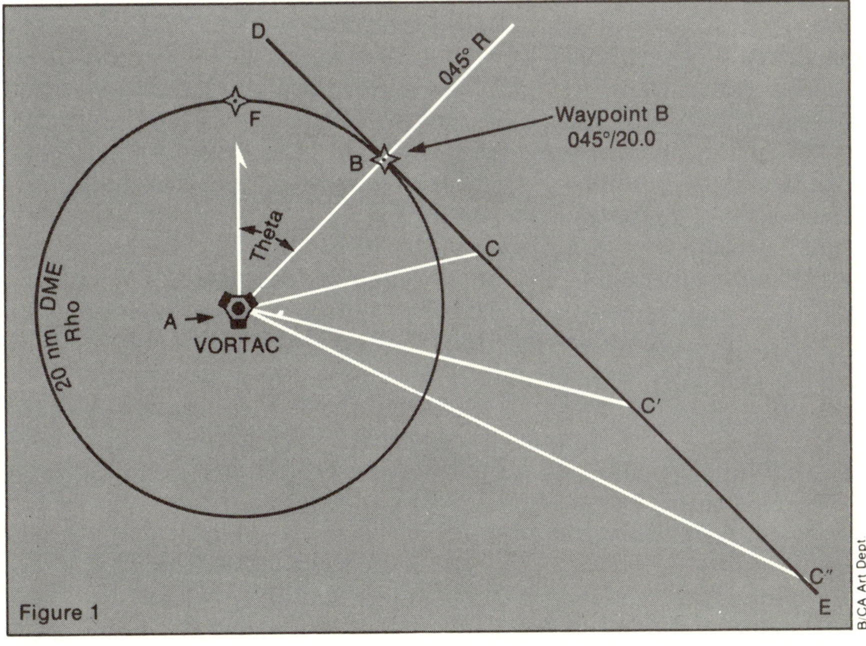

arrow-straight line from the reference facility on out to the limits of reception. But in the real world, electronic, topographic and atmospheric gremlins tweak the radial rope, causing it to shimmy and bend. VOR radials plotted on a chart are properly called *geographic radials.* The things you fly are *electronic radials.* Ideally, the electronic radials will correspond precisely with the geographic radials, but in actuality, they rarely do. Bends and scalloping can come and go as atmospheric and topographic conditions change. (The change of seasons causes topographic variations. The amount of foliage, snow coverage and ground conductivity can all affect electromagnetic wave propagation.) There can also be errors within the ground station itself; that is, the radial may not be aimed exactly where it should be.

FAA electronics experts say that the VOR ground station error will rarely be more than plus or minus 1.9 degrees, and for RNAV error calculations, it's assumed that the VOR ground station error will *never* exceed 1.9 degrees. That error doesn't sound too large, but when you apply the one-nm-per-degree-at-60-miles rule, the error becomes pretty sizable.

As it happens, DME is much more accurate than VOR. Maximum DME ground station error is plus or minus 0.1 nm. Unlike VOR, accuracy of the ground-based DME station is not affected by the distance of the airborne equipment with respect to the station.

Airborne VOR/DME equipment—The second source of RNAV error is the airborne VOR receiver (and related components) and the DME system. These errors are quite independent of the ground station errors. The error contributed by the airborne VOR equipment is assumed to be a maximum of plus or minus 3.0 degrees. (We'll be looking at this number more closely later.) Airborne DME equipment is assumed to have an error no greater than 0.5 nm or three percent of the range. The DME error figure probably looks familiar to you. It's the accuracy figure you see on the specification sheets of most low-to-medium-cost DMEs.

RNAV equipment—The airborne RNAV computer itself has accuracy limits like any other man-made device. Manufacturers are required to build these computers to perform within an accuracy of plus or minus 0.5 nm.

Flight technical error—This source of error is you, the pilot. When a pilot flies raw data, he has to wait for an error to develop before he can take corrective action. Or, stated more simply, if the needle is centered, the pilot does nothing. If it starts to move right or left, he'll usually wait for some measurable deflection—perhaps one dot—before taking a cut back toward the course. Most general aviation RNAVs are calibrated to present a one-nm-per-dot deviation in the en route mode and a one-quarter-nm-per-dot deviation in the approach mode. With these sensitivities in mind, the FAA has made the assumption that the flight technical error will not exceed two nm when operating en route and 0.5 nm when conducting an RNAV approach. It is assumed that along-track flight technical error is zero because distance-to-waypoint is presented digitally and therefore requires no pilot compensation.

Slant-range error—Slant-range error always causes the aircraft to err from its selected track toward the VORTAC. The error is actually induced by the DME, which measures the slant-range distance to the VORTAC rather than the geographic distance from a point directly under the aircraft. Published waypoints are predicated as geographic distances. Some of the more sophisticated two-dimensional RNAV systems and all of the three-dimensional systems have a means of getting rid of slant-range error by inserting the elevation of the VORTAC.

Slant-range error is relatively small at all altitudes and negligible when the aircraft is relatively close to the ground; therefore, you needn't worry about slant-range error during execution of a published RNAV approach. (See Figure 2.)

To understand how all these individual error sources combine to produce total system error, we must first review some basic RNAV terminology. Figure 3 shows an RNAV course constructed through a waypoint that has been established relative to a VORTAC *reference facility.* We'll assume that the cockpit instruments indicate the aircraft is crossing the waypoint. The aircraft symbol represents the actual position of the aircraft. Note first that the aircraft is right of course. Deviation left or right of course is called *cross-track error.* Note also that although the cockpit instruments indicate the aircraft is at the waypoint, it is actually short of the waypoint. An error in position along the course is called *along-track error.* The *tangent point*

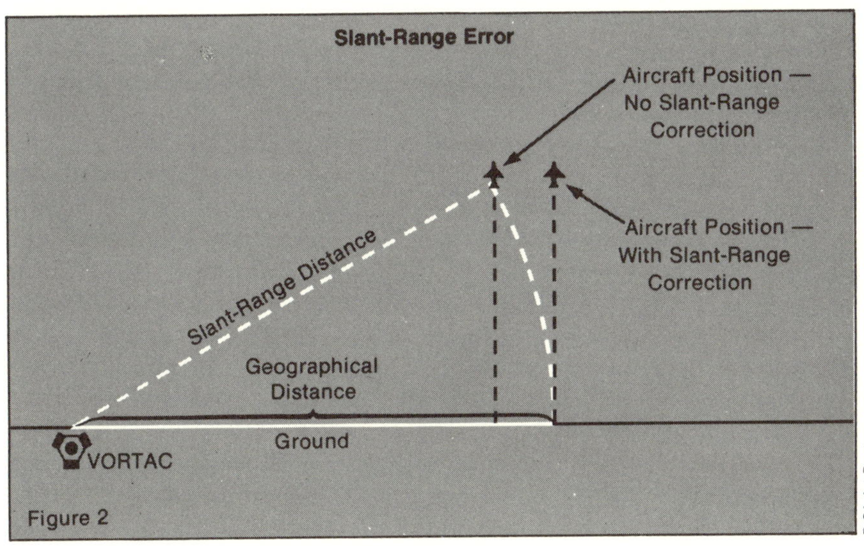

Figure 2

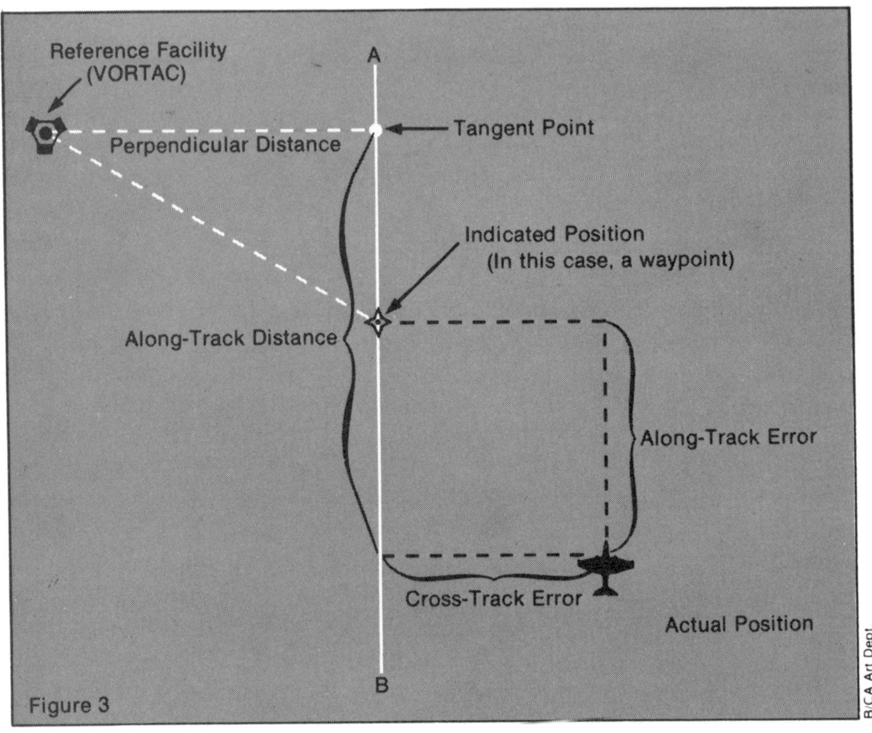

Figure 3

is that point at which the course comes closest to the reference facility. The distance from the tangent point to the reference facility is called *perpendicular distance*. The distance from the tangent point to the aircraft position is called *along-track distance*. Tangent point, perpendicular distance and along-track distance are all important considerations in discussions of RNAV accuracy.

Refer again to Figure 1 for a moment to see why this is so. Assume first that we've established a waypoint at B and we are located over the reference facility, RNAVing to Waypoint B along the course A-B. As we fly toward Waypoint B, the RNAV computer is using DME and VOR input to establish our position relative to B. The geometry of this situation is such that DME information is determining our along-track position and VOR is determining our cross-track position. Because DME ground and airborne equipment is inherently more accurate than VOR ground and airborne equipment, we could rightly expect that our along-track position will be more accurate than our cross-track position.

Now suppose that having reached Waypoint B, we decide to intercept RNAV route BE. That is, we're flying outbound from Waypoint B along BE. We'll let C, C' and C" represent our positions as the flight progresses.

You'll remember that the RNAV computer is continuously solving the triangle ABC, ABC′ and ABC″ to figure our position. The VOR/DME information used for the solution is represented by the lines AC, AC′ and AC″.

When we were outbound from A to B, along-track position was determined primarily by DME information; cross-track position was determined by VOR input. However, as soon as we intercept RNAV route BE, along-track position becomes a function of VOR input (and therefore accuracy) and cross-track position becomes a function of DME input.

As we leave Waypoint B, which in this case is coincident with the tangent point, you'll notice that the error geometry again changes. The closer we get to E, the more important DME is to the solution of the along-track problem and the more important VOR is to the solution of the cross-track problem.

The point is that RNAV accuracy depends not only on distance from the reference facility but upon the geometry of the specific RNAV problem. We'll see shortly how we can check our RNAV system accuracy using knowledge of the tangent point and perpendicular and along-track distances to solve the accuracy triangle. But for the moment, let's return to our discussion of error contributions of the various RNAV system components.

We've already decided that government and industry engineers believe the individual error contributions fall within these tolerances:

Ground VOR: ± 1.9 degrees

Ground DME: ± 0.1 nm

Airborne VOR: ± 3.0 degrees

Airborne DME: ± 0.5 nm or three percent of the range

RNAV computer: ± 0.5 nm

Flight technical: 2.0 nm en route; 0.5 nm approach (cross-track only)

Slant range: Forget it.

If all these errors regularly lined up in the same direction, RNAV as a method of navigation wouldn't be of much use at all, unless, say, you were in California looking for the Pacific Ocean.

Happily, these error contributions rarely line up. To the contrary, they actually tend to cancel each other out. Statisticians have a way of combining the individual errors to come up with an error probability for the system as a whole. (The method says it's 95 percent probable that the total error will not exceed the root of the sum of the squares of the individual error contributions.)

Flight technical and slant-range error are not figured in, but rather are additive to the total system error.

Because the individual error contribution depends on the geometry of the specific nav problem, calculation of total system error gets pretty tricky.

Area Navigation Error Table (95% Probability)

	DISTANCE ALONG TRACK FROM TANGENT POINT														
	0	5	10	15	20	25	30	35	40	50	60	70	80	90	100
0 (x trk)		.6	.8	1.1	1.3	1.6	1.9	2.2	2.5	3.1	3.7	4.4	5.0	5.6	6.2
(alg trk)		.7	.7	.7	.8	.9	1.0	1.2	1.3	1.6	1.9	2.2	2.5	2.8	3.0
5 (x trk)	.7	.7	.8	1.1	1.4	1.6	1.9	2.2	2.5	3.2	3.8	4.4	5.0	5.6	6.2
(alg trk)	.6	.7	.8	.8	.9	1.0	1.1	1.2	1.4	1.6	1.9	2.2	2.5	2.8	3.1
10 (x trk)	.7	.8	.9	1.1	1.4	1.7	2.0	2.3	2.6	3.2	3.8	4.4	5.0	5.6	6.2
(alg trk)	.8	.8	.9	.9	1.0	1.1	1.2	1.4	1.5	1.7	2.0	2.3	2.6	2.9	3.1
15 (x trk)	.7	.8	.9	1.2	1.4	1.7	2.0	2.3	2.6	3.2	3.6	4.4	5.0	5.6	6.3
(alg trk)	1.1	1.1	1.1	1.2	1.2	1.3	1.4	1.5	1.6	1.9	2.1	2.4	2.7	3.0	3.2
20 (x trk)	.8	.9	1.0	1.2	1.5	1.8	2.1	2.3	2.6	3.2	3.8	4.4	5.1	5.7	6.3
(alg trk)	1.3	1.4	1.4	1.4	1.5	1.6	1.7	1.8	1.9	2.1	2.3	2.6	2.8	3.1	3.4
25 (x trk)	.9	1.0	1.1	1.3	1.6	1.8	2.1	2.4	2.7	3.3	3.9	4.5	5.1	5.7	6.3
(alg trk)	1.6	1.6	1.7	1.7	1.8	1.8	1.9	2.0	2.1	2.3	2.5	2.7	3.0	3.2	3.5
30 (x trk)	1.0	1.1	1.2	1.4	1.7	1.9	2.2	2.5	2.7	3.3	3.9	4.5	5.1	5.7	6.3
(alg trk)	1.9	1.9	2.0	2.0	2.1	2.1	2.2	2.3	2.3	2.5	2.7	2.9	3.2	3.4	3.7
35 (x trk)	1.2	1.2	1.4	1.5	1.8	2.0	2.3	2.5	2.8	3.4	4.0	4.6	5.2	5.8	6.4
(alg trk)	2.2	2.2	2.3	2.3	2.3	2.4	2.5	2.5	2.6	2.8	3.0	3.2	3.4	3.6	3.9
40 (x trk)	1.3	1.4	1.5	1.6	1.9	2.1	2.3	2.6	2.9	3.4	4.0	4.6	5.2	5.8	6.4
(alg trk)	2.5	2.5	2.6	2.6	2.6	2.7	2.7	2.8	2.9	3.0	3.2	3.4	3.6	3.8	4.0
50 (x trk)	1.6	1.6	1.7	1.9	2.1	2.3	2.5	2.8	3.0	3.6	4.1	4.7	5.3	5.9	6.5
(alg trk)	3.1	3.2	3.2	3.2	3.2	3.3	3.3	3.4	3.4	3.6	3.7	3.9	4.1	4.3	4.5
60 (x trk)	1.9	1.9	2.0	2.1	2.3	2.5	2.7	3.0	3.2	3.7	4.3	4.8	5.4	6.0	6.6
(alg trk)	3.7	3.8	3.8	3.8	3.8	3.9	3.9	4.0	4.0	4.1	4.3	4.4	4.6	4.8	5.0
70 (x trk)	2.2	2.2	2.3	2.4	2.6	2.7	2.9	3.2	3.4	3.9	4.4	5.0	5.5	6.1	6.7
(alg trk)	4.4	4.4	4.4	4.4	4.4	4.5	4.5	4.6	4.6	4.7	4.8	5.0	5.1	5.3	5.5
80 (x trk)	2.5	2.5	2.6	2.7	2.8	3.0	3.2	3.4	3.6	4.1	4.6	5.1	5.7	6.2	6.8
(alg trk)	5.0	5.0	5.0	5.0	5.1	5.1	5.1	5.2	5.2	5.3	5.4	5.5	5.7	5.8	6.0
90 (x trk)	2.8	2.8	2.9	3.0	3.1	3.2	3.4	3.6	3.8	4.3	4.8	5.3	5.8	6.4	6.9
(alg trk)	5.6	5.6	5.6	5.6	5.7	5.7	5.7	5.8	5.8	5.9	6.0	6.1	6.2	6.4	6.5
100 (x trk)	3.0	3.1	3.1	3.2	3.4	3.5	3.7	3.9	4.0	4.5	5.0	5.5	6.0	6.5	7.1
(alg trk)	6.2	6.2	6.2	6.3	6.3	6.3	6.3	6.4	6.4	8.5	6.6	6.7	6.8	6.9	7.1

The row-label column is labelled **PERPENDICULAR DISTANCE TO TANGENT POINT**.

To find the cross-track and along-track error at point A, enter the table with tangent distance and distance along track from the tangent point; for example, when the distance to the tangent point equals 30 miles and the distance along track equals 20 miles, the cross-track error is 1.7 miles and the along-track error is 2.1 miles.

Figure 4

At least we're lucky that someone has already done the work for us.

Figure 4 is a table showing the results of such calculations to determine area navigation error within a 95 percent probability.

The importance of this table to the pilot is that manufacturers build RNAVs to these tolerances; the FAA certificates airborne equipment to these tolerances; airways and approaches are designed assuming these tolerances; and your avionics shop aligns your equipment to these tolerances.

In other words, if your area navigation system is demonstrably accurate within the tolerances shown in Figure 4, your equipment is working as it should. If it doesn't perform within these tolerances, your equipment is unsafe (and illegal) in the IFR environment.

Surprisingly, there is no requirement in the FARs that RNAV equipment be checked periodically for accuracy. (We're talking about the type of operational check required for VOR receivers.) The theory behind not requiring these checks is that an RNAV unit is merely a computer that manipulates input data. If the input data is correct, the RNAV output will be correct. The VOR input *is* checked under the FARs. The nature of DME is such that errors will be noticed immediately by a pilot in the course of routine operations.

Our experience at B/CA using relatively simple RNAV systems in the IFR environment has been that the question of RNAV accuracy and stability is not as simple as the manufacturers would have us believe. Most low-cost RNAV computers are analog devices that suffer a degradation of accuracy over a period of time. (The newer digital RNAVs don't. Like all digital electronic devices, they either work or they don't work.)

We've also had our system bench aligned and discovered that it worked better before the alignment than after.

In short, our experience has convinced us that regular checks of the system in VFR conditions are absolutely necessary. One of the worst feelings imaginable is shooting an RNAV approach into a small airport with no other facilities while wondering if your RNAV system is really telling you the truth.

If they had their druthers, the members of the FAA's Flight Standards group would probably regulate some kind of RNAV system checks. In the meantime, they have gone on record suggesting procedures for maintenance, inspection and tests. Among other things, the FAA suggests that "following repair or alteration, the system should be checked before predicating any operation on its use." We heartily concur. Other suggestions from Flight Standards include these:

• Compatibility of area navigation system replacement components should be assured unless the replacement is of the same make and model as those upon which original approval was based.

• Operators using aircraft under IFR with an RNAV system not maintained under an approved procedure should establish procedures that will be used to inspect and test the equipment periodically to determine that it is operating in accordance with at least the accuracy specified in Figure 4.

• Test and inspection procedures and intervals should be adjusted in accordance with the results of the analysis.

Exactly when to formally check your system depends almost entirely on how much you use it. For example, if you use your RNAV regularly, you'll develop a gut feel for its accuracy and you'll notice immediately when things start to go bad. However, if you only turn the system on once in awhile, you'd better set up some sort of formal check routine. That is, once a month, fly it around VFR and see what it can really do. So far as bench checks are concerned, the manufacturers of analog-type RNAVs recommend that you get the system aligned every 18 months or so. It is important to make sure the shop is *approved* by the manufacturer to work on its RNAV equipment.

The first step in checking RNAV accuracy is to make sure the raw data going to the RNAV computer is good. This means flight checking your DME and ground checking (VOT or ground check point) your VOR equipment. To flight check a DME, simply overfly a convenient VORTAC as low as possible. Multiples of 600 feet are good because each represents one-tenth of a nm. For example, if you overfly the station at 1200 feet, the DME should count down to two-tenths as you approach the station and count up from two-tenths as you depart the station. Remember, the ground station is considered accurate to within plus or minus one-tenth, and analog airborne DME equipment is considered accurate to plus or minus five-tenths. So, if you cross the station and the system reads five-tenths or one-tenth, you're probably doing OK.

FAR 91.25 requires periodic checks of the airborne VOR equipment. In the opinion of most RNAV designers, the plus or minus four-degree tolerance allowed in the VOT or ground check tests, while all right for straight VOR navigation, is too much for good RNAVing. We suggest that you tolerate a maximum VOT indicated error of plus or minus two degrees.

So, summing up the raw data checks, if your DME is within a couple of tenths of where it should be and your VOR is within a plus or minus two-degree limit on a VOT check, the raw data going into your RNAV computer is fine.

Checking the entire RNAV system takes a bit of preflight preparation. You'll need a large-scale VFR chart (a sectional is good, a local area or TCA chart is better), a protractor and a compass. You'll also need a plate for a published RNAV approach in your area.

Start with the chart and select two VORTACS within 30 nm of each other and plot a course between them. Be sure to check *AIM* to make certain that the signals you're working with are OK. Next, define the location of each in terms of distance and bearing from the other as precisely as possible. (Estimate tenths of miles and tenths of degrees.) Now put that chart aside and go to the RNAV approach plate. Using the plate as a reference, plot a model of the approach on another piece of paper. Your plot will be similar to that shown in Figure 5. Don't run away. It's not as tough as it looks.

First make a point on the paper representing the position of the reference VORTAC; then draw a vertical line straight up from the point to represent magnetic north. Now, using the protractor, construct two radials from the VOR representing the published bearing of the final along-track fix way-point (Island in our example) and the missed-approach waypoint (MAP). Then, using any appropriate scale, measure out the published mileage on

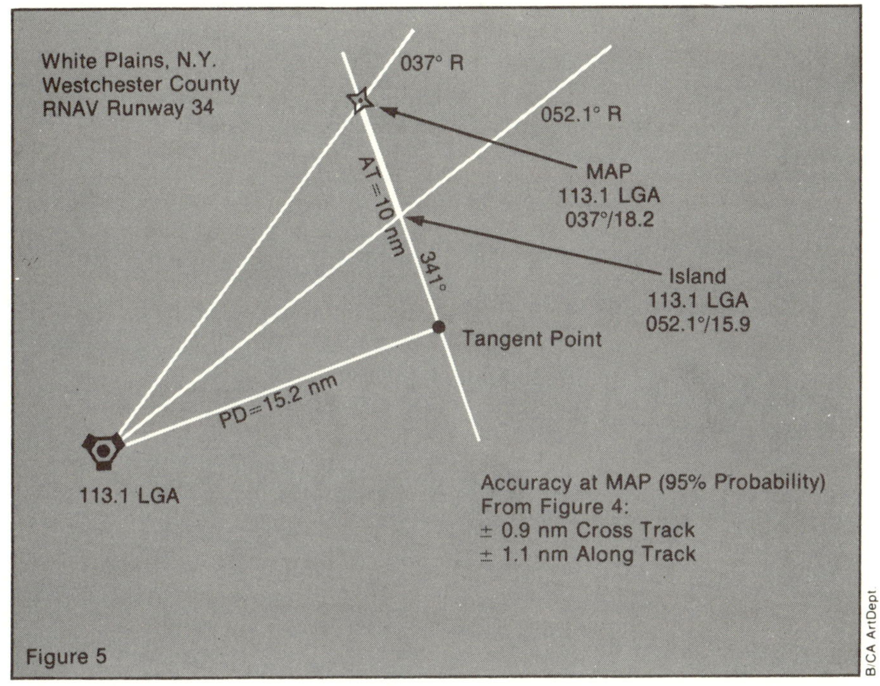

each radial and draw in the waypoint positions. The straight line determined by the two waypoints you've drawn is the final approach course
depicted on the approach plate. Next, extend the final approach course line
in either direction for a couple of inches. Finally, using the compass, determine where the final approach course line (or its extension) comes closest
to the reference VORTAC. This is the *tangent point* discussed earlier.
Now, using the same scale you used to plot the positions of the waypoints,
determine the *perpendicular distance* (distance from VORTAC to tangent
point) and the *along-track distance* (distance from the tangent point to the
missed-approach waypoint).

When we did this at B/CA for the RNAV Runway 34 approach at White
Plains, we came up with a perpendicular distance of 15.2 miles and an
along-track distance of 10 miles.

Using these numbers in the table in Figure 4, we determined that at the
missed-approach waypoint, the total system error could be as much as 0.9
miles cross-track and 1.1 miles along-track.

You may wish to show this error graphically by plotting it on the airport
diagram provided with the approach plate for the airport. We've done that
in Figure 6. Note that the cross-track error probability of plus or minus 0.9

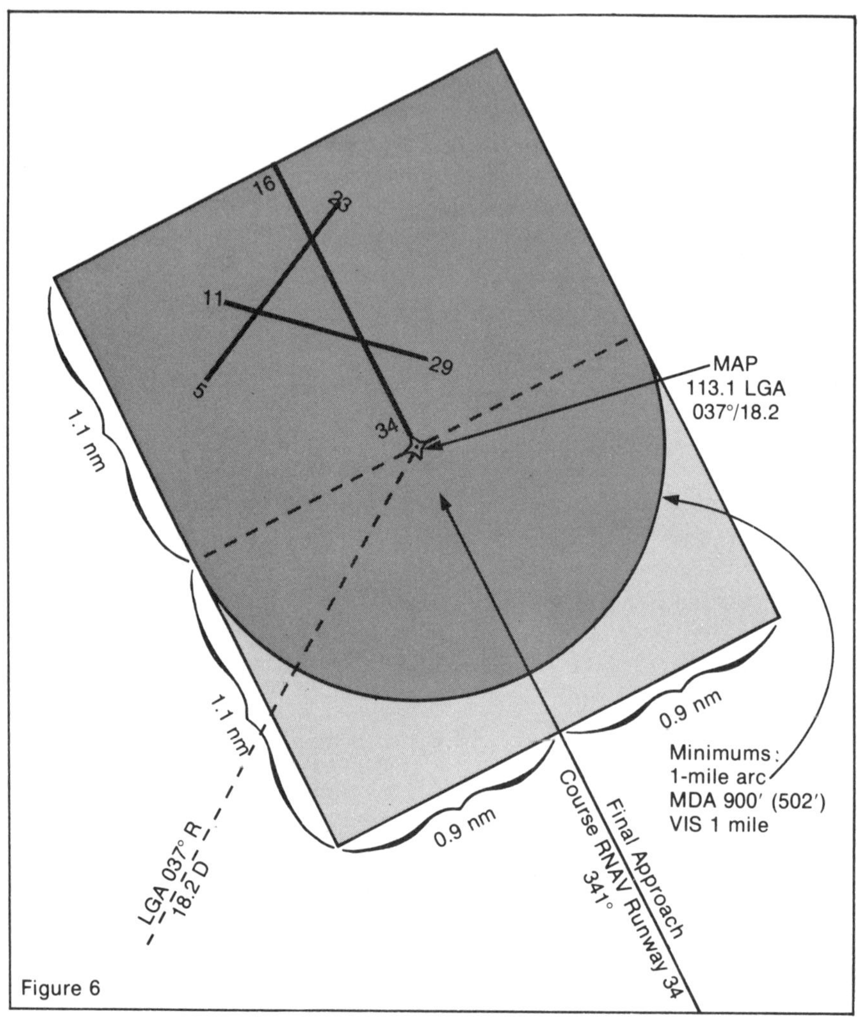

Figure 6

miles and the along-track error probability of plus or minus 1.1 miles when plotted produce a rectangle.

The significance of this rectangle is that you should end up well within its boundaries when your RNAV says you've reached the missed approach waypoint . . . most of the time.

Similar rectangles can be plotted on the VFR chart at each of the selected VORTACs. (During the test flight, each of the VORTACs will be overflown as a waypoint using the other VORTAC as a reference facility.) In this case, the tangent point is at the reference facility, so the perpendicular distance is zero. If the VORTACs are 20 miles apart, the maximum probable error

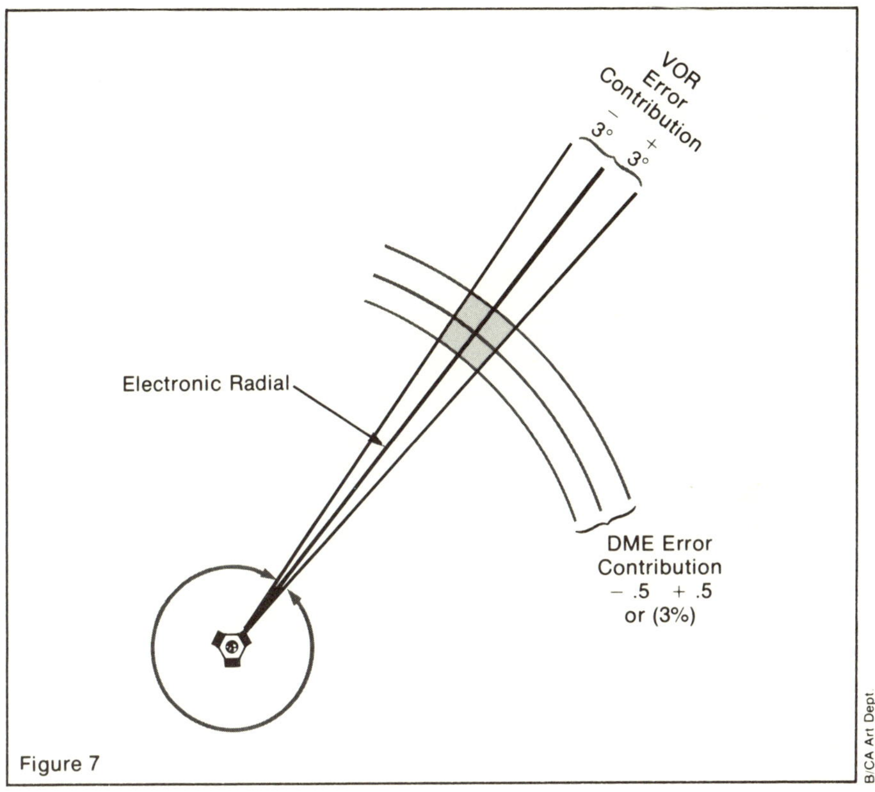

Figure 7

The airborne VOR and DME receivers both contribute to RNAV error. Up to 5/163.0 degrees for the VOR, and 5/160.5 nm for the DME are within tolerances.

over each VORTAC will be (from Figure 4) 1.3 miles cross-track and 0.8 miles along-track. Thus, the sides of the rectangles would be 2.6 miles and 1.6 miles respectively.

With all this plotted, it's time to go out and fly the check. Fly to the first VOR using raw data; then, using that VORTAC as a reference facility, establish a waypoint at the second VORTAC. Fly the RNAV course to the waypoint and eyeball your position relative to the second VORTAC antenna when the RNAV indications show a waypoint arrival. If your chart has a large enough scale, you'll be able to plot the actual position relative to the theoretical position.

Next, switch to the approach mode and overfly the actual location of the second VORTAC while making minor adjustments to the distance/bearing knobs on the RNAV to zero the indications directly over the VORTAC position. Fly a cloverleaf pattern through the waypoint from all compass points and note any deviation in waypoint position.

Finally, using the second VORTAC as reference, establish a waypoint over the number-one VORTAC and repeat the procedure. (Some RNAV checkers like to establish a third geographical fix and check waypoint accuracy at that point relative to the two reference VORTACs.)

Now it's time to shoot the RNAV procedure that you plotted. Use normal procedures and try the approach a half-dozen times. Plot the aircraft position when instrumentation indicates arrival at the missed-approach waypoint.

It's time to think about Figure 4 again. We said earlier that the individual error elements usually combine in such a way that the actual total system error is less than the total of *possible* system errors. Remember that Figure 4 says only that there's a 95 percent probability that the total system error (discounting flight technical error and slant-range error) will be within the limits for the appropriate perpendicular and along-track distances. It's been our experience, and indeed the experience of most RNAV users we've talked to, that system accuracies are a lot better than Figure 4 would indicate, even with the least expensive single-waypoint RNAV units.

A mathematician looking at the error calculations for Figure 4 would tell us that since the error probability is actually distributed along a bell curve and therefore, in a large number of approaches, spread out over a large number of days, only a few of the approaches would end up near the edges of the rectangle. If you plotted each sample approach, you'd find the plots densest near the waypoint and most thinned-out toward the edges of the error rectangle.

That's the long way of saying that most of your test approaches should end up within a half mile or so of the missed-approach waypoint. If they consistently end up near the edges of the rectangle or all over the rectangle during any series of approaches, you've probably got problems. The same is true for your tests with the two VORTACs.

On an RNAV approach plate, the given waypoint coordinates (distance/ bearing) are geodesic rather than electronic. For example, cartographers say that the MAP in Figure 6 should be 18.2 miles out on the La Guardia 037 degree radial. But, as we saw earlier, the electronic LGA 037 degree radial on a given afternoon might not precisely overlay the geographic 037 degree radial. Therefore, suspicious test results in your flight check should be confirmed by repeating the checks with other facilities. If the waypoint plots still look poor, it's time to take your RNAV into the shop for a checkup.

An RNAV—even a low-cost, single-waypoint system—can be a marvelous aid to IFR operations, but only if its operator knows its limitations and, at the same time, has confidence in its accuracy.

Checking your equipment using these techniques should go a long way toward achieving those ends.

How to Choose a Radio Altimeter

33

by J. Mac McClellan

Spend an evening with a group of pilots and the last thing you'll hear discussed will be the merits of radio altimeters. Even if you can move the conversation away from women and sports, there's little chance that radio altimeters will stand a chance against other avionics.

The lowly status of the radio altimeter is reemphasized when it comes to laying out the panel. The indicator is usually located at the bottom of the cluster so the pilot's knee makes viewing it difficult if not impossible. Burying the radio altimeter has long been a pet peeve at B/CA. We'd like to see it up where it can save a life.

Although it's not a major conversational piece, a controversy does surround the radio altimeter. It will never rank up there with the first Ali-Frazier fight, but there is a real difference of opinion about the best design concept.

The argument starts with the very name. Some systems are called "radar" altimeters and that is an accurate description of the way they operate. Others are called "radio" altimeters and that more accurately describes their system design. In settling on one term that defines all the systems, we at B/CA have selected "radio" rather than "radar." Our logic is that all systems, whether pulse or continuous wave (CW), use signals in the radio frequency spectrum.

There are the three different ways in which the altimeters operate, with claims and counter-claims of superior performance from each faction.

To gather data on the various methods of operation, B/CA talked with engineers at all the major altimeter manufacturers. The CW technique is used by all Arinc format system makers and in business aviation systems by Collins and King. Sperry, and recently Hoffman, use a pulse technique similar to radar. Bonzer uses a modified pulse technique. We'll discuss each system in turn.

The CW technique uses a low-power continuous signal that is modulated by an FM cycle. The signal is directed toward the earth and is reflected back to the aircraft. Because the frequency of this signal is being constantly varied, the system can determine the time it's taking for the signal to make a round trip by comparing the frequency presently being received with that of the one being transmitted. It's as though you were bouncing a bunch of variously colored balls off the ground from a second-story roof. You'd know how long ago you threw the one that's just bounced up by looking at the color of the one you're about to throw down. (Granted a very quick mind, which a radio altimeter has.)

While the basic technique is simple, the electronics to accomplish it are complicated. The transmitter must be stable and the receiver sensitive to the weak reflected signal. The advantage of the FM/CW system is that low transmitter power is required; therefore the entire system can use solid-state components with no final transmitter tube.

Pulse systems, such as those from Sperry, work much like radar. A pulse is fired toward the ground. When it's received, its round-trip time is divided by two and the speed of light to get the distance above terrain. Now you're throwing down one ball at a time off that second-story roof and timing its journey.

The advantage of the pulse concept is that each pulse provides an individual measurement, rather than the average reading of CW, for greater theoretical accuracy. However, to generate the high peak power for the pulse transmission, a tube must be used.

Bonzer, as mentioned, uses a modified pulse technique. The Bonzer altimeter fires its pulses at a much greater rate than other systems and listens continuously for their return. The pulse pattern ranges out, searching for the ground through various "windows." The system constantly searches at various distances and displays the shortest return, which is the ground or an object on it. Bonzer claims this technique provides greater accuracy.

How do you decide between the various systems? First, consider what kind of display you want to see in the cockpit. A nice, smooth needle that reacts much as your barometric altimeter, right? If every time the aircraft flies over trees or a large building the needle jumps, confidence in the system will be eroded.

To avoid that, the manufacturers of all three systems provide some dampening to steady the display needle.

Pulse manufacturers claim that even with indicator dampening, their systems offer a more accurate topographical presentation than the CW systems. Because the pulse systems use a series of individual measurements instead of a constant average, we'd have to agree, but when you pass over a levee at 100 plus knots, it translates into little more than a twitch on the needle, so what good is it?

From a practical sense we can't say one system is better than the other and sincerely doubt that one can tell the difference between a pulse and CW system of equal quality. For what it's worth, the makers of CW systems seem more ambivalent toward the question than the pulse makers, who are quite evangelical. Other factors, such as price, interface considerations and your attitude toward a manufacturer and his support, are more important considerations than the pulse versus CW controversy.

The difference between TSOd and non-TSOd altimeters is something we were able to get a much more general agreement on. The consensus is that the radio altimeter TSO, C87, is the toughest standard in avionics. A TSOd altimeter is going to cost double the price of a non-TSOd version, but in contrast to the affect of many other TSOs, the extra cost is going to be returned in a capability of the altimeter to accommodate more function and accuracy demands.

A major requirement of the TSO is that the system must be accurate within five percent from three feet to 500 feet above the ground. Obviously, to do that the system must read to the ground and it's those last 50 feet or so that cost a lot of money in engineering and material.

The major problem in measuring radio altitude close to the ground is that the reflected signal must be recovered and a very tiny difference in time measured. With radio waves traveling at the speed of light it doesn't take long to cover 50 feet and obviously zero feet is impossible to time.

To resolve that, two antennas are used to provide a longer delay between the transmitted signal and its reception. Remember that the system is measuring the time radio waves, either in a continuous fashion or in a pulse, travel from the transmitter back to the receiver. It can't measure zero time, so a delay line is used. For example, somewhere in the transmitter/receiver/timer loop, 50 feet of wire may be inserted. Thus the signal must travel those 50 feet plus the distance to the ground and back. If the ground is at zero, the signal will travel the 50 feet through the cable and the system can time that, figure the total distance, then subtract 50 feet to get the actual distance.

That delay line, a second antenna and very stringent accuracy requirements are what drive up the cost of a TSOd system. While the overall accuracy requirement, including the indicator, is ± 5 feet for the first 100 feet under C87, the accuracy requirement for the transmitter/receiver/timer portion is ± 3 feet or three percent for the first 500 feet. That is extremely accurate and requires demanding design and component selection. Also, at the top end of the range of measurement C87 requires more gain to assure adequate performance over terrain with poor reflectivity. That is an important consideration when using the altimeter with a ground proximity warning system.

But what's so important about reading all the way to the ground? Who's going to be looking at his radio altimeter 50 feet above the runway?

Those are important questions that only you can answer, but there are some valid reasons for a readout capability below 50 feet.

Radio altimeters, or at least the Arinc format systems, received their biggest boost in the early days of the CAT II and later CAT III landing certification craze. The radio altimeter was viewed in part as a backup to the glideslope for approaches below 200 feet. The idea was that at least one crewmember would be watching the altimeter for those last few hundred feet. Rising runway symbology was incorporated into flight directors to put that last 200 feet of radio altitude into perspective.

Beyond the capability to drive a rising runway, what does the extra cost of a system that functions accurately below 50 feet buy you? Safety, certainly. We think that on any tight approach one crewmember should have his head inside all the way to touchdown, whether it's CAT I or CAT II, and the radio altitude should be part of the scan for two reasons.

First, it's a backup to the glideslope down to DH. Second, even after passing through DH the man with his head in should monitor radio altitude closely to make certain the continued descent to touchdown is progressing smoothly and logically. Many accidents result from optical illusion or an undetected increase in sink rate inside the middle marker and the one-head-in technique will resolve that. A readout capability below 50 feet is obviously necessary, however.

On nonprecision approaches, especially at night, the radio altimeter will help fight off that unconscious tendency to get too low when visual clues are confusing and a VASI isn't available. Again, it's probably going to require a two-pilot operation to get the most benefit out of the last 50 feet of radio altitude information, so that capability may not be of concern to single and light-twin operators.

Finally, maybe the nicest thing about a radio altimeter that reads all the way to the ground is heightened credibility. There's no better way to build confidence in the system than to see it reading zero as you taxi out. No amount of self-test whistles or bells can make up for that acid test.

While we can offer no firm advice as to whether TSO is right for you, we can say that you definitely get something for your money. You get more coverage and greater accuracy. But only you can decide if that is worth double the price.

Another big price jump in the radar altimeter market is between general aviation systems and Arinc format systems. Although the Arinc 552 and 552A systems may have more power, they cover the same altitude range as general aviation systems costing half as much. The majority of that extra money is spent on extensive monitoring and fault isolation. Remember that these systems were designed for use in coupled approaches leading to an automatic landing. For that use, concern about undetected faults is great. Therefore Arinc systems have nearly two complete systems to compare outputs and monitor for a possible fault. Unless you plan to certificate for CAT III, it's difficult to see the need for this extra monitoring, expense and weight. Accuracy is no greater and reliability, due to the extra parts required, is probably less.

The self test and monitoring in most TSOd altimeters for business aviation is quite good. Most systems will generate a test signal that is injected into the receiver as though it were coming through the antenna. This signal should drive the pointer to a predetermined reading if the system passes its self test. Again, in the non-TSOd systems the monitoring and self-test feature will be less complete.

No matter which radio altimeter you select, it is going to be extremely installation sensitive. Although all avionics require a good installation, the radio altimeter is even more sensitive than other components. But the installation problems are similar for all radio altimeter types and any good avionics center can cope with them.

Your major installation concern will be antenna location. All antennas, except for the Bonzer, are designed to be mounted flush with the skin. The antennas should never be painted. The antenna must be surrounded by as large an area of skin that is free of protrusions—such as landing gear, steps and other antennas—as possible. It is especially important to keep the radio altimeter antenna away from pulse antennas such as those for the transponder and DME. Also, the minimum distance between antennas in a two-antenna system is critical and the manufacturer's specification must be observed.

As far as choosing between several radio altimeters is concerned, the major installation consideration is the interface problems with other equipment.

For people with complex flight control systems, the radio altimeter interface is of considerable importance in making a selection. Sophisticated flight control systems use radio altitude input to activate such things as ILS gain changes, flare computation and the rising runway display. While virtually all TSOd system makers say they can interface with any flight control system, there are some differences that must be compensated for by the installation shop. Check your installer on this point before making a selection.

Radio altimeter installation in helicopters can be a problem mainly because of the restricted space for antenna mounting. It's difficult to get the antennas far enough away from skids and unique helicopter problems, such as the rotor modulation that can effect VOR reception. All makers of TSOd systems offer a special helicopter indicator that has an expanded scale for the last few hundred feet to take advantage of the unique flight characteristics of rotor-wing aircraft.

Decision height annunciation in most altimeters includes a light on the indicator, plus outputs for lights on a flight director or aural alerts. Some, such as the Bonzer Mark 10, have a built-in aural alert.

Radio altimeter manufacturers themselves, as well as the manufacturers of other equipment, offer alternative radio altimeter displays and you must consider that when making your selection.

Be certain the one you pick will interface with the digital readout in your flight director if you have one. Also, if you plan to install one of IDC's RADBAR barometric altimeters, make certain the interface is compatible.

In any event, if given a choice, try to pick a radio altimeter that allows you to remote a second readout which can be placed where you'll be looking during the approach, such as on or near the altimeter, flight diretor, HSI or even in the windshield.

When it comes down to making the buying decision on a radio altimeter, we'd leave the pulse versus CW argument to the engineers and consider TSO versus non-TSO, availability of service when and where it's likely to be needed (where being a special consideration for overseas operators), installation and interface problems and price versus functions and accuracy required.

If there's a question in your mind about different classes of systems, we recommend that you fly one of each before making a decision.

Radar Maintenance 34

Weather radar interpretation has so many variables that the last thing you want is variation in the radar system itself. Radar is the only constant we have for measuring the ever-changing weather around us. Weather radar isn't perfect, since it can only see precipitation and not turbulence or wind shear, but it's our only yardstick.

There are many things to consider and weather radar interpretation is part art, part science and part intuition. Since that art, science and intuition must be based on what the radar shows you, it is obviously essential that it present a stable, consistent reflection of precipitation patterns. If it doesn't paint a storm today precisely as it did that same storm yesterday, last month and even last year, you have no opportunity to develop either art, science or intuition in your interpretation of the radar picture.

Solid-state electronics have all but done away with regular avionics maintenance. Current thinking by both manufacturers and avionics maintenance shops is that avionics boxes should be left alone until they quit. Often, removal and test bench handling can cause more problems in a piece of avionics gear than it uncovers.

But weather radar is in a different class than most avionics equipment. If a transceiver partially fails or degrades, someone will tell you your transmission is breaking up. Or you can hear the reduced performance in your receiver. Nav receivers are also easy to keep tabs on. If you're not getting the signal when you should, something obviously is wrong.

Nearly every avionics system communicates, interrogates or in some way receives a signal from outside the aircraft. If performance drops off, the degradation is obvious. Again, the exception is radar. It's like some people—it talks to itself—and it alone listens for replies to its own questions. Thus if its interrogations become slurred or its hearing is poor, who's to know?

Weather radar lives in its own little world, sending out electronic pulses and listening for those that bounce back from something. If a radar runs amuck, it will simply tell us that nothing is out there, whether true or not. Of course, a total failure is easy to spot because ground returns won't paint. But what about a partial failure? A degradation in performance? Are you really seeing that storm as it is, or does it appear weak only because the radar transmitter power is down, or the receiver is not working properly, or the radome has a flaw? You can't be sure without a regular radar checkup.

Manufacturers and avionics shops agree that the radar system needs an inspection prior to the start of each severe storm season. The key word is "system." Weather radar is made up of four major components: the indicator, receiver-transmitter, antenna/radome and the waveguide plus other connections between the major components.

Not all elements of the radar system require the same degree of scrutiny to be certain of proper operation. The indicator is not likely to fail without giving a visual indication on the screen. All current indicators use solid-state power supplies so there is little or no degradation in performance there. Digital indicators are complex units that gauge, record and display the returned echo. They use semiconductor memory chips and precise timing circuits to perform their function. If those components fail, they take enough of the system with them to enable you to observe the failure on the screen.

But that is not true of other components in the radar system. The RT, antenna/radome and intercomponent connections can all suffer partial failures or reduced performance through aging without an apparent visual warning on the indicator. That's why they require care and regular examination.

Step one in the inspection process is a close visual check, first by yourself and then by the avionics technician. As you know, the X-band radar signal can't be carried by a wire but must be transmitted from the RT unit to the antenna along a pipe called a waveguide. Just like any plumbing, the waveguide is susceptible to cracks, kinks and loose joints. Flexible lengths of waveguide can become brittle or worn from chafing. A good visual examination is required to be certain the entire waveguide and all its connections are tight and free from defects.

Waveguides are often pressurized with cabin air in jet aircraft to prevent arcing at high altitudes. However, since cabin air is dirty and loaded with moisture, in order to prevent undesirable elements from entering the waveguide along with the cabin air, a desiccator is inserted in the line to dry and clean the air. This desiccator should be changed, or at the very least inspected, to keep the waveguide clean and moisture free. A dirty waveguide will attenuate the signal and in the extreme may cause a bad storm to not be displayed at all.

The antenna is another element that requires close visual examination. The antenna is a purely mechanical device and after a year of banging back and forth against its stops, it may require minor adjustments or lubrication of the bearings and gears. The antenna should be examined by a qualified repairman for proper sweep angle and alignment with the aircraft's longitudinal axis. The stabilization system should be checked, if the radar system has one, to be certain the antenna is maintaining a constant sweep relative to the horizon during aircraft maneuvering within the correction limits.

The owner or pilot should examine the antenna system himself between visits to the radar shop. When the nose cone is off, a general examination of the antenna will reveal any loosening of attachment bolts to the bulkhead or the bolts joining the antenna to the sweep mechanism. Abnormal wear in the bearings or sweep drive can be easily spotted by the owner or pilot who has taken the trouble to know the system and what the normal play in the bearing is. The antenna is an expensive and complex component in the radar system and it is certainly worth a little preventive maintenance and care.

The radome is an element frequently overlooked in the radar system and that should not be. It's easy to inspect, requiring no technical expertise beyond that normally possessed by a pilot. It is also the component of the total system most likely to cause reduced performance of the sort not easily detectable by just looking at the display.

The radome is nothing more than a faired window through which radar pulses go out and return to the antenna for processing in the receiver. No radome is perfect, that is, none allows 100 percent of the signal to be transmitted and returned. Radomes that pass more than 80 percent of the signal are considered good, although some well-designed units have transmission ratings in the high 90 percent range.

Radomes are usually made of a honeycomb structure covered on both sides with a plastic skin. The goal is to keep the thickness, and therefore the electronic transparency, equal over the entire surface of the radome. The thickness of the honeycomb and its bonded inner and outer skins is also important, but those are factors established in the design and production of the unit.

The number-one enemy of any radome is water. Any puncture, or hole caused by abuse, collision or static discharge, can allow water to seep into the honeycomb. Of course, since detection of water is what a weather radar does, if the electronic pulse senses water inches away in the radome, it will look no further and simply bounce back to the antenna. What's worse, the strong signal bouncing back may glance off the bulkhead behind the antenna itself and then bounce around several times and finally show up on the indicator as a ghost storm.

Also, once water seeps into the honeycomb, freezing and thawing as the aircraft passes through freezing levels and weather cycles will delaminate the bonded skin and ruin the transmissivity over an increasingly larger area.

Visual inspection, both by the pilot during preflight, and by the shop during the radar's annual, will reveal many possible defects such as holes and delamination. But not all flaws will be visible even to the trained eye. The only way to be certain of the electronic transparency of a radome is to have it removed and checked on a special test range. This should be done only if you're having problems that aren't obviously caused by some other element of the system. Hand-held devices can be used to measure the transmissivity of spots on the radome, but there is no way to get a complete picture of transmissivity without removing the radome and sending it to a test range.

The most common cause for substandard radome transmissivity, believe it or not, is a rubber or plastic anti-erosion boot or cap on the nose. They keep the nose looking sharp, but they dull the radar picture significantly.

The cap can cause problems in two ways. First, it changes the carefully designed and controlled thickness of the radome, which is vital to optimum transmissivity. The radar signal will pass through the area with the cap or boot over it differently than it does the rest of the radome. Secondly, moisture can and often does seep behind the erosion cap. If enough moisture gets behind the cap, it will knock out a large share of the system. The water simply blocks the signal and prevents it from leaving on its search for more sinister forms of water. Moreover, water trapped behind the cap is like water that has seeped into the honeycomb. It bounces back part of the signal, which may then be reflected off the bulkhead and around the radome to confuse the picture and make troubleshooting the system very difficult.

One radar design engineer bluntly told us, "If it were my airplane, I wouldn't have one of those caps or boots on it." It doesn't take much water to degrade radar performance if it seeps into the wrong place.

If you feel you must use a nose cap, during the preflight inspection make sure the glue joint all the way around the cap is tight and impervious to moisture. Neoprene anti-erosion shoes are better than the plastic caps. They don't change transmissivity as much and they remain glued tighter to the radome than plastic caps. However, neoprene shoes also can trap water next to the radome. Be sure to check the seal at the edge of the shoe frequently and avoid washing the area with solvents that could dissolve the adhesive.

The best alternative to using caps or shoes is to paint the radome with anti-static/anti-erosion coatings made by various manufacturers. The best and most protective of these coatings are flat black. Unless you or somebody in your company has a hangup about a black nose, we recommend it.

However, protective coatings can't be layered onto the radome time after time without degrading transmissivity. When it becomes necessary to repaint, you'll have to either remove the coating with a special solvent designed for neoprene-type finishes or sand it off if no solvent is available for your particular coating. Sanding must be done very carefully to avoid digging too deeply and weakening the surface of the radome.

Each time the radome is removed, painted or treated, care should be taken to make sure the lightning arrestor strips are bonded to the airframe. Also, it's best not to paint the metal strips. The paint can interfere with their conductivity.

All of these measures are time consuming and therefore expensive, but your radar is helpless without a good radome. The more you count on your radar, the more time and money you should spend maintaining your radome.

Finally, there's the heart of the radar system—the receiver-transmitter. This black box generates the pulse of energy sent out and then receives the echo returned from precipitation or solid objects. It does that at rates of up to 400 times each second, although current radars fire their pulses at a rate generally between 100 and 200 times each second. Each pulse of transmitted energy lasts from one microsecond, or millionth of a second, to five or six microseconds, depending on the design, range and function of the radar system. Many sophisticated radars use a longer or wider pulse on long ranges to transmit more energy over the greater distance and then narrow the pulse width on shorter ranges. The narrower pulse width provides better resolution, so the short-range, high-resolution radar systems designed for helicopters have pulse widths of less than a microsecond. But that type of pulse will not paint weather well because not enough energy is transmitted to provide a good echo off other than solid objects.

Radar pulses are generated by a vacuum tube-like device called a magnetron. There are three general types of magnetrons used in current production radars—vane axial negative cathode, vane axial positive cathode and simply coaxial. Technical differences are of interest only to design engineers, but there are performance differences in the three types that are important to all radar operators.

The vane type negative magnetron dates back to World War II in its basic design. It is well proven and has been built by the thousands, so it is relatively cheap and offers predictable performance. But recently a new type of vane magnetron came into use in airborne weather radar—the positive pulsed type. The positive pulsed unit is smaller and lighter and makes possible such small RT units as the Bendix RDR-160, which is being fitted onto single-engine aircraft.

The positive pulsed magnetron is limited to less than 10 kilowatts peak power output, so it is found only in smaller, lighter types of units designed for piston and turboprop aircraft. Larger, more powerful units must be fitted with either a negative cathode vane type magnetron, or the superior coaxial type magnetron.

The important consideration when operating a vane type magnetron is to understand its degradation characteristics as opposed to those of the coaxial type. The vane magnetron will gradually lose power output over its entire life. Many of the vane magnetrons start out with a little more than their rated power, then degrade over a rather steady slope. However, the radar will continue to operate normally, or what appears to be normally, even though the power is continually growing weaker. With less and less power output, less and less of the weather ahead will be depicted as it really is, especially at longer ranges. The differences may be sinisterly subtle. Storms that may have contoured at a certain range last year won't contour at the same range this year. That's important information to know.

You will notice the power loss first at long ranges, but there should be plenty of power left within the shorter ranges where the STC (sensitivity timing control) takes over. At a certain range, depending on the design of the radar, the receiver sensitivity is gradually turned down to prevent nearby targets from painting larger than they actually are. Within this range even a degraded magnetron should have enough power to give you a good picture of the precipitation. But you need to know how much power is left in your unit to gauge storms at a distance and have confidence in your system in general.

At some point on that degradation curve, probably at the minimum power output specified in the system handbook, the vane type magnetron should be replaced. However, you may wish to consult with your avionics shop and replace it before it degrades to that minimum level to be assured of adequate performance throughout the entire spring or summer storm season.

The company that makes the magnetron (which is not the same company that builds the radar) places a warranty life on the device. If the vane type magnetron has gone past its warranty period and has degraded close to the minimum specified output, it would seem wise to replace it.

The beauty of the more expensive coaxial magnetron used in most current top-line equipment is that it doesn't degrade gradually as the vane type does. The coaxial unit will continue to transmit near peak-rated power throughout nearly all of its life. Then, just before it fails totally, power output will drop off sharply and the magnetron will conk out. With the coaxial type, if the radar system is working at all, you can have a great degree of confidence that the signal output is right up near the rated power.

RCA is so pleased with the performance of the coaxial magnetrons it uses in its top-line equipment that one company engineer told us he doubted that a test could determine any degradation in power output until just a few hours before the magnetron fails totally. Total life of a coaxial magnetron is also several times that of the vane type. A coaxial type costs a great deal more than a vane type, but there is universal agreement among manufacturers who don't use it, as well as those who do, that a coaxial magnetron is far superior in power output consistency and life expectancy.

Other problems that can be encountered in the RT unit are frequency drift in the transmitter and possibly a change in the AFC (automatic frequency control). Compared with other avionics transmitters, the signal transmitted by a radar is very dirty and unstable. The signal drifts over several hundred kHz while com transmitters remain within a few kHz.

Since the transmitted signal is drifting over this wide range of frequencies, the receiver must be listening for echoes over the entire range. If the transmitter and receiver are not on the same frequency or within the specified range, the echoes are going to be unheard and unpainted no matter how big the thunderstorm in front of you is. Current production receivers are all solid state and quite stable, so there's little chance of error there, but frequency drift in the transmitter is not uncommon at all.

Testing an RT unit to uncover these possible maladies is no simple matter. Manufacturers and avionics shops agree that any avionics unit should be disturbed as little as possible. A piece of avionics should be removed and taken to the bench only as a last resort if all applicable tests in the aircraft fail to turn up the trouble. Carefully documented airline experience has shown that 50 percent of all avionics removals fail to solve the squawk. The box checks out well on the bench but won't work when it's returned to the aircraft.

Radar systems have an even worse record of unwarranted squawks and removals than avionics in general. Radar is more complex, is partly mechanical (with respect to the antenna and waveguide) and operates in a different spectrum than any other piece of avionics onboard. The record has been so poor on radar removals that one airline went to the trouble and expense to build a ramp tester that could be wheeled up in front of the aircraft for testing radar in place. This was more complex than it may sound because radiation from the radar had to be captured and contained to prevent injury to people working on the unit and even to those nearby. The experiment wasn't successful enough for any other shops or airlines to follow suit.

Nevertheless, a ramp test of the total system is the only meaningful way to measure power output. Since radar is a system, if the RT unit only is taken to a bench and tested for power and receiver performance, there is still no guarantee that the antenna output is up to par.

The only really valid check of RT output is at the antenna. To accomplish this, the waveguide is disconnected at the antenna and a dummy load and couplers are installed. The dummy load confines the radiation for safety. Couplers then make it possible to attach a device called an echo box. Part of the transmitted pulse is directed into the echo box. It simulates a target

276

and reflects a signal back to the receiver. In this way the waveguide, all connections, the RT and the indicator are checked. Instruments at the dummy load and couplers can measure power output, frequency and receiver settings. Nothing is removed from the aircraft and only one waveguide joint is opened.

Well-qualified radar shops will have the equipment necessary to conduct this test and so will the radar manufacturer's service centers. We believe from talking to radar experts that you should insist on this kind of ramp check so the system will be disturbed as little as possible.

What you should be looking for in the report from the avionics shop is the power output as a percentage of radiated power. If it's a marginal case, you may want to be in on the magnetron replacement decision. Get a report on what other things the shop found wrong, if anything. Keep and examine records from year to year to compare and see if the system is performing as well as it did last season.

Now, let's run through the steps the experts believe are necessary and best for a complete radar checkup.

First, examine the display visually yourself. You spend more time looking at the radar than anybody else and should be able to spot anything unusual. You don't need to know what's causing the problem, but if you can point the symptom out in great detail, the shop will have a much easier time troubleshooting the system.

Next, you and the shop technician should examine the display together if there's anything you wish to point out. Experts can isolate a great many radar faults simply by looking at the display.

Third, the technician should visually examine the entire system, including the indicator, RT, waveguide, antenna and radome. Waveguide joints should be clean and tight. The guide itself should be free of kinks or sharp bends. The antenna may require lubrication or adjustment. Radome repairs other than a simple refinishing of the protective coating require the special attention of an expert.

Finally, the system should be ramp checked using an echo box to check general performance. Power output should be recorded, receiver parameters checked and frequency stability monitored. But ask that the system be disturbed as little as possible.

Be certain to get full reports on your radar checkup. Something like an "all OK" doesn't give you much to compare against when the radar comes out of the shop next year. Also, you'll want to know if your radar is operating at 100 percent power output or only 90 percent, because it will make a difference when you view a long-range target.

Keep in mind the type of magnetron your system uses. If it is the vane type, decide how far you will let it degrade before replacement. If it's the coaxial type and it's still operating up near 100 percent of rated output,

277

leave it alone until it quits. No one can predict when that might be. If, on the other hand, its output is down even as little as five percent, it probably will die a sudden death within the very next few hours and you should consider replacing it if it's the middle of the thunderstorm season or an extensive international trip is coming up.

These checks will give you confidence that your radar is showing you the same picture it did last year and thus will remove one of the variables of weather interpretation.

Some fleet operators may wish to have all their radars adjusted alike so that when pilots change aircraft they will see a similar picture on each indicator. We talked to radar manufacturers about the feasibility of this practice and they told us it isn't really a problem if the fleet is equipped with radars of similar power, range and general performance. Even if you cross brands, if you stay on the same relative price and performance level, all the radars will display weather systems in much the same way. It's rather like the difference between Scotch whiskies. There is a difference between premium brands and inexpensive booze, but it takes a connoisseur to tell the difference. There may be differences between the way the information is displayed and other features of the system, but basic weather information presented by systems of equal price and performance will tend to be very similar.

Lower-powered systems and lower-cost systems, however, go about things differently. That's not to say that low-powered and low-priced radars are no good, but there's no way a $7000 system is going to paint a weather situation as well and as exactly as a $20,000 system. So there's no way an avionics shop can adjust the two so they'll show identical pictures of the same storm. Therefore, the best advice for an operator equipping a fleet is to install radars of a similar quality level in all aircraft so there won't be a potential problem when pilots change from one to the other. Ideally all aircraft in a fleet should have the same type radar, but because aircraft are added to a fleet rather slowly and radar technology and type designations change so fast, that isn't always possible.

When you find a shop that maintains and checks your radar to your satisfaction, it's a good idea to take your whole fleet there regardless of brand. If all systems are set up in the same way by the same shop, you should get good, consistent performance across the fleet and each radar should paint approximately the same picture of identical storms.

Radar maintenance requires good coordination between the operator and the shop. The system should be treated with as much care as any other safety device on the aircraft because that's exactly what it is.

Maintaining Your Radome

35

by Richard N. Aarons

Perhaps you've been lucky to date and haven't discovered what a radome costs. To give you an idea, here are some list prices (from Norton Plastics and Synthetics, the largest manufacturer of general aviation retrofit radomes) for replacement nose cones: Aero Commander, $1265 to $2028; Beech King Air, $1263; Beech Baron, $1548; Cessna 310, $1338 to $2323; Cessna 400 series, $1051 to $1377; Piper Aztec and Navajo, $1238 to $2223. Radomes for turbojets are not much more expensive. A Sabreliner nose cone, for example, costs $1480, and one for a 1123 Westwind goes for $2166. And all of those prices are up considerably since these 1976 quotations.

It's obvious, then, that crunching a radome carries much more economic impact than crunching a plastic wingtip. Yet it would seem radomes rarely get more attention than wingtips during a preflight walk-around.

Recently, B/CA did a quick survey of our own pilots (and some of our friends) and asked but one question: What are you looking for when you check your radome during a preflight walk-around? In each case, we got an answer something like this: "Well, er . . . ah . . . ah . . . I . . . ah . . . make sure it's there and that it doesn't have any holes in it. You know . . . bird strikes and that sort of thing. And . . . ah . . . well, that's about it."

That type of inspection would be good enough if a radome were simply a fiberglass lay-up designed only to keep the radar antenna from blowing away. But the fact is a radome is a relatively sophisticated—and, as we've seen, expensive—part of your avionics installation. Its structure is complicated and delicate. A radome can be damaged by trauma yet show no external signs of that damage. And it can fall victim to an insidious disease that eats away at its innards, ultimately causing complete destruction.

Several kinds of radome abuse—caused by operator ignorance—can ruin a radome also. Painting it with the wrong kind of paint can destroy a radome's electromagnetic transparency; plastic ablative shields can cause beam distortion and create back-reflections that generate ghost storms.

These shields can also make it more difficult for the radar system to discriminate intensity levels and, in some cases, can prevent the system from contouring cells that it should.

The point is that radomes deserve careful attention and preventive maintenance—the former because they have a significant effect on radar performance and the latter because they are expensive. In this chapter, we'll look at radome inspection and preventive maintenance, but to understand these procedures we'll have to look briefly at radome construction.

From a design viewpoint, radomes must be physically tough because they form an important part of the aircraft structure. They must be appropriately contoured to optimize appearance and drag characteristics, and they must be (so far as is possible) transparent to the electromagnetic energy leaving and returning to the radar antenna. The latter requirement is the most important because it directly affects the performance of your radar system.

General aviation radars typically transmit pulses at three to eight kilowatts, then listen for returns as the radiated pulses bounce off precipitation. Both the outgoing and the returning signals must pass through the radome. If the radome were 100 percent efficient, there would be no attenuation of the signal by the radome either going or coming. However, no one has discovered how to make a practical, 100 percent efficient radome. Good ones have efficiency ratings well above 80 percent. Poorly made or poorly maintained radomes may have efficiencies below 50 percent. In the case of one with 50 percent efficiency, you'd only get half the performance from a radar set through no fault of the black boxes. (In fact, you'd get less than half because the system would have trouble differentiating intensity levels of the precip it did see.)

All the turbojet manufacturers fit their aircraft with relatively efficient radomes, either fabricated in-house or made by a vendor such as Norton. Piper, Beech and Cessna all make radomes in-house. Only Beech offers a choice between an in-house radome and one supplied by an outside vendor. In all cases the radomes are constructed of inner and outer fiberglass skins bonded to a honeycomb core. The core, like the fiberglass skins, is nonconductive (dielectric).

The thickness of the skins and core is carefully controlled to assure maximum efficiency. If the skins are too thin or too thick, portions of the transmitted radar energy are reflected back into the antenna or nose cone area to be reflected out again in a random pattern. This situation not only reduces the efficiency of the main beam, but it can cause confusing returns if the misdirected energy is reflected back to the antenna after its second bounce.

The independent makers of radomes argue that their nose cones are generally more efficient and less susceptible to side-lobe radiation than those made by the airframe manufacturers, primarily because radome manufacturers specialize in a single product. We won't spend any time on that debate other than to tell you how to get a free check of your radome efficiency, regardless of who manufactured it. Norton Plastics and Synthetics will provide free efficiency checks (as long as the demand is not excessive) at its radome test range in Akron, Ohio. The test requires about one day downtime.

At the heart of radome problems is the integrity of the bonded honeycomb sections of the unit. If the radome has been fabricated correctly, each honeycomb cell is airtight and has no connection with adjacent cells. It's critical to keep these cells airtight and, thus, watertight. Water is an excellent reflector of radar energy, which, of course, is why we can use radar to detect the presence of precipitation. It stands to reason, therefore, that we could render a radar system useless if we filled each of the radome honeycomb cells with water, thus causing all the energy radiated by the antenna to be reflected back into the aircraft immediately.

Water is the insidious killer of radomes—insidious because water contamination can begin in a single honeycomb cell through a tiny pinhole and spread from cell to cell with no external indication that the deterioration has begun. The process usually begins when a static discharge perforates the outer skin of the honeycomb sandwich. Moisture is condensed out into the cell just as it is in fuel tanks during a temperature cycle. As the aircraft ascends through a freezing level, the water in the cell expands and ruptures the seal to adjacent cells. As the process continues, the patch of water-contaminated cells multiplies and radar efficiency decreases. If the process is caught in time, the deteriorated patch can be refabricated at relatively little cost—a few hundred dollars at most. However, if the deterioration continues unnoticed, replacement of the entire unit may be necessary.

Here's how to catch the water disease before it spreads beyond repairability.

• Inspect the radome exterior daily for pinholes. If the radome is painted, pinholes caused by static discharge will normally be surrounded by a smudge mark or a little area of charred paint. If a pinhole is discovered, cover it immediately with plastic electrician's tape and get it to an avionics shop as soon as possible.

• Periodically check the inside of the radome. A logical time to make these checks is whenever the radome is swung open for work on the radar antenna system. Delamination will appear as a chalky area. If you discover such an area, show it to an avionics technician immediately.

• If you've got a friend in the maintenance department of a large fleet operator, he may have access to a radome water probe—a hand-held electronic device that detects the presence of moisture in the honeycomb cells.

281

The test is nondestructive and can be performed in minutes. Some larger avionics shops also have this equipment.

It's possible to get delamination without water contamination, that is, a delamination where the inner or outer skin pulls away from the honeycomb core. This situation distorts the shape of the radome cross section and can cause a deterioration of radome efficiency. The most common cause of this problem is trauma.

Obviously, if there's a hole or a dent in the radome, you've got delamination problems. However, radomes are relatively flexible and often spring back to their original shapes after impact. Therefore, during the preflight inspection, look for smudges and scrapes. A greasy smudge could indicate a bird strike. Scratches and scrapes indicate possible collisions with fuel trucks, hangar doors and the like. In any event, smudges and scrapes call for further investigation.

One trick you can use to check for delamination is to tap the radome with a coin and listen to its sound. Start at the rear of the radome and tap in concentric circles. Your taps should have a live, resonant tone. A flat, dead response is bad news. The technique of testing radomes by ear is similar to that used for checking a boat hull for rot. Good areas are resonant; the bad respond with a dull thud. Mark suspected delaminated areas and get the radome to a shop for an inspection.

Delamination, like water contamination, spreads. A small patch of delamination will grow, largely through mechanical flexing, and ultimately the radome will be destroyed.

Too often, operators put off needed radome repairs for the same reason they put off needed trips to the dentist—they simply don't have the time. Repairing a radome is time-consuming. Rebuilding a delaminated or water-contaminated section can take a few days or several weeks. However, like putting off the dentist, the longer you wait, the longer you'll be out of operation when the situation gets critical. The answer, of course, is a standby radome. One way to take advantage of a bad situation when your factory-installed radome has to go into the shop for repairs is to buy a replacement immediately and have the old unit fixed up as a spare. Sometimes loaners are available, but usually only for large aircraft where the radome fasteners have been installed on precision jigs. In light aircraft installations, the mounting holes are usually drilled wherever the field installer decided to stick them, so interchangeability becomes a problem.

Some operators of similar aircraft pool their resources to buy a single spare radome. It's unlikely that any two operators in the group will need a spare at the same time.

Radome engineers tell us that operators do as much to ruin the efficiency of radomes as do errant line technicians, static discharge and careless birds. The one thing that seems to disturb radome engineers the most is the installation of plastic ablative nose caps. Said one engineer, "The first thing you do when you install one of these things is change the cross section of the radome and do away with all the careful engineering we did to establish the cross section in the first place. The second, and probably worst, thing that happens is that moisture collects behind the cap, causing reflection problems."

Most radome manufacturers do approve of neoprene erosion shoes, as opposed to plastic shields. (Check your avionics technicians for sources.) If you have such a shoe installed, don't allow solvents to be used to clean the radome because the adhesive bond between the outer skin and the shoe can be dissolved.

As an alternative to shoes and shields, radome manufacturers recommend the anti-static/anti-erosion coatings made by Goodyear and Olin. The Goodyear product is 23-57S neoprene coating; the Olin product is Astrocoat 7200 polyurethane coating. Both are designed to protect the radome from erosion while preventing buildup of static charges, which can lead to discharge damage.

These anti-static/anti-erosion coatings are black, and some operators just can't abide a black nose on an airplane. If you insist on painting the nose cone, use Alumigrip AA-92, made by U.S. Paint Lacquer and Chemical; Cat-A-Last 600 polyurethane from Bostik-Finch Paint & Chemical; Imron Polyurethane enamel from DuPont; or Prestec polyester-based coating manufactured by Presto Chemicals. A good epoxy primer is Bostik-Finch's 463-6-1 green primer.

Be sure to remove old paint and protective coatings before repainting a nose cone. Paint buildups can cut efficiency. The neoprene-type finishes can be removed by soaking in special solvents. Epoxy, polyester and polyurethane finishes must be sanded off, but special care must be exercised to prevent damaging the radome laminate.

Radomes for high-speed aircraft often have metal strips on their surfaces to conduct static buildups (and lightning) away from the front of the radome to a grounding bus at the rear. If you can live with it aesthetically, don't paint over the strips; they are more effective when left unpainted. (Radomes have been destroyed by the sudden evaporation of painted strips when struck by lightning.)

Be sure to check the continuity of the lightning strips regularly. Ungrounded ones generate static charges, thus entirely defeating their purpose.

If these few cautions and rules are followed, your radome should continue to give good service for the life of the radar itself. Inspect it often, repair it properly, keep it clean and have it checked by a competent shop periodically. Preventive care is quick and painless; the penalty for not doing it can be very expensive in both dollars and downtime.

AVIONICS: OPERATIONS VIII

Avionics components are inevitably delivered with a neat little operating guide to describe the function of each knob and switch. Beyond that immediate information there is a wealth of operating techniques which normally evolve from thousands of hours of operator experience. This section will let you in on some of those unofficial but valuable skills.

More and more aircraft are being delivered with autopilots. More and more autopilots are designed with sophisticated functions like autocoupling and even autolanding. "How to Finesse Your Autopilot" goes far beyond the manufacturers' guides to help you get the most from that sensitive device.

As business aircraft operations continue to expand worldwide, constant voice communications between home base and the flight crew is essential. "Long Range, Air-Ground Communication" takes a look at communication services and facilities available to the international corporate aircraft.

And speaking of long-range voice communication, high-frequency radio is still the predominant method. "HF Stuff" is a short piece which summarizes the most common quirks of that very different radio.

Avionics "off" flags are an integral part of all VOR and DME receivers as well as many other components. As it turns out, those flags have a split personality, which will make its appearance in "The Case of the Bragging Flag."

Weather radar also requires close watching; therefore, it is essential that the radar picture be standardized as much as possible for each flight. "How To Prepare Your Radar for Flight" describes the basic preflighting techniques that will allow you to maximize that valuable weather avoidance equipment.

How To Finesse Your Autopilot

36

by Dan Manningham

Instrument flying has been in a steady process of evolution for over 50 years, and there's no sign of a letup in the future. Approaches to 200 and a half have long been routine, but that last 200 feet presents an enormous challenge for engineers and pilots alike. The engineers are doing their jobs well already. Autoland is a fact, and the normal progression in state of the art will result in even more sophisticated autopilots in smaller and smaller aircraft. Therefore, future reductions in landing minimums will come only through increased dependence on more sophisticated automatic flight control systems, and, we, as both businessmen and professional pilots, need to begin now to develop skill and facility with autopilots and couplers in preparation for CAT II (1200 RVR) and CAT III (700 RVR) minimums in even the smallest business aircraft.

Autocoupled approaches markedly change the pattern of cockpit business and introduce several unique and critical failure modes. Autopilot operation is as much an art as is good stick and rudder work, and you need to begin with an intimate knowledge of the equipment in your airplane. Sometimes that information can be difficult to obtain because autocoupler design is still largely a black art. One designer we spoke to freely admitted that he didn't believe in telling pilots how the thing worked because his job was to exclude pilots from the loop anyway. Be persistent, get the information somehow, because you must understand the hardware in order to capitalize on its idiosyncrasies. The best advice you'll ever get on how to interface with autopilots is: Do not let yourself become a passive button puncher.

There are many approaches to autocoupler design, but there are some common elements. If you are flying a high-performance airplane with a sophisticated coupler, it works something like this: Up to the point of localizer and glideslope intercept, the autopilot functions as a stability platform to keep the aircraft in level flight at some preselected altitude. Localizer intercept is usually possible up to 45 degrees, and at least 20 degrees of intercept angle is desirable to ascertain that the beam has been captured. With some autopilots, glideslope capture is possible only from below. Know those characteristics of the one, or ones, you fly. Be especially cautious of coupled approaches initiated from an on-course, on-glidepath position because you will have no intercept maneuvering to confirm that beam capture has triggered the appropriate autopilot responses. We have seen couplers engaged from a needles-centered situation only to find out too late that one channel or the other was not really engaged. The airplane was tracking near center line only by coincidence.

Localizer capture is pretty straightforward, although there may be some scalloping as the electrons adjust to crosswinds, airplane trim and signal idiosyncrasy. Glideslope intercept is often a two-stage process involving an initial pitch-over to some specific rate of descent followed by actual beam capture. Autopilots that use that logic need to be carefully monitored to assure that sequencing doesn't fail after the initial push-over. If conditions are just right, that primal rate of descent can keep the airplane very close to the glidepath until it's too late to reengage. In both cases, allow the autopilot some pretty substantial oscillations during the first 30 seconds after intercept for normal adjustments to wind, temperature, airplane trim and speed. During that half minute, look for progressive stabilization in both axes and recheck the annunciation panel for appropriate indications.

After capture, continue to keep a skeptical eye on mode indications. Some autopilots will silently *un*couple if the navigational signals are momentarily interrupted or if displacement from the on-course position exceeds certain limits. We have experienced that sort of uncoupling due to a large truck passing near the ILS shacks and distorting the signals.

Somewhere around the outer marker your equipment may begin a timed gain reduction of the LOC and/or G/P signals. Autopilot engineers call this feature attenuation, and it is used to reduce signal sensitivity so that coupled responses are progressively softened as those beams narrow down to critical sizes. Attenuation is good for you, but it's even better if you know where it begins and what happens if it doesn't. Depending on the manufacturer and model, attenuation may begin at glideslope intercept, middle marker reception, some predetermined value of radio altitude, or not at all. Each of these different configurations presents its own failure possibilities.

Glideslope programming may include another little goody, known as glidepath extension. By the time you get to 200 feet or so, the glideslope beam is so narrow that any aberration in the signal could cause a gross disturbance to the airplane's flight path. Glidepath extension is simply a programming device within the autopilot computer that allows a memory circuit to complete the last few hundred feet of vertical guidance.

So what can you do about it after you have researched your own equipment? You can practice and learn how to tweak those black boxes for optimum performance. We have found several tricks that allow the pilot to maximize the airframe/autocoupler combination.

It is always necessary for the autocoupling procedure to initiate well within the prescribed speed envelope because some autocouplers just don't have the authority to correct for gross speed changes and none of them do it well. Try to give the autopilot its best shot at flying a smooth, stabilized approach. Avoid large flap movements for the same reason.

Once established in the approach, you may find that the coupler functions appreciably better at a speed 10 to 12 knots above minimum weight V_{REF} and that the added speed is justified for this automated operation. For instance, a Sperry SP-30 instrument does its best work at or above 140 knots, although V_{REF} can be as low as 120 knots.

During the approach you have no direct control over localizer or glide-slope tracking, but it is possible to cheat a little when the coupler needs persuasion. Asymmetrical thrust, or just a foot on a rudder pedal, used judiciously, will often coax the airplane over to an on-track condition when the coupler insists on tracking to one side or the other. Similarly, small glidepath displacements can sometimes be corrected by increased or decreased power, especially in those airplanes with a substantial pitch response to power changes. Both of those deceptions are increasingly effective as attenuation progresses.

As you approach DH, mentally establish the runway picture you can expect, based on crab angle and on-course location. When the runway is in sight, resist the urge to disconnect until you have taken a moment to become familiar with the visual environment. You are your own worst enemy for the first few seconds.

Below DH, the pilot not flying ought to announce speed and sink rate until the wheels are on. After touchdown, he should be ready to track the localizer during rollout in the event that fog, rain or blowing snow obscures the runway.

Don't ignore that autocoupler. Start practicing now, and by the time you really need it you will probably understand each other.

Long-Range, Air-Ground Communication   37

by Arnold Lewis

Almost anywhere in the world—wherever U.S. flag carriers fly—the corporate pilot can key his mike and establish virtually instantaneous communications with his home base.

Ironically, however, while navigating the North Atlantic with push-button accuracy unheard of 20 years ago, the pilot employs a communications system that has remained relatively unchanged in recent times. While inertial navigation can trace the world independent of surface facilities, long-range voice communications continue to be tied to a complex network of worldwide radio facilities, all requiring people at the other end. This is despite Arthur Collins' development of the single side band (SSB) capability in the 1950s that injected new life into high frequency (HF) communications and led to subsequent development of light-weight, solid-state airborne communications equipment.

The only major improvement on the horizon in long-range communications is AEROSAT, an aeronautical satellite program being fostered jointly by the United States and European countries for air-ground communications, initially across the North Atlantic. However, the program has been mired in controversy over the issue of UHF versus VHF air-ground frequencies, with the Europeans insisting on UHF. U.S. airlines—seeking compatibility with existing airborne equipment—have apparently won a compromise and there are now provisions for VHF as well as L-band transponders aboard the AEROSAT satellite.

Short of AEROSAT, existing SSB technology is thought to be adequate. "I don't think we can go much further until we have the satellite," B/CA was told by Pan Am communications expert George Crandall. "Our existing capability is sometimes greater than is used. Sometimes the cockpit crew doesn't work as hard at it as they might. It's a question of how hard they want to talk to us. I think communications have kept up with the aircraft to the extent necessary—they're adequate. The next big step is the satellite," Crandall said.

It is clear that as business aircraft operators continue to expand their activities worldwide, utilizing more and more sophisticated equipment, the day-by-day, minute-by-minute operational control of these aircraft from home base becomes increasingly important. Some already are reporting off times, fuel load and general condition of the aircraft, whether it be departing from Johannesburg or Teterboro.

Commercial air carriers, from their very birth, have spent billions of dollars fostering and developing complex long-range communications capabilities for the operational control of their fleets. Domestically and throughout most parts of the world, this task is handled through the airline-owned Aeronautical Radio Inc. (Arinc) and its vast communications network. These facilities are readily available to corporate aircraft operators.

Arinc was founded by some of the early airlines in 1929 when the government told them that if they wanted to establish a voice air-ground communications system, they would have to do it themselves. Since 1929, Arinc has grown into a nationwide system of more than 1,600 VHF ground stations, of which 400 are interconnected into 69 communications networks by 76,000 miles of telephone lines.

Internationally, Arinc offers wide Atlantic HF SSB coverage from New York and superb Pacific coverage from a little-used Honolulu station. Beyond that coverage, flag airline facilities include wide-ranging Pan Am HF SSB stations at Beirut, Hong Kong and Monrovia. Localized airline VHF frequencies also are available worldwide. In no case are these HF SSB communications facilities tied to any air traffic control function. The FAA does utilize Arinc VHF and HF facilities at the gateway points of New York, Miami, San Juan, San Francisco and Honolulu for air traffic control. These include 16 special high-powered, extended-range VHF stations.

It is through the 69 VHF networks—tied to nine communications centers at New York, Chicago, Washington, Miami, Fort Worth, Denver, Los Angeles, San Francisco and Seattle—that Arinc provides operational communications for the airlines and corporate aviation.

A typical Arinc network stretches from Miami to Chicago with remote, unmanned ground stations located at West Palm Beach, Orlando, Jacksonville, Tampa, Bainbridge (Georgia), Atlanta, Chattanooga, Nashville, Louisville and Indianapolis. Each of these remote stations transmits and receives on 131.0 MHz and is tied to the Miami communications center via telephone landline. A pilot talking to Arinc in the Louisville area is actually talking to a radio operator in the Miami center. As an added capability, many remote stations are located on airports—Miami, West Palm Beach, Tampa, Atlanta and Chattanooga in this case—enabling crews to communicate with home base while sitting on the ground.

Once the Arinc operator receives a message from an aircraft, there are

several ways it can be handled. The airlines and the larger corporate operators have their own Arinc private-line teletype terminals. As the Arinc
operator receives the message, he types it out on his teletype and it is
automatically routed to its destination through the company's unique electronic switching system (ESS), billed as the largest private message switching system in existence.

For less frequent Arinc users, the message can be relayed by telephone,
or an actual phone patch can be quickly established between the aircraft
and the (authorized) party being contacted, whether it be the dispatcher or
the vice president in charge of stuck landing gears.

The remaining 1,200 Arinc ground stations are local area facilities—
sometimes mistakenly referred to as "company frequencies"—assigned
through special lease-contract agreements to airlines, commuters, corporate operators and FBOs. These stations are "off-net" facilities and are not
tied to any of the 69 Arinc networks. They generally consist of a simple
10-watt base station and are only good for limited-range, line-of-sight communications.

But let's slow down for a minute. There is a catch to the system. Not
just anyone can dial up and use an Arinc frequency. Arinc's services are
highly regulated by the FCC and they do cost money.

"There is no such thing as a company frequency," declared Jim Mulhern,
Arinc director of service administration. "These frequencies are 'aeronautical en route' frequencies. They belong to everybody. In the United States,
use of these frequencies is managed by the FCC. Arinc is only a licensee
of ground stations," he explained. Proper loading or allocation of frequencies is obtained according to the airline or company flight operation, but
under a lease-contract agreement, frequencies are simply operated *for*
Arinc, he added.

In order to use an Arinc frequency, the airborne radio station must be
licensed by the FCC, which represents no major obstacle. The application
for an aircraft radio license contains a list of frequency categories that are
to be used, such as private aircraft, air carrier and aeronautical en route.
The applicant must specifically check the aeronautical en-route category
and list the frequencies under that category he plans to use. Or he may
simply cite the 127 VHF frequencies contained in section 87.295(b) of the
FCC's rules and regulations. The application form also requires that the
applicant have a "valid agreement" with the licensee of aeronautical en-
route frequencies—in other words, Arinc.

"Anybody who desires to do business with Arinc should get in touch with
this office [2551 Riva Rd., Annapolis, Md. 21401]. Then he's got to sign a
service agreement with us," Mulhern said.

Arinc charges are nominal. For the infrequent user, the cost is $4 per
contact ($4.50 for international contacts) plus the telephone toll charge for

messages from the communications center to their destination. Extensive users pay a specific rate each month—regardless of the number of contacts—computed on a cost sharing basis. This may run approximately $100 per month.

There are a couple of options for the operator of a lease-contract station. He may buy his own base station equipment for approximately $1,000 and have it licensed by Arinc for $7 per month. Or, Arinc will install and maintain the equipment for a monthly charge of $20 to $30, depending upon the type of maintenance plan selected. Those utilizing private teletype terminals obviously must pay for the terminal, telephone landline and a small message switching charge.

In addition, all users pay a "unit service charge" to compensate for industry-related Arinc costs not directly related to communications; for example, Arinc's role in standardization of airborne communications equipment and racks to assure compatibility of black boxes and aircraft installations. The charge is based on type and number of aircraft. A Learjet operator would pay $12 per month, for instance, compared with $14 for a Gulfstream II operator.

There is one more catch to dealing with Arinc: "A limitation on the kinds of traffic we can handle," Mulhern said. "The message must relate to the operations of the aircraft. We are not authorized to handle public correspondence." Thus, while airborne telephones may infringe somewhat on Arinc business—at least domestically—airborne telephone manufacturers have nothing to worry about in terms of Arinc competition.

In all, by the end of 1973, Arinc had 741 customers, of which an amazing 60 percent (446) fell under the category of general aviation. "Corporate members range from General Motors' aircraft (two heavy jets plus 15 turboprops) down to light twins—every kind of operator; many are owner-pilots," Mulhern said. The company's 46 U.S. airline customers and 122 foreign carriers, however, account for 80 to 90 percent of the contacts. Other customers included 83 commuter air carriers, 24 FBOs and 20 air freight forwarders.

FBO customers have posed a particular problem to Arinc lately because of nonauthorized aircraft using the lease-contract frequencies. The problem has been especially prevalent in Florida, where FBOs have advertised their Arinc frequencies without qualifications and where the FCC has an especially vigilant listening post (Fort Lauderdale). Several such unauthorized aircraft operators have recently been cited for violations by the FCC, much to their surprise. FBO Arinc stations certainly provide a viable alternative to frequently congested Unicom frequencies—if the aircraft is authorized to use them.

Operational control of aircraft and flight following must be an important consideration for any corporate operator in the process of expanding the scope of its operations internationally. Here the key is HF single side band, not only for operational communications, but also for air traffic control in many parts of the world.

Developed by Collins in the 1950s and first used to any extent by the Strategic Air Command, SSB takes modified HF (short wave) signals and literally sends them around the world by bouncing them off the ionosphere. SSB is subject to atmospheric interference occasionally, but is still eight times more efficient than conventional HF.

In the old days it would have taken a whole room full of equipment to produce and decipher SSB signals. Today Collins has brought its all-solid-state 718U-5 SSB unit down to under 34 pounds with 100 watts of peak envelope power.

There is one more piece of equipment that should be seriously considered both for domestic and international long-range communications. It's called SELCAL and enables a ground station to contact an aircraft through a combination of audio tones that illuminate a light on the instrument panel of only the aircraft being contacted. This means the crew does not have to continually monitor a given HF or VHF frequency.

There is one problem with SELCAL: SSB signals are incompatible with SELCAL signals. Many aircraft HF SSB transceivers are designed to detect SELCAL transmitted in the full carrier mode even though the aircraft transceiver mode selector is in the single side band (SSB) position. Aircraft transceivers not designed and built with this feature must have the selector switch in the full carrier mode to be able to detect a SELCAL signal. In addition, the appropriate Arinc ground station must know the aircraft's SELCAL code assignment in advance.

Arinc's Honolulu HF facilities were described by Mulhern as "one of the finest radio stations in the world. It has five high frequencies and very special antennas with omni-directional coverage." He said that during a recent test operation, an aircraft on the ground at Sydney was patched to a Sydney telephone number through the Honolulu facility. The only problem is that no one is using it.

Mulhern believes that the Honolulu facility is little used because corporate operators "don't like the toll charge from Honolulu to the mainland. The fact that it could save him [the pilot] $1,000 in operational delays doesn't seem to enter his mind. The same guy won't use New York either."

The New York Arinc station has some antenna problems and does not provide the wide coverage of the Honolulu facility. It does, however, offer good coverage across the North Atlantic and is used to a much greater extent than Honolulu. In fact, three New York area operators—American Cyanamid, Executive Air Fleet and Texaco—recently got together and had HF transceivers remoted to their bases from Arinc's Long Island antenna farm. They now can remain in constant voice communication with their aircraft all the way to Europe through Arinc's facility.

Pan Am offers its entire spectrum of communications and ground servicing facilities to the corporate operator—including private teletype, air-ground communications, weather, flight planning and fueling. The airline charges for each of its stations used, plus a per-manhour fee for any ground services provided, such as clearing through customs. Weather and flight planning cost additional. Most companies operating internationally, however, subscribe to their own weather and flight planning services and receive information via the airline's teletype system. Pan Am provides flight following services through its own HF and VHF facilities as well as through various government owned and operated ATC facilities around the world.

As an example of Pan Am's activity in this area, the carrier during the last three months of 1973 averaged 120.3 corporate flights per month representing 52.3 companies. "The majority are European, but there is a lot of South American activity and West African activity among the oil companies. A number seem to go around the world a lot," a spokesman said.

So why go through all this for one or two quick international trips a year? Nothing in the regulations requires installation of an HF transceiver. The FARs only state that the aircraft be equipped with whatever is necessary (two of everything under Part 121, but Part 91 operators can get by with one). You can skip across the North Atlantic via Goose Bay, Narsarssuak and Reykjavik quite adequately with VHF only, or island hop down the Caribbean chain to South America. Even JFK-San Juan direct at FL 230, according to one crew, takes you out of VHF range for only eight minutes.

On the other hand, perhaps the NBAA's Fred McIntosh put the question in the proper perspective. "If somebody comes to us and says they're going to fly to Jo-burg every Thursday, I tell them to go see Pan Am and do exactly what they do."

HF Stuff 38

by Dan Manningham

My first substantial cross-country was in a Navy Beech 18, more affectionately known as a Secret Navy Bomber after its official designation of SNB. That trip from Pensacola to Minot, North Dakota was pretty routine except for tremendous headwinds that held our groundspeed below 100 knots the entire way, with one leg averaging only 88 knots.

What I remember best are the long conversations with individual radio facilities—ATC centers were not completed then—as we sought a more favorable route or altitude in the face of that strong northwest wind. All of those conversations took place on the old HF common frequency of 3023.5 KC.

High frequency communications were and are a mixed bag. Nothing else provides the sheer range of voice communications, although reception is often disappointing or nonexistent due to skip or interference.

When the signal leaves an HF transmitter, it splits into two segments. One part remains near the earth's surface and is called a *groundwave*. Broadcast stations rely on the groundwave to carry their signal to distances around 100 miles. A second part of the HF signal heads for outer space but is reflected back by the ionosphere, which acts like a giant mirror. These reflected signals, called *skywaves*, are more common in the upper portion of the HF band used by aviation, and at night. That, in fact, is the reason you can often hear distant broadcast stations on your AM radio after dark.

Since the ionosphere's reflective capabilities vary greatly with time and season, it can be helpful to remember the most obvious changes.

• Higher frequencies (10 to 30 MHz) are generally more usable during the day. I use the mental guide "high freq at high noon."

• Lower frequencies (2 to 10 MHz) are more useful at night although everything is likely to be open on summer nights.

• During winter months there will be a really pronounced shift at sunset, and the low frequencies will tend to have extraordinary strength and range on winter nights.

Fading is an HF phenomenon in which the signal strength increases and decreases at rates from several times per second to once every several minutes. Fading is most pronounced below 6 MHz and may often be eliminated by selecting another frequency. Fading is often very different for any two frequencies, even those very close.

Skip occurs when the skywave signal is reflected over or past a station. If you don't get an immediate response, try repeating the call in a few minutes when your transmitter and/or receiver may be better positioned to take advantage of the skip.

Forecasts of HF signal propagation are given over Station WWV, the National Bureau of Standards time signal broadcasting facility, at 14 minutes after each hour. WWV can be received on the following HF frequencies: 2.5, 5, 10, 15, 20 and 25 MHz. These are short-term forecasts of propagation conditions in the North Atlantic, but are generally applicable to the Northern Hemisphere. The actual announcements are given in the form of a code that uses one phonetic word and a single digit. The word identifies the radio propagation at the time the forecast is issued (0100, 0700, 1300 and 1900 zulu-time). The numeral indicates the quality expected during the ensuring six hours. The codes have the following meanings:

"Whiskey"—propagation disturbed
"Uniform"—propagation unsettled
"November"—propagation normal
"1"—quality useless
"2"—quality very poor
"3"—quality poor
"4"—quality poor-to-fair
"5"—quality fair
"6"—quality fair-to-good
"7"—quality good
"8"—quality very good
"9"—quality excellent

If, for example, propagation conditions are disturbed and forecast to be fair during the next six hours, the coded forecast announcement would be "whiskey 5."

At the same time, 14 minutes after each hour WWV broadcasts K-index values and solar flux data. K index is a measure of disturbances in the earth's magnetic field that have a strong effect on HF signal propagation. The K figures broadcast by WWV range from 0 (very quiet) to 9 (extremely disturbed). A K figure of 5, for instance, would mean that the earth's magnetic field was moderately active and likely to degrade HF communications proportionately.

The solar flux value is a measure of radio activity being received from the sun. This index is not related to an arbitrary scale like the K index, but is an actual measure of received energy on some specific frequency. The lowest solar flux index ever recorded was 64 and readings near 150 are considered high. When the solar flux index is low, HF communications above about 10 MHz are likely to be impaired. As the index increases, those higher frequencies become more usable. Solar flux index is just a rough handle on your maximum usable frequency.

A typical complete announcement at 14 minutes after the hour would sound something like this:

"The radio propagation quality forecast at 1300 is good. Current geomagnetic activity is normal. The coded forecast is November 7. The K index at 1300 is 2, tending to increase. The 2800 MHz solar flux index is 70 units, tending to remain constant."

The National Bureau of Standards handbook providing complete time and frequency information is available from the Government Printing Office, Washington, D.C. 20402. Its order code is SD CAT C13.10:432.

HF communications has come a long way from the old coffee grinders, and it continues to get better and more reliable. If you are expanding into an over-water operation, that long-range radio will be a must for air traffic control, company communications, weather information and time data. If your experience has been limited to domestic VHF communications, find a friend with some solid HF experience and pick his brains before flying that first long trip.

The Case of the Bragging Flag

39

by Richard N. Aarons

A while back, two B/CA editors were playing the did-you-know game with then Narco President Chuck Husick while waiting for a couple of lobsters in a harborside fishery at Groton, Connecticut. The conversation got around to VOR and DME equipment and displays, and Chuck won all the prizes. Several of his did-you-knows were so thought provoking, we decided to pass them along. We'll do it in a narrative form, but with thanks to Chuck for giving us some fun insights into the intricacies of electronic navigation.

Course width and the bragging flag—There are times when you can get a good solid TO or FROM indication on a VOR display but do not have a good navigation signal. How do you check for that? First, we've got to go back into the books and determine what the avionics designers and TSO writers have in mind when they talk about *course width* and *flags*. We'll look at the flag situation first. If the avionics designer wants to, he can so adjust the nav display that the nav flag disappears as soon as a signal of even the weakest strength is picked up by the nav receiver. But the signal could be so poor at this point as to be useless. Super-sensitive flags do nothing for the pilot other than to give him a false sense of security. Husick calls these fine-adjusted indicators "bragging flags" and says that some manufacturers have gone the bragging flag route (on non-TSOd equipment) simply to make their boxes look better.

Perhaps of greater interest is that some *malfunctions* can create a bragging flag. So, in the presence of a bragging flag, or in the absence of any flag at all, how can you tell if you're receiving useful navigation information? *Course width* is the answer.

VOR displays are designed typically with a small circle in the center of the presentation and four dots to either side of the circle. Course width, in the context we're using it here, is the displacement of the OBS setting required to move a centered course deviation needle to either outside dot of the display. The TSO for conventional VOR indicators states that this course width shall be 10 degrees plus or minus one degree with a full flag and 20 degrees plus or minus two degrees with the flag just beginning to appear.

For example, suppose the OBI is showing a full TO flag and you're close enough to the ground station to be guaranteed a good strong signal. Suppose further that you center the OBS and it reads 090 degrees indicating that your aircraft is on the 270-degree radial. If you were to displace the needle to the outermost left dot by moving the OBS, you should find the OBS now reading 100 degrees. The course-width in this case is right on the button at 10 degrees.

If you were to fly across the VOR ground station in the example above and continue to fly away from it, while repeating the experiment, eventually you'd find that as the signal strength weakens the course width becomes wider than 10 degrees. At this point, the signal should be considered too weak for accurate navigation. Of course, if your indicator's flag system is working properly, the TO/FROM flag should get nervous at the point where the course width grows larger than 10 degrees and should disappear when the course width grows to 20 degrees.

Checking audio idents—When was the last time you tuned in a familiar VOR and checked the audio ident? Chances are it was a while ago. With digital tuning, the chances of mistuning a VOR or VORTAC are relatively remote. But digital tuning has not changed the fact that listening to the audio ident is the only way to verify that the ground station is functioning properly. It is also a good way to help your avionics shop isolate problems in your VHF nav equipment should they develop (we'll see how in a moment).

For our purposes, you can think of the VOR signal as a pipe with measurable limits. Navigation information is continuously coming up the pipe and it requires about 60 percent of the pipe's capacity, leaving the other 40 percent for voice communication and ident.

This 60/40 ratio is good to keep in mind when you're trying to use a VOR ground station for voice communication. All other factors being equal, the VOR collocated voice facility will be about one-third as strong as regular voice communication facilities. That's because only 40 percent of the nav station "pipe" is used for voice as opposed to 100 percent of the com station's "pipe."

Anyway, identifying the ground station is a must. High altitude aircraft often get within range of two VOR facilities using the same frequency. You'll hear gobbledygook on the ident when this is the case. You'll remember, of course, that the FAA warns pilots when a station is down for maintenance by removing the ident from the broadcast.

Typically, an airborne VOR system consists of a receiver, VOR converter, LOC converter and an indicator of some sort. The nav receiver is very much like a com receiver in that it picks up the ground station signals, removes the intelligence and sends it off for processing. In the case of a com receiver, the intelligence is removed from the signal and sent to a cabin speaker which changes electrical energy into sound energy which the pilot interprets for himself. In the case of a nav receiver, the intelligence is sent to the VOR and LOC converters where it is processed for use by the indicator.

We said earlier that getting into the habit of identifying stations can help your avionics shop troubleshoot the system and therefore save you money. Here's how. Suppose your system works fine on the LOC frequencies but does not work on the VOR frequencies. If you've been checking idents and you're getting them, chances are your receiver is functioning. As long as the indicator works on the LOC frequencies, there's no reason to suspect the indicator itself. If the LOC frequencies work, the LOC converter must be working, so the trouble is in the VOR converter. It's a lot easier to check all this stuff in the aircraft under actual failure conditions than on a shop bench at $14 an hour. Obviously, the ident check is only one of a series of observations made in the above case, but it is an important one.

When you turn your radio off, where should the needle go? It should center. If it does not, you've got problems with the needle movement which will introduce errors into the system when it's turned on.

Ground checks with Doppler VOR—We've heard much about the super accuracy of Doppler VOR, but accuracy really isn't one of Doppler's fortes. Actually, all the advantages of Doppler VOR accrue to the installer, not the pilot. Doppler is used primarily to minimize ground station siting problems. It produces a signal which only approximates the VOR signal. That point should be emphasized.

Airborne VOR receivers are designed to work with the ground signal from conventional VORs. A Doppler ground station tricks the airborne system into thinking it's looking at a conventional VOR signal, when, in fact, it is not.

For very complex reasons, no two nav receivers function exactly alike when listening to Doppler VOR. Since there are no bench checks to determine how a given VOR receiver will function when listening to Doppler, you can't find out how well your equipment is doing in this respect. It's possible to have two matched VOR receivers fully peaked and within all VOR bench-check tolerances and discover that although they zero out on a VOR check, they will differ by as much as five degrees when tuned to the same Doppler ground station. Keep this in mind when you're checking your receivers for compliance with the IFR check provisions.

Living with DME—Distance measuring equipment is in a world by itself. Ask any pilot which of his black boxes gives him the most problems and he'll probably say DME. How come? Well, simply stated, DME is the most complex avionics box in the aircraft. First, its transmitter and receiver work on frequencies averaging eight times higher than the com and nav frequencies, and techniques for handling those frequencies are just not as good as those available for the lower com and nav frequencies.

A second factor in DME's poor reputation for reliability is that there are

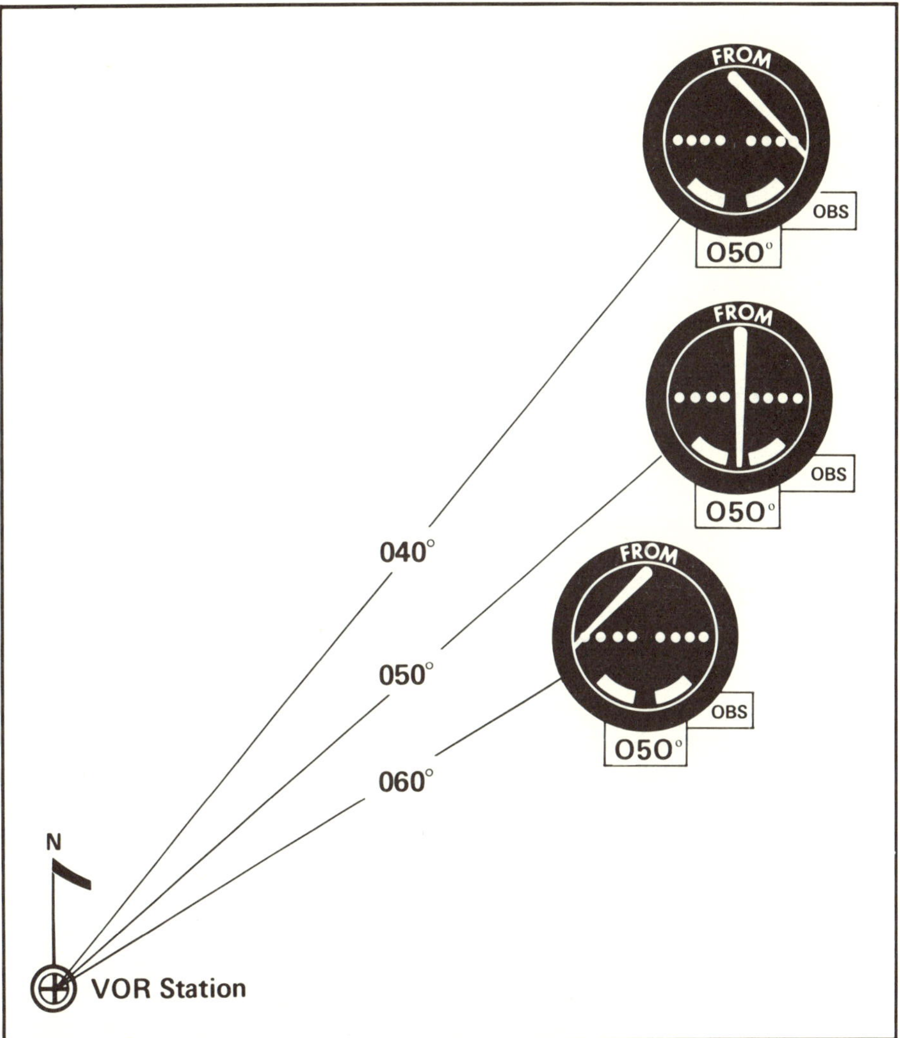

When the flags are working properly, course width (a needle movement from center position to a full left or right deflection) is about 10 degrees. If the TO/FROM flag appears before course width has narrowed to 10 degrees, you've got a bragging flag. Reliable nav information is available only when course width is in the 10 degree range. Anything more can lead to serious error. (Not to scale.)

not as many DMEs in service as nav and com radios. Less than a third of the nation's civil aircraft fleet is so equipped. This means that shops see fewer DMEs (despite higher failure rates) than navs and coms, and simply are not as experienced when it comes to fixing them.

The final factor in DME reliability problems is presented by the task we ask this box to perform. To get a feel for its complexity, consider first the ATC air-ground *communication* system. The pilot's voice is impressed on a carrier and shot off to the ground, received, removed from the carrier and presented as voice to the controller. The controller has a pretty good idea what the pilot is going to say so he can interpret the pilot's message even if the signal-to-noise ratio is very poor and a goodly part of the pilot's message is blocked by another aircraft's transmission. The controller sends a message back to the pilot and the pilot has a pretty good idea what the controller will say and thus can pick the message out of noise and other transmissions with little difficulty.

Now consider what we ask the DME to do. First the intelligence to be transmitted is a rather complex series of pulses. These must be transmitted to the ground where they are heard and processed. (Remember, the ground station could be listening to dozens of DME transmissions at the same time.) The DME ground station processes our signal, adds a time delay and sends back an identical signal which must be received in its entirety and sorted out from the signals destined for other aircraft. Then the airborne equipment measures the roundtrip time, subtracts the ground station delay and divides by two. The result must be converted and displayed. If any element in this complicated system isn't working properly, the distance measuring function will not work.

It's apparent that with all this back and forth "talk" between the ground station and airborne equipment there must be a saturation point—a point where the ground station just can't listen to any more where-am-I-requests. Typically, this point is reached when about 100 aircraft are interrogating the same ground station simultaneously.

DME ground stations are pretty smart, though, and do the same thing under the above circumstances that we do when we're at a noisy party and attempting to listen to one pretty girl. We turn our ears off to all conversations but hers. The DME ground station, when saturated, lowers its own receiver gain and thus closes its ears until it hears only the number of aircraft it can handle. This means that guys with weak airborne DME transmitters operating at the fringes of the DME's range are going to be left out in the cold. This doesn't happen too often, but it can and does happen from time to time in high-density terminal areas.

DME idents—Do you know that you can and should check DME ground stations aurally just as you do VORs? The problems and cautions mentioned for VOR ident checks are valid for DME. The problem is that the

DME ident feature is not wired up in many aircraft installations. Says Husick, "That's criminal." Therefore, check your system and get it fixed if need be.

Time for review—If you're at all like the two B/CA editors who found Husick's did-you-knows interesting and, in some cases, surprising, it might be a good idea to get back into the books for a bit of review. We did.

How to Prepare Your Radar for Flight

40

by J. Mac McClellan

When the thunderstorm season comes upon us, it's time to be sure the radar is turned on, tested and the controls properly set up to avoid that bane of summer flying. That is important even early in the year because the thunderstorm season arrives much sooner in many parts of the country. While pilots in the Northeast can still look forward to a couple of final bouts with ice, those in the Southwest are already dodging heavy springtime thunderstorms.

Weather radar is one piece of equipment that requires a great deal of understanding if one is to interpret properly what it's trying to say. Unlike a DME or VOR, or any other piece of avionics gear, the radar requires interpretation and appropriate manipulation of the controls to provide the desired information.

Let's review the basic use of system controls and some ground and inflight checks you can perform to confirm the performance and physical condition of the radar system.

The place to start is with a physical inspection of the radome. Winter is the worst time for radomes because any moisture that enters the honeycomb structure freezes and expands, which tends to break down the internal structure and laminations. Look for any exterior holes that could have allowed moisture into the radome and also check the inside of the unit for irregular areas, either in color or smoothness. The presence of those symptoms can mean that the radome has suffered delamination, which can block some or all of the transmitted energy. If you find any indication that the radome has suffered from moisture damage, the services of an expert repairman from a qualified shop are needed.

Visual inspections of the receiver-transmitter unit, waveguide and antenna are also in order. Look for loose waveguide fittings, cracks, loose or kinked wires and indications that the antenna mounting has worked loose.

The self-test function of most current radars is very good and you should get out your owner's manual and re-read the self-test regime to be certain you understand all of the ramifications of this function. The self-test exercise will tell you much about the condition of the indicator of a digital system by displaying all three levels of weather returns, plus the alphanumerics and range marks. Many systems display a noise band to confirm that the receiver is working properly.

In a digital radar, the antenna stepper motor is critical and if it should fail to synchronize with the indicator, your system will certainly fail the self test. Again, the important thing here is to review the manual to be certain you perform the self test properly and analyze all of the parameters it is testing.

One common maladjustment of a digital radar is the display intensity or brightness. If the brightness control is set too high, it will be impossible to detect all three levels of weather return on a digital display. Yet, we're amazed at how often we see a pilot turn the brightness knob full up the instant the ambient cockpit lighting goes up.

The only way to properly set the brightness is during the self test so you can be certain the levels of weather intensity can be distinguished. So every time the brightness knob is adjusted, even in flight, select the test function and increase the brightness only enough to solve the problem, but not enough to obliterate the three levels. If you still can't see the display, shade it with a map or your hand, don't turn the brightness up any more.

Remember, if the brightness is not set properly, it will be easy to assume that the display is showing only weak level-one returns when it is in fact showing level two and three weather.

Gain control should be set in its pre-set detent position prior to takeoff or during flight until a weather target is acquired. Gain changes can be very helpful in analyzing a target, but it is important that the control be left in its normal position at all other times. If it's turned down, significant weather may not paint.

The position of the gain control is so vital that Bendix, Collins and King don't offer an adjustable gain in the weather mode. While the gain control is very useful in making a detailed analysis of a target, its misuse can lead you down the garden path. When the gain control is turned down, very intense cells show up as weak returns on the display—or not at all— misleading the crew, possibly dangerously.

We firmly believe that gain control in the weather modes should be available to flight crews because it can be so useful in weather analysis, but it is just like retractable landing gear—if it isn't where you think it is, you're in trouble.

After completing the test-mode checks and adjustments, the radar should be set up for flight. Begin with the tilt control. Turn it full up (for reasons that will be discussed later). Next, select the map or weather mode as appropriate. Finally, select the appropriate range.

One precaution in all this: Leave the system in the standby mode until clear of the ramp. Depending on the radar type, that may preclude switching to weather or map mode, or selecting a range, until taxiing out. On some radars the search modes or ranges and standby are interconnected by knobs or push-buttons in such a way that you can't have both. In that case, the final action in preparation for flight must come just before taking the runway.

The next decision is *what* weather mode? Many pilots prefer to consistently leave the radar in the contour mode so their attention will be drawn to any intense target. Others prefer to leave the system in its normal weather mode, using contour and gain control to analyze a target should it become necessary. Either method works well and both should be used to analyze a target once it appears on the display.

The only possible danger in continuous contour operation is that part of a return may be blanked if the rain gradient is very steep. When the heaviest rain is very near the edge of a radar return, it indicates a potential area of extreme turbulence. However, when the rain goes from none, to light, to very heavy in a short distance, the radar has a difficult time displaying that narrow band of light precipitation in contour mode and thus may show only a blank spot, giving you no indication of where the actual edge of the precipitation return is.

Cyclic contour modes of the digital radars get around this problem by cycling the display back and forth between contour and normal modes. RCA has eliminated this problem in the contour mode with a feature it calls "contour edge enhancement." Its digital systems artificially create an outline of the contoured areas, even though they may not otherwise show up on the display.

Without a doubt, the most important control on a radar is the tilt adjustment. Tilt control enables you to adjust for all of the various flight altitudes and attitudes to display weather rather than the clear sky above storms or the ground. Tilt management should be a continuous operation while flying in areas of severe weather. This is especially true during takeoff and departure, and arrival and landing, when altitudes and the aircraft attitude are constantly changing.

Tilt management is quite different for systems with antenna stabilization compared to those that don't have it. Vertical gyro inputs correct the scan pattern of a stabilized antenna to keep it parallel to the horizon. The non-stabilized antenna simply scans relative to the attitude of the aircraft, which requires that the pilot correlate the tilt angle control with aircraft attitude in order to zero the antenna scan angle relative to the horizon. The gyro in a stabilized system, within limits, performs this function for the pilot.

With either system, the tilt should be kept full up during ground operations. With the antenna tilted up it's possible to scan the immediate area of flight and this should be done just prior to takeoff to be certain you're not about to launch into severe weather. Another reason for keeping the tilt full up is to prevent the radar beam from striking another aircraft or building, which could reflect a dangerously strong return back to the receiver, possibly damaging it.

Of course, the radar transmitter should never be operated during aircraft fueling or when ground personnel are nearby. Keep the system in standby until you have taxied clear of buildings, fuel trucks and other aircraft. The danger from microwave radiation becomes apparent when you recall that an average microwave home cooking oven has between 0.5 and one kilowatt of power and can cook a roast in minutes. An airborne weather radar can easily have 10 times that much power and so can do a great deal of harm if these safety rules aren't observed.

As we've said, you'll want to have the tilt full up, or nearly so, to scan the vicinity prior to and during takeoff. However, with a non-stabilized system it will be important to turn the tilt angle down after rotation because the pitch angle of the aircraft will be added to the antenna tilt angle and as the aircraft climbs the radar beam could easily scan over the weather.

A stabilized antenna will continue to scan relative to the horizon at the tilt angle selected regardless of the deck angle, within limits. So as the aircraft climbs, tilt on it too must be reduced to avoid looking over the weather.

With both stabilized and non-stabilized systems, the antenna tilt will have to be changed several times during the climb to cruise altitude and the non-stabilized system will need an extra adjustment when cruise altitude is reached to compensate for lowering the aircraft nose to cruise attitude.

Most experts advise that in clear air the radar should be set to its longest range and the tilt adjusted to provide maximum line-of-sight range. To achieve the proper tilt adjustment at cruise altitude, turn the tilt down until receiving solid ground returns, then slowly adjust it upward until the solid ground returns just disappear. At 5000 feet the antenna will be tilted up 5° or 6° with a maximum line of sight of about 87 nm. At FL400 the antenna will be tilted up about 1° for maximum line of sight, which is about 246 nm. The maximum line-of-sight setting is used to provide the earliest detection of weather. But once it's detected, shorter ranges and tilt adjustments will be necessary to gather as much information as possible about the target.

Tilt adjustments also provide one way of checking the performance of your radar in flight over level ground. As described above, you should tilt the antenna down and slowly raise it until the ground targets disappear. The ground target farthest away should be displayed near the limits of line of sight if the radar is working properly. If the system is not painting ground targets to within about 80 percent of the line-of-sight range for your altitude, something is wrong with the radar and it should be checked by a shop.

You can also perform airborne checks of your antenna stabilization system. At some altitude above 10,000 feet over level ground, turn the stabilization system off with the aircraft in level flight and adjust the tilt down until it displays an even band of ground return at the longest possible range. Now, turn the stabilization system back on and, if it is working properly, the image should not change.

With the same image on the display, roll the aircraft 20° right and then left and raise and lower the nose. Through all those maneuvers the image should not change appreciably. If the ground return grows on one side when a wing is lowered, or fades or builds as the pitch angle is changed, you know the stabilization system is not performing right. Slight shifts are normal, but full stabilization systems are accurate to within 2° in unaccelerated level flight.

The antenna stabilization system is affected by all of the usual gyro errors, and because the antenna beam is looking so far ahead, tiny gyro errors loom large on the radar display.

Gyro precession will take place during takeoff acceleration and can take as long as five minutes to correct itself. Also, gyro precession can be introduced by making shallow banked turns with less than 6° of bank angle. That precession will cause improper antenna scan patterns that will not be parallel to the horizon and that will, in turn, cause a lopsided image on the radar display. The best course is to avoid shallow turns and, realizing that the gyro will have precessed during the takeoff, give it time to settle down.

Stabilization systems have limits of authority, which means they can correct for only so much aircraft roll and pitch, and combinations of the two, and still keep the antenna scan parallel to the horizon. Those limits are typically a combined pitch and/or roll of 25° or 30°. If the aircraft is pitched up 10° while in a 25° bank, it will have exceeded the stabilization limits of a 30° system. When the limits are exceeded, the display will show ground returns on the low wing side, just as a non-stabilized system does, but the scan-angle error will be only that which is in excess of the stabilization limits.

One final factor to remember with a stabilized antenna is that the scan will need to be checked and possibly readjusted whenever the aircraft vertical gyro system is repaired or adjusted. If the antenna scan isn't checked relative to the readjusted gyro, the antenna could scan an erroneous pattern or not be aligned with the tilt control index.

In an effort to insure that our own radar pretakeoff check is complete, we have come up with a saying that may not go down in history with

GUMP, Cigar Tips, or I Can Fly This Fool Airplane Safely, but it does the job.

It is: This Is Going To Work Right Fine. The T in This is for Test, the I for display Intensity, G for Gain, T for Tilt, W for Weather mode, R for Range selection and F for the Freeze or hold feature on digital radars.

If you've Tested it, set the Intensity, checked the Gain setting, adjusted the Tilt, put it in Weather mode, selected a range and made certain the Freeze or Hold mode is off, it probably will work right fine. Right?

THE AIRFRAME IX

There is a great irony in the study of aircraft systems. Because they have multiplied so much and because they have become so complex, there is a tendency to overlook that most primitive system, the airframe itself.

Airframe design is an intricate and demanding task. That basic structure must be fashioned to withstand all reasonable static loads and to resist fatigue over the life of the aircraft. Promotional material often bandies about the buzz words "fail-safe" or "damage-tolerant." Sometimes they mean a great deal. Sometimes they are empty promises. You will know the difference after reading "Fail-Safe, Safe-Life, Damage-Tolerant." Furthermore, after an encounter with severe turbulence or a very hard landing, you may wonder about the structural integrity of your airplane. "The Structural Failure: How To Prevent It," describes the available inspection methods to set your mind at ease.

Fuel is expensive and sometimes scarce. In the future it is likely to be more of both. With careful attention to maintenance details it is possible to reduce consumption by measurable amounts. "Airframe Maintenance for Fuel Conservation" catalogues the many and fascinating individual steps which can be taken on the ground to optimize fuel in the air.

Summer sun can turn your aircraft fuselage into an efficient greenhouse, with inside temperatures which soar far above the hundred mark. "Tips for a Hot Ramp" tells what the business pilot can do to protect his fuselage interior and good will on those steaming summer ramps.

Fail-Safe, Safe-Life, Damage-Tolerant

41

by Dan Manningham

Every profession has its overworked and misused terms. Laymen use coronary to describe every type of heart failure when that term is intended only to describe the specific instance of blood clots in the heart. Recently, the aviation community has adopted a new pet term, fail-safe, which has been widely misunderstood and, in some cases, grossly abused.

Understand that the term fail-safe has no intrinsic meaning. It is a coined idiom intended to describe systems or structures designed to minimize risk in the event of damage, fatigue, corrosion or some other form of malfunction. Fail-safe design does not in any way eliminate failures or guarantee safety, despite occasional subtle inferences in advertising copy. Fail-safe is a basic design philosophy usually, but not always, desirable and often misunderstood by those outside of airframe and system design teams.

Essentially there are two quite different disciplines of fail-safe design. One area deals with the fatigue requirements of airframe structures and is the bread and butter of aviation structural engineers. The second area has to do with systems design for the prevention of catastrophe, the total loss of system functions or personal injury in the event of a failure. Each of these two fail-safe applications—structures and systems—is so different they bear separate description.

Basically, the structural engineer has two problems. He must design the critical airframe parts—wings, control surfaces, tail section—to withstand the maximum expected *static loads* and include enough *fatigue resistance* to give the aircraft a reasonable service life. Static testing is relatively easy. An applicable part is subjected to measured loads in a laboratory environment until, at the ultimate load, the structure breaks. When that ultimate load-carrying capability has been established, appropriate safety factors are applied to determine reasonable static load limitations.

Prior to World War II, structural designers thought that generous static strength would provide sufficient protection against the fatigue effects of innumerable small loads. After the war, when the same philosophy was used for long-life civil transports, there was an epidemic of fatal accidents caused by fatigue failure. Big, strong wing spars do not necessarily have good fatigue resistance.

The immediate remedy was to establish safe-life time limits on critical structural parts. The longer term solution was a trend to redundant fail-safe structures in which a single failure would result in some tolerable reduction in overall strength. Today, safe-life and fail-safe are acceptable alternatives to the structural designer. Each one represents a different approach to a common problem. FAR 25.571 allows manufacturers the option of designing to one or the other and details the requirements for fatigue evaluation of flight structures.

Safe-life fatigue evaluation depends on repeated and extensive load testing to establish some safe-service life-limit, usually expressed in thousands of hours, for a given component. Typically, an airframe part, such as the wing, will be subjected to prolonged fatigue testing in a laboratory environment agreed to by the FAA. Such tests involve shaking and vibrating the wing under varying loads corresponding to the expected operating conditions for the actual aircraft. Several assumptions have to be made in terms of expected aircraft utilization, frequency and level of applied loads and numbers of ground-air-ground (GAG) cycles. (One GAG cycle represents the sum of large stress changes that occur once per flight due to the low positive loading of the aircraft while on the ground, variable loads while taxiing, positive loads in flight, gust and maneuver loads, fuel burnoff and landings.)

When the test structure has been fatigue-cycled over some number of simulated flight hours, the FAA applies a scatter factor, sometimes called an insurance or ignorance factor, to compensate for unknowns. If, for instance, the ground test vehicle is tested for a simulated 15,000 hours of fatigue, and the FAA applies a scatter factor of three, that airframe would be assigned a legal safe-life of 5000 hours, three hours of testing for each hour of safe-life.

In actual practice, the scatter factor is a negotiable item based on the extent and accuracy of the laboratory and operational experience. Factors as low as three may be used against full scale spectrum testing of approved ground vehicles, while a factor of eight may be necessary where the designer uses only theoretical data to support his fatigue analysis. In any event, the safe-life limit is the legal maximum lifetime and is never to be understood as a guaranteed performance minimum.

A pure and simple safe-life design would involve single structural elements without any load-carrying redundancy. That design would then be

313

subjected to fatigue evaluation using mathematical analysis and laboratory cycling to establish a reasonable limiting or "safe" life.

Actual failure of any single component could be catastrophic, but the structure would still be adjudged safe because it had undergone actual fatigue verification. Generally, such verification is an ongoing process so that safe-life limits can be progressively extended, where possible, to stay ahead of the high-time aircraft. When an aircraft component does reach the prescribed safe-life, it must be replaced or reworked in a prescribed fashion. In reality, few structures are now designed without some fail-safe characteristics, even though they may be certificated for safe-life.

The essence of fail-safe design is to insure that a failure from some cause can occur without catastrophic failure or excessive structural deformation. Implicit in the fail-safe concept is the idea that such structures need not be assigned a legal life-limit because they are not prone to catastrophic failure even in the event of fatigue damage. Some manufacturers use the terms "no life-limit" or "infinite-life" in place of fail-safe. In fact, engineers are slowly replacing the term "fail-safe" by the more accurate term "damage-tolerant" and the FAA is now writing structural regulations around the damage-tolerant concept.

There are at least four elements to any damage-tolerant design.

• Fatigue-critical primary structures must be tested to establish the service life at which fatigue cracking can reasonably be expected. Just as in safe-life evaluation, every effort is made to design the part so it will have the longest possible trouble-free life.

• When that time frame is established, the structural components are tested to determine how fast those fatigue cracks are likely to grow. Every effort is made to reduce crack propagation to a minimum through the use of alternative materials and crack stoppers.

• It must be demonstrated that even in the cracked condition, the structure will retain enough residual strength through redundant members to withstand the prescribed load.

• Finally, potentially critical damage must be detectable at an early stage by (preferably) visual inspection.

In order to verify the design concept, failures to critical parts are induced purposely. Wing spars or pressure bulkheads may be scratched or cut or drilled while under stress to determine crack propagation rates as well as the residual strength of the remaining structure. In some instances, explosive charges are detonated at critical points, and the FAA has even required that .45 caliber bullets be fired at critical parts while they are under stress.

On the basis of those tests, inspection procedures and periods are established to assure that any actual damage is recognized and corrected within a reasonable time.

Imagine the challenge of hanging a picture in a travel trailer. Static loads will be compounded by the fatigue problems associated with the constant bumping and jostling of road travel.

The solution would be to grab a big nail and presume that its tremendous static strength would compensate for any strength loss due to fatigue and aging. Unfortunately (at least in aircraft) that logic has often been fatal, so it is necessary to provide more explicit protection against fatigue.

Using the safe-life approach, you, as the picture hanger, would select a nail and some wire known by test and experience to withstand the anticipated loads for at least 3000 hours, and use those to hang the picture. During that 3000 hours you would undertake further tests and analysis to extend the life-limit, if possible. Following the classic aviation methodology, you would set up a test device that would jostle and swing the picture and its attachments exactly as they would move in the trailer. You would set the test in motion and let it run. Assuming a value of three for a safe-life factor and a desired safe-life of at least 1000 hours, after the test had run 3000 hours you would stop it and then begin tracking the number of hours on the high-time trailer in the fleet. As it approached 1000 hours, you would set the test in motion again to extend the safe-life. You might extend the test to 4500 total hours to insure a safe-life of 1500 hours, then wait until the high-time trailer reached almost 1500 total hours before beginning the test again. Thus you would keep the safe-life out ahead of the high-time unit.

If the wire or nail should fail at any point in the test, you would be forced to issue a service directive. If the wire should break at 900 hours into the test, but the nail and other points of attachment remained in good condition, you would send out a directive requiring replacement of the wire at or before 300 total hours.

Finally, at some point, you might cease the testing, say 6000 hours for a safe-life of 2000 hours, and require that all the picture attachments be replaced with new parts at 2000 hours.

The engineer who espouses the damage-tolerant (once called fail-safe) philosophy would take a different approach. He would select a nail and a wire that from experience he knows will withstand some acceptable time in service and would hang the picture with two such nails and wires. He thus would know that failure of a nail or a wire would not jeopardize the picture because he provided redundant load-carrying paths for the critical parts. He would then require periodical inspections of the suspension because failure of any one of those components would compromise his damage-tolerant design. Damaged or broken nails or wires would be replaced on demand. Note that the nails and wires do not have any fixed service life-limit.

A more sophisticated engineer might employ a more modern technique. Instead of two wires, for instance, he would use a single braided wire with

315

some factor of excess strength. Inspections would reveal a broken strand so the braided wire could be replaced before total failure. Instead of two wires, each capable of sustaining the load, which would result in 100 percent excess structure and weight, the braided wire might have 10 strands and be only 30 percent stronger than the minimum necessary. In that case, up to three strands could break before the strength would become critical. Thus there would be a 70 percent gain in structural efficiency and a resultant saving in weight.

For a nail, the sophisticated engineer might select one with 50 percent excess capacity rather than two, each of which would carry the full load. He would then split that one nail from head to point in three equal parts and bond them back into a single unit. Thus his sophisticated nail would be lighter, would require half the effort to install and yet it would carry the required load should any one of its three parts fail since its total strength would be 50 percent greater than necessary. Inspections would reveal that partial failure so the unit could be replaced.

Those sophisticated techniques in fact are used in aircraft to create damage-tolerant structures. Laminated wing spars are common and in some cases forged parts are actually split lengthwise and bonded back together to form a single, but redundant, part.

The current trend among structural engineers is to employ damage-tolerant techniques wherever possible, and to establish safe-life limits only when necessary. In general, damage-tolerant design is not appropriate for inaccessible or blind areas, or for structural components such as landing gear that cannot be designed with alternate load-carrying members. In other areas, such as in primary wing structures, control surfaces, tail sections and pressure cabins, the damage-tolerant approach is desirable.

There is at present an international effort to develop a set of certification standards that will satisfy all parties. It appears now that the emphasis of those new rules will be to encourage use of the damage-tolerant/fail-safe approach. Manufacturers will be required to employ fracture mechanics to establish design materials and configurations that will have satisfactory crack propagation characteristics. A key requirement will be that damage be "inspectable" for perhaps two inspection periods prior to becoming unable to sustain some given loading condition. In places where damage-tolerant techniques are not feasible, parts would be certificated under appropriate safe-life guidelines.

Damage-tolerant and safe-life are two very different approaches to the demands of airframe fatigue protection. Current FARs allow manufacturers to select one or the other as the basis of certification, but the FAA itself is leaning toward the damage-tolerant philosophy. Philosophical debate over these two alternatives is still very much alive in the engineering community, however, with many proponents of each approach. The truth

316

is, either approach, by itself, has limitations. The ultimate answer would be a comprehensive damage-tolerant design subjected to complete fatigue testing. The point is, pilots and prospective purchasers should not be too easily swayed by the terms themselves. Damage-tolerant or safe-life may be less important than the integrity and expertise of the manufacturer.

With respect to systems, fail-safe is probably a more accurate term than damage-tolerant, although a fail-safe system may have many damage-tolerant features.

Fail-safe systems are related to damage-tolerant structures only in terms of design purpose. Both are intended to reduce damage or risk.

Systems design does not lend itself to the alternative approaches of safe-life versus fail-safe techniques, but life-limited components are often fail-safe systems, which afford the best of both worlds.

It is important to understand that fail-safe systems need not provide for full system operation. Their purpose in order of priority is:

- First to protect people from harm.
- Second to prevent damage to equipment.
- Last of all to prevent loss of system function or degraded operation.

To accomplish one or more of those purposes, fail-safe system designs are sub-categorized into these three types:

- Fail-passive arrangements reduce the system to its lowest energy level. Fail-passive devices such as circuit breakers and fuses deactivate the system to prevent damage or injury from the original failure. They render the system safe by de-energizing it.

- Fail-active design provides an energized condition to keep that system in a safe operating mode until corrective action is possible. Some fuel systems incorporate standby electric pumps that come on line automatically when a main pump fails. This results in a fail-active situation in that it keeps the powerplant in a safe operating mode until appropriate action restores operation of the main pump. Some warning lights incorporate a blink circuit activated by failures in the basic warning circuit. These devices provide fail-safe protection by energizing at the time of failure to warn or compensate.

- Fail-operational is the most desirable arrangement and the one pilots tend to recognize. This type of design provides for system function even in the event of a failure. Aircraft hydraulic landing gear are always designed to be fail-operational. When hydraulic pressure is lost, gravity and airstream forces provide the necessary power to lower and lock the undercarriage.

Redundancy should not be confused with fail-safe design. Redundancy or duplication of systems is an effective and very desirable means of reducing the probability of total failure. If one generator fails, a second or third picks up the load to keep the system functioning. Nevertheless, if they all fail the system fails, possibly causing an accident. Fail-safe protection entails the prevention of damage or injury when the system fails. Redundancy reduces the chances of failure.

Damage-tolerant or fail-safe is a valid structural and system design criterion for minimizing damage and risk.Fail-safe itself is a catch word,too glibly bandied about in promotional talk. Damage-tolerant is a better term and pilots and operators would like to believe that their aircraft are comprehensively fail-safe in a damage-tolerant fail-operational fashion. But that ultimate goal is an illusory extension of someone's vivid imagination.

Damage-tolerant, fail-safe and safe-life are nothing more nor less than sound engineering applied with good common sense to *minimize* the potential for catastrophic damage and injury in the event of a failure, not make a catastrophe impossible. Any claims to the contrary should be carefully evaluated by pilots and customers.

The Structural Failure: How To Prevent It

42

by Gerard M. Bruder, Jr.

Next to a sudden, catastrophic accident such as a midair collision or explosion, the specter pilots probably dread the most is inflight structural failure. The reason for that concern is simple; structural failure often is tantamount to an irrevocable loss of control. Heavy icing over the mountains, an engine failure on takeoff, fuel starvation over the ocean, an inflight fire, total electrical failure at night all leave the pilot at least a few options, however desperate, and thus a chance to escape. But structural failure can destroy an airplane's ability to fly, and when that happens, there are no options except prayer.

Thanks to stringent FAA aircraft certification standards, structural failures are relatively rare—and of those that do occur, according to an NTSB spokesman, "a substantial number" are caused by pilot error such as exceeding the airspeed redline.

NTSB statistics show inflight structural failures accounted for only 63 of 4237 general aviation accidents in 1975. In 1974 the figures were 78 out of 4425 and in 1973 they were 66 out of 4255.

There are other pertinent statistics. About 83 percent of the structural failures in 1975 involved fatalities. More than 60 percent were fatal in 1973. In each of those years, the fatality rate for all general aviation accidents was around 16.5 percent.

Thus, the implication clearly is that while it is unlikely you will experience a structural failure—especially, if you retain control of your aircraft —your chances of surviving such an incident are not very good.

Therefore, after you've flown through severe turbulence, made a back-wrenching landing or subjected your aircraft to some other extreme stress, you may well feel uneasy about the possibility of hidden damage. Following such an experience, you should insure that the aircraft is still airworthy before you take off in it again. That much is obvious. What is not so obvious is how best to obtain an airworthiness determination. The boys in the hangar can strip your plane down to its frame and examine every inch of metal, but that is expensive and time-consuming and is neither practical nor necessary.

A much better approach is to utilize modern "non-destructive testing" (NDT) techniques. As the name implies, NDT involves testing that does not impair usefulness. Bending a piece of metal to measure its breaking point is an example of destructive testing and certainly is not appropriate to an airplane you wish to operate in the future.

In its most elemental form, NDT has been practiced for centuries. Every time a Viking swordsmith snapped his finger against a new blade to evaluate the ping, he was using NDT because the tone of the ping told him whether or not the blade contained a flaw.

You use elementary NDT when you push, pull, twist and thump an airframe each time you conduct your pre-flight walk-around inspection. Unless the aircraft has been abused or ill-maintained, such an inspection is adequate for pre-flight airworthiness assurance.

But if abuse has taken place and you suspect damage, that sort of NDT may not be enough. For one thing, many primary structural components are not easily accessible. For another, the unaided human eye cannot detect certain flaws such as minute cracks.

Here is where modern NDT techniques are invaluable. Through *radiography* (X-rays), for instance, a technician can examine critical areas of an airplane with a high degree of reliability, but with little or no disassembly. Airlines have used X-rays for preventative maintenance for years, and FAA airworthiness directives (ADs) often specify the use of X-rays for inspections. For instance, the Beech 18 became the subject of an AD requiring X-rays after defects were discovered in the inner steel tubing and welds of its wings.

Most parts of an airplane—including engines—are "seeable" via X-rays and, of course, by using them dozens of man-hours can be saved over the tear-down, visual inspection method. One drawback, however, is that X-ray film is rather small—a typical size is 14 by 17 inches—and sometimes problem areas are missed simply because the film did not encompass them.

Ultrasonic testing, in which sonic devices introduce high-frequency acoustic energy into a part, is another form of NDT and is similar to X-rays in that it is a "see-through" method. Reflected vibrations or echos reveal defects as signals on a cathode-ray tube. Wheels, wing plank splices, pneumatic ducts and landing gear struts are examples of aircraft areas often inspected by ultrasonic testing. Ultrasonic devices are more expensive than X-ray machines and usually require more training for effective operation.

A third NDT method is the use of *dye penetrants,* phosphorescent liquids that are coated on a cleaned surface and then wiped off. If any cracks or flaws are present, the residue dye will have seeped into them, revealing their presence. The penetrant is usually red and often a white powder is applied on top of it at suspected points to reveal a tiny crack. Dye penetrants are limited in that they can be used only on whole parts, as opposed to assemblies, but they are inexpensive and in common use in most maintenance shops.

A modern NDT method that is also employed in maintenance shops is called *magnetic particle* testing. Here, the subject part is magnetized and a liquid or powder solution of phosphorescent iron particles is sprinkled or sprayed on it. Under ultraviolet light, defects show up because they cause disruptions in the magnetic field and alter the patterns of the particles. Magnetic particle testing has been used for more than 50 years, but one limitation is that the object part must be of ferro-magnetic material, which eliminates aluminum.

Eddy current testing is the fifth major NDT method used for aircraft inspections and involves the circulation of small electrical currents in the subject part by a coil in a hand-held probe. The magnitude of the currents is read on a meter, and cracks and other flaws cause deflections in the meter needle since they act as a barrier to the currents. Eddy current testing was developed primarily to inspect landing gears but can also be used to detect heat damage and other defects in the structure.

Through the use of ADs, the FAA may dictate what NDT to use on a certain aircraft to discover a specific problem.

Which of these NDT methods are appropriate for a post-trauma inspection depends on your airplane and the nature of the trauma. Your first step, therefore, should be to seek advice from sources familiar with your model. The mechanic who normally works on your plane is not necessarily the wisest choice unless he is an expert on that model and knows specifically what to look for. Otherwise, he'll probably check for damage in a general sense. In other words, he'll perform the same inspection on your plane as on any other model, not knowing that, perhaps, the trailing edge ribs in your aircraft model are prone to cracking internally in heavy turbulence and should be minutely inspected.

The point is, airplanes are individuals, and yours may need special attention in certain areas. The manufacturer should know what those areas are and is a better source. But keep in mind that manufacturers are partial to their products and may intentionally or unintentionally provide undue reassurance.

All the general aviation manufacturers B/CA consulted said NDT procedures usually are not necessary after flying through severe turbulence, making a hard landing or subjecting one of their aircraft to other extreme stress. Instead, they recommend having "a good mechanic" check the plane over. If no indications of damage are evident, they said, the plane probably is safe to fly.

One manufacturer even said it is okay for the pilot himself to examine external surfaces for such signs as popped rivets, buckled skin or chipped paint and that the absence of those signs indicates there is no internal damage.

We consider this attitude too cavalier for something as critical as structural airworthiness. In many cases—perhaps in most—absence of external damage indications does indeed signify that everything is sound inside. But not always. Just as a pilot can suffer from high blood pressure with no overt symptoms, an airplane can sustain invisible damage that can quietly worsen and, like a heart attack, strike suddenly and devastatingly.

Also, the eyes of most pilots are not trained to detect subtle damage indications, especially if the plane is old and shows signs of wear anyway.

We recall the story of a commuter twin in Texas that lost a wing during flight in low-level turbulence one day because of undetected damage to a primary structure in the nacelle area. The practice of shutting down the engine on that wing—which invariably produced heavy vibrations at each stop and start—while passengers climbed in and out combined with hundreds of hours in low-level turbulence weakened the structure. The aircraft was not built for that kind of use, so the manufacturer's inspection methods did not stress the affected area.

The point is, the owner or pilot's knowledge of how his airplane has been used—or abused—is a part of a past incident inspection, but it must be supplemented with other expertise.

We do not mean to imply that the manufacturer should not be consulted. The manufacturer's engineers and maintenance people can provide valuable information and advice, and, of course, their recommendations should be followed as far as they go. The maintenance manual for the Piper Cheyenne, for instance, lists specific areas that should be checked after a hard or overweight landing. They include:

• The wings for wrinkled skins and loose or missing rivets.

• Fuel leaks around the nacelle fuel tanks and fuel fittings throughout the wings.

• Wing spar webs, bulkheads, nacelle skins and attachments, firewall skin and wing and fuselage stringers for any signs of overstress or damage.

• A possible alignment check to clarify any doubt of damage.

The Cheyenne manual says a severe turbulence inspection should include a check of the same items, plus the top and bottom of the fuselage for loose or missing rivets and wrinkled skins, and empennage skins and attachments.

The guidelines stop there. The manual does not state that the airplane is airworthy if those checks are negative, but the absence of such a statement implies that it is, or at least that flight thereafter is at the pilot/owner's discretion.

Some discretion is obviously necessary, since there are degrees of stress and unique circumstances, such as the general condition of the plane, that render each situation different. Therefore, you should contact another (or even a third) qualified source as well as the manufacturer for information and advice the latter might not have or impart.

Your local FAA General Aviation District Office (GADO) is an excellent and impartial source. We do not always concur with the administrative actions the FAA takes, but we welcome the aircraft research and testing it conducts, as well as the knowledge field inspectors have built up about particular aircraft. That research and testing has produced a wealth of data on all models, and GADO personnel can either pass it on to you directly or put you in touch with an FAA office that can.

Rest assured that contacting the FAA will not automatically ground your airplane or incur red tape or procedural hassles. The FARs contain no provisions for specific post-trauma inspections (though, of course, some ADs do). The most pertinent FAR is 91.29, which states that "No person may operate a civil aircraft unless it is in airworthy condition," and "The pilot-in-command of a civil aircraft is responsible for determining whether that aircraft is in condition for safe flight. He shall discontinue the flight when unairworthy mechanical or structural conditions occur."

Unless there is obvious damage to your airplane, therefore, the FAA's response to your inquiry will be mainly advisory. Since the FAA's primary purpose is to enhance flight safety, your inquiry will be welcomed and assistance provided.

Contacting the FAA is also worthwhile if you acquire or are considering acquiring an old airplane and wish to determine its state of airworthiness. The manufacturer may be out of business or unable to offer more than general information on that model. The FAA, on the other hand, will likely be able to furnish considerable safety data it has accumulated over the years.

Unlike the manufacturers, the FAA has great faith in the value of NDT methods and is the most convenient source for a list of maintenance shops and testing laboratories that offer NDT in your area. The GADO with jurisdiction over the area in which B/CA has its editorial offices, for instance, informed us there are six nearby testing laboratories with X-ray services.

Most testing laboratories that work on general aviation aircraft have mobile inspection units and thus can perform inspections at your home base. Of course, there usually is a service charge for mileage. Industrial Heat Testing of Indianapolis, for example, charges a mileage fee. But

Consolidated Testing Laboratories of New Hyde Park, New York, does not charge a mileage fee within a 50-mile radius of its base.

It is not always necessary to have the technicians come to you. If your plane shows no signs of damage and the manufacturer, the FAA or a qualified mechanic believe a ferry flight is acceptable, you can save mileage charges as well as time by flying to an airport near the testing laboratory's base.

Other than mileage charges, what costs are involved in having NDT done on your aircraft? Factors such as the nature of the stress, the age of the plane and the extent of NDT required determine how much you'll have to pay, and these are so variable that the testing laboratories B/CA contacted quoted sample charges reluctantly.

Consolidated Testing Laboratories said it probably would charge $250 for an eight-hour inspection of a Bonanza that had been flown through severe turbulence, plus $3 for each 14-by-17-inch X-ray film required.

Industrial Heat Testing quoted a sample charge of $20 an hour in addition to the same $3 fee for X-ray film.

NDT technicians usually can give you an evaluation of damage within minutes of an inspection. X-ray film, for example, often is processed on site and evaluated 10 minutes after exposure.

Since evaluation of NDT results is critical to a proper airworthiness determination, it is crucial to have that evaluation made by competent technicians. ADs have been issued calling for a reinspection of an old problem because of improper NDT analysis procedures. Testing laboratories that work on general aviation aircraft do not have to be licensed by the FAA, but the better ones are FAA-certified, much as superior flight schools are. Any names of testing laboratories you receive from a GADO, of course, will be FAA-certified.

NDT technicians usually are not licensed airplane mechanics because they do not work on aircraft in the sense that a mechanic does. They merely perform inspections, and most testing laboratories require that any necessary disassembly be done by non-company personnel. Also, aircraft NDT is typically a small part of a testing laboratory's business; some labs don't get involved with aviation at all, and most do many kinds of industrial work.

Although testing laboratories that perform NDT inspections on aircraft are not required to be approved by the FAA, they are subject to regulation by other agencies. A lab that uses radioisotopes, for example, must be licensed by the Nuclear Regulatory Commission.

Most of the labs certified by the FAA belong to the Society for Nondestructive Testing, 914 Chicago Avenue, Evanston, Illinois 60202. The Society can furnish you with literature or answer questions on NDT if you so request.

NDT can save a lot of money and time when a post-trauma inspection is necessary, but it has limitations. NDT cannot detect metal fatigue, although it can reveal stress points and areas that have been overheated.

Also, as we mentioned earlier, X-rays can miss important defects if inspection by that method is limited. Some parts of an airplane such as the central spar structure in a thick wing and heavy landing gear require more exotic cobalt or isotope testing methods, which some labs are not geared to do.

Of course, NDT is not always necessary for a post-trauma inspection. The stress trauma you subjected your aircraft to may not be as serious as you thought. There is no point in engaging the services of a testing laboratory if the FAA or some other qualified source says a simple external inspection is sufficient.

But remember, you were there, they weren't. Also, they probably won't be onboard to test their opinion on the safety of the aircraft the next time you encounter heavy turbulence. You will. If you're genuinely concerned, invest in peace of mind and obtain a thorough inspection.

Incidentally, Impact-O-Graph of Bedford, Ohio, makes a device that records G loadings. Such a device takes the guess out of how bad the turbulence was and so could be a worthwhile investment. It's a simple, spring-loaded inertial gauge that requires no electrical connection. You simply mount it to the aircraft structure, then visually inspect it from time to time to see if it has been tripped.

NDT methods are constantly being improved and expanded and NDT by laser beam is currently under development. NDT undoubtedly will play a larger role in general aviation as time goes on.

"If you operate an airplane, you'd just about better get ready for NDT, because it's here to stay," one FAA engineer told us.

Airframe Maintenance for Fuel Conservation 43

by Dan Manningham

There are no secrets left on the subject of fuel conservation, but operational, maintenance and bookkeeping techniques, taken together, can minimize wasted fuel, extend the useful range of any airplane and result in a significant reduction in the annual cost of aircraft ownership. Although many of these techniques are derived from relatively sophisticated engineering principles, the line pilot can capitalize on all of them with a single resource, his patience.

Fuel conservation is simply a state of mind. There is no magic formula for conserving that increasingly precious commodity, fuel. On the contrary, it is a compendium of seemingly insignificant tasks that save fuel one pound at a time. The necessary actions are often tedious and occasionally discouraging, but professionalism has always urged such attention to detail, and economics increasingly require it.

The subject of fuel conservation lends itself to three broad subdivisions: maintenance, operations and record keeping.

Maintenance realities are too often overlooked in favor of operating tricks, such as the use of lower power settings, which yield quicker and more dramatic results. But many times maintenance attention can yield really significant returns on only minimal investments. Our system involves several.

Total aircraft performance is degraded almost exclusively by aerodynamic drag. There are some areas of powerplant operation and care which can maximize performance, but drag is the real common enemy. Airlines have found through careful record keeping that the performance of a new aircraft deteriorates at a predictable rate as misrigging, pressurization leaks, airframe dents and insidious weight increases contribute to drag. They also know that close attention to each of those minor details results in a profitable tradeoff as maintenance dollar investments are quickly returned by operational economies resulting from drag improvements. There are several very specific maintenance checks vis-à-vis drag that should be part of any total conservation program.

• *Rigging* is crucial in a maintenance program directed at fuel conservation. At regular intervals, entrance doors, baggage doors, emergency exits, landing gear doors, oil cooler doors, engine reverser buckets and doors, cowl flaps, wing flaps, flap leading edge devices and spoilers/speed brakes should be checked for alignment and adjusted as necessary. Any one of those items not precisely aligned will create drag. Many of the items are particularly sensitive because any misrig requires compensating control inputs that compound the drag rise.

All control surfaces should be rigged to precise tolerances to prevent unnecessary drag-producing displacements. Trim tabs must be checked against cockpit trim position indicators to allow accurate trim adjustments, especially when flight conditions preclude the sort of precise trimming that yields minimum control drag. The importance of precise rigging cannot be over-emphasized and that is true for all classes and sizes of aircraft. A 10-to-15-knot airspeed loss due to rigging errors is common in aircraft with 1000 or more hours total time. Even new aircraft can be made more efficient with a carefully controlled rerigging program.

As a very rough rule-of-thumb, a 25 man-hour rerigging program conducted by a knowledgeable mechanic should result in a five-knot increase in cruise speed, or the equivalent in reduced fuel flow to achieve a given Mach number, for most aircraft. Normally, by the end of a year there will begin to be a return on that 25 man-hour investment in the form of fewer en route hours or lower fuel and turbine maintenance costs.

• *Cockpit instrumentation* should be periodically calibrated so that flight crews can operate with accurate information. Speed instruments such as IAS, Mach and TAS can introduce errors that make a joke of sincere cruise control efforts. Even groundspeed readouts from INS, area navigation and DME units should be checked because they often influence inflight decisions. Outside temperature indicators, whether OAT, RAT or SAT, can introduce both flight planning and power setting errors.

Sideslip indicators such as ball and spirit levels are frequently subject to installation errors, with the end result that the aircraft is operated in a constant out-of-trim condition. These primary trimming aids need to be large, easily interpreted and adjusted for absolute precision.

Fuel quantity indicators can influence fuel conservation in several insidious ways. When totals are erroneous, it is impossible to operate at optimum speeds and altitudes because gross weight calculations will be consistently inaccurate. Lateral or longitudinal fuel gauging errors may require drag-producing trim corrections. Any known or suspected error is likely to influence the pilot's fuel load decisions, usually in favor of additional fuel to compensate for uncertainties.

• *Pressurization leaks* can be a prime cause of excess drag. When cabin differential pressure squirts out through door and window seals, antenna mountings and around loose rivets, it forms plumes of escaping air that create drag just like any other appendage in the slipstream. Sealing those leaks is as important as removing unnecessary physical structures on the airframe and can be done quite easily in most cases, once they are located. Finding those leaks can be done by a microsonic leak detector that converts the motions of accelerating gases to an audible sound. A lightweight head-set plugs into a small detector unit, which is activated by a single on/off/volume control. In perfectly still air, there is no audible sound through the earphones. Accelerating air currents produce the sort of hissing sound made by blowing into a microphone, but with a distinct difference. The detector hears *only* that sound because others are precisely filtered out, and it hears those hisses at very low volume levels. Radios, engine noises and conversation are all excluded so that all you hear is the telltale hissing of a pressure leak, when present.

We tried such a detector on several flights in large pressurized aircraft with cabin differentials between eight and nine psi. In every case it was very easy to find some really substantial pressure leaks around windows and doors. On one trip a side cockpit window developed a serious inflow of water bubbles between the inner and outer panes and we could just make out the point of pressure transfer along the window frame.

On the ground, the unit can be used outside the aircraft to detect unwanted outflows from a pressurized cabin. Pressure differential should be above four psi for this check, but it is an excellent way to detect leaks around antenna mounts, temperature and angle-of-attack probes or any other device that penetrates the pressure hull but is not directly accessible from inside.

Unpressurized aircraft can be checked for drag-producing air leaks either inflight or by using a special tone generator. The miniature, transistorized generator is placed inside the aircraft where it produces a tone, compatible with the detector. When all the doors are closed, the detector is used outside to listen for any escaping sound from the generator which would indicate a faulty seal.

One more word about pressurization leaks. They do not, as some people imagine, decrease available engine power. Cabin pressurization systems are designed with a constant mass air input which far exceeds the basic requirement of maintaining differential pressure. That excess air mass flows through the cabin for ventilation before passing through the outflow valve, which is often designed and situated to capitalize on the small thrust vector created by cabin air exhaust. Pressure leaks in the hull do not affect that total mass air bleed from the engine. They simply exhaust some of the airflow before it gets to the outflow valve while total airflow remains constant. You take a twofold penalty in parasite drag and reduced outflow thrust, but engine performance is unaffected. However, when used with caution and discretion, there is a technique that will yield substantial economy. It consists of simply shutting off one bleed air valve from a turbine compressor or piston engine turbocharger. If the pressure vessel is tight, the appropriate pressure differential will be maintained and the efficiency of that one engine will be increased significantly. Two major precautions must be borne in mind, however. First, if the other bleed air source is suddenly lost, due to engine failure or some fault in the valving or ducting, the cabin will depressurize. Second, the total airflow through the cabin will be less, so smoke and odors may not be dissipated properly.

Surface contours must be maintained to very high standards for minimum drag. On some particularly sensitive areas of the airframe, airflow can be significantly disturbed by very small changes from the design contours. Leading edges of the wing stabilizers, the fuselage nose and cockpit area, and engine cowlings on jet airplanes require very careful maintenance to avoid disproportionate drag contributions from nicks and dents.

Control surface and flap gap seals are installed on some airplanes to prevent leakage, or pumping, of air from high pressure areas to those of lower pressure, which leads to a loss in aerodynamic efficiency. When those seals deteriorate and leak, that loss of design efficiency must be overcome with more power which results in the use of excess fuel. Obviously then, gap seals should be maintained in perfect condition.

Antennas are an operational necessity but they often have a way of proliferating as new and improved avionics are added to the original package. There are at least three specific possibilities for reducing the drag associated with antennas.

• Remove unnecessary antennas completely. Elementary? Yes, but how long has it been since you've conducted an antenna audit? While you're at it, make sure the antennas on the aircraft are the most efficient available. Recent advances in antenna design can contribute to decreased drag to a degree that will return a profit on replacement costs within a relatively short time.

• Consider combining some pairs of antennas to reduce the total number of drag producers.

• Carefully check the installation of those antennas that *are* necessary to make sure that they are properly aligned, tightly sealed to the fuselage or tail surface and located in areas of lowest possible pressure.

While you're assessing the exterior, consider which handholds, steps and lights could be removed. You can get some idea of the problem the next time you pass a Boeing 727 on the ground. The little retractable tail skid under the far aft fuselage of that aircraft produces a very remarkable drag penalty if it fails to retract. In fact, the drag penalty from that minute appendage requires 25 percent additional climb fuel and 10 percent additional cruise fuel. Cruising speed is reduced by 20 knots and the airplane must be altitude planned as though it were 20,000 pounds (about 15 percent) heavier. Another example is the retractable step on older Mooneys. If it fails to retract, the drag penalty is seven knots or about five percent of the indicated airspeed.

Check your airplane carefully for such unnecessary drag producers. Steps that you could get along without, assist handles, door stops, fasteners on access panels and temperature probes in high pressure areas all contribute drag. (But coordinate with the FAA before moving items, because it doesn't take much to constitute a major alteration requiring approval and flight test.)

Airframe cleanliness is generally taken for granted in corporate aviation. That cosmetic nicety, however, also reduces drag in a rather subtle fashion. Dirt accumulation on the wings acts just like frost to reduce the kinetic energy of the boundary layer. This reduced kinetic energy effectively increases drag and coincidentally increases stall speeds by some small amount. Keep it clean and you will save a little fuel.

Weight reduction is an often overlooked option. Every added pound of weight requires an additional pound of lift with a corresponding increase in induced drag. The formula is so basic and simple that professional pilots and mechanics may forget the very immediate and direct benefits associated with any weight reduction.

Many operations could benefit from a thorough audit of all aircraft equipment and furnishings to identify those that are no longer necessary. When Bill Lear designed the original Learjet, he is reported to have said that he would sell his grandmother to save just one pound. In fact, that became the byword of the design staff as they pursued ways to save one more "grandmother." Try it with your airplane. We bet you will find several grandmothers with a minimum of effort such as:

• Cabin supply items of marginal or outdated usefulness.

• Drinking water supplies, especially in those aircraft having central water tanks. Airlines have recently begun to carry only as much water as is necessary for each trip.

• Specialized equipment for long range or overwater trips. Rafts, survival kits, HF radio and Loran can be stored elsewhere when the trip in question does not justify their presence.

Weight reduction in turbines also offers more immediate climb to higher, more efficient altitudes.

Drag reduction, in all its many forms, is a most fruitful area of fuel conservation, but it must be cost effective. One knot added to the speed of a jet should be worth well over $500 in one year. Similar figures for other categories would be $350 for a turboprop, $100 for a twin and $20 for a single.

Those figures are predicated on the accumulated time savings resulting from a one-knot speed increase; hence the saving is a reduction in the total direct operating cost, not just the cost of fuel saved. If you intend to operate the airplane for three or four more years, simple multiplication will provide the breakeven figure for any given modification. If, for instance, you could add one knot to your piston twin by combining two antennas at a total cost of $200, you will see an actual dollar return in the third year while enjoying the immediate benefits of slightly reduced trip times and some added range.

Drag reduction may be the most productive area for maintenance action in a fuel conservation program, but engine maintenance can produce other significant results. Pressurization leaks may not detract from engine efficiency but pneumatic system leaks do. Leaks in pneumatic anti-ice plumbing, fuel heaters, expansion turbines or any other pneumatic users will divert air that was intended for the power producing combustion process. Aircraft performance is calculated with pressurization bleeds taken into account. Similarly, appropriate flight manual charts will reflect the performance penalties associated with normal bleed usage. Any unknown leakage from the compressor section, through faulty pneumatic plumbing, will detract from thrust, raise turbine temperatures and cost fuel.

Careful maintenance action to preclude pneumatic leaks contributes to fuel economy and engine condition. Once again, the EI-500 was most useful in tracing pneumatic leaks and minimizing that loss.

Most turbine engine manufacturers have established procedures for periodic washing of the compressor. This simple action is designed to remove the residue of airborne contaminants adhering to blades and stators, which reduces their efficiency. Compressor wash usually involves motoring the engine with the starter while water or a special preparation is sprayed into the inlet. The job is simple and brief, and ought to be a part of any maintenance effort for fuel conservation.

Piston engine operators should frequently check and adjust the plugs, magnetos and fuel injectors. Injected engines can be run at optimally lean settings only when all the injectors are within close tolerances. Otherwise the engine can only be leaned for the one or two leanest cylinders. Exhaust system maintenance will pay dividends in added volumetric efficiency and some consequent fuel savings.

There is simply no way of knowing how much fuel is being wasted by unnecessary drag and inefficient powerplants until you undertake a comprehensive audit of your own aircraft. When you do, it is a sure bet you will find your aircraft has not been as efficient as it could be.

331

Aircraft Bonding   44

by Robert Stangarone

One predictable sequence of events in the aviation industry is the technological hand-me-down process that occurs from military to airline to general aviation. Sometimes it only takes a couple of years for military spin-offs to find their way into business aircraft, but usually, it requires decades, if not generations.

We've seen it on various levels: DMEs, radars, turbine power and in the growing popularity of a process known as adhesive bonding.

Bonding is by no means a new technology to general aviation aircraft manufacturers. Beech got its feet wet back in the late 50s when it started bonding assemblies such as rudders and speed brakes for a variety of military aircraft ranging from the F-4 to the F-102, and airliners like the Convair 660 and 880.

More recently, Beech has been bonding assemblies on JetRanger fuselages, which it produces for Bell and has also been using the process on many of its own aircraft subassemblies, both structural and nonstructural.

Cessna is currently boasting an all-bonded wing on its 421C and is incorporating the process into its assembly line for components on almost all models. Extensive bonding will be employed on Cessna's new 441 turboprop and future aircraft not yet announced. Bonding was nothing new for Grumman American; that company used the sophisticated gluing process extensively since the first Yankee way back in the early 60s.

Obviously, the recent widespread use of adhesive bonding implies certain virtues attractive to both manufacturer and operator.

What is bonding? Very simply, bonding is a method of joining two surfaces with a chemical adhesive. The process is sophisticated, in that the adhesive itself must be prepared with precision and handled with perfection. Surfaces to be bonded must be properly prepared to accept the adhesive, etched in an acid solution and handled with the utmost of care. Finally, the bonded assembly must be cured through a baking process in an autoclave.

Up to this point manufacturers have been somewhat reluctant to use bonding on major stress-bearing aircraft components, primarily because of a lack of experience and confidence in the process, and more importantly, because a huge commitment in capital and expertise is required. Beech, Grumman American and Cessna have been exceptions. Over the past several years, all of the manufacturers have developed a confidence in the process for an increasing number of applications, which is why we are seeing an increase in the popularity of bonding. But it is still being approached cautiously.

Manufacturers we spoke to were reluctant to say just how much they plan to increase their bonding activities, but most agree that increases will be conservative and will take place only after studies prove it feasible from economic and manufacturing standpoints.

Unlike Beech's military origins in bonding, Cessna first began in the late 60s using bonding as an improvement on engine cowlings and other nonstructural components. With the Citation came Cessna's first venture into structural bonding; the process is used in the Citation carry-through spar, spar caps and horizontal stabilizer.

There are two main disciplines to consider when a change such as switching from riveting to bonding is anticipated: engineering and manufacturing. For an airplane that's been in production over a period of years, the cost of engineering, tooling and personnel training have been amortized. To make a change to bonding requires hours of reengineering, retooling, a new learning curve for production people and partial or complete recertification of the airplane. That means a lot of dollars to any manufacturer.

What are the payoffs for the manufacturer if he does elect to go to bonding? They are numerous.

Primarily, a manufacturer can, in the long term, expect to reduce the number of man-hours needed to join materials. He can also expect to produce a stronger product and get a more representative test of the component's strength.

The reduced number of man-hours is possible because bonding is done by panels or sections. Unlike the one-at-a-time riveting process, which requires many short-term repetitions, bonding is the result of fewer, longer-term operations, creating a better flow in mass production. Thus, preparation, acid etching, adhesive application and baking require, overall, fewer man-hours than riveting.

Strength is increased considerably with bonding, more than four times over that of rivets, estimates one manufacturer. The reason is that stresses are evenly spread throughout the bonded joint, which is untrue of a riveted joint since the stress is concentrated at each rivet location.

Testing of a joint is improved in bonding because a test panel is run with every batch of materials being bonded and each sample panel is destructively tested to assure that the batch is satisfactory. All bonds are also tested ultrasonically to locate possible flaws.

From a cost standpoint, manufacturers find that production line costs are

333

lower with bonding, but the cost of quality control is higher. All agree that the quality testing is more rigidly controlled and disciplined because it is a relatively new technique.

Also, the noise level in a plant where bonding is the attachment method is extra quiet compared with a plant where riveting is taking place. By going to bonding, noise levels can be reduced, which results in production people being more efficient and fewer management hours being spent in meeting environmental complaints.

What may seem the obvious advantages of bonding to the aircraft operator do not turn out to be advantages in actuality. By eliminating rivets, you would think drag would be reduced, giving a noticeable increase in airspeed. Naturally, you would think weight would be decreased.

The fact is, the reduction in drag is so minute the airspeed increase is not noticeable, and the weight of a bonded part can sometimes be greater than the weight of the same part riveted.

The real advantages to the aircraft owner and operator lie in the strength and longevity of a bonded part. Discounting collisions, it takes quite a bit to tear an airplane apart, probably nothing short of a severe thunderstorm, and most pilots stay far away from these. Nevertheless, if the aircraft operator can have added strength at no additional cost, he's getting more for his money. There's some disagreement here, however. Several engineers told us that airplanes are strong enough as they are now and to add any additional strength would be "overkill." Other engineers disagree, saying, "Why not have all the strength you can get, if it's not costing you weight, performance or dollars?"

A look at 1973 accident reports shows there were only three cases in which an airframe failure was the cause of an accident (not counting landing gear failures.) One was caused by a skin/attachment failure and two by failure of horizontal stabilizer attachments. This implies that our production airplanes are strong enough for most operations. But since the three above accidents were related to severe weather situations, the question remains open—if strength can be increased without any loss of performance, weight increase or additional cost, should we move in that direction? From our discussions with manufacturers, they are not quite ready to answer that question because of a trade-off potential. We mentioned earlier that bonded parts are sometimes heavier than nonbonded ones. That's true if no changes are made to the part other than a trade of chemical adhesives for rivets. But when a subassembly is carefully designed for bonding from inception, some or all of the strength gained can often be traded for lighter weight.

If it is possible to reduce the weight of an aircraft by going toward bonding more extensively—and most manufacturers agree that with time it will be possible to reduce the weight by about 25 percent—we can expect what is known in engineering circles as "configuration impact" to evolve. By reducing aircraft weight, the engineer can reduce wing area; because of the reduced wing area, the weight would reduce again. This weight reduction falls out as a need for less fuel to go the same distance, making another reduction in operating weight. The end result could be airplanes with the same strength factors as today's riveted versions, but with much greater efficiency.

Another advantage of bonding is a result of the noise characteristics of a bonded honeycomb structure. On the Lear 35 and 36 the bonded honeycomb engine inlet, because it has better noise-absorbing characteristics than its aluminum counterpart, reduces fan noise coming out the front of the engine, a growing advantage in today's noise-conscious environment.

Lear also found that bonding was the key to some of its space saving requirements. Back in 1963, the Learjet design incorporated single wheels for the landing gear. When the decision was made to go to double wheels, extra space had to be found to stow the larger-volume gear when it was retracted. The solution was to use a bonded honeycomb panel instead of a thick aluminum floorboard, which increased the space available for gear storage the necessary few inches. As a bonus, the honeycomb floor yielded a significant weight saving.

In this age of the wet wing, bonding provides a much better seal against fuel leakage. Cessna engineers made maximum use of that fact when they removed the tip tanks from the 421 and put the fuel in the wing bays.

Another distinct benefit of bonding is that longevity of the part is increased. Because the stress in a bonded part is evenly distributed throughout the bonded surface, the cracks, commonly found in riveted parts after service ranging from one to several thousand hours, are not expected to appear on bonded assemblies. For that reason we can expect reduced maintenance with bonded components.

One less tangible but very real advantage of bonding to the operator is the aesthetic appeal. After seeing bonded wings and fuselages, rivets appear as eyesores. Moreover, that sleek surface is easier to keep clean, so paint should last longer. When the finish does require renewal, the absence of rivet heads will make removal of the old paint easier and less costly.

The configuration impact of bonding, coupled with recent technological developments such as the GAW wings, hydrogen injection and more advanced, fuel efficient engines, all point to the fact that the aircraft we'll be seeing in the coming years are certain to be more efficient and will represent a better business investment.

Tips for a Hot Ramp 45

by Gordon Gilbert

It is only 0900 hours but already it's 30 degrees C as you step out of your light twin after a two-hour business flight. You lock the aircraft up, making sure none of the window vents are open. You are worried about someone reaching in and swiping something, and thunderstorms are frequent this time of year. As you walk away from the plane, your attention switches to the business appointment you have that will tie you up until about 1800.

Situations like this occur many times daily at airports across the country where mid-day summer temperatures are commonly 30 to 40 degrees C. A businessman-pilot locks up his light twin and proceeds about his appointments unaware that he has also locked in a potential temperature rise in his airplane that could reach 71 degrees C or more, which is about 20 degrees above the avionics' TSO heat limitations. When he returns in the cool of the evening and takes off for home, it may not occur to him that the sun and heat have been cooking away the life of his radios, instruments, seat covers and just about everything else that lies under the glareshield.

Single-engine airplanes and cabin twins offer greater visibility for both pilots and passengers than larger corporate-size aircraft. This is a safety factor for the former and a convenience for the latter, but your avionics and interiors pay dearly.

Some of you may even be unaware of just how hot it can get in that cabin. After all, many times you park the aircraft in the morning—when it's cool —and return in the evening—when it's cool. In between, you have been subjected to an air-conditioned rental car or taxi, restaurant and conference room. Unless you've returned to your aircraft in the middle or late afternoon on a warm sunny day and felt the oven-like blast when you opened the door, you really can't appreciate the heat your aircraft suffered through. The point is, whether you've experienced this situation or not, when your aircraft is sealed-up on even a "warm" ramp, heat and sun are playing havoc with its insides—unless you have taken certain protective measures (that we'll discuss in a moment).

We talked to several avionics manufacturers and interior shops to find out what happens to light aircraft radios and interiors under hot-sun conditions. So, before we get into things you can do to protect the equipment and interiors, here is what avionics and interior experts reveal about the problem.

"Heat is without a doubt the worst enemy of radios." This is the consensus of all the major avionics manufacturers. Constant heat cycling does damage. For instance, "physical damage can occur to electrical connections as leads expand and shrink with extreme temperature changes," says one manufacturer. "However, proper design and installation standards usually consider this and call for leaving a strain release, like a loop of wire, at the connection point."

Another manufacturer: "We know that long-term high temperature will deteriorate component dielectrics, condensors and things like that. You can figure as a rule of thumb that for every 10 degrees increase in temperature above 50 degrees C, life of dielectrics is cut in half."

All manufacturers concurred, though, that long-term deterioration as a result of excessive heat would depend on the condition of the radio and how well it was being treated and serviced.

Long-term degradation may be hard to measure, and the only indication you might have is a vague feeling that your radios are not playing to full capacity. Short-term effects of heat are immediate, but not always evident. For instance, you might climb into a hot cabin, switch on the transmitter (the place where a heat-induced failure is most likely to take place), call ground control and wonder why they don't answer. This problem, which can be heat-induced, has deceived many pilots into thinking that their aircraft is just in a bad reception position. So they fire up and taxi to what they think is a better position. While they are doing this, the open door and air stirred about by the props will cool the transmitter. Ground is called again and this time they answer. The problem is quickly forgotten, but damage has been done because the problem wasn't location, it was a transmitter failure due to heat. B/CA has conducted experiments to demonstrate this is so.

There is also a psychological reason why many of us have not associated radio problems with heat. "The fallacy of a few years ago—when transistorized equipment came on the scene in a big way—was that avionics technicians and pilots thought, 'Boy, we're getting away from the high-heat environment of tubes. Solid state is smaller, uses less voltage and has no tubes or filaments to glow and heat up.' But heat is just as big a problem nowadays because more of everything is put in a smaller package and this develops *more* heat than the old tube radios. As a result of this myth, operators and service technicians alike at first didn't advise ram-air cooling and did not consider heat a factor when installing the radio stack." This is the candid opinion of one major avionics firm.

What exactly is "excessive" heat? Any long-term exposure to temperatures over 55 degrees C. How can we be so exact? Easy. TSOd avionics should work for an indefinite period to 55 degrees C. Near, at or above this temperature, "reliability will suffer over the long term as compared with operating the radios in an ambient of, say, 25 degrees C."

Unfortunately, for the operator there are no plans to increase the heat tolerance of radios. In fact, radios are going to get smaller and do more. Avionics manufacturers will be providing more detailed installation instructions to prevent overheating, but protection measures will still be the responsibility of the operator. In fact, most warranties include a caution: "Avoid mounting close to any high external heat source. If this is done, no air cooler will be required." This covers a multitude of sins. One manufacturer admitted that on a hot day, a glareshield would be considered an "external heat source."

Electric gyro instruments are adversely affected by cabin heat buildup to a much larger degree than non-electric instruments. According to one instrument company: "In any gyro that has electronics associated with it, like a yaw damper, turn coordinator or RMI, heat effect will be the same as on the radios," that is, long-term deterioration and short-term failure or false indications. Condensation on the inside of the instrument glass is another problem resulting from the heat and humidity in a tightly closed cabin.

Here are hot-ramp tips you can follow to make your avionics work better and last longer.

(1) Cover *all* the windows. Use covers custom-made expressly for this purpose. Anything else you use might scratch the glass. Proper covers are lined on the inside with flannel, bonded to white (reflective) Naugahyde. They are preshrunk and fire-proofed. Be certain you wipe windshield and windows clean before attaching the cover.

(2) If you don't already have them, add vent ports in the glareshield directly above the avionics stack. (But don't go chopping holes before making sure the shield is not an integral part of the aircraft structure.) Properly installed vents will provide a chimney effect for the trapped hot air at the top of the stack.

(3) Allow about ¼ to ½ inch between radios for air circulation. This may go against your sense of panel aesthetics, but the space will reduce heat transfer and associated heat-rise to the top radio in the stack.

(4) Add ram air cooling to the avionics stack. This should be distributed through a plenum, or "piccolo" (a vertical pipe along each side of the stack with holes cut out along it) which will provide air circulation around all radios. This system will provide immediate cooling to the radio stack when you start the engine. Beech, Piper and Cessna provide a method of cooling the radios, but the operator who has a non-manufacturer custom installation may not get this feature if the installer believes the myth associated with solid-state avionics.

(5) Open windows, doors and vents prior to preflight. By the time you finish your walk-around, the cabin will be measurably cooler and the thermal shock will be less when the radios are turned on.

(6) Park into the wind and open wing or fuselage vent doors.

(7) Have a qualified shop put a tiny screened hole in the glass of electric instruments to prevent fogging if that is a problem. Fogging is nothing more than condensation caused by a temperature differential between the air inside the instrument and the outside air. After you take off from that hot ramp, the air inside the cabin will become cooler than the trapped air inside the instrument. The screened filter simply allows a continuous flow of air between the instrument and the cabin to keep the temperature the same. Aviation Intrument Manufacturing of Houston does this routinely on installations operating in hot, humid areas.

(8) Stack your radios in a manner to protect them from heat. Since radios are usually stacked in logical order of use and ease of operation, this tip may not be feasible for some operators. Avionics technicians say, "If we had our way, we would try to get the hotter units on top and the cooler units at the bottom so they wouldn't heat everything up on the stack." You may wonder what this tip has to do with a hot ramp. Suppose the radios already are over 55 degrees C when you climb in the cockpit. As soon as you turn the radios on, you may get a 20-degree rise inside them. In this case, that top radio (usually your nav/com) may not perform to full specifications or work until it cools down.

(9) Delay turning on nonessential avionics as long as possible. On VFR days (which is usually when the danger of overheating is greatest) taxi out with a single transceiver turned on, then activate and check other equipment in runup position. Inertial systems, radar and other long-warmup-time devices may have to be excepted.

(10) Begin to taxi as soon after starting engines as you can. With or without ram air cooling, the heat around the radios will dissipate much faster as you are moving. This tip goes along with the engine manufacturer's unofficial suggestion that engine life and efficiency can be increased by little or no warmup period during the warmer months.

Upholstery, carpets and curtains suffer more from the direct rays of sun than heat buildup. Curved windshields intensify the sun's rays more than flat ones. Most business aircraft manufacturers have weeded out the less durable fabrics and are using rayon acetates, nylon, leather synthetics and (best of all) wool. They hold together real well, but "sun will fade even the finest of materials over a period of time," warns one interior specialist.

Without exception, all the experts we talked with said stay away from Herculon. It feels good and is inexpensive, but it falls apart in a relatively short time.

If you are in the market for a new aircraft or are going to refurbish your old one, wool holds up best against heat and sunshine (as well as being the most flame resistant). Nylon too withstands fading a longer time than some of the other materials, but it is difficult to flame-proof.

Good interiors should last at least five years without noticeable deterioration (short of fading), according to most interior shops. Waxing may help preserve such materials as leather, but does nothing to prevent fading.

In addition to covering the windshield, which will add several years to the life of your interior, opening air vents, facing the aircraft into the wind and following some of the other tips covered under avionics, here are some specific do's and don'ts to prolong the life of your interior in the face of sun and heat:

(1) Do keep your upholstery clean. Dirt and grime act like sandpaper and in combination with heat, moisture and sunlight, will tear up the fabric.

(2) Do fix even the smallest leak that might let water seep onto the fabric from those frequent summer thunderstorms. This will spot fabric. Worse, after that summer shower, the closed cabin begins heating up again. That little puddle of water lying in the seat mates with the high temperature and causes mildew. "Mildew deteriorates cloth fabrics right away," emphasized one expert.

(3) Do select lighter colors if you are considering reupholstering your aircraft. They absorb less heat and although not really more fade-resistant than darker colors, they will show the fading less.

(4) Do cover your seats with an ordinary white bed sheet when the aircraft is closed up on a hot ramp. This will reflect some of the sunlight and heat away from the fabric. When considering the effects of heat in your choice of fabric, remember this trade-off: a hard-finished texture is hotter to the touch than a soft finish, but the hard wears better and the soft is a little more expensive.

(5) Don't "protect" your seats with a clear plastic cover. It'll get extremely hot for one thing, but more important it will cause serious fabric damage. Like the windshield, plastic covers will intensify the sunlight burning into the fabric. When it cools down in the aircraft, dry rot will occur under the plastic. If at the end of summer you decide to remove the seat cover, you may take the fabric with it.

(6) Don't leave plastic items such as sunglasses and plotters on the seats. Direct sunlight can not only melt them, but fuse them into the fabric.

(7) Don't cross your seat belts over the seats. This practice may be traditional, but sunlight will damage the nylon webbing of the belt. In addition, fade lines can appear if the sun has been cooking the entire seat area except for that covered by the belts.

Besides avionics, instruments and interiors, sunlight and heat cause other harm in a hot cabin, not the least of which can be personal injury. Seat buckles lying on the seat and exposed to the sun can get hot enough to give that mini-skirted passenger (or your tennis-attired boss) a bad burn. They may not be easy to find when first climbing into the seats, but safety belts should be stowed out of sunlight even if it means stuffing them under the seats.

It should not need saying, but cameras, plotters, sunglasses and similar items will self-destruct if left on the glareshield. Even professionals forget this basic rule once in a while. If you have to, don't be too proud to add "Glareshield clear?" on your after-shutdown checklist.

LESSER SYSTEMS

Aircraft systems seem to go on and on. Just when you think that there is nothing left to talk about, you discover several new ones. It is a matter of definition, to be sure, but even the most paltry aircraft fixture can have considerable safety and operational significance. When viewed as individual systems, those fixtures assume their proper importance.

It may be difficult to picture a tire as a system. It is easier when you realize that a plain old tire is comprised of eight separate components. Tires are essential to safe landings and ground maneuvering. Poorly maintained tires can induce hydroplaning, reduce crosswind capability and seriously compromise accelerate-stop distances. This section in part explains all the known ways to make your tires last longer and perform better.

Can there be an aircraft fixture more petty than the fuel filler cap? Would you believe that there are at least a dozen kinds? Do you know if your cap can protect your tank—and your airplane—from lightning? Read on, and you'll find that they are not so petty after all.

Similarly intriguing and safety connected things can and will be said about windshields, recognition lighting, heaters, and pressurization. These are things we hardly notice until they fail or threaten to when we need them. It's amazing how often and how much we need them.

Tire Conservation 46

by Gordon Gilbert

When we began researching this study the rubber industry was in the middle of a labor strike that had virtually shut down all major tire manufacturers. With the possibility of a tire shortage, we felt it was essential to hustle on our research and get into print suggestions and tips on tire conservation. That strike has now ended, but in view of what was described as an "expensive" settlement, prices for new tires are expected to rise sharply. So it is just good economic sense to make our tires last as long as possible.

Aircraft tires are among the toughest pneumatic products made. They have to be, to stand up to the requirements we expect of them and the abuse they too often receive. The heavy loads, impacts and speeds they are subjected to mean that aircraft tires must be designed to flex, or distort from their normal shape, 32 percent which, for your appreciation, is nearly twice as much as is asked of auto tires.

However, there's a tradeoff—although flexing enables tires to withstand hard landings better, it causes internal stress and friction as they roll down the runway. This, in turn, causes heat. *It's the heat, not the impact of hard landings, that places the toughest demand on airplane tires.*

Recent developments in lighter tires, made of materials with increased heat resistance, has helped combat the heat problem, but pilots must still guard against heat buildup by avoiding, where possible, long ground runs, rapid taxi speeds, excessive braking and, especially, improper tire inflation.

For illustrative purposes, aircraft tires can be broken down into eight major components. Most of those components are individually fabricated by hand. Tires are one of the few aircraft accessories not mass produced. They must be built up and fitted one part to another much like clothing is because, like clothing, a tire is composed of layers of fabric. But being hand-made has its drawbacks. The most significant one for pilots is that not all tires are exactly matched in size or perfectly round.

The eight components of an aircraft tire are:

(1) *The tread*—This is the only component that is supposed to be in contact with the ground. It's the wearing surface of the tire, fabricated with a highly abrasion resistant rubber compound specifically formulated

to optimize wear, minimize heat generation and protect tires from bruises, cuts and moisture. Tread depth varies from 0.180 inch in a 600 × 6 tire (Cessna 182 size) to 0.400 inch in a 49 × 17 tire (B-727 size.)

(2) *The undertread*—This special rubber compound, between the tread and casing plies, provides for adhesion of the tread itself to the cord body. The undertread also facilitates retreading as well as providing protection against cuts and bruises.

(3) *Cord body*—This component of the tire is made up of rubber-coated nylon cords. Since a single layer of these cords—called a ply—has all its strength in only one direction, the cords of every succeeding ply run diagonally to each other to give balanced strength. Small aircraft tires typically have four plies. The number of plies in large tires can be as many as 20.

(4) *Bead*—This is the only component that is supposed to be in contact with the wheel. The bead consists of layers of steel wire embedded in rubber and wrapped with nylon fabric. The bead provides a base around which the plies are anchored and it insures a firm fit on the wheel.

(5) *Chafer strip*—This is a layer of rubber and nylon to protect the cord plies and bead area from damage due to chafing against the wheel.

(6) *Sidewall*—The sidewall protects the cord body against ozone damage and other injuries. Sidewalls are constructed of a rubber compound surrounding a nylon fabric.

(7) *Inner liner*—In tube tires, a thin rubber inner lining is incorporated to prevent tube chafing. In tubeless tires, a thicker inner lining of specially compounded rubber acts as a built-in tube to prevent air seepage through casing plies. Although it's done, it is not good practice to put a tube in a tubeless-type tire. Such a tire often lacks the proper anti-chafing qualities.

(8) *Fabric tread reinforcement*—This component adds durability to the tire, particularly by increasing stability for high-speed operations.

The greatest threats to tire life and performance are under-inflation, heat and foreign object damage (FOD).

Under-inflation is the most serious because it causes the tire to be more susceptible to the second and third threats. Some of the potentially dangerous, as well as harmful effects of under-inflation are:

• Under-inflated tires are much more likely to creep or slip around the wheel when the brakes are applied after a landing.

• Tube valves can be sheared off from slippage, and the complete tire, tube and wheel can be destroyed.

• Under-inflation causes rapid or uneven wear at or near the edge of the tread.

• Sidewalls or shoulders of tires may be crushed by wheel rim flanges during a landing or when the tire strikes the edge of a runway or taxiway pavement while taxiing.

• Under-inflated tires may flex over the wheel flange causing damage to the bead and lower sidewall area.

• A bruise, break or rupture of the tire cord body may result from under-inflation.

• Under-inflation allows a tire to deflect beyond its design tolerances, which causes severe heat problems.

This last point should be emphasized. Internal and external heat is generated every time the tire rolls over. As we noted previously, heat is caused by the continuous deflection of the tire carcass and tread as the tire rotates. This flexing action of the nylon fabric is similar to the rapid bending of a piece of wire back and forth. First it gets hot, then breaks. The same thing happens with the fabric in aircraft tires if the deflection is too great, *and the deflection is always too great when the tire is under-inflated.*

With proper air pressure the tire will perform at peak efficiency at a deflection of no more than 32 percent. An under-inflation that allows a 42 percent deflection can create more than triple the heat that would have resulted from the normal 32 percent. (See Figure 1.)

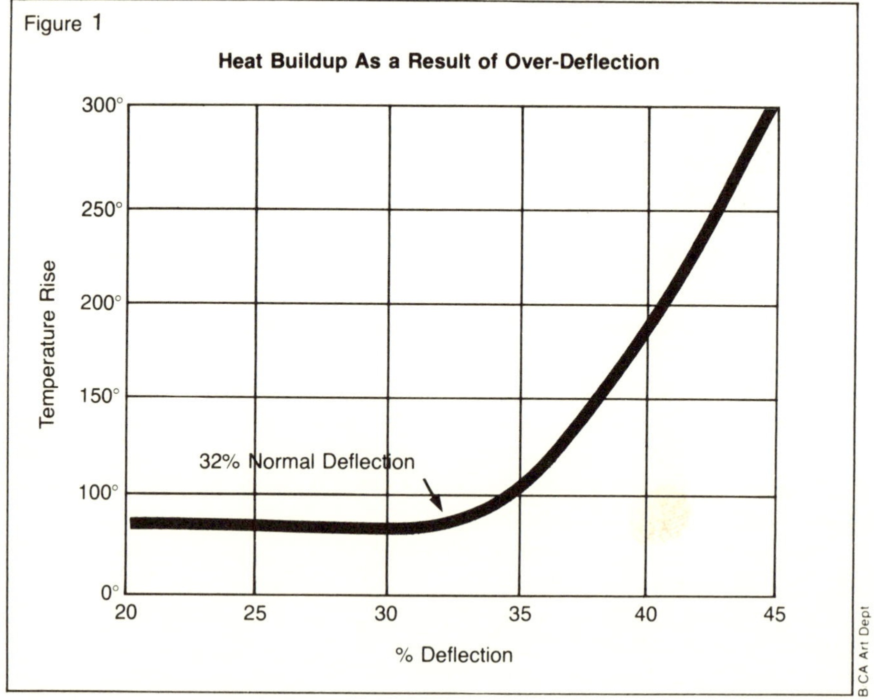

A combination of over-deflection (under-inflation) and heat buildup causes excessive shoulder tread water, a weakening and breakdown of carcass plies and bead bundles, and eventually a dangerous tire.

Turning to external heat, it comes mainly from the transfer of heat from the brake through the tire bead to the carcass of the tire itself. That's why heavy braking should be avoided. The scuffing of a tire against a runway or taxi surface is actually less damaging than the brake heat resulting from the skidding stop—unless, of course, the tire actually slides on an abrasive surface.

It was shown in tests that during the rejected takeoff of a DC-9, in which brakes were applied at a groundspeed of 175 knots to bring the aircraft to a complete stop in 18 seconds, the tremendous energy absorbed by the brakes caused rapid heating of the metal parts to cherry red within 12 seconds. Flames were expected to develop in four more seconds if stopping attempts had continued.

Even after a wheel has stopped turning, heat buildup in the brake area continues to dissipate first from the brake to the wheel, then to the bead area of the tire, and ultimately, to the air pressure chamber in the tire. Heat expansion will then cause the internal pressure to rise dangerously. Tires are fitted with fuseplugs—a kind of safety valve—to relieve really excessive pressures due to heat rise.

Rejected takeoffs and brake fires are rare, but short of this, heavy braking can still cause irreparable damage. In some cases, the damage is very obvious—blown fuseplugs and scorched bead areas. In other cases, tires may look perfectly normal under visual inspection, but the inside may be in dangerous condition due to excessive heat. The only safe course of action following heavy or prolonged braking is to remove the tire, wheel and brake assemblies for a detailed inspection.

Premature tire death can also result from foreign object damage (FOD).

Now that we know how tires are made and what their biggest enemies are, let's get on to some of the things pilots can do to increase tire service life and insure safe operation.

The recommendations and points that follow were gathered by B/CA from a wide variety of industry sources, including tire manufacturers, retreaders, service centers, aircraft manufacturers and operators.

Proper inflation is undoubtedly the most necessary maintenance function for safe, long service for aircraft tires. This universal truth, expressed by nearly every expert we talked with, is the most important single factor in tire life. Here's what to do to insure proper inflation:

Use valve caps—If you don't, dirt and moisture can get into the valve causing leaks and deterioration.

Tire pressure should be checked regularly—It's recommended it be checked before each flight, using an accurate gauge, preferably the more precise dial type. Note that the gauges need checking regularly too. If tires are not checked this frequently, a slow leak could go unnoticed until a serious air loss occurs. Such a leak can result in significant pressure loss in two or three days, or sooner if aggravated by operations. The tires on an inactive aircraft should be checked and aired once a week.

Air pressure should be checked when tires are cool—This will mean at least two hours after a flight (three hours after a hot weather flight). When the aircraft tire is hot, the pressure indication will be higher than that for the same tire at ambient temperature.

A newly mounted tire and/or tube should be checked daily for several days, after which the regular inflation control schedule described in the second item should be followed. This is necessary because air is usually trapped between the tire and the tube at the time of mounting, giving a false pressure reading. As this trapped air seeps out under the beads of the tire and around the valve hole in the wheel, the tire may become severely under-inflated within a day or two.

In tubeless tires, the maximum allowable air loss is five percent for any 24-hour period—A tire showing a pressure drop over 10 percent during the first 12 hours after mounting should be disassembled and checked for the cause.

Newly mounted tires should not be used immediately—They should be left to stand at least 12 hours after being mounted and inflated to regular operating pressure. This is good advice because the nylon cord used on all aircraft tire bodies stretches under tension, causing a possible five to 10 percent drop in air pressure within the first few hours of installation. After the 12-hour waiting period, the air pressure should then be readjusted to compensate for the decrease in pressure caused by the stretching of the cord body.

Keep tire pressures equal on each dual-wheel landing gear—Unequal pressure between dual tires, whether on main or nose gear, generally means that one tire is carrying more of a load than the other. A pair of tires of unequal pressure will tend to throw the wheel assembly out of alignment, possibly causing a pull in one direction, thus making the ride on the ground potentially dangerous as well as uncomfortable. (Incidentally, to prolong the life of tires on dual-wheel systems, they must be matched according to their diameter. See Figure 2.)

Tire pressure must be adjusted for the load it's supporting—Pressure ratings recommended in tire manufacturers' specifications and aircraft flight manuals are not for aircraft loaded to maximum gross weight. Instead, the tire pressures shown are for an aircraft sitting on the ramp, empty, except for some residual fuel. To compensate for the weight of the aircraft in a full gross situation, the recommended inflation pressure shown in the service specifications must be increased by four percent. Applying this formula insures that the tire deflection is 32 percent or less.

In cases where the aircraft is flown at less than full gross weight, this means the tires will be slightly over-inflated for that load situation. But

Matching tires on dual wheels is necessary so that each tire will have the same contact area with the ground and thereby carry an equal share of the load. Only those tires with inflated diameters within the tolerances listed above should be paired together on dual-wheel systems.

Figure 2
Dual-Wheel Matching Tolerances

Outer Diameter (in.)	Tolerances (in.)
Up to 24	¼
25 to 32	5/16
33 to 40	⅜
41 to 48	7/16
49 to 55	½
56 to 65	9/16
66 and up	⅝

experts say it is far better for the tires to be slightly over-inflated than under-inflated, even though the ground ride won't be as soft as with properly or under-inflated tires. Over-inflation insures that the optimum deflection of 32 percent is not exceeded; over-inflated tires will have some margin in the event a gradual leak is not immediately detected. Also, on a dual-wheel assembly in the event of a tire failure, the adjacent tire, being at a relatively high inflation pressure, will take the overload with a deflection factor closer to 32 percent than would otherwise be the case with proper or lower inflation.

Tire pressure must be adjusted for temperature extremes—When flying from a hot climate to a cold climate, or even when bringing an airplane out of a heated hangar into the cold air of winter, the air pressure inside the tire drops. To compensate for this, more air must be added. Prior to a flight to a destination that is colder than the departure airport, tires should be over-inflated or they will be subjected to excessive flexation when landing at the other end. The rule when flying from a warm area to a cold area, is that for each 2.5°C differential in expected temperature, add 1 percent above proper inflation pressure. Note: It does not follow that when flying from hot to cold you should *deflate* your tires a corresponding amount to compensate for the expected overpressure at the other end. Rather than take off in an *under*-inflated condition, it's best to land in an *over*-inflated condition.

Consider using nitrogen instead of air for inflation—Nitrogen will not burn, is less corrosive on metal and reduces oxidation of the inner tire walls. Jet aircraft, because of their higher weights and takeoff and landing speeds, and the fact that most of them use tubeless tires, use nitrogen regularly. It's preferable, but not essential, for lighter aircraft tires. A drawback in using nitrogen is that some FBOs charge for it. If you want to make the change immediately, go ahead. Air and nitrogen may be added to each other without ill effects.

With respect to aspects of tire care in addition to proper inflation, here are four more steps operators should be aware of.

Prevent flat spots on the tires of aircraft that are to remain idle or stored—If the aircraft is going to sit for longer than three days, it should either be moved every day or put on blocks so that no weight is on the tires. For most businessmen operators, that is not practical. Fortunately, those flat spots are usually temporary, disappearing by the end of a taxi run, but not always. If they don't, the tires can generally be reshaped by over-inflating them 25 to 50 percent of recommended pressure and moving the aircraft until the flat spot is on the upper side. The over-inflation should only be necessary for an hour or so.

Tires should be kept clean and free of contaminants—Certain minerals and chemicals, such as oil, brake fluid, grease, tar and degreasing agents have a deteriorating effect on rubber. If any of these contaminants unavoidably get on tires either in storage or mounted on aircraft, wipe it off with a gasoline dampened cloth and then wash the tire with soap and water.

Protect tires from weather extremes—Weather checking (usually in the form of oxidation) of the sidewall is going to occur to every tire. The rate at which checking will develop, and the severity, will fluctuate from operator to operator, area to area. Weather checking does not impair performance unless plies or fabric are exposed. The sidewall is merely a covering, a protective fairing as it were, and does not contribute to overall strength. But weather checking can eventually become so severe you will have to replace the tire, even though the tread has lots of wear left. Weather checking can be slowed somewhat by placing protective covers (ideally with a light color or aluminized surface to reflect sunlight) over the tires when the aircraft is going to be exposed for several hours or longer outside.

Airport and FBO authorities should keep aircraft movement areas free from debris—Unless runways, taxiways, ramps and floors are clean of rocks, glass, nails, rivets, bolts, hose clamps, hand tools and other items, FOD is assured.

Assuming you are following the standards for good preventive maintenance outlined above, your second line of defense is the preflight. Besides checking inflation using the techniques already discussed, preflight inspections should include the following checks and actions:

Check for valve leaks—You do this the same way you've checked for leaks on bike and auto tires. Apply a small amount of water or saliva to the end of the valve stem and watch for air bubbles.

Carefully remove objects that you find embedded in the tread—You will probably find glass, stones and metal objects, among other things.

350

(Caution: When prying out objects, use a tool with one hand and use your other hand to guard against the object flying into your face.)

Use the quick-touch test between flights—By briefly touching the treads and sidewalls, exposure to excessive temperatures on the preceeding landing may be determined.

Check for uneven wear—This malady may be the result of long-term under-inflation, over-inflation, uneven alignment, an out-of-balance situation, faulty brakes and anti-skid, or a combination of any of these. Tires showing uneven wear should be demounted, turned around and remounted to even up the wear. Cause of the uneven wear, of course, needs to be determined and eliminated as soon as possible.

Insure proper tire/wheel clearance— Make sure nothing is caught between the tire and the landing gear. Look for marks on the tire that might be a sign of rubbing due to inadequate clearance when the gear is retracted.

Be especially alert in checking inflation of dual-mounted tires—In a dual-wheel setup, one tire may be deflated, but it may not appear that way when eyeballing them because the aircraft weight is being supported by the good tire in the set.

Include a check of slippage marks in preflight inspections—Slippage marks, which should be mandatory on all tube-type tires, indicates if the tire has rotated on the wheel. Tire slippage damage, or suspected damage, should be a no-go item until a detailed inspection confirms a lack of damage and eliminates the cause of the slippage. Incidentally, markings should be applied using a permanent-type paint and contrasting colors, such as white, red or orange.

Recognize when a tire must be removed—A tire must be replaced if it has a cut that exposes or penetrates the cord body, or if it extends across more than 50 percent of any rib. Severe blistering of the bead, bulges anywhere or an area of loosened tread are all fatal injuries to tires.

This is your final chance to insure longer and safer wear for your tires. From this point on, it is no more just a question of economics—safety and passenger comfort now come into consideration. You will notice that some of the practices outlined below seem contradictory. That is because different circumstances call for different, and sometimes opposing, techniques.

For instance, although short ground runs and soft landings are normally recommended to reduce tread wear and prevent flat spots, there are some circumstances—like a landing on a grooved runway—that call for just the opposite procedure.

Be aware of the hazards of grooved runways—The ridges of concrete created by some grooved runways can cause a type of tire damage known as "chevron cutting." The high-pressure tires used on jets are particularly vulnerable to this hazard. These cuts get their name because they are at

351

right angles to the tread ribs. In confirming the cause of chevron cutting, the Air Force concluded after conducting a series of tests using a Lockheed P-3C (anti-submarine version of the Electra) that a greater degree of cutting was encountered during normally defined good, soft landings. Hard or firm landings reduced the damage by spinning the tires up to speed faster.

Smooth, light touchdowns increase tread life (landings on grooved runways excluded, of course)—In addition, such a technique eases the strain on tires at the moment of impact and gives passengers a nice ride.

Use minimum approach speeds and full runway length—The object here is to reduce heat damage due to excessive braking. Minimum use of brakes also lessens the probability of flat spots on tires and excessive tread wear on rough runways.

Don't always make your "quick-turnarounds" so quick—This suggestion is for the purpose of allowing hot brakes and tires to cool down to insure an acceptable performance level in case you must abort the next takeoff. It's a good suggestion, but it's only essential when your landing gross weight is in excess of a specific amount that is variable, depending upon runway gradient, temperature, use of landing flaps and other factors. Unfortunately, only large jet aircraft are required to have a chart that tells you what the quick-turnaround weight limitations are. That information— at least for lighter business jet operators—should be available from the engineering departments of aircraft manufacturers.

Taxi runs should be no longer than necessary—Taxi speeds of less than 20 knots should be used.

Use as little brake as possible for pivoting and turning—When an aircraft is turned by locking one wheel, the tire on the locked wheel is twisted on the pavement, generating considerable shear forces that severely strain the casing, plies, sidewalls and beads. A small piece of rock or stone that would ordinarily cause no damage can, in such cases, be literally screwed into the tire. To prevent this on tight turns, allow the inside wheel to roll on as large a radius as possible.

Delay as long as possible braking application on landing—This suggestion is obviously easier followed in jets with reversers. In a jet, the pilot can wait until the aircraft has settled firmly and finally onto the runway and than apply reversing before brake application is necessary. (If, however, community noise is a problem, it's good public relations to just burn up a little rubber for the sake of less noise.)

In smaller aircraft, in which runway length is normally a less critical factor, use aerodynamic braking as much as possible; land nose high and continue to hold the control wheel full back through the rollout. This technique will both increase aerodynamic braking and minimize the risk of sliding the tires by increasing the weight on the mains. Ideally, flaps should be left full down until wheel braking begins, then dumped to decrease lift and thus increase the weight on the mains. But flap techniques ultimately depend on the characteristics of the flap system and the aircraft.

Avoid landing with brakes on—This is obviously a good general operating practice. For the sake of tire conservation though, here are the specifics on why: brakes-on landings can result in flat spotting, severe heat generation at the point of contact between ground and tire tread and it may melt the tread rubber—an injury known as skid-burn. In addition, heat buildup within the tire may literally devulcanize it.

When it comes time to replace your aircraft tires, you should consider the purchase of retreads, or the economics of having your own worn tires retreaded versus buying new ones. Retreaded tires cost about half the price of new ones. Whether or not a tire should be retreaded depends on its age, condition and downtime considerations. If you send your own tires to be retreaded, the aircraft might be down a couple of weeks. In terms of wear potential, retreaded tires will give as much service as new ones because of the FAA standards they must meet. If you experienced poor wear performance from your old tires, you will experience the same performance with the retreads unless you change your area of operations, maintenance practices or operational techniques.

The main thing to be wary of with respect to retreaded tires is the outside diameter and roundness. Operators have reported to us that retreads are frequently slightly out-of-round and thus can get jammed in wheel wells of some aircraft when the gear is retracted. While retreading is done extensively with airliner tires, business jet operators as a group tend to just replace with new. Part of the reason for this, of course, is that they don't go through tires as fast as airliners, and each corporate operator doesn't have a large fleet that might have up to 16 wheels per aircraft. Retreading has worked for the airlines, and it can possibly work for you.

Operators of small business aircraft normally average much longer on tire wear than either corporate jet operators or airliners, but the cost of tires for light aircraft is greater, relatively, than those for the jets. In addition, replacement costs of small tires have skyrocketed over the past years. Therefore, the use of retreads on these aircraft has become more attractive.

If you do decide to go the retread route, be sure and make the decision before your tires get too worn or suffer catastrophic damage. Tires to be retreaded should be removed not later than when tread design is no longer visible in any one area and before any carcass ply cord shows.

The FAA says tires having injuries of the following types may be repaired:

• Bead injuries where only the chafe resistant material is damaged or loose, or where minor injuries do not penetrate into more than 25 percent of the tire plies, up to a maximum of three damaged plies.

353

• Injuries in tread or sidewalls may be repaired by the spot repair method. These injuries include cuts in the tread area that are smaller than 0.5 inch in length and do not penetrate into the cord body more than a specified percentage of the total plies.

The FAA is equally specific in enumerating conditions that it "recommends" should be cause for not retreading or repairing a tire: flex breaks, bead injuries that exceed the limits outlined above, separation between plies or around bead wire, kinked or broken beads, weather or radial cracks extending into the cord body, heat damage or blisters, cracked, deteriorated or damaged inner liners of tubeless tires.

B.F. Goodrich says that tires that have been run flat, or partially flat, due to failure of fuseplugs, should normally be scrapped even though there may be no visible evidence of damage to the tire. The only exception would be if it is known that the fuseplug leaked air because of a defect in the plug itself, and the tire was not run in an under-inflated condition.

Sometimes retreaded tires can be retreaded again. There is no rule on how many times a carcass can be retreaded, but the wide variation in tire operating environments that affect total carcass life and serviceability makes it inadvisable to prescribe arbitrarily the maximum number of times a tire should be retreaded. This aspect, therefore, is best left to the retreader.

Aircraft tire performance has tripled over the past 10 years; that is, pilots are getting three times more takeoffs and landings per tire than they did in the early 1960s, according to studies conducted by the manufacturers. And more improvements are on the way.

It's difficult to discuss all of the research that is going on in the laboratories of tire manufacturers because the researchers are, understandably, highly secretive for competitive reasons. But a couple of programs that have been underway for some time have come to light. For instance, Firestone Tire and Rubber Company is experimenting with a new material called Kevlar that may eventually replace the nylon now used in all tires. Harry E. Davis of the company's aircraft tire engineering department said that Kevlar has about twice the heat resistance of nylon. No field tests had been scheduled, and it will be a few years before this material sees production.

A joint study by the University of Akron and NASA is underway to find better rubber materials to make aircraft tires even tougher than they are now. The study is looking at friction coefficients and abrasion characteristics of new polymer materials. Polymerization construction is to tire strength as bonding is to aircraft structural strength.

Aircraft tires—they are probably the only components on the aircraft that are on duty when the aircraft is *not* flying. In fact, when they are in the air, they are dead weight that subtracts from the payload capability of

354

the aircraft. But unless aviation totally takes to seaplanes, tires will continue to provide the cushion between aircraft and ground, and therefore shouldn't be neglected. As costs continue to rise, the expression, "let's kick the tires and go" is certain to take on a new and significant meaning for all pilots.

Fuel Filler Caps 47

by Gordon Gilbert

"There's more than meets the eye" may be a hackneyed expression, but it is nonetheless applicable to aircraft fuel (and oil) caps and adapters. Few of us pay much attention to them other than to make sure they are where they're supposed to be and that the little tab on top is down, indicating the cap is properly secured. The fact is, however, fuel caps are a lot more sophisticated than you may think.

We recently visited Shaw Aero Devices, which supplies most of the caps used on business aircraft, more in curiosity than because we expected a story to grow out of it. We expected to have lunch with Jim Shaw, vice president of the company, and learn all there is to know about caps in 20 minutes. We were 180 degrees off course. We spent an entire afternoon in Shaw's Long Island plant seeing how caps are designed, put together, tested and mated to an assortment of adapters.

It develops there are a bunch of different kinds and sizes of caps, and they must be properly cared for if they are to do the job.

Each cap (except the simple, all-metal, twist-off kind found on many single-engine machines) is designed, manufactured and tested to strict military specifications. Mil specs establish operating-temperature extremes, special pressure ratings, corrosion controls, locking and removal torque ratings and quality assurance inspections.

The most impressive test is one to demonstrate the resistance—or lack of resistance—to internal sparking when a cap is struck by lightning. In simplified terms, the setup consists of a box that simulates a fuel tank, one side of which has a hole and adapter to accept a test cap, plus two tiny monitoring holes. Inside the box is a Polaroid camera focused on the bottom of the cap. Banks of high capacity condensers (looking like something out of Dr. Frankenstein's laboratory) are employed to create simulated strikes.

The camera tells the story. A lightning-safe cap will produce no arcing inside the tank. This is verified by a totally black picture with nothing but two small dots of light shining through the monitoring holes to indicate the camera didn't malfunction.

But you ought to see what happens when lightning hits a fuel tank unprotected by a lightning-safe cap. Shaw demonstrated this for us and the photo came out as white as your knuckles would become if you saw a real lightning strike on *your* fuel tank. There was so much sparking in the test box when the lightning struck, the bottom of the cap wasn't even visible in the photo due to extreme overexposure of the film. The irony is that if you were lucky enough to look at the topside of a non-lightning-safe cap after a strike, all you'd see in many cases would be a tiny, innocent looking black mark.

Although there are at least a dozen different kinds of fuel and oil caps available from several manufacturers, the majority of business aircraft designers opt for only one or two types. But a particular operation may make a completely different kind of cap more desirable. Here is a list of several caps and adapters that are being manufactured and the kinds of operations they are especially suited for:

Locking caps. Locking caps come in two basic kinds: lightning safe and non-lightning safe. Both have locks built into the flip-up tab, and a protective cover. Interestingly, cap manufacturers tell us lockable caps became popular long before the energy crisis made fuel precious. When you stop to think about it, the reason becomes obvious. With all the sump and tank drains an aircraft must have, there's no way short of a locked and guarded hangar to prevent fuel theft. About all a lockable cap can do for you is prevent vandals, or persons with a more malevolent intent, from putting something *into* the tank. A couple of years ago, when malevolency towards certain corporations became rampant, lockable cap sales soared.

The lock itself fits flush in the tab; the protective cover, which is removed for flight, prevents water from accumulating around the lock then freezing and making both it and cap inoperable.

Non-siphoning caps. "Non-siphoning cap" is really a misnomer because in virtually every instance it is the adapter that is non-siphoning. Such adapters are available for both oil and fuel tanks. The most common type for fuel tanks is an adapter fitted with a one-way, spring-loaded flapper valve that opens only in a downward direction. The flapper is pushed open by the fuel nozzle. When it is withdrawn, the flapper itself closes the tank. Even if you lose the cap, fuel can't siphon out. Non-siphoning fillers for oil tanks are similar, but usually it is the weight of the oil that opens a flapper or check valve. This cap and adapter are desirable, of course, for all filler openings. Were they standard, a significant number of incidents and accidents would be prevented each year and in fact recent amendments to FAA regulations require that newer aircraft designs be fitted with some sort of siphoning prevention device on fuel filler openings.

Gloved-thumb caps. More properly referred to as an Arctic cap, the gloved-thumb cap is designed for operations anywhere it is cold enough to require that line service personnel wear gloves. The primary feature of it is its over-sized latch to allow easy operation by a gloved thumb.

Bleed-valve caps. This type is recommended for high-altitude operations by aircraft equipped with fuel bladders inside the cells. A bleed-valve cap looks like an ordinary one except for a small valve with a pin-hole through its center mounted on the cap's topside. This valve automatically equalizes pressures inside and outside the tank to prevent a partially filled bladder from collapsing.

Lightning-safe caps. Perhaps the most important from the standpoint of safety are caps designed to eliminate sparking inside the cell. Mounted in the proper (mil spec) adapter, these caps will withstand a direct lightning strike without conducting any of the fire into the tank. They are easily identified by the notched top plate and the total absence of metal on the interior side of the device. All internal parts, including the lanyard that secures the cap to the aircraft, are made of a high strength, non-conductive plastic. They are especially recommended for aircraft having fuel filler outlets located near the wing tips and on tip tanks.

Unfortunately, knowing which type of cap is best in your operation does you little good because you can't run to the nearest FBO, buy it and replace your old ones. Lockable caps are available that will exchange with the current caps on some aircraft, but lightning-proof and non-siphoning ones require that the adapter also be replaced. In most instances that is a major modification requiring an STC and for some reason no enterprising entrepreneur has yet developed the kits necessary. However, Piper, on some models, offers a regular cap (standard) or a non-lightning one (optional), with no adapter change necessary.

"Caps last a long time even when horribly mistreated," Shaw told us. He was referring to the almost universal practice of tightening the adjustment nut a turn or two to prevent leaks, then smashing the tab down with the heel of the hand and prying it up with a big screwdriver. A properly adjusted cap, occasionally treated with a dab of grease under the tab, can be easily closed and opened with the fingers. If the adjustment must be tightened more than that to prevent leakage, the problem is in the seal between cap and adapter; check the O-ring for cuts, nicks and deterioration. The latching fingers should be inspected for uneven wear and the adapter seat itself for deep scratches, roughness and uniformity.

Most cap problems are the result of mistreatment during the refueling process. If the lineman bangs a heavy nozzle into the O-ring seat, he will gouge or bend it, making a proper seal difficult to maintain. Since filler openings are usually on top of the wing in a low-pressure area, siphoning is a frequent result.

Normal maintenance is limited to keeping the area around the tab clean, and periodic inspections. On later caps, the metal plate under the heel of the tab is impregnated with a lubricant to make turning and locking easier. A touch of grease every now and then will suffice to keep it working freely.

If a screwdriver must be used, the tab should be pried up with caution, otherwise the metal plate itself may be lifted and bent. Should a cap be damaged it's best to replace it rather than repair it in the field. A repairable damaged cap can be returned to the manufacturer through your airframe customer service department and used as a spare after its return.

To sum up cap care and cautions:

(1) Every now and then—at least once each 100 hours—pull the cap, inspect the O-ring and adapter seat carefully, clean the tab-well thoroughly and put a dab of grease on the metal plate under the tab.

(2) If lightning-safe caps are installed, inspect the non-metallic parts extra carefully for cracks. The non-sparking feature may be compromised if this assembly is damaged.

(3) With no care whatsoever, a cap can be expected to go about 1000 hours and five years with perhaps a new O-ring or two; with a minimum of attention it'll go at least twice that long before overhaul. If a cap does need major attention, return it to your airframe manufacturer for service.

(4) If your aircraft has non-siphoning filler adapters, inspect the flapper valves occasionally by reaching in and checking for spring tension, side play in the hinge, dings and wear at the seating surfaces.

(5) Non-lightning-safe adapters are usually carbon steel (rather than stainless) protected against rust and corrosion by cadmium plating. If the plating is worn away, other protective techniques may have to be employed.

Compared to the cost and aggravation almost everything else on an airplane causes the operator, fuel and oil caps are saintly. Give them just a little TLC and they'll outlast the airplane.

Windshields 48

by Gerard M. Bruder, Jr.

The highest tribute a pilot can pay to his aircraft windshield is to make no comment about it at all. Of course, that observation is from a major transparency manufacturer. That golden silence indicates the windshield is safely and inconspicuously providing adequate visibility through a wide range of flight conditions. In other words, it is doing its job.

Thanks to modern technology, windshields usually receive years and thousands of hours of quiet approval. Like other components, however, they are not immune to defects, abuse, accidents, fatigue or Murphy's Law, and thus trouble occasionally develops.

When trouble strikes a windshield—especially in a high-speed, pressurized aircraft—flight safety can be jeopardized. This is not to say a crash or emergency will immediately take place; in fact, windshield-related crashes are extremely rare. But the potential for an incident is increased, most often because of the restriction, or danger of restriction, to visibility.

Reducing that potential by repairing or replacing the windshield is expensive and time-consuming, but obviously it must be done. Windshield reliability, problems and maintenance, therefore, are of concern to all pilots and flight departments.

In the infant days of flying, a windshield was literally only that—a glass or acrylic screen designed to protect the pilot from wind, bugs, oil, water from a boiling over radiator and whatever else came at him. Goggles offered a fail-safe backup for the eyes.

With the advent of planes with enclosed cockpits, windshields assumed the role for which they are responsible today: providing visibility. At first, it was an undemanding role. Cruising speeds were low, instrument flight was limited and altitudes were well within the realm of liveable air. Hand-cut, two-ply safety glass filled the bill on even the most sophisticated airliners.

As sophistication of aircraft and flight continued, the conditions under which windshields must work grew increasingly complex. Today, while providing clear, undistorted visibility, windshields must also withstand the stress of abrupt temperature and pressure changes and large temperature and pressure differentials. They must tolerate systems that inhibit and repel ice, rain and fogging on windshield surfaces. Often they must serve as part of the structure. And they must resist impacts by birds, hail and other objects.

These are not merely desired capabilities; in more technical language they are cited in Part 25 of the FARs, which governs airworthiness standards for aircraft in the transport category. (Part 23 standards for aircraft under 12,500 pounds are less stringent, but so are the demands placed on windshields of such aircraft.) Interestingly though, there are no Technical Standard Orders (TSOs) for windshields.

It is not surprising, then, that the design and construction of a modern windshield—or transparency, as manufacturers prefer to call that misnomer—is a complex, meticulous science. Makers of light, fixed-gear aircraft typically fabricate the windshields themselves. Windshields for corporate category equipment, on the other hand, are the result of team effort: airframe manufacturer engineers develop specifications and the transparency manufacturer takes it from there. Sometimes airframe engineers visit several transparency manufacturers before selecting the design they believe is superior.

Pittsburgh Plate Glass Industries (at its Huntsville, Alabama plant) and the Sierracin Corporation (Sylmar, California) are the major domestic manufacturers of aircraft transparencies. PPG, the world's largest manufacturer of aircraft transparencies, makes a variety of products for about 250 military, commercial and general aviation models, including 27 corporate planes such as the Sabreliner, JetStar and Falcon. Sierracin provides windshields and other transparencies for about 40 aircraft. They include most Beech and Cessna heavy twins and turboprop models and a number of military and commercial planes.

Other U.S. aircraft transparency manufacturers are Swedlow Incorporated. Garden Grove, California; Goodyear Aerospace Corporation, Litchfield Park, California; Texstar Corporation, Grand Prairie, Texas; and Libbey-Owens-Ford Company, Toledo, Ohio.

Triplex Safety Glass Company Limited, London makes transparencies for the Hawker-Siddeley 125 and Lucas Aerospace Limited of Bedfordshire, England manufacturers them for the Hansa Jet.

Since airplanes are individuals, they require individual windshields based on considerations such as weight, structural participation and altitude and cruise speed certification. Windshields for most small, unpressurized aircraft are of simple acrylic construction, but higher speed and pressurized models require multi-layered transparencies that provide the strength and heating capabilities necessary for all-weather and high-altitude flight.

According to PPG, about 95 percent of all electrically heated windshields are made of laminated glass because glass is superior to acrylic in heat conductivity. Also, glass is more resistant to abrasion and is not sensitive to the action of wipers.

Acrylic, however, is more pliable, which is one reason Gates selected it for the Learjet. (On the Learjets and the Cessna Citation, which also has an acrylic windshield, heat and rain removal are provided by an external bleed air system.) Another advantage of acrylic is that it is less prone to delamination and cracking due to its greater compatibility with the plastic interlayer used to bond windshield layers. Acrylic is also more resistant to impacts.

Although most windshields today are of either glass or acrylic, the trend is towards a composite construction to combine the best characteristics of each material.

We've chosen two representative business aircraft—the Grumman G-II and Cessna 421—to briefly illustrate the windshield manufacturing process.

After design, the first step is obtaining raw materials. PPG makes its own glass and vinyl for the G-II, and rejection at this point (up to 15 percent) is liberal because innate defects can be more costly later on. If the raw glass passes inspections for thickness, optical quality, surface finish and other considerations, it is machine cut into pattern size. Materials for curved windshields are formed on a mold through heat and gravity.

Next, the edges are dressed to discourage bending and cracking during tempering, a process in which glass is gradually heated and cooled to toughen it. During tempering PPG applies *Nesa*, an electrically conductive transparent film the company developed in 1946 to provide anti-icing, de-icing and de-fogging capabilities when the windshield assembly is connected to the aircraft electrical systems. Bus bars, electrical braids and temperature sensors are bonded to the glass in preparation for this connection.

For airplanes with limited electrical capacity, PPG provides for electrothermal windshield heating via a mesh of nearly invisible wires embedded in the interlayer. *Nesa* film is applied on the inner face of the outer ply to serve as an anti-static force.

Now the interlayer (or layers), prepared and cut in a separate process, is added to the glass. Most interlayer material is vinyl, but the G-II windshield instead uses *112*, a stronger, more flexible material PPG developed about two years ago. The need for *112* in the G-II windshield will be explained later.

Assembly of the glass and interlayer is one of the most critical steps in construction because even a slight misfit undermines the integrity of the final product. In fact, assembly is the highest blue-collar job at the PPG plant.

After assembly, the components are placed in an autoclave where they

Windshields of smaller pressurized aircraft may
have as many as three layers.

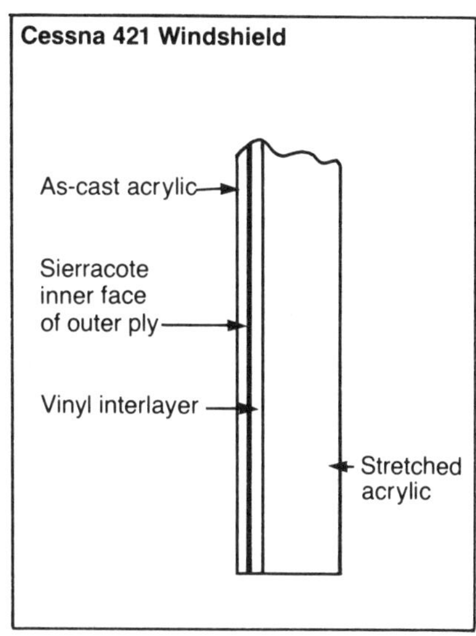

This is the layout of a windshield for a large jet, in
this case the Gulfstream II.

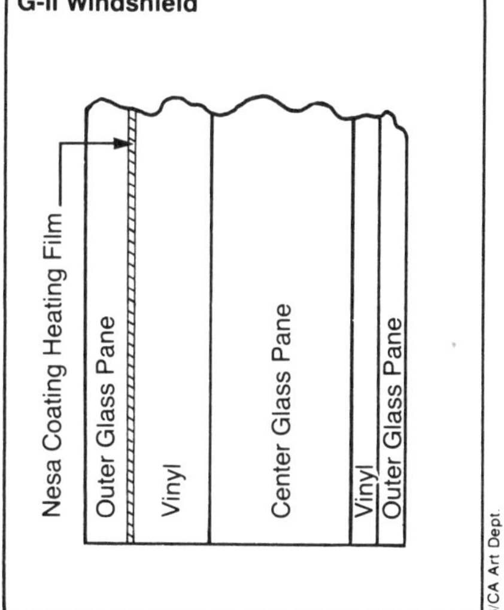

are heated under pressure to complete the bonding process and thus become a single laminated unit. The G-II windshield is then one and seven-sixteenth inches thick overall and consists of three tempered glass plies and two layers of interlayer. The middle glass pane is the structural member.

All that remains is to add seals and retainers, drill bolt holes and apply other finishing touches. Finally, four months after the start of the process, the windshield is packaged and shipped.

The 150 construction steps include numerous inspections (one is an optical check by laser beam), and quality control procedures are followed (for instance, sterilization of certain preparation rooms) to insure a reliable product. Also, each component is given an identity number so it can be monitored throughout the fabrication cycle. Records of each windshield are maintained in case future problems require an investigation. In the case of the G-II, problems did arise.

The two plies of the Cessna 421 windshield are made of acrylic that Sierracin purchases outside. One of the plies is processed to form stretched acrylic, which is superior in strength and flexibility to the unstretched, or "as-cast," material. However, the latter is a more effective conductor of electricity and, since Sierracin provides heat via its patented electrical film *(Sierracote)* on the inner face of the outer ply, that ply is not stretched.

After the plies are machine cut and formed, the *Sierracote* is applied and the plies are assembled and laminated using a vinyl interlayer. Primary finishing to enhance optical qualities is the next step.

Trimming, drilling of attachment holes and application of sealant then take place, and electrical terminals are installed. More polishing is done and, finally, the windshield, seven-sixteenth inches thick, is ready for shipping and installation. In all, the process involves 12 steps (including exhaustive tests at four inspection stations) and takes eight weeks.

Unlike the G-II windshield, the 421 unit does not have to meet a bird impact requirement for certification. If it did, the inner main ply would be layered and thicker than its three-eighths inches.

Manufacturers submit windshields to tests that produce more stress than they are likely to encounter in flight. It is impossible to simulate flight conditions exactly, however, and whether of glass or acrylic, windshields occasionally fail in operational situations. Delamination, a separation of components that usually begins in a corner and produces opaqueness, often in the form of bubbles, is the most common type of windshield failure. Those comprised of laminated glass seem to be most susceptible. It is always progressive, but the rate varies according to age, stress and other factors.

PPG says moisture penetration is the major cause of delamination, followed by stress between layers. Sierracin attributes it mainly to heat differential, with moisture and stress acting as aggravating forces.

B/CA asked a number of mechanics for their opinions, and most cited stress and moisture. One said manufacturing defects are responsible while another mentioned faulty installation procedures.

A second windshield woe is cracking—almost always in the outer ply. Again, moisture and stress were blamed, and impacts and manufacturing defects were included. Cracking can constitute a single longitudinal line, but it can also come in the form of a sudden, dice-like shattering of the entire ply. When an inner ply shatters on a glass windshield, according to the manufacturers, it is usually the result of the interlayer contracting at cold temperature and chipping the adjacent, more rigid, glass. Cracking, especially the shattering variety, is often accompanied by an explosive sound.

Failure of heating elements in windshields is frequently a ramification of delamination or cracking. For example, a crack can damage the *Nesa* coating and cause electrical arcing. On the other hand, trouble with the heating elements can damage the windshield. One contributor to the "Feedback" section of NBAA's monthly *Maintenance and Operation Bulletin* reported that arcing had prompted delamination of the outer glass of a HS-125-600. Likewise, a malfunctioning sensor can damage a windshield through improper heat control.

Fatigue, manufacturing defects and electrical system trouble are other factors that can lead to heating element failure.

Another problem that occasionally befalls a windshield is impact by a foreign object. Some years ago a White Plains, New York-based corporate pilot was flying a Super Ventura when the left prop spinner separated and smashed into the windshield "like a cannon," causing a severe crack. Once in a while a prop or gust of wind will hurl a stone into a windshield and, inside the cockpit, tossing or shoving a metal clipboard against the windshield can create a stress point.

But the most common impact danger is from birds. Few pilots who fly regularly have escaped at least one collision with a bird, and the law of averages demands that a certain percentage of such encounters take place on the windshield. A windshield that runs into a sparrow at 120 knots does not always crack, but subtle damage can occur that will later develop into an overt problem.

A Hansa pilot told B/CA that the copilot's windshield would not heat the day after a strike by a small bird during an approach. There was no apparent damage, but the windshield had to be replaced.

Damage is immediate and substantial, of course, when a windshield and an eight-pound goose collide.

There is no need for a causal investigation when a goose and a windshield meet; the reason for the damage is evident. Determining the reasons for delamination, cracking and failure of heating elements, however, is often a different story. Knowing that moisture under the seal, the stress of temperature and pressure differentials, fatigue and manufacturing defects are suspects does not reveal which—if any—of these factors was directly or indirectly responsible for the damage.

In fact, the culprit usually gets away without an indictment for lack of evidence. As long as the problem is not regular, flight departments are content to order the windshield changed and grudgingly dismiss the incident as part of the expense and attrition of operating a high-performance aircraft.

But when an airplane has chronic windshield woes, corrective action must be taken. Windshields are expensive and replacement requires at least two maintenance people and grounds the aircraft for one to three days. If the maintenance department is unable to resolve a chronic windshield problem, the aircraft and transparency manufacturers should be consulted. In this sense, the definition of "chronic" is a matter of opinion; some operators say a windshield should last indefinitely; others are satisfied if they get three years or several thousand hours out of one. If you think your windshields are failing too often, you have a chronic windshield problem.

Detective work leading to arrest of the cause is often a time-consuming process. Months and months can pass, for instance, before it becomes apparent that using a different type of sealant is not going to stop delamination. Then another long period is necessary while the use of a different torquing technique during installation is evaluated.

Sometimes windshield failure is found to be more a factor of aircraft use than of defects. Boeing 707 windshields are about twice as durable as Boeing 737 windshields because 707 flights are longer and involve fewer temperature and pressure changes.

PPG reports it took six to eight months to discover why almost all of Mohawk Airline's F227 windshields had to be replaced in the late 1960s while F227s operated by Ozark and Piedmont flew on and on with little windshield trouble. Engineers eventually discovered that the paint Mohawk used was chemically attacking the seals, permitting moisture to launch its own attack. Ozark and Piedmont were using a different type of paint.

On investigation also ensued when some G-II operators began complaining about cracks and other problems that required windshield replacement. One G-II pilot told us both windshields once cracked on the same leg (though not at the same moment) on a flight to Rio de Janeiro.

"We've replaced every panel at least once and some at least three times," the pilot added.

Other pilots and maintenance people also related G-II windshield stories, but there may be many G-IIs that still have original panels.

The G-II takes the same windshield as the G-I, which historically has not been as troublesome. However, the G-II is certificated for flight at 43,000 feet and a pressure differential of 9.45 psi at a cruise speed of 0.85 Mach.

No apparent pattern of G-II windshield failures was related by pilots during the troublesome period. Some occurred during taxi, some took place during climb, some occurred at cruise and some happened during descent.

Grumman American told B/CA it and PPG made a number of changes

366

in an effort to halt the failures. One change was installation of a second sensor to better control heating and cooling, but that didn't work. Also tried —again without success—was a gradual application of heat during ground warmup.

Use of PPG's *112* instead of vinyl for the interlayer and an improved seal in the windshield frame eventually granted longer life to G-II transparencies. G-II pilots and maintenance people say they have had few problems since those changes were made.

Another indication that G-II windshield problems may be over is that of 52 cockpit comfort improvements suggested by G-II operators in a Grumman survey, only six involved transparencies.

The German-built Hansa also incurred a certain notoriety for problems with its windshields, which consist of two three-eighths-inch plies, one of acrylic and the other of polyester. One Hansa pilot told us both of the windshields on his aircraft once cracked on the same flight.

The Hansa windshield history was not a major problem—except to those who maintain them—simply because there are so few in the fleet. But the solution sheds some light on a potential solution to problems in other installations.

Since it was the outer polyester ply that usually failed, Sierracin (which does repair work on the Lucas fabricated windshields) replaced that ply with as-cast acrylic, which is less brittle and less prone to moisture penetration. Hansa operators say windshield problems have diminished with the use of the as-cast acrylic outer ply.

The Beech King Air is an example of a turboprop model on which windshield problems—mostly delamination—were experienced. These windshields are constructed of glass. PPG said stress was the main cause and that over the years it and Beech made 24 changes, including the use of a different seal to deter future trouble.

Changes were also made in Federal Express's Falcon 20 windshields to correct failures and installation difficulties. A company representative, who noted that Federal Express operates 32 Falcons at near maximum utilization, said PPG designed a new windshield as the result of its experiences that was more flexible, provided better heating characteristics, was cheaper to purchase and easier to replace.

The fact that we've singled out G-IIs, Hansas, King Airs and Falcons to illustrate windshield problems and solutions should not imply that other aircraft models do not or did not suffer windshield problems as well. They do. Cessna, for example, made several false starts with its Citation windshield until it discovered that a single acrylic ply worked best. And the windshields in earlier HS-125s were sometimes so notoriously troublesome that Hawker-Siddeley makes certain everyone understands the new 125-700 will have edge-heated panels, similar to those in Hawker's own Trident airliner, which purportedly will give seven times better service than the old 125 units.

Occasionally, however, an airframe and windshield are so nicely matched —by luck as well as by design—that windshields seem to last indefinitely if they escape accidents and abuse. PPG says no Navajo or Cheyenne windshields (both made of glass) have ever been returned to its repair station for delamination, though some have been sent in for other minor reasons.

Side cockpit and cabin windows, of course, also crack and delaminate, but not as frequently as windshields. One reason is that the former are of less complex construction and thus there is less to fail. Another is that cabin windows and many cockpit side windows are unheated.

How serious are inflight windshield problems? To meet certification standards (including, for appropriate aircraft, the ability to withstand without penetration the impact of a four-pound bird at a relative velocity equal to the plane's design cruise speed), transparency manufacturers build damage-tolerance (fail-safe) systems into their windshields. The inner ply or plies serve as structural components so that if other plies fail, disaster will not take place.

Deaths or injuries due to windshield failure, therefore, are extremely rare. The NTSB reports there was just one fatal accident involving windshields of business aircraft from 1971 to 1975. In that incident, a Mitsubishi MU-2G crashed shortly after takeoff from Atlantic City, New Jersey, after one or both pilots apparently were incapacitated when geese struck the acrylic windshield. Geese weigh more than four pounds.

The only other business aircraft crash involving a windshield in the period, according to the NTSB, concerned a Cessna 310K. The pilot aborted a takeoff in Mississippi after an engine failed and collided with a helicopter and other objects on the ground. The NTSB said a dirty, foggy windshield was partially responsible for the collision.

The fact that windshield-related crashes are infrequent does not mean that windshield failure is of no concern. On two different occasions involving Cessna 421Bs recently, copilot windshields have fractured and separated completely from the frame. There were no serious injuries in either incident, but that might not have been the case had the planes been higher than 19,000 and 21,000 feet.

Investigation of the two incidents revealed that both were caused by cracks at critical windshield bolt holes in which the bolts were bearing against the acrylic. The FAA issued an AD requiring windshield inspection of all 421B and 421C aircraft.

Numerous pilots have told B/CA of other sudden, pulse-quickening inflight windshield failures. One pilot reported that the outer panel on his HS 125 shattered "with a big bang" at 41,000 feet, obscuring vision and "scaring the hell out of the passengers—and me." The pilot said his copilot had to land the aircraft.

Again, however, we emphasize that damage-tolerance systems minimize the possibility that delamination or cracking will cause an entire windshield to blow out. The danger, instead, is that visibility will be restricted or obscured through the affected panel. Assuming that both windshields do not fail on the same flight, a landing can still be executed, but of course, collision avoidance is jeopardized.

(Although dual failure is rare, it does happen. We've already reported two cases in this article. A third involved a Boeing 747 that had to be landed at Heathrow in London with the autoland system after an outer panel delamination on both windshields obscured forward visibility.)

To reassure JetStar pilots that windshield failure does not automatically result in an emergency situation, Lockheed has issued a report on the structural damage tolerance of its windshields after conducting tests under a sustained pressure loading of 150 percent of maximum operating conditions.

"Should all three glass panes fracture," the report reads in part, "the two layers of vinyl plastic will carry the pressure loads by bulging and acting as a hoop tension diaphragm. . . . We recognize that when any glass cracks, a loss of cockpit visibility will occur and the captain must make his own decision as to his flight plan. . . . We can only do our best to relieve the crew of the worry of sudden decompression."

Some flight manuals contain recommended procedures should a windshield problem develop. These, of course, should be followed—just as you would follow instructions for electrical system failure, fuel pressure surging or other abnormal inflight condition.

JetStar pilots, for example, are advised to slow to 250 knots below 14,000 feet if the heat fails. This is because components in an unheated glass windshield lose some of their impact resiliency. The HS 125 has a speed limit of 220 knots below 6000 feet with inoperative heat.

Acrylic windshields, according to Sierracin, do not lose their resiliency when cold, but the MU-2 manual states that the vinyl interlayer in its acrylic windshield is part of the bird impact proofing when heated.

Incidentally, the Lear 24 has a speed restriction of 300 knots below 14,000 feet while the Lear 23, which has the same acrylic windshield, has no such restriction. The simple explanation is that the 24 model was certificated under Part 25, large aircraft certification rules, which contain a bird impact resistance requirement, and its older brother was certificated under the old CAR 3 rules, which did not.

Windshield cracks, according to the Cessna 421C manual, restrict that plane to unpressurized flight. The HS 125 manual instructs pilots to reduce pressure to five psi within 10 minutes and turn off the windshield heat if the center glass panel fails. The JetStar manual says delamination does not seriously affect the strength of its windshield panels, but notes that it can restrict visibility.

If the manual for your airplane does not include windshield failure procedures, we suggest you contact the airplane and transparency manufacturers and find out what to do for various contingencies. Then make your own windshield failure additions to the emergency procedures section of your manual.

During the interim, consider the following points and suggestions:

The most serious consequence of most windshield failures is a restriction or potential restriction to visibility. Therefore, if your windshield cracks and you do not have a copilot, it would be wise to move to the right seat if that is feasible. The depressurizing cycle and the temperature changes as you descend to land may cause the fault to spread rapidly, causing obscured vision on approach to landing or at some other awkward time in the flight. Sometimes a crack that does not initially restrict visibility will quickly progress to the point that it does.

• If visibility is totally obscured out of your windshield, advise ATC.

• If a windshield cracks or chips, do not panic, but do descend and/or reduce pressurization as a precautionary measure as soon as feasible—especially if the failure takes place in the structural panel.

• Remember that windshield failure can cause heating element failure. Monitor the heat to detect subsequent heating element failure. Turn the heat off if an element malfunctions. Of course, following discovery of a windshield fault during flight, you should anticipate failure of the anti- or de-ice system and plan the remainder of the flight accordingly. You shouldn't continue into potential icing conditions.

• Remember that loss of heat in a glass windshield reduces impact strength.

• To de-fog a windshield after the heating system has failed, turn up the cockpit heat or open the air vents.

• Delamination usually progresses more slowly than a crack and is less serious because the failure is in the lamination rather than in the panel. You can continue your flight, but check with a mechanic at your next scheduled stop and request this evaluation. PPG advises pilots to use the windshield the way it's intended when delamination occurs (that is, operate under normal flight conditions) and replace the windshield when the delamination progression begins to affect visibility or reaches the limits specified in the airplane maintenance manual.

• A dice pattern indicates cracking; a milky, bubbly or opaque discoloration indicates delamination.

• If an impact causes substantial windshield damage, the damage-tolerance system may have been affected. Reduce pressurization as much as possible and descend.

With windshields, as with most things, an ounce of prevention is worth a pound of cure. Inspect the windshield sealant frequently and make sure it inhibits moisture penetration.

Keeping a windshield clean is important, of course, but cleaning agents can cause trouble if the seal is not tight or complete. Remember that plastic scratches easily, so use non-abrasive materials to clean acrylic.

Scratches on acrylic can also be discouraged by taxiing slowly in dusty, rocky or windy environments and by keeping clipboards and other solid objects off the glareshield.

With either acrylic or glass windshields, be sure to use an approved agent to polish the frame; some frame cleaners are acidic and can chemically alter the electrical heating coat.

Speaking of heating, the use of heat year round—at least with a glass windshield—will promote long windshield life because heat keeps the plastic interlayer fairly pliable. Heat is less important in acrylic windshields since acrylic and interlayer components have more common expansion properties.

Both to assure that you have heat when it's needed and to preclude heat-induced failures, check heating and electrical system elements frequently. Checking the electrical system is especially important if you've just replaced a windshield; a problem in the system may have prompted the windshield failure in the first place and will likely do it again if it's not corrected.

Flight departments can assist in the promotion of long windshield life by scheduling longer flights, if possible; the more often a plane climbs and descends, the more often its windshield panels are going to be subjected to the stress of environmental changes.

If your airplane manual doesn't contain windshield maintenance tips, try the maintenance manual. PPG advises, "treat the windshield as a $2500 piece of equipment—which it is."

Sierracin has developed a windshield-mounted heater assembly for aircraft with 28-volt electrical systems. PPG has developed its *112* interlayer and more effective edge attachments for longer life and high reliability. Some jumbo jets now have windshields that provide more panoramic visibility and better aerodynamic characteristics than their predecessors and this innovation will eventually work its way down to corporate aircraft.

Those are a few of the advances made possible by aerospace technology in recent years, and there is no reason to believe progress will not continue.

Manufacturers, for instance, are becoming increasingly interested in applications of polycarbonate, a relatively new material that is superior to glass and acrylic in impact resistance, ductibility and performance at tem-

371

perature extremes. Polycarbonate is highly susceptible to scratching and attack by solvents, but with improvements it could become the transparency material of the future. It is now being used in windshields and canopies of some military jet fighters, but it is not yet approved by the FAA.

As superior materials are developed, windshield visibility will likely become more panoramic and less interrupted by posts and structural members.

New material and design concepts will be necessary as business aircraft become more sophisticated. Already the Lear 24F and 25D/F models are certificated for flight at 51,000 feet, although no windshield changes were necessary for that achievement.

If windshield technology keeps pace, delamination, cracking, heating element failure and damage from eight-pound geese might someday be relegated to the aviation history books.

The Search for a Lighting Standard

49

by Richard N. Aarons

Hypothesis—If you see conflicting traffic soon enough, you won't hit it.

It seems pretty simple. If you make airplanes conspicuous under all conditions and build cockpits with unlimited visibility, you'll have no mid-airs.

Obviously we've been able to do neither in 40-or-so years of trying. If anything, cockpit visibility is decreasing in newer aircraft as panel real estate wins priority over windshield area. Worse, complex external lighting systems seem to confuse the conspicuity situation rather than improve it. Next time you're flying in a relatively high-density area at night (or dusk), check to see what you pick up first in your traffic scan. Do you see the strobes first and then the anti-collision lights? Or is it the beacon that catches your eye, followed by the strobes? What about the nav lights, when do you see them? You'll find, as we have in a year-long informal study of the situation, that the answer to all those questions is: "It depends."

Now ask yourself these questions after you've picked up the traffic, regardless of the type light you see first. How far away is the target? Is it at my altitude? In which direction is it traveling? Is it a threat?

That's silly, you point out. We ask these questions *every time* we see traffic, and often we ask those questions verbally. "Hey, Joe, which way is that guy going?" "You got that traffic?" "Is he in a turn toward us?"

Well, it has occurred to some aircraft lighting experts that pilots really shouldn't have to ask those questions—at least consciously. The subconscious is perfectly capable of working out the collision-potential problem instantaneously if it gets enough data to work with. Ideally, aircraft lighting systems should provide that data.

The red, green and white position lights used on aircraft are straight out of the Christopher Columbus era. Red to port, green to starboard and white at the masthead. In the mid-1950s, anti-collision lights were added in the form of rotating beacons. (United and American were the first to use them.) Then in the 1960s strobe lights were added as "supplemental" lighting systems, and finally, in the 1970s, tail lights (the type that illuminate the vertical stabilizer) appeared in both the airline and general aviation fleets.

But the development has been hodge-podge. If the goal of lighting system designers is to provide instantaneous information on size, speed and direction, some type of uniformity in aircraft lighting would seem essential.

B/CA called for a scientific evaluation of supplemental light systems in October 1973, and since that time many others have suggested similar studies. The latest proposal is by the FAA's Systems Research and Development Service. The office suggests a two-part study of aircraft exterior lighting. Part one would deal with night VFR and part two would consider low-visibility daylight operations. The study is expensive—$1.3 million— but researchers think it's necessary. The draft proposal for the study says, in part:

"In recent years, the FAA has allowed supplemental lighting to be added to aircraft. Presumably, the purpose of the supplemental lighting was to aid pilots in seeing other aircraft. Under the provisions of the supplemental lighting regulation, a vast array of different lighting configurations has been installed on all types of aircraft in the United States. The fact that aircraft are flying various lighting configurations can lead to confusion on the part of pilots. They must first make a decision as to what it is they are looking at, and then, secondly, make a decision as to whether or not a threat exists.

"There can be no doubt of the fact that standardization, in the sense that all aircraft are flying similar, easily identifiable lighting configurations, is a desirable goal. . . ."

The study would "objectively determine whether there are significant differences among the lighting configurations tested with regard to their ability to convey accurate and timely information to a pilot which may assist him in avoiding a midair collision or near-midair event."

Certainly, the study's goal is well stated, but is it worth $1.3 million? We'll look at that in a moment.

In simple terms, the FAA experimenters want to fly airplanes at each other under controlled conditions while pilots attempt to sort out the collision potential based on the lights they see. Specifically, they'll be looking at the relative performance of:

• Incandescent anti-collision rotating beacons versus anti-collision strobe lights of approximately equal effective candlepower.

• White versus red strobe anti-collision lights of equal power input.

• White anti-collision strobes of varying intensities.

• Steady-burning versus strobe position/navigation lights.

• Steady-burning position/navigation lights of various intensities.

They want to determine if there is an interaction between position/navigation lights and anti-collision lights as a function of either type of intensity of light.

The FAA's John Reed, one of the researchers who originally proposed the day/night lighting study, believes the program may already have been scuttled by user objection. The Air Line Pilots Association (ALPA), NBAA and AOPA officially objected to the expenditure of $1.3 million on this study.

Fred McIntosh, the NBAA's director of operational services, told B/CA, "I can't for the life of me at this stage in aviation see us spending that kind of money to find out if strobes work. We know they do. I don't in any way believe the expenditure of $1.3 million is justified—not when we're talking about adding three, four or five cents a gallon to the cost of fuel to pay for everything else. . . ."

Ted Linnert, director of ALPA's Engineering and Air Safety Department, was just as adamantly opposed to the study—or at least the expenditure of $1.3 million on a study: "Strobe lights have unquestionably proved themselves over the last 16 years. So far as we can determine—and we've made a study of it—there have been no midair collisions involving aircraft *showing* strobe lights. That's not to say that strobes would have prevented the collisions that have occurred had they been there, but we still think it's significant. The FAA and the military have been studying aircraft lighting for decades. It's time they stop studying and start doing something."

In 1970 ALPA requested the FAA to mandate strobe light installations on all aircraft—airline and general aviation. (Surprisingly, only about 60 percent of the commercial airline fleet is strobe-equipped.) Says Linnert, "In our proposal to the FAA that everybody be strobe-equipped, we suggested that the agency take economics into consideration. We know the little guy can't afford a lot of money for exterior lighting—but he can get a fully acceptable strobe light system for under $500. That doesn't seem to be too much money, considering what we're talking about."

When asked about user objections, Reed agreed that a lot of work has been done in lighting research, but he insists prior research has looked only at elements of the problem and never at the entire situation broadly enough to provide a "bench mark or base line" for (1) the standardization of lighting systems, or (2) a starting point for evaluation of still-to-be-devised lighting systems.

The question is really whether the FAA should continue to base lighting system regulations on an intuitive feel that strobes are terrific or collect objective analytical data on the subject.

"That's surely the crux of it," says Reed. "We still don't have any objective data on the benefits to strobe lights. The agency has never done any work in this area. They did all the incandescent and rotating beacon stuff years ago, but nothing on strobe lights. So all the comments we have are subjective. ALPA, for example, is strong on strobes. Its 40,000 pilots think strobes are the greatest thing in the world. In their night flying, they say, they see strobe lights long before they ever see rotating beacons, and, conceivably, this might be right. But from an eyeball and scientific standpoint, if the effective intensity of both rotating beacons and strobes were the same, I'm not sure there would be any difference. In most cases, the effective intensity is different because of the red lens (on the beacon) and the white lens (on the strobe). Naturally, you're going to see something different.

"Intuitively, I'd say that you ought to be able to detect strobe lights much better than the rotating beacon, and, of course, you're going to be able to detect strobes in your peripheral vision long before you'll see a beacon."

To this point, we've been talking about a study to compare the relative merits of various lighting systems in night VFR circumstances.

The second part of the proposed study package would look at the conspicuity benefits of strobes in daylight conditions. This part of the proposed study was requested by the FAA's Flight Standards Service, which is considering requiring strobe lighting for both day and night operations. In the daylight study, flight tests would compare the detectability of four intensities of white strobes and three intensities of red strobes with the detectability of aircraft without exterior lighting.

Given the same light source, the intensities of aviation red strobes are about 15 percent of white strobes because the aviation red filter reduces the light output by 85 percent. A white strobe, intense enough for daytime collision protection, often produces too much backscatter for night use.

The researchers admit that some analyses have indicated that strobe lighting would not be effective during daytime flight, but they believe "there is sufficient theoretical and practical reason to conclude that daytime strobe lighting may enhance visual detection." The draft proposal for the daylight study goes on to comment: "Should the results indicate that visual detection is enhanced in daylight flight through the use of strobe lighting, Flight Standards may wish to change the FARs dealing with aircraft exterior lighting. Using the data obtained in the proposed flight test, Flight Standards could, if it deemed it to be in the interest of safety: (1) require that all aircraft be equipped with strobe lighting of specified color and intensity, and (2) require that the strobe lighting be used in day, as well as night, flight."

Therein lies the AOPA's basic objection to the study; that is, besides a $1.3-million expenditure, the AOPA doesn't want more equipment regulated onto light general aviation aircraft.

The NBAA doesn't go as far as the AOPA in its fears of strobe regulation, nor is it pushing the FAA for mandatory strobes, as is ALPA. Says

McIntosh, "There's been adequate work done to prove strobes are beneficial. We've asked the FAA for years to do a simple thing like encourage
the use of strobes by making them completely interchangeable with any
other type of lights. . . ."

In the absence of scientific data on merits of the various lighting systems, defining what's good and bad in these lighting systems isn't easy.

Lighting engineers tell us that, if you want to be seen a long way off (day
or night), you need only flash an intense white light. How intense should
it be? When it comes to strobes on light aircraft the FAA says 400 effective
candlepower is enough, which is good for about five or 10 miles on a clear
night, but useless in daylight or heavy haze conditions. Conversely, the
widebodies are flying with strobes that bang out 3000 effective candlepower and can be seen for 30 or 40 miles. But is that good? On a clear night
in the New York area, for example, the pilot's scan is often cluttered with
dozens of aircraft that are not factors in his traffic problem.

We explored this subject with Paul H. Greenlee, chairman of the SAE's
external aircraft lighting committee and engineering director for Grimes
Manufacturing.

"There's no question about it," says Greenlee, "we need a standardized
lighting system with perhaps some different intensities for different categories of aircraft. With a standardized system, the pilot would be able to
judge much more quickly the size, speed and direction of flight of his
traffic."

Greenlee maintains that the basic problem with our existing lighting
systems is not initial recognition, but rather interpreting what the observed
light means.

As a first step, Greenlee would put as many lights as would fit on the
aircraft's wing tips and tail. "If you put white lights—both forward- and
aft-looking—on the wing tips, you get an awful lot more attitude information on the aircraft. Picture the situation where you're following an aircraft
with only a single white tail light in the pattern at night. When he starts
turning onto base or final, it takes a while for you to determine that his light
is moving off. However, if he had white lights on the trailing edge of the
wing tips, you could tell immediately that he was turning." (The widebodies
and most of the B-727 and DC-9 series are already equipped with aft-
looking wing-tip lights.)

B/CA couldn't agree more with Greenlee's contention that we need better aft-looking light systems. A single white light mounted on the tail cone,
even when accompanied by a red anti-collision light, simply doesn't do the
job.

Consider the midair collision between an Aero Commander 680T and an
F-111A, the latter involved in an attempted aerial refueling operation.

The refueling operation was being conducted between FL180 and 210.

The Commander was VFR at 17,500 feet and had just requested an IFR clearance at FL180. Before the clearance could be issued, the collision occurred. From an NTSB report on the accident comes this comment: Initially, the lead F-111A (a flight of two was involved) had navigational difficulties because of a malfunctioning inertial nav system and TACAN while attempting a rendezvous with the tanker. Immediately following a change of lead, the F-111A flight began to join up when the pilot established visual contact with a flashing red light, which appeared to emanate from an aircraft operating within the blocked airspace. Unfortunately, the red light was on the Aero Commander and not the tanker."

Another midair, similar in many ways, involved a National Guard F-106 and a Piper Comanche.

The F-106 pilot was unable to recall the events preceding or immediately following the midair, except he did recall "seeing a bright red light and tightening his turn right before the collision." According to the NTSB report, the F-106 pilot "could not recall exactly where in his visual scan the red light became visible."

In the first case, the aircraft lighting systems involved were not good enough to enable the F-111A pilot to distinguish between a Boeing KC-135 tanker and an Aero Commander. In the second case, the "red light" did not warn the F-106 pilot soon enough for him to avoid the collision with the Piper Comanche.

One lighting scheme, suggested to prevent midairs such as those described above, is the "Tel-tail" or "Logo Light." These lighting systems, designed and sold in kit form by DeVore Aviation, illuminate the surface of the vertical stabilizer. The idea of lighting the vertical tail is not new. It was first used on President Roosevelt's airplane—"The Sacred Cow"—to light up a flag insignia. Three decades later, Hugh Hefner specified tail floods to illuminate the giant white Playboy Bunny that adorned the vertical tail of his all-black DC-9.

DeVore designed and STCd the Playboy light—nobody remembers who did "The Sacred Cow." Shortly after the Playboy light appeared, TWA and Pan Am opted for similar lighting systems to call attention to their corporate logos. Gil DeVore, developer of the system, admits that his tail floodlights began more as an advertising medium than as a safety feature; however, he claims that the tail lights—with or without advertising messages—go a long way toward improving aircraft conspicuity at night.

"With tail surface lighting," explains DeVore, "the observer knows immediately the size of the aircraft and its direction of travel and speed. The problem with radiational lighting systems is that they are points of light. All pilots have been in the situation where they've lost contact with traffic as the traffic overflies clusters of ground lights. With full-tail illumination

378

there is no loss of contact because the lighted surface stands out against the background lights."

Some ALPA pilots believe DeVore's tail lights are as useful—if not more so—on the ground as in the air. One ALPA type told B/CA, "When you're taxiing around in a sea of lights, it's really pretty easy to run over somebody, especially when the visibility is down and there's a lot of light scatter. But you never have that problem when the guy in front of you has his tail floodlighted."

DeVore has installation kits and STCs for virtually all airline and business aircraft down to the light twins.

On large, swept-wing business jets, the tail is illuminated by spotlights mounted in customized fiberglass wingtip attachments or in bullets attached to the trailing edge of the flap-track housings. On straight-wing jets and all turboprops and piston twins, the lights are mounted on the horizontal tail.

To date, about 25 corporate turbojets have been equipped with the tail floodlights. Beech offers them as a factory-installed option on its Super King Air, the only manufacturer to do so.

Both the NBAA and ALPA like the idea of area illumination of the vertical stabilizer on the basis of "the more lights the better." However, neither organization is pushing for universal installation of these systems.

Another scheme for enhancing the conspicuity of the *overtaken* aircraft is simply increasing the intensity of the tail cone light, perhaps to an effective intensity matching that of the taxi lights. Most pilots have involved themselves voluntarily in the program to show a light (day or night) when operating in high-traffic areas. Therefore, most pilots are already well aware of the conspicuity benefits derived from the use of landing or taxi lights as running lights. Taxi and landing light coverage is limited to head-on and near head-on situations because of the relatively narrow beam width; the same would be true, of course, of high-power tail lights. The most critical collision potential, however, seems to be in head-on or overtaking situations.

FAA researchers told B/CA they'd like to include logo lights and landing lights in their proposed lighting study, but to do so at this point "would confuse the issue." Specifically, on the subject of landing lights, the draft proposal states: "Although landing lights are used in the vicinity of airports and may differentially affect the performance of the various (other) lighting combinations, their use has been excluded from this study for the sake of economy and simplicity of relative comparisons of anti-collision and position lights."

The entire point of improving aircraft lighting systems is obviously collision avoidance, and there are many elements in the collision-avoidance equation other than lighting. But one significant tie should be kept in mind.

379

Despite the fact that the FAA believes the basic collision prevention tool should be ground-based radar or cooperative collision-warning systems (CWS), many commenters, including the NBAA and ALPA, still are hoping for a proximity warning indicator (PWI) system based on detection of infrared radiation from strobe lights. The beauty of such a system, say its proponents, is simplicity: all airplanes would be equipped with strobes. Those operators who wished to make an additional investment would purchase a PWS, which detects the proximity of strobe lights, and thus, other airplanes. (Several infrared detection systems have been proven under experimental conditions, and one was offered for sale to the general public a year ago. However, the sales effort was aborted.)

Completely outfitting the night-flying fleet with strobes is not as big a task as it sounds. It's estimated that, of the 130,000 registered civil aircraft, 40,000 already have strobe lighting systems of one kind or another.

The fact is that we've all got gut feelings about various external lighting systems, but no one seems to be in a position to reduce those gut feelings into engineering and (if necessary) regulatory terms.

There is *no* question that $1.3 million is a lot of money and that *all* proposed R&D projects deserve vigorous user scrutiny because, after all, the users in one way or another will have to pick up the R&D tab. While we are not suggesting that the $1.3-million night/day aircraft lighting study be undertaken, we do believe a lesser sum should be expended on a modified version of the draft plan.

Certainly, the use of strobes for daylight recognition should be studied, especially the red/white system used by the Air Force. Some thoughtful standardization of lighting systems beyond that in the current regulations should be pursued.

Combustion Heaters 50

by Richard N. Aarons

Most piston twins are equipped with gasoline combustion heaters and most piston-twin pilots distrust them. There's just something about burning raw fuel in the nose section which worries us. (How may times have you toggled your heater switch and waited apprehensively for something other than heat to happen?)

Although we at B/CA had all heard horror stories about combustion heaters blowing aircraft out of the sky, none of us ever actually *knew* anyone who fell victim to an errant combustion heater. (There was that DC-6 problem back in 1948, but that wasn't the heater's fault. Heater intake scoops were in a position to catch the overflow from the fuel tanks when fuel was transferred. The overflow fuel was sucked past the cherry-red combustion chamber and ignited. That was clearly an airframe problem.)

To settle the matter, we asked the NTSB to query its computer for us: take a look at general aviation accidents over the last five years and identify those in which combustion heaters were involved. We expected 10 yards of readout with many grim accounts of heater fires and explosions.

Out of thousands of accidents on the tape there were two heater incidents, one clearly attributable to airframe plumbing, the other a "possible" catastrophic combustion heater malfunction.

In the first case, an air taxi cargo flight in a Beech C-45G was aborted when an aluminum fuel supply line to the cabin heater failed causing a fire in the left wheel well.

The second case involved an Aztec that hit trees during an off-airport landing after one engine quit due to fuel starvation. The NTSB said the pilot mismanaged the fuel system while under the influence of carbon monoxide poisoning. Inadequate maintenance and inspection were factors because heater cracks went undetected and that allowed exhaust gas to escape into the cabin, said the investigators. (Both major manufacturers of combustion heaters say the NTSB is wrong for reasons we'll see later.)

The only conclusion we could reach from this computer run is that combustion heaters *are* in fact quite safe. Even if you allow the Beech C-45G and Aztec incidents to count as black marks against them, you must at the same time concede that proper inspection and maintenance could have prevented these two records in the NTSB files.

Airborne combustion heaters have kept thousands of pilots warm for countless thousands of hours over the last three decades, apparently quite safely. But rather than let the matter drop there, we visited the two major manufacturers of these devices—South Wind Division of Stewart-Warner and Janitrol Aero Division of Midland-Ross—to find out how their products work and why they're so dependable and safe. As it turns out, simplicity is the answer.

Combustion heaters are, by no stretch of the imagination, new. They've been around since the early 30s in automobiles and since World War II in aircraft. And they haven't changed much over the years except for increased efficiency and reliability.

Both South Wind and Janitrol admit there is little difference between their products from the layman's viewpoint. The two products function identically and it would take a practiced eye to identify either heater by manufacturer without looking at the name plate. Janitrol heaters are on all Piper, Beech and Rockwell piston twins. Janitrol also provides the combustion heater and pressurization system for Cessna's 337P. South Wind heaters are on all other Cessna twins.

Since South Wind and Janitrol heaters are identical in principle of operation, we'll use only one diagram to describe their components and flow system.

From the outside a gasoline combustion heater looks like a section of stove pipe with a couple of cans glued to it. The cross-section in Figure 1 shows the insides of the heater. (For the experts, this cross-section more nearly represents the South Wind heater.) You'll notice first that the outside "stove pipe" is just that—a stainless steel pipe through which ventilating air moves. Ventilating air is pulled in the left end by the ventilating air blower and moves past the heat exchanger to the right end where it enters the aircraft ventilation ducts. If you examine Figure 1 carefully, you'll see that the heating section is a can within the "stove pipe" which is entirely sealed off from it. There is no mixing of ventilation air and combustion air or exhaust.

Combustion air is pumped into the combustion air inlet and ducted into the burner assembly. Fuel is supplied to the burner assembly by a constant pressure pump (usually about seven psi). Ignition is provided by a continuous duty spark plug which is sparking whenever the heater switch is in the "on" position. The spark plug is activated by a vibrator-ignition coil system housed in a can mounted on the external surface of the heater case. Exhaust gases are ducted out of the burner assembly and thereafter overboard.

Note the drain on the bottom of the burner assembly. This allows un-

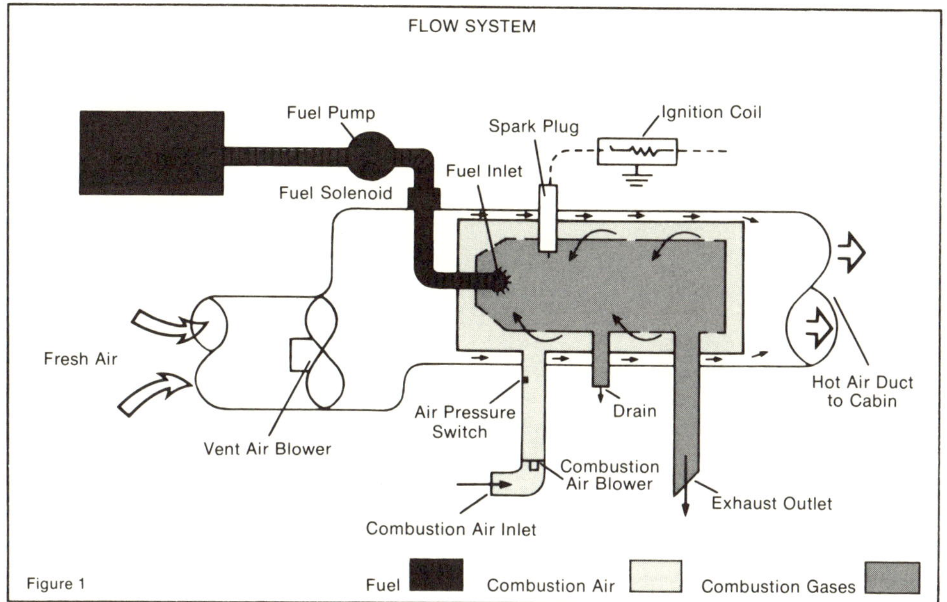

An aircraft combustion heater is similar in operation to the home oil heater. Walls of the combustion chamber form a heat exchanger by which ventilation air is forced. The ignition system is a continuous duty type. Fuel flow is either "on" or "off" as dictated by simple thermostat and safety controls.

burned fuel to run out of the heater unit and overboard.

The heater is controlled by various switches and valves, all designed to interface in a manner that will provide fail-safe operation. We'll look at these controls individually.

Fuel solenoid—This device opens or closes the fuel supply to the combustion chamber.

Overheat switch and duct limit switch—These temperature-limiting switches are mounted on the heater case. The duct limit switch is normally closed, but opens when ventilation air reaches a preset temperature— approximately 102 degrees Centigrade in a typical installation. When it opens, it de-energizes the fuel solenoid thus cutting off fuel supply to the combustion chamber. The duct limit switch, as its name implies, is designed to protect the ventilation air ducts.

The overheat switch is the ultimate overheat protection system. Preset to operate between 148 and 177 degrees Centigrade, the opening of this switch will cut off the fuel supply, ignition and combustion blower. It is manually reset but only with access to the heater itself. It cannot be reset by the pilot inflight.

Airflow switch—This pressure switch senses combustion air pressure and will open to shut off the heater if combustion air flow drops below a preset level.

Cabin controls—Typically there are but two combustion heater controls in the cockpit. One is a three-position "On-off-fan" switch and the other a rotary thermostat control knob. The controllable thermostat is a bimetal device that varies heat output—or maintains it at the selected level—by varying the fuel solenoid.

The relationship of these switches can be best understood by following the sequence of events when the heater is activated.

Placing the heater switch in the "on" position energizes the fuel pump and both the ventilating air and combustion air blowers. As the combustion air blower comes up to speed, combustion air pressure increases causing the air flow switch to close, which in turn energizes the ignition system. It also energizes the fuel solenoid if the contacts of the cabin temperature thermostat are closed. Fuel then sprays into the combustion chamber.

Since the ignition system is working, ignition is instantaneous and an intense flame is established. The hot gases flow through the heat exchanger and are exhausted overboard. Ventilation air passes along the outer surface of the heat exchanger where it is heated and then ducted into the cabin.

When the cabin thermostat opens, the fuel solenoid is de-energized, shutting off the fuel supply. Residual heat is drained away from the heat exchanger by ventilation air, the thermostat contacts close re-energizing the fuel solenoid, and the entire process begins anew.

In most installations the ventilation air blower is hooked up to a squat switch, so it is taken off line when the aircraft becomes airborne. At that time, ventilation air is supplied by ram air. But the combustion blower is on and operating at all times.

Janitrol and South Wind engineers say carbon monoxide contamination of cabin air is virtually impossible because a positive pressure differential is always maintained between the vent air and combustion air sections of the heater. If a crack develops in the combustion can, air flow is from the ventilation side into the can and then overboard with the exhaust.

The logic of the system controls prevents other possible hazards. Consider these:

(1) If the combustion air blower stops or the combustion air intake is blocked, the air pressure switch senses this and shuts down the system.

(2) If the spark plug fouls or the ignition system fails, fuel is not ignited and is drained overboard.

(3) If the system overheats for any reason, the duct switch or overtemp limiting switch turns everything off.

All aircraft combustion heaters are TSOd and among the TSO requirements is a test that subjects the heater to 50 explosions. The test is accomplished by filling the combustion chamber with an explosive fuel/air mixture and activating the spark plug. The heater must withstand 50 explosions without any damage—internal or external.

In the course of a typical flight, the pilot activates the heater switch, adjusts the cabin heat thermostat and then forgets about the heater for the duration. Meanwhile, the heater's ignition system fires continuously and the fuel solenoid cycles hundreds of times turning the fire on and off. On the ground, the beginning of this cycle can be heard sometimes as a breathy "pumrhh." In the air, the heater's operation cannot be heard over engine and airflow noises.

By now you're probably pretty convinced that combustion heaters are indeed safe if all the various controls and circuits are functioning. This brings up the subject of heater maintenance—probably the most overlooked aspect of environmental system care.

B/CA asked South Wind and Janitrol engineers to name the number one cause of heater problems. Both groups said without hesitation, "maintenance." Not poor maintenance, but the total lack of it. (We checked with the first half dozen light-twin operators we met after talking to the heater manufacturers and asked each to tell us how he maintained his heater. All six said they were not aware that their heater required any maintenance, or even inspection, and they had never seen replacement parts show up on annual inspection bills. We also checked bills for inspections on B/CA aircraft and found that the only mention of heater maintenance was in reference to a heater squawk several years ago.)

Well, to set the record straight, heaters *do* require regular inspection and preventive maintenance. We'll start with preflight:

• Before each flight during which the heater will be used, check the air duct inlets, the exhaust outlet and the heater drain outlet for clogging, ice, carbon and mechanical obstructions. Pay particular attention to the drain outlet. It's a small pipe easily damaged and it's one of the key safety devices on the heater.

• After each flight, ideally while the aircraft is on short final or during rollout, make sure to heed the checklist warning to move the heater into the "fan" mode for a while before shutdown. The fan will cool the combustion chamber thus preventing an overheat condition caused by the lack of vent air after shutdown.

• Periodically—(50- or 100-hour inspections) the heater fuel filter should be cleaned and all fuel connections should be checked for security and leaks.

• Annually—before the beginning of each heating season—the entire heater should be inspected. This includes removal, cleaning and gapping of the spark plug, and testing the fuel pump, which may have been adversely affected by gumming of fuel over a prolonged shutdown period.

• Every 1000 hours of heating-season flying, remove and overhaul the entire heater.

There is little a pilot can do to troubleshoot his heater or fix it inflight. If the heater fails inflight, recycle it *once*. If that works, you're in business. If it doesn't, there's probably something wrong that requires the attention of a mechanic. In this case, the safety features have shut down the heater and there's no sense trying to outsmart the cutouts by repeated attempts at starting.

Make sure, however, that you record the conditions under which the heater failed including altitude and OAT. This information can be helpful to the mechanic.

Both South Wind and Janitrol make heaters ranging in output from 20,000 BTUs to 55,000 BTUs per hour. A 40,000 BTU unit, used in most six-to-eight place piston twins, burns about three pounds of avgas per hour.

Heaters for pressurized twins follow the same principles of operation described above, except the ventilating air comes from the cabin rather than outside the aircraft. Therefore the ventilating side of the heater is at cabin pressure and the heater case is carefully sealed to avoid leaks.

Today the use of combustion heaters is restricted to piston twins. (Turboprops and turbojets use bleed air for heating.) But the day may soon come when combustion heaters make a reappearance on the piston singles.

That's right—reappearance. The first use of combustion heaters in general aviation aircraft was on the old Navion. Later they showed up as an option on the Cessna 195 and then as standard equipment on Piper's Apache and Cessna's Model 310.

Airframe manufacturers use muff heaters on single-engine aircraft, simply because they're cheaper by a factor of about three. Certainly, installation of combustion heaters is no problem. They're relatively light—a 20,000 BTU system capable of heating a single-engine aircraft weighs only 14.5 pounds—and they can be mounted anywhere.

Airframe manufacturers will make the switch as operators of single-engine aircraft demand greater creature comfort from their expensive machines.

Combustion heater manufacturers also believe a degree of safety could be added to single-engine operation if combustion heaters replaced the muff types. There's no way of telling how many pilots have fallen victim to carbon monoxide from leaky muff systems. Combustion heater engineers think the number is greater than the statistics indicate.

In any event, well-maintained combustion heaters *are* safe and dependable, and don't seem to have half the malevolence we originally credited them with. To the heaters in our company twins, which have never let us down or blown us up, we apologize.

The Ups and Downs of Pressurization

by Richard N. Aarons

The mechanics of pressurization are not at all difficult to understand. To get a feel for just how uncomplicated the systems really are, consider the fact that all the specialized hardware required for pressurizing an aircraft —controllers, outflow valves and plumbing—costs the airframe manufacturer less than $2000.

But before we discuss this relatively inexpensive hardware in detail, let's talk about the general theory of pressurization systems.

First, let's build ourselves a big rigid airtight box like that in Figure 1 and put a passenger in it to remind us that what we're really looking at is the pressure vessel of an aircraft.

For starters we'll look at the box at sea level with the outflow door (upper right side) open. The pressures inside and outside the box are equal as long as the door is open and the box is not moved. The pressure of the atmosphere at sea level on a standard day is about 14.7 psi. Thus the pressure inside and outside the ventilated box is 14.7 psi. One way of describing this situation would be to say there is no difference between the inside and outside pressures; or, more simply, the *pressure differential* is zero.

If we were to lift the open box to 10,000 feet msl, the outside and inside pressures would decrease at the same rate and end up at 10.1 psi, the ambient atmospheric pressure at that altitude. And of course, we could run the box on up to a higher altitude, say 18,000 feet msl, and observe again that the pressure differential is still zero in that outside and inside pressures are now stabilized at the 18,000-foot ambient of 7.3 psi.

At 35,000 feet msl the inside and outside pressures are about 3.5 psi, one-quarter of that at sea level. And if we were to lift the box on up to 40,000 feet, we'd find that the inside and outside pressures had dropped to only 2.7 psi.

It's obviously much more desirable for physiological reasons to maintain the inside pressure relatively high as the box is lifted.

One way of doing this is to close the door and seal it at sea level, thus

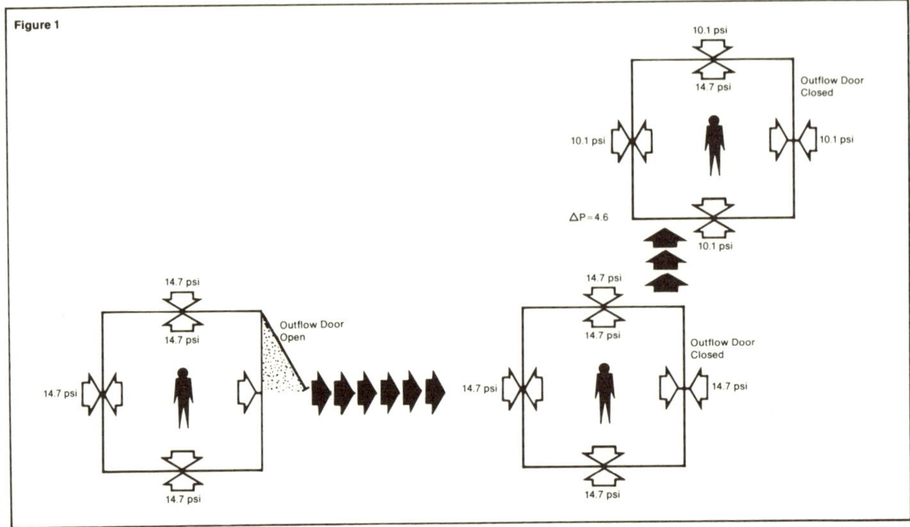

A simple pressurization system can be made by sealing a box at sea level where the ambient pressure is 14.7 psi. When the sealed box is lifted, the inside pressure remains at sea level while the outside pressure drops, thus creating a pressure differential.

establishing the inside pressure at 14.7 psi. If the sealed box is lifted to 10,000 feet msl, the outside pressure will drop to 10.1 psi, but the inside pressure will remain at 14.7 psi. The *pressure differential* in this case is 4.6 psi (14.7 − 10.1 = 4.6).

Lifting the box to 30,000 feet where the ambient pressure is 4.4 psi increases this pressure differential to 10.3 psi.

Although the closed-door technique is relatively simple, this approach to pressurization has its limits. The obvious one is a lack of ventilation. No one has figured out how to build a perfectly airtight airplane cabin.

Adding wings and engines to the box produces unavoidable leaks. Control cables, push rods and wires must exit the pressure vessel to reach the components they operate. And no matter how carefully holes around cable throughways are packed and no matter how cleverly gaskets are designed for doors and windows, some leakage will be present.

We'll return to our box now with these new limits in mind. First, a way must be found to exchange air inside to keep the passengers healthy; and second, we must find a way to compensate for leaks. Typically, pressurized light aircraft cabins have leak rates of about four pounds per minute at sea level at maximum pressure differential.

388

Figure 2 shows our box outfitted with a ventilation source (fan), outflow valve (flapper door) and controller (passenger). Assuming the fan is adjusted to deliver fresh air to the cabin at a constant rate of 14 pounds per minute, the situation shown in Figure 3 will exist before the box is moved, i.e., the inside and outside pressures are at 14.7 psi; 14 pounds of air are entering the box each minute via the fan and 14 pounds of air are exhausted each minute because the outflow door is wide open.

If we were to close the outflow door, the cabin would begin to pressurize as the weight of air in the cabin increased at a new rate of 10 pounds per minute. (Fourteen pounds per minute would be delivered by the fan while four pounds per minute escaped because of leaks.) And of course as the amount of air in the cabin increases, the pressure of the cabin air increases. We can stop this pressure change in the cabin by opening the outflow door just enough so the air escaping through it, and the air escaping via the leaks, equal the amount of air provided by the fan. For our purposes then, we would open the outflow door until air exited at that point at the rate of 10 pounds per minute. The leaks would account for another four pounds per minute; thus we'd have a stabilized condition of 14 pounds per minute in and 14 pounds per minute out. If we were to raise the box now, outside pressure would decrease and a pressure differential would begin to develop between the inside and outside environments. The amount of pressure differential would be controlled entirely by the amount of air escaping from the cabin through the outflow door and we could open or close this door at will to control the internal box pressure. Any time more air is entering than

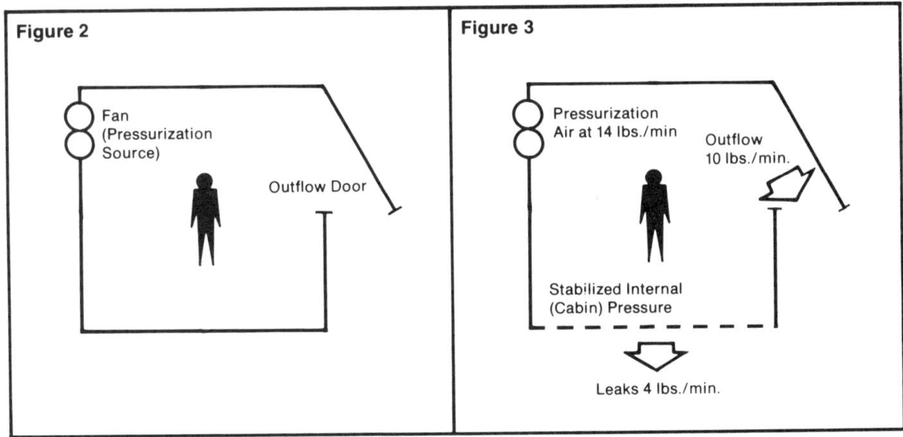

Figure 2: The problem with the pressurization system in Figure 1 is its lack of ventilation. One way to solve this problem is to exchange the air in the box by pumping air in then exhausting it at controlled rates. Figure 3: A stablized cabin pressure (altitude) will result if the entering (pressurization) air equals the weight of air lost through leaks and controlled outflow.

leaving, the internal pressure increases, thus decreasing internal altitude. Whenever more air is escaping than entering, the pressure inside the box decreases and the internal altitude of the box increases.

The box in this example (Figure 3) has functioned exactly like the pressure vessels and pressurization control systems in current production piston twins. The fan in our example is replaced in the aircraft by engine-driven turbochargers and the outflow door in our box is represented in aircraft hardware by a pair of outflow-safety valves. We used the passenger to control the outflow door in our system; production aircraft use automatic controllers, which we'll discuss in detail.

The outflow-safety valve is really the heart of the general aviation pressurization system and a clear understanding of how it functions is essential to the understanding of the pressurization system in its entirety. (Unless noted we'll be talking about AiResearch equipment, which is installed on all but a few general aviation aircraft including the business jets.)

These valves are produced in several diameters depending on the amount of airflow required. They are mounted on a bulkhead of the pressurized portion of the cabin so that outflow of cabin air is achieved whenever the cylindrical valve is off its seat. Figure 4 shows the outflow valve in cross section. Cabin air normally occupies the space in chamber A and a reference pressure from the cockpit controller is applied to the space in chamber B. A muscle diaphragm attached to the valve poppet separates the two chambers. If the reference pressure in chamber B falls below the cabin pressure in chamber A, the muscle diaphragm will begin to open the valve. (The delicately balanced valve starts to open when the difference between the cabin pressure and the reference pressure is about one inch of water and reaches its full open position when that differential is about six inches of water, which is just about the same negative pressure you apply when you sip a Coke through a straw.)

The valve will stay open as long as there is a significant difference between reference pressure and cabin pressure. As cabin pressure decreases (valve open) the force on the muscle diaphragm decreases and the valve begins to close. By varying the reference pressure the valve position can be regulated and thus the cabin pressure can be regulated at any given altitude. This function of the valve provides isobaric control. It is this mode of operation that enables the controller to modulate the reference pressure to maintain cabin altitude at a given level.

The valve must provide differential pressure protection also. This function is accomplished by the mechanism in chamber C, which is open to outside air pressure at one end and separated from the reference pressure chamber by a diaphragm at the other. A spring loaded valve similar to an automobile tire valve is mounted in the diaphragm so that it contacts a set screw when the diaphragm extends far enough in an upward direction. This

390

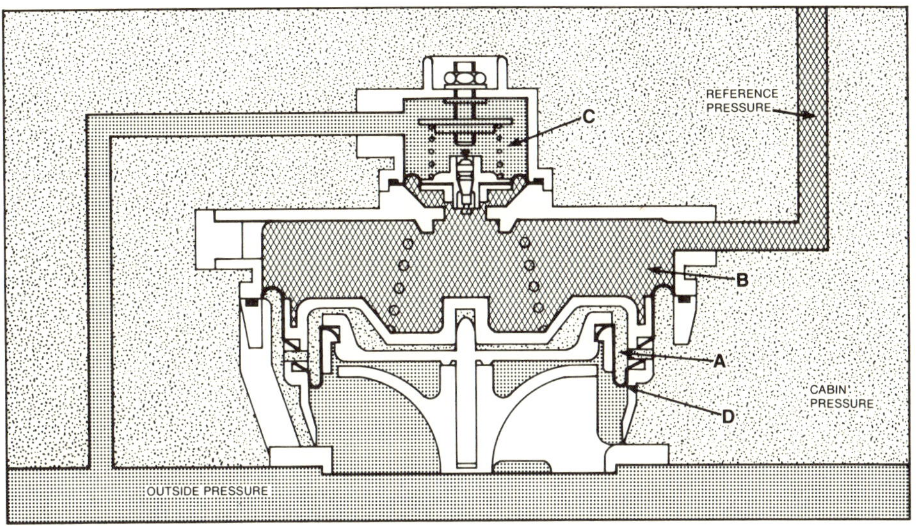

Figure 4: This cross-sectional view of an outflow valve shows its operation. The reference pressure in chamber B and the cabin air pressure in chamber A work together to control the valve's position.

set screw is adjusted to open the valve between the reference pressure chamber and outside air when the difference between cabin air and outside air pressures reaches the maximum permissible differential. You can see that venting the reference pressure to ambient pressure will quickly cause a large difference between the reference pressure and cabin pressure chambers and open the main valve to reduce cabin pressure.

Finally, the valve must provide negative pressure differential protection. Aircraft pressure vessels are designed to maintain a pressure differential only when the cabin pressure is greater than outside pressure. If outside pressure were to exceed cabin pressure (i.e., the cabin gets higher than the aircraft), the fuselage might crush inwards.

The diaphragm at D (Figure 4) takes care of this problem. This diaphragm and the areas of the valve face are designed in such a manner that a negative pressure differential will be sensed here immediately, causing the total pressure applied against the reference pressure to overcome the lightly loaded spring in chamber B and open the valve.

Most general aviation pressurized aircraft are equipped with two outflow-safety valves. One (sometimes called the "outflow" valve) is connected. The other, identical in internal mechanism, is hooked up so its

391

reference pressure chamber (B) is vented to the aircraft vacuum system through a hard line and to cabin air pressure through a restricted aperture. The line between this valve (sometimes called the "safety valve") and the vacuum system includes a solenoid operated shutoff valve activated by a gear squat switch and (sometimes) a cockpit switch. In the differential pressure relief mode the safety valve functions identically to the outflow valve. The connection to the aircraft vacuum line keeps the safety valve open whenever the aircraft is on the ground (squat switch) or the pilot selects "dump" on a panel switch. However, the safety valve has no function in isobaric control. The job of maintaining the cabin at a preselected altitude is handled solely by the outflow valve which is connected to the cockpit controller.

Manufacturers of pressurized piston twins usually provide fixed-schedule controllers as standard equipment and offer variable-schedule controllers as options. We strongly recommend that you go with the option and we're sure most buyers do. But we'll take a look at the operation of both systems in case you're living on a tight budget.

AiResearch systems are completely pneumatic. Other than the solenoid between the control head of the safety valve and the vacuum system, there is no requirement for electrical power. The uncomplicated fixed-schedule (fixed cabin altitude) pressurization system begins to work as soon as the engines are started and electrical power, running through the squat switch, opens the solenoid between the vacuum system and the safety valve. The safety valve strokes open and allows turbocharger compressor bleed air, which is entering the cabin at a rate near 14 pounds per minute, to flow overboard. Immediately after liftoff the squat switch opens, deenergizing the solenoid which in turn disconnects the vacuum source from the control head of the safety valve. As cabin air seeps into the safety valve control head via the cabin air orifice, the reference pressure in the control head nears that of the cabin and the spring in chamber B closes the safety valve. Of course, this all happens a lot faster than it takes to say it. The outflow valve has been closed all along, so momentarily at least, both valves are closed and the cabin begins to pressurize. (The pilot will notice a slight descent rate on the cabin climb indicator.) The fixed-schedule controller is designed to begin cabin pressurization only when the aircraft reaches a factory-set altitude, typically 8,000 feet. So the controller must open the outflow valve after takeoff to keep the cabin from pressurizing prematurely and it does this by venting the control head of the outflow valve to the outside. The slight pressure difference between cabin and ambient will open the valve and keep it open until the controller orders isobaric control at 8,000 feet. As the aircraft reaches 8,000 feet, the isobaric control begins to modulate the pneumatic signal to the outflow valve. And as the airplane climbs above 8,000 feet, the controller maintains a fixed-reference pressure to the outflow valve and the valve automatically regulates cabin altitude to 8,000 feet until the maximum permissible cabin pressure differential is reached. When this point of maximum cabin differential is reached, the differential pressure relief mechanisms (chamber C) of both valves take over to maintain the preset maximum differential.

Figure 5 might make understanding this process a little clearer. (The striped line represents a fixed-schedule cabin pressurization profile.) Here, we're assuming the fixed-schedule controller is set to provide an isobaric cabin at 8,000 feet with outflow-safety valves set for a maximum pressure differential of 6.5 psi. During the unpressurized climb to 8,000 feet there is a slight cabin pressure differential on the order of 0.5 inches Hg. This is necessary to hold the outflow valve open. Once in the region of isobaric control, the system keeps the cabin at 8,000 feet until the differential pressure reaches 6.4 psi. (That will occur at an aircraft altitude of about 27,500 feet.) As the aircraft climbs higher than 27,500 feet, the differential control portions of the outflow valves take over to maintain the 6.4 psi

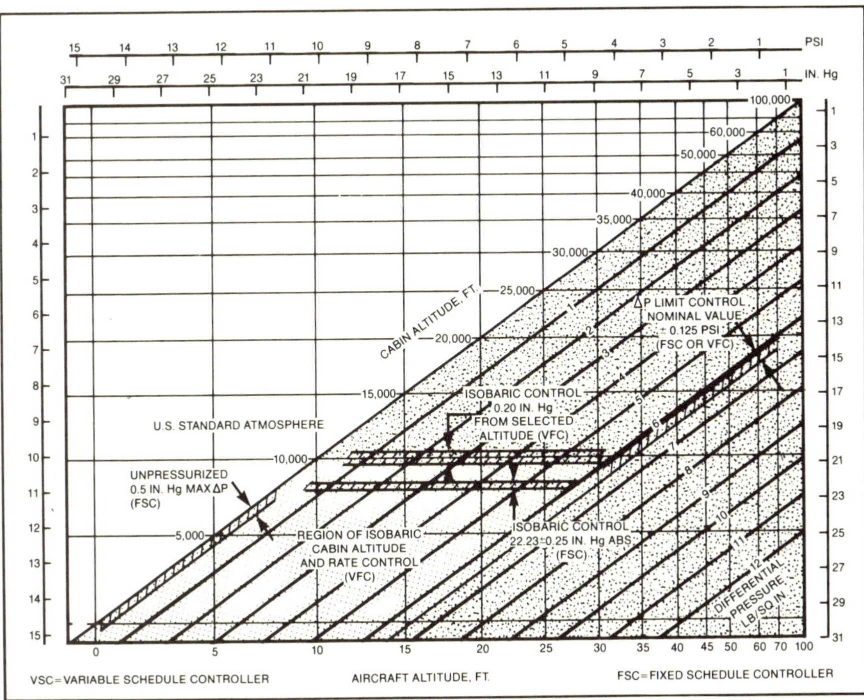

Figure 5: Profiles of aircraft versus cabin altitude for fixed-schedule controllers (FSC) and variable-schedule controllers (VSC) are shown here. The FSC operation is limited to the striped line. The VSC operates throughout the isobaric (shaded) area.

differential and the cabin climbs along with the aircraft. On the way back down, cabin pressure differential hits zero at an aircraft altitude of 8,000 feet and the cabin descends to sea level along with the aircraft.

The variable-schedule pressurization controller functions similarly to the fixed-schedule unit except that the pilot can select the end cabin altitude as long as it's within the maximum pressure differential limits. He can also select the rate at which the cabin climbs or descends to the selected altitude.

Variable-schedule controllers are really black art devices probably fully understood by only a half dozen guys locked up in rubber rooms. Suffice it to say that its diaphragms, bellows, rate orifices, springs and check valves all work to modulate the pressure in the reference line between it and the control head of the valve. The pilot need only concern himself with the front of the device. Happily, the system is pretty simple to operate. The left knob moves through a 270-degree arc and controls cabin rate of climb or descent over a range of 50 fpm at full counterclockwise to 2,000 fpm at full clockwise rotation. The 12 o'clock position corresponds to about 500 fpm. The knob on the right moves the big pointer on the dial face. It's used to select cabin altitude. The little window at the bottom of the instrument shows the maximum aircraft altitude at which the selected cabin altitude can be maintained (pressure differential limit).

Figure 5 also shows the characteristics of a variable-schedule system. Here we're assuming a maximum cabin pressure differential of 6.5 psi and that we're not going to select cabin altitude higher than 10,000 feet. Notice first that we can opt to set the cabin altitude selector at sea level and that we can maintain a sea level cabin until the aircraft reaches a little over 15,000 feet, at which point we've reached maximum pressure differential. Once we hit that limiting differential the cabin will climb with the aircraft. In this case, for example, cabin altitude would be almost 3,000 feet as the aircraft went through 20,000 feet.

There's nothing really wrong with flying a pressurization system in this manner, i.e. dialing a sea level cabin and forgetting the rest, and it's probably the preferable way of operating the system as long as you keep the aircraft altitude below maximum differential. Figure 5 also shows us that we can maintain a sea level cabin while avoiding a maximum differential situation up to about 14,800 feet. And it's good operating practice to stay away from that maximum differential point and thus leave control of cabin altitude to the pressurization control unit which is designed to provide a well modulated cabin. If we reach max differential, the differential sensing elements of the outflow valves control cabin pressure—not the cabin pressure controller which was designed to do the job. If we are "riding the outflow valves," any minor aircraft altitude excursion will result in a proportional cabin altitude excursion.

Therefore the best practice is to set the number in the aircraft altitude

394

Standard Atmosphere Pressure Relationships

Altitude (ft.)	Inches Hg	PSI	O_2 (partial pressure psi)	
Sea level	29.92	14.7	3.09	1 atmo-sphere
1,000	28.85	14.2	2.98	
2,000	27.82	13.7	2.88	
3,000	26.81	13.2	2.77	
4,000	25.84	12.7	2.67	
5,000	24.89	12.2	2.56	
6,000	23.98	11.8	2.48	
7,000	23.09	11.3	2.37	
8,000	22.22	10.9	2.29	
9,000	21.38	10.5	2.21	
10,000	20.58	10.1	2.12	
11,000	19.79	9.7	2.04	
12,000	19.03	9.3	1.95	
13,000	18.29	9.0	1.89	
14,000	17.65	8.6	1.81	
15,000	16.98	8.3	1.74	
16,000	16.29	8.0	1.68	
17,000	15.60	7.6	1.60	
18,000	14.88	7.3	1.53	½ atmo-sphere
19,000	14.33	7.0	1.47	
20,000	13.75	6.7	1.41	
21,000	13.18	6.5	1.37	
22,000	12.63	6.2	1.30	
23,000	12.10	5.9	1.24	
24,000	11.59	5.7	1.20	
25,000	11.10	5.5	1.16	
27,000	10.16	5.0	1.05	1/3 atmo-sphere
30,000	8.88	4.4	0.92	
33,000	7.70	3.8	0.80	
35,000	7.03	3.5	0.74	¼ atmo-sphere
40,000	5.54	2.7	0.57	

window to a level 1,000 feet above your cruising altitude. The resulting cabin altitude will be well within the maximum differential limits and you will be letting the controller do the work it was designed to do.

The next concern is climb and descent rate. Assuming you're flying the cabin somewhere above sea level (or takeoff airport elevation), you'll have to climb the cabin to the desired altitude; the best technique is to climb the cabin as slowly as possible and yet still keep from "riding the outflow valves." Maximum passenger comfort is realized at climb rates below 500 fpm. And most guys we've flown with set the rate knob to the 500-fpm position, then monitor the climb on the cabin altitude, cabin rate and differential pressure instruments. Here again, the goal is to keep the system off the outflow valves. You do that by preventing the aircraft from climbing away from the cabin at a rate which would develop a maximum cabin pressure differential before the aircraft leveled off at cruise altitude. There are several approaches to management of this problem. Today's pressurized cabin twins are not really super climbers so it's rare that a 500-fpm cabin climb will not be sufficient to keep off the outflow valves. You can check this by glancing at the differential pressure gauge during the climb. If the needle seems to be getting too close to the red line, increase the cabin climb rate a tad and you'll have no problems.

Management of the variable-schedule system during descent takes a bit of thought. The maximum cabin descent rate for ideal passenger comfort is about 300 fpm. Much faster and you start popping eardrums.

So if you normally descend your aircraft at 2,000 fpm, it becomes obvious that you'll have to start the cabin down a bit before the aircraft leaves cruising altitude if the cabin and the aircraft are to meet at some altitude near pattern altitude. If you start the cabin down too early, it will descend until maximum differential limit is reached and then wait for the aircraft.

The best technique for the pressurized piston twins is to set the cabin altitude pointer to an altitude about 500 feet above airport elevation (assuming relatively standard baro conditions) a few minutes before you expect to begin the descent. Adjust the rate knob to produce a cabin descent rate of about 300 fpm. This will give the cabin a head start, and as long as you keep the aircraft altitude above the indicated cabin altitude, the cabin's rate of descent will be about 300 fpm. If ATC should stop you on the way down, the cabin (on the AiResearch system) will continue to descend until max differential is reached. This needn't bother you much because you only ride the outflow valves for a short time. Once you start down again, the cabin will begin down at 300 fpm.

If you catch up to the cabin on the way down, the valves will open and the cabin will descend at the same rate as the aircraft. Since this could pop some eardrums, the best technique is to try to keep the aircraft from catching up with the cabin until the aircraft is only a few hundred feet above the ground.

So far we've discussed only the AiResearch system because that system is found on over 95 percent of the pressurized general aviation aircraft flying. And at that, we've been talking about the old AiResearch system. (It's the same system used on the Electra, DC-9, most business jets and all the turboprops.) In 1972 AiResearch introduced a new system for general aviation aircraft which is said to be every bit as accurate and reliable as the older systems. But it's much smaller than the older system and is significantly lighter. In fact the entire system—controller, outflow valves and solenoid weighs only 6.49 pounds.

Current production Beech Dukes and Pressurized Navajos use an electro-pneumatic variable schedule pressurization system manufactured by Dukes Astronautics, a small California company. Although the reference pressure signaling circuits of the Dukes system differ from the AiResearch system, the general principles discussed above apply.

The Dukes controller has a cabin altitude selector knob and a rate knob like the AiResearch system, but it also has an ascend/descend switch. The AiResearch system automatically starts the cabin moving (up or down) whenever the cabin altitude selector is repositioned. With the Dukes system the pilot must order the cabin to ascend or descend by moving the appropriate toggle switch. The desired cabin altitude is selected first, of course. The electrical component of this electropneumatic system is a motor controlled by the ascend/descend switch. (The rate knob on the Dukes controller modulates the speed of this motor.) The motor turns a metering screw which in turn modulates the pneumatic signals to the outflow valves. In the event of an electrical system failure, the pilot can manually "twist the cabin down" by turning the inside knob on the cabin altitude selector. A Dukes spokesman told B/CA the company will soon introduce a new controller with an automatic cabin ascend/descend function which, from the pilot's viewpoint, will function in the same manner as the AiResearch system.

Finally, the failure modes of these systems are pretty uncomplicated. A check of the NTSB files could produce no account of a general aviation accident directly attributable to a faulty pressurization system. But a thorough study of your flight manual is imperative for the safe operation of your pressurization system.

A Final Word

Airplanes--even light, single-engine airplanes--are incredibly complex devices. Whether we fly small aircraft or some of the larger, enormously complicated machines, we are wedded to that machinery in a union of self preservation.

Aircraft systems are the vital, largely self-contained elements of the total machine. The serious pilot needs to understand the workings and limitations of those systems, because each system makes a unique contribution to the safety--or hazards--of flight. In recent years, for example, major aviation disasters have resulted from tire failures, door-hardware malfuntions and drinking water leakage. All aircraft systems are as vital to aviation safety as good pilot training and careful flight planning.

We hope that these pages have helped to improve your understanding of the systems that serve your aircraft. We know that this enhanced knowledge will contribute to your flying safety and pleasure.